$1.50

THE
End of Ideology
Debate

THE
End of Ideology
Debate ❧ EDITED,

WITH AN INTRODUCTION
BY *Chaim I. Waxman*

Funk & Wagnalls *New York*

IN MEMORY OF

The Reverend Dr. Martin Luther King, Jr.

1929–1968

FOREWORD

The essays and articles in this book constitute, in the main, a debate that began during the early 1950s and continues, to some extent, to this day. The purpose of presenting them in a single volume is for a clarification of the positions with the hope that each side will gain some appreciation of the other, and the end-of-ideology debate will not congeal into a war between two dogmatically rigid ideologies. The papers are presented more or less in the order in which they were originally published because part of their flavor derives from the time during which they were written.

I should like to express my sincere appreciation to all the authors and publishers who so generously permitted me to reprint their material; to Miss Rachel Whitebook of Funk & Wagnalls, for her editorial and technical assistance; to my colleagues, Professors Ernest D. Lehman, Jack Lucas, John G. Rommel, and Franklin J. Watson, for their critical comments; to Lucinda Camara, for her clerical assistance; and to my wife, Chaya, and our children, Ari and Shani, to whom I had originally intended to dedicate this book.

The manuscript was completed on the morning following the brutal assassination of a bright light in a cave of darkness, and it is to him and all for which he stood that this book is mournfully dedicated.

CHAIM ISAAC WAXMAN

New Haven, Connecticut
April 5, 1968

CONTENTS

THE
End of Ideology
Debate

INTRODUCTION

To a large extent the end-of-ideology debate is due more to the lack of a common definition of the term "ideology" than to a disagreement over basic issues. Almost no two writers maintain the same definition. The following is a sample of various definitions:

HENRY DAVID AIKEN: "Now political ideology is nothing but political discourse . . . on its most general, formative level. It is, that is to say, political discourse insofar as the latter addresses itself . . . to the guiding principles, practices and aspirations by which politically organized societies . . . ought to be governed" (1964), p. 251 in this volume.

RAYMOND ARON: ". . . ideology . . . is *a pseudo-systematic formulation of a total vision of the historical world*" (1967, p. 144).

DANIEL BELL: "Ideology is the conversion of ideas into social levers. . . . It is the commitment to the consequence of ideas. . . . What gives ideology its force is its passion. . . . For the ideologue, truth arises in action, and meaning is given to experience by the 'transforming moment'" (1962), p. 96 in this volume.

ROBERT A. HABER: "Ideology is an intellectual production describing the society" (1962), p. 186 in this volume.

JOSEPH LAPOLAMBARA: "Ideology . . . tends to specify a set of values that are more or less coherent and that seek to link given patterns of action to the achievement or maintenance of a future, or existing, state of affairs" (1966), p. 320 in this volume.

KARL MANNHEIM: "We speak of a *particular* and of a *total*

3

conception of ideology. Under the first we include all those utterances the 'falsity' of which is due to an intentional or unintentional, conscious, semi-conscious, or unconscious, deluding of one's self or of others, taking place on a psychological level and structurally resembling lies. . . . The sociology of knowledge, on the other hand, takes as its problem precisely this mental structure *in its totality*, as it appears in different currents of thought and historical-social groups. . . . Since suspicion of falsification is not included in the total conception of ideology, the rise of the term 'ideology' in the sociology of knowledge has no moral or denunciatory intent. It points rather to a research interest which leads to the raising of the question when and where social structures come to express themselves in the structure of assertions, and in what sense the former concretely determine the latter" (1955, pp. 265–6).

TALCOTT PARSONS: "An ideology . . . is a system of beliefs, held in common by the members of a collectivity, i.e., a society, or a subcollectivity of one—including a movement deviant from the main culture of the society—a system of ideas which is oriented to the evaluative integration of the collectivity, by interpretation of the empirical nature of the collectivity and of the situation in which it is placed, the processes by which it has developed to its given state, the goals to which its members are collectively oriented, and their relation to the future course of events" (1951, p. 349).

EDWARD SHILS: "*Ideologies* are characterized by a high degree of explicitness of formulation over a very wide range of objects with which they deal. . . . Complete individual subservience to the ideology is demanded of those who accept it, and it is regarded as essential and imperative that their conduct be completely permeated by it. . . . All adherents of the ideology are urgently expected to be in complete agreement with each other. . . ." (1968).

4

And yet, the problem of definition is far from the entire issue.

The end-of-ideology thesis involves two basic premises. The first, and in this most agree, is the statement of actual situation; namely, the absence of ideological politics in modern industrial society. The interesting point here, at least insofar as the United States is concerned, is not that we have reached the end of the ideological age, but rather that there almost never was an ideological age in America. The United States in the 1950s and 60s is the outgrowth of what Michael Harrington has termed "the *accidental* century"; our contemporary crises are the result of unplanning technologically, economically, and politically.

The second premise at least implicit in the end-of-ideology thesis is a positive value-judgment about this reality: "We've reached, or at least are well on our way to reaching 'the good society,' and ideology can only serve to hinder the progress we are making." It is primarily on this point that the debate ensues.

There are those who maintain that the recent significant growth of the "New Left" is evidence of a rebirth (or birth) of ideological politics in the United States. This may be so, but only to a very limited degree. When one probes more deeply, what he finds is a number of lefts which unite to some extent on certain specific political issues, such as the demand to halt the bombing of North Vietnam. But these very same lefts are as divided as possible on other issues, such as the Arab-Israeli war of June, 1967. What we have is a number of *protest* organizations, protesting various policies and issues, which have just enough in common to combine forces and present a united front, as, for example, in the 1968 Coalition for a Democratic Alternative.* But, there is a world of difference between pro-

* As of this writing, Senator Robert F. Kennedy has announced his candidacy, and President Lyndon B. Johnson has taken himself out of the

test groups, or even *a* protest movement, and a positive political theory or ideology. Not one of these groups has come up with a new positive alternative based upon a new political philosophy or social theory. Certainly there is no political theory which they all share.

The end of ideology is due not to our good fortune in having achieved the great society, but rather to our great misfortune in concentrating on what the late C. Wright Mills called "abstracted empiricism," that is, concentrating on the very minute particles within the total framework. Just as abstracted empiricism in the social sciences "is not based upon any new conception of the nature of society or of man" (1959, p. 55), so too, political protest as it is currently manifested in the United States is actually not based on any new conceptions of society or of man, especially political man.

This should not, by any means, be taken as in concurrence with the position of George Kennan that the "rebels without a program" should either "put up or shut up," that they should either state positively "in what way this political system should be modified, or what should be established in its place" (1968), or else they should hold their peace. Quite the contrary; protest and dissent are essential, lest we become "a nation of sheep," lest we regress to the abysmal apathy of the 1950s.* But the "thoughts of young radicals" must not remain confined to protest as an end in itself. They must not expend all their efforts on protest and neglect the more critical realm of socio-political theory. This is the most important area, and

---

race. The "united front" was indeed short-lived. We now see at least a three-way split on the left: those who support Kennedy, those who retain their loyalty to Senator Eugene McCarthy, and those who denounce both as "Establishment" candidates.

* Protest and dissent are not to be confused with violence and destruction. Those who advocate the violent destruction of the institutions of our society, here and now, have no proclaimed plans for their replacements and are too hasty to forget that things *can* become, and in fact, *were* worse.

yet, increasingly in modern technological society, this is the most difficult.

As the result of the bureaucratization of society which Max Weber so accurately forecasted, modern society has become compartmentalized. Each of us is, in the words of Herbert Marcuse, a "one-dimensional man." Social science is broken down into particular social sciences, and each of these is composed of a growing list of specialized areas. We are, increasingly, a society of specialists, and the specialist in one area is not expected to "infringe" on the domain of another. It becomes a self-fulfilling prophecy. Ultimately, we have lost the capacity to envision another social order. We can no longer think in broad terms; we are only capable of concentrating on specifics.* Certainly none of us would dare attempt to think in terms of a new overall political philosophy-theory. No single specialty can possibly encompass all the areas involved in such a theory. We are afraid of making mistakes and thus loosing our claim to expertise. We have forgotten the warning of Alfred North Whitehead that "the panic of error is the death of progress" (1958, p. 22).

What we lack and what we desperately need is a new ideology, not of the fanatical, closed-system character which Aron and others understandably reject, but most certainly a broad, plastic ideology (corresponding somewhat with what Mannheim defines as "Utopia") which will enable us to transcend our current stagnation.

Now there are those who tell us that ideology is now passé, because the expertise of the social engineer can provide us with the solutions to all of our problems. The benevolence of the social engineer is taken as a foregone conclusion. Being so much more enlightened, he certainly knows what is best for the general welfare. He has been trained to be value-free, to be

---

* A cursory examination of what is passed off as "pure research" would suffice to demonstrate the paucity of even what Robert K. Merton calls "theories of the middle range."

completely objective. He is part of Mannheim's free-floating intelligentsia. He is different in nature from the "Guardians of the Vested Interests" who seek only the maximization of their own interests. Regretfully, it is a cruel irony that in the not-too-distant past, this same type of faith was held by Thorstein Veblen in another sort of engineer, and we now know only too well that "it was Veblen, and not the Guardians of the Vested Interests, who was deceived" (Bell, 1963, p. 17).

When we look at what our "policy sciences" have to say about any of our social problems, we find that none of them has discovered anything even approaching a concrete solution. Each of the sciences focuses on a particular aspect of the problem, and each of the solutions is derived from the unique disciplinary "ideology" of those proposing that solution.

The late eminent social-psychologist Kurt Lewin cautioned that "Unfortunately, there is nothing in social laws and social research which will force the practitioner toward the good. Science gives more freedom and power to both the doctor and the murderer, to democracy and Fascism. The social scientist should recognize his responsibility also in this respect" (1948, p. 213).

Engineering of any type can be no more than a tool, and until we have developed the ideology with which we can guide the use of that tool, it stands as a potential threat to all of us.

BIBLIOGRAPHY

AIKEN, H. D.: "The Revolt Against Ideology," 1964 (pp. 229–258*).
APTER, D. E.: *Ideology and Discontent,* New York: The Free Press, 1964.
ARON, R.: "The End of the Ideological Age?," 1957 (pp. 27–47); *The Industrial Society,* New York: Frederick A. Praeger, 1967.
BELL, D.: "The End of Ideology in the West," 1962 (pp. 87–105);

* Page numbers refer to this volume.

Introduction to Thorstein Veblen: *The Engineers and the Price System,* New York: Harcourt, Brace and World, 1963.

BERGER, P. L. and LUCKMANN, T.: *The Social Construction of Reality,* New York: Doubleday, 1966.

BOTTOMORE, T. B.: *Critics of Society,* New York: Pantheon, 1968.

HABER, R. A.: "The End of Ideology as Ideology," 1962 (pp. 182–205).

HARRINGTON, M.: *The Accidental Century,* New York: Macmillan, 1965.

KENNAN, G. F.: "Rebels Without a Program," New York *Times Magazine,* January 21, 1968.

LAPALOMBARA, J.: "Decline of Ideology: A Dissent and an Interpretation," 1966 (pp. 315–341).

LEWIN, K.: *Resolving Social Conflicts,* New York: Harper & Row, 1948.

MANNHEIM, K.: *Ideology and Utopia,* New York: A Harvest Book, 1955.

MARCUSE, H.: *One-Dimensional Man,* Boston: Beacon Press, 1964.

MILLS, C. W.: *The Sociological Imagination,* New York: Oxford University Press, 1959.

OFFENBACHER, D. I.: "Men, Machines and Moral Indignation: The New Radicals and the Technological Society," unpublished paper, 1968.

PARSONS, T.: *The Social System,* New York: The Free Press, 1951.

SHILS, E.: "Ideology," in *The International Encyclopedia of the Social Sciences,* New York: Macmillan, 1968.

WHITEHEAD, A. N.: *Modes of Thought,* New York: Capricorn Books, 1958.

KARL MANNHEIM

❦

*Utopia in the Contemporary Situation**

Editor's note: Mannheim has defined as utopian a state of mind which transcends reality. A crucial distinction between the ideological and utopian states of mind, both of which are incongruous with and transcend reality, is that the latter (utopia) is transformed into actual conduct and tends to shatter the prevailing order of things, whereas the former (ideology) conceals the chances of social progress and does not shake the *status quo.* The problem with which Mannheim is herein involved is that of being able to determine what was considered ideological and what was considered utopian at a given period in history. C.I.W.

At the present moment the problem has assumed its own unique form. The historical process itself shows us a gradual descent and a closer approximation to real life of a utopia that at one time completely transcended history. As it comes closer to historical reality, its form undergoes functional as well as substantial changes. What was originally in absolute opposi-

* From *Ideology and Utopia* by Karl Mannheim, Harvest Books edition, pp. 248–263. Reprinted by permission of Harcourt, Brace & World, Inc. and Routledge & Kegan Paul Ltd.

tion to historical reality tends now, after the model of conservatism, to lose its character as opposition. Of course, none of the forms of these dynamic forces which emerge in an historical sequence ever disappears entirely, and at no time is any one of them indisputably dominant. The coexistence of these forces, their reciprocal opposition, as well as their constant mutual interpenetration, bring into being forms from which the richness of historical experience first emerges.

In order not to obscure what is decisive by an excess of details, we purposely stressed only the important tendencies in all this variety and overemphasized them by portraying them as ideal-types. Even though in the course of history nothing actually ever is lost of this multiplicity of things and events, it is possible to show with increasing clarity various degrees of dominance and alignment of the forces at work in society. Ideas, forms of thought, and psychic energies persist and are transformed in close conjunction with social forces. It is never by accident that they appear at given moments in the social process.

In this connection there becomes visible a peculiar structural determinant, which is at least worth indicating. The broader the class which achieves a certain mastery of the concrete conditions of existence, and the greater the chances for a victory through peaceful evolution, the more likely is this class to follow the road of conservatism. This signifies, however, that the various movements will have relinquished the utopian elements in their own modes of life.

This is demonstrated most sharply in the already mentioned fact that the relatively purest form of modern Chiliastic mentality, as embodied in radical anarchism, disappears almost entirely from the political scene, as a result of which an element of tension was eliminated from the remaining forms of the political utopia.

It is, of course, true that many of the elements constituting the Chiliastic attitude were transmuted into and took refuge in syndicalism and in Bolshevism, and were assimilated and incorporated into the activity of these movements. Thus the function devolves upon them, particularly in Bolshevism, of accelerating and catalyzing rather than deifying the revolutionary deed.

The general subsidence of utopian intensity occurs in still another important direction, namely that each utopia, as it is formed at a later stage of development, manifests a closer approximation to the historical-social process. In this sense, the liberal, the socialist, and the conservative ideas are merely different stages, and indeed counter-forms in the process which moves continually farther away from Chiliasm and approximates more closely to the events transpiring in this world.

All of these counter-forms of the Chiliastic utopia develop in close connection with the fate of those social strata which originally espouse them. They are, as we have seen, already moderated forms of the original Chiliastic ecstasy but in the course of further development they discard these last utopian vestiges and unwittingly approach more closely to a conservative attitude. It appears to be a generally valid law of the structure of intellectual development that when new groups gain entry into an already established situation they do not take over without further ado the ideologies which have already been elaborated for this situation, but rather they adapt the ideas which they bring with them through their traditions to the new situation. Thus liberalism and socialism, as they entered a situation more conducive to conservatism, did intermittently take over the ideas which conservatism offered them as a model, but on the whole preferred to adapt the original ideologies that they brought with them to the new situation. When these strata had come to occupy the social position previously held by the conservatives, they quite spontaneously developed a feeling for life and modes of thought which were structurally related to conservatism. The initial insight of the conservative into the structure of historical determinism, the emphasis, and, wherever possible, the overemphasis of the silently-working forces, the continuous absorption of the utopian element into everyday life appeared also in the thinking of these strata, sometimes in the form of a new and spontaneous creation, sometimes as a reinterpretation of older conservative patterns.

Thus we note that, conditioned by the social process, there develops a relative departure from the utopia at many points and in various forms. This process, which has already a dynamic quality of its own, is accelerated even further in its tempo and intensity by the fact that different coexistent forms of utopian mentality are destroying one another in reciprocal conflict. Such a reciprocal conflict of the various forms of the utopia does not necessarily lead to the annihilation of utopianism itself, for struggle in and by itself only heightens the utopian intensity. The modern form of reciprocal conflict is nevertheless peculiar in that the destruction of one's adversary does not take place on a utopian level, a fact which is most clearly perceptible in the way the socialists have gone about unmasking the ideologies of their antagonists. We do not hold up to the adversary that he is worshipping false gods; rather we destroy the intensity of his idea by showing that it is historically and socially determined.

Socialist thought, which hitherto has unmasked all its adversaries' utopias as ideologies, never raised the problem of determinateness about its own position. It never applied this method to itself and never checked its own desire to be absolute. It is nevertheless inevitable that here too the utopian element disappears with an increase in the feeling of determinateness. Thus we approach a situation in which the utopian element, through its many divergent forms, has completely (in politics, at least) annihilated itself. If one attempts to follow through tendencies which are already in existence, and to project them into the future, Gottfried Keller's prophecy—"The ultimate triumph of freedom will be barren" [1]—begins to assume, for us at least, an ominous meaning.

Symptoms of this "barrenness" are revealed in many contemporary phenomena, and can be clearly understood as radi-

[1] *"Der Freiheit letzter Sieg wird trocken sein."*

ations of the social and political situation into the more remote spheres of cultural life. Indeed, the more actively an ascendant party collaborates in a parliamentary coalition, and the more it gives up its original utopian impulses and with it its broad perspective, the more its power to transform society is likely to be absorbed by its interest in concrete and isolated details. Quite parallel to the change that may be observed in the political realm runs a change in the scientific outlook which conforms to political demands, i.e. what was once merely a formal scheme and abstract, total view, tends to dissolve into the investigation of specific and discrete problems. The utopian striving towards a goal and the closely related capacity for a broad perspective disintegrate in the parliamentary advisory council and in the trade-union movement into a mere body of directions for mastering a vast number of concrete details with a view to taking a political stand with reference to them. Likewise in the realm of research, what was formerly a correspondingly unified and systematized *Weltanschauung* becomes, in the attempt to deal with individual problems, merely a guiding perspective and a heuristic principle. But since all the mutually conflicting forms of utopia pass through the same life-cycle, they become in the realm of science, as in the realm of parliamentary practice, less and less mutually conflicting articles of faith, and more and more competing parties, or possible hypotheses for research. Whereas in an age of liberal ideals philosophy best reflected the social and intellectual situation, today the internal condition of the social and intellectual situations is reflected most clearly in the diverse forms of sociology.

The sociological view of classes acceding to power undergoes transformation along particular lines. These sociological theories, like our contemporary everyday conception of the world, embody the conflicting "possible points of view" which are nothing but the gradual transformations of earlier utopias. What is peculiar to this situation is that in this competitive struggle for the correct social perspective, all these conflicting approaches and points of view do not by any means "discredit" themselves; i.e. do not show themselves to be futile or incorrect. Rather it is shown with increasing clarity that it is possible to think productively from any point of view, although the degree of fruitfulness attainable varies from position to position. Each of these points of view reveals the interrelationships in the total complex of events from a different angle, and thus the suspicion grows that the historical process is something more inclusive than all the existing individual standpoints, and that our basis of thought, in its present state of atomization does not achieve a comprehensive view of events. The mass of facts and points of view is far greater than can be accommodated by the present state of our theoretical apparatus and systematizing capacity.

But this throws a new light upon the necessity of being continuously prepared for a synthesis in a world which is attaining one of the high points of its existence. What had previously grown up in random fashion from the particular intellectual needs of restricted social circles and classes suddenly becomes perceptible as a whole, and the profusion of events and ideas produces a rather blurred picture.

It is not out of weakness that a people of a mature stage in social and historical development submits to the different possibilities of viewing the world, and attempts to find for these a theoretical framework which will comprehend them all. This submission arises rather from the insight that every former intellectual certainty has rested upon partial points of view made absolute. It is characteristic of the present time that the limits of these partial points of view should have become obvious.

At this mature and advanced stage of development, the total perspective tends to disappear in proportion to the disappearance of the utopia. Only the extreme left and right groups in modern life believe that there is a unity in the developmental process. In the former we have the neo-Marxism of a Lukács, with his profoundly important work, and in the latter the universalism of a Spann. It would be superfluous at this time to demonstrate the differences in the sociological points of view of these two extremes by referring to the differences in their conceptions of totality. We are not interested in completeness in this connection, but rather in a provisional determination of the phenomena which are symptomatic of the present situation.

Unlike those mentioned above, who regard the category of totality as an ontological-metaphysical entity, Troeltsch used it as a working hypothesis in research. He employed it in a somewhat experimental fashion as an ordering principle for an approach to the mass of data and, resorting to different lines of attack on the materials, he sought to uncover the elements which at any one time make it a unity. Alfred Weber seeks to reconstruct the whole of a past historical epoch rather as a *Gestalt*—a configurational unity by means of what can be intuitively observed. His method stands in decided contrast to rationalist dogmatism which relies upon deduction. That Troeltsch and Alfred Weber, as democrats, stand between the two extremes of Lukács and Spann is reflected in their respective mental structures. Although they accept the conception of totality, the former avoids any metaphysical and ontological assumption when speaking of it, and the latter rejects the rationalistic attitude usually connected with it as used by radicals.

In contrast to those who are associated with Marxism or the conservative-historical tradition in their conception of totality, another element in the middle group attempts to disregard entirely the problem of totality, in order, on the basis of this renunciation, to be able to concentrate its attention more fully on the wealth of individual problems. Whenever the utopia disappears, history ceases to be a process leading to an ultimate end. The frame of reference according to which we evaluate facts vanishes and we are left with a series of events all equal as far as their inner significance is concerned. The concept of historical time which led to qualitatively different epochs disappears, and history becomes more and more like undifferenti-

ated space. All those elements of thought which are rooted in
utopias are now viewed from a skeptical relativist point of
view. Instead of the conception of progress and dialectics we
get the search for eternally valid generalizations and types, and
reality becomes nothing but a particular combination of these
general factors (cf. the general sociology of Max Weber).

The conceptual framework of social philosophy which stood
behind the work of the last centuries seems to disappear with
the faith in utopias as collective ends of human strivings. This
skeptical attitude, in many ways fruitful, corresponds primarily
to the social position of a bourgeoisie already in power, whose
future has gradually become its present. The other strata of
society manifest the same tendencies in the measure that they
too approach a realization of their aims. Nevertheless, the concrete development of their present mode of thought is also to
some extent sociologically determined by the historical situation in which they had their beginnings. If the dynamic conception of time is cancelled out of the Marxian sociological
method, here too is obtained a generalizing theory of ideology
which, since it is blind to historical differentiations, would relate ideas exclusively to the social positions of those who hold
them irrespective of the society in which they occur or of the
particular function they may there fulfill.

The outlines of a sociology which is indifferent to the historical time-element were already perceivable in America, where
the dominant type of mentality became more completely and
more quickly congruent with the reality of capitalistic society
than was the case in German thought. In America, the sociology derived from the philosophy of history was discarded at a
rather early date. Sociology, instead of being an adequate picture of the structure of the whole society, split up into a series
of discrete technical problems of social readjustment.

"Realism" means different things in different contexts. In
Europe it meant that sociology had to focus its attention on the
very severe tension between the classes, whereas in America,
where there was more free play in the economic realm, it was

not so much the class problem which was considered as the "real" center of society but the problems of social technique and organization. Sociology for those forms of European thought which found themselves in opposition to the *status quo,* signified the solution of the problem of class relations— more generally, a scientific diagnosis of the present epoch; to the American, on the contrary, it meant the solution of the immediate, technical problems of social life. This helps to explain why, in the European formulation of sociological problems, there is always asked the uneasy question about what the future has in store, and similarly it throws light on the closely related drive for a total perspective; likewise it is possible to explain, on the basis of this difference, the type of thought involved in the American formulation of the problem, as represented by the following: How can I do this? How can I solve this concrete individual problem? And in all these questions we sense the optimistic undertone: I need not worry about the whole, the whole will take care of itself.

In Europe, however, the complete disappearance of all reality-transcending doctrines—utopian as well as ideological— took place not merely through the fact that all these notions were shown to be relative to the social-economic situation, but also by other means. The sphere of ultimate reality rested in the economic and social sphere for it was to this that Marxism, in the last analysis, related all ideas and values; it was still historically and intellectually differentiated, i.e. it still contained some fragment of historical perspective (due largely to its Hegelian derivation). Historical materialism was materialist only in name; the economic sphere was, in the last analysis, in spite of occasional denial of this fact, a structural interrelationship of mental attitudes. The existent economic system was precisely a "system," i.e. something which arises in the sphere of the mind (the objective mind as Hegel understood it). The process which first started by undermining the validity of spiritual elements in history proceeded further to disturb that sphere of the mind, and reduced all happenings to functions of human drives which were completely detached from historical and spiritual elements. This, too, made possible a generalizing theory; the reality-transcending elements, ideologies, utopias, etc.—were now no longer relative to social group-situations but to drives—to eternal forms in the structure of human impulses (Pareto, Freud, etc.). This generalizing theory of drives was already adumbrated in the English social philosophy and social psychology of the seventeenth and eighteenth centuries. Thus, for example, Hume, in his *Enquiry concerning Human Understanding,* says:

"It is universally acknowledged that there is a great uniformity among the actions of men, in all nations and ages, and that human nature remains still the same, in its principles and operations. The same motives always produce the same actions. The same events always follow from the same causes. Ambition, avarice, self-love, vanity, friendship, generosity, public spirit: these passions, mixed in various degrees, and distributed through society, have been from the beginning of the world, and still are, the source of all the actions and enterprises which have ever been observed among mankind." [2]

This process of the complete destruction of all spiritual elements, the utopian as well as the ideological, has its parallel in the most recent trends of modern life, and in their corresponding tendencies in the realm of art. Must we not regard the disappearance of humanitarianism from art, the emergence of a "matter of factness" (*Sachlichkeit*) in sexual life, art, and architecture, and the expression of the natural impulses in sports—must all these not be interpreted as symptomatic of the increasing regression of the ideological and utopian elements from the mentality of the strata which are coming to dominate the present situation? Must not the gradual reduction of politics to economics toward which there is at least a discernible tendency, the conscious rejection of the past and of

[2] Hume, *Enquiries concerning the Human Understanding and concerning the Principles of Morals.* Ed. by L. A. Selby-Bigge, 2nd ed. (Oxford, 1927), p. 83.

the notion of historical time, the conscious brushing aside of every "cultural ideal," be interpreted as a disappearance of every form of utopianism from the political arena as well?

Here a certain tendency to act on the world is pressing forward an attitude for which all ideas have been discredited and all utopias have been destroyed. This prosaic attitude which is now dawning is in large measure to be welcomed as the only instrument for the mastery of the present situation, as the transformation of utopianism into science, as the destruction of the deluding ideologies which are incongruent with the reality of our present situation. It would require either a callousness which our generation could probably no longer acquire or the unsuspecting naïveté of a generation newly born into the world to be able to live in absolute congruence with the realities of that world, utterly without any transcendent element, either in the form of a utopia or of an ideology. At our present stage of self-consciousness this is perhaps the only form of actual existence that is possible in a world which is no longer in the making. It is possible that the best that our ethical principles have to offer is "genuineness" and "frankness" in place of the old ideals. "Genuineness" (*Echtheitskategorie*) and frankness seem to be nothing more than the projection of the general "matter-of-factness" or "realism" of our time into the realm of ethics. Perhaps a world that is no longer in the making can afford this. But have we reached the stage where we can dispense with strivings? Would not this elimination of all tension mean the elimination also of political activity, scientific zeal—in fact of the very content of life itself?

Thus, if we are not to rest content with this "matter-of-factness," we must carry our quest farther and ask whether there are not, besides those social strata who by their satisfied attitude promote this decreased psychological tension, other forces active in the social realm? If the question is put in this manner, however, the answer must be as follows:

The apparent absence of tension in the present-day world is being undermined from two sides. On the one side are those strata whose aspirations are not yet fulfilled, and who are striving towards communism and socialism. For these the unity of utopia, point of view, and action is taken for granted as long as they are outsiders in relation to the world as it now exists. Their presence in society implies the uninterrupted existence of at least one form of utopia, and thus, to a certain extent, will always cause the counter-utopias to rekindle and flare up again, at least whenever this extreme left wing goes into action. Whether this will actually happen depends largely on the structural form of the developmental process which confronts us at present. If, through peaceful evolution, we are able, at a later stage, to reach a somewhat superior form of industrialism, which will be sufficiently elastic and which will give the lower strata a degree of relative well-being, then they too will undergo the type of transformation which has already been evidenced by the classes in power. (From this point of view it makes no difference whether this superior form of social organization of industrialism, through the arrival at a position of power on the part of the lower strata, will eventuate in a capitalism which is sufficiently elastic to insure their relative well-being, or whether this capitalism will first be transformed into communism.) If this later stage in industrial development can be attained only through revolution, then the utopian and ideological elements in thought will flare up once more with fresh vigor on all sides. However this may be, it is in the social power of this wing of the opposition to the existing order that there is to be found one of the determinants upon which the fate of reality-transcending concepts depends.

But the future form of the utopian mentality and of intellectuality does not depend only on the vicissitudes of this extreme social stratum. In addition to this sociological factor, there is yet another which should be reckoned with in this connection, namely, a distinct social and intellectual middle stratum which, although it bears a definite relation to intellectual activity, has not been considered in our previous analysis. Hitherto all classes have included, in addition to those who actually represented their direct interests, a stratum more oriented towards what might be called the realm of the spirit. Sociologically, they could be called "intellectuals," but for our present purpose we must be more precise. We are not referring here to those who bear the outward insignia of education, but to those few among them who, consciously or unconsciously, are interested in something else than success in the competitive scheme that displaces the present one. No matter how soberly one looks at it, one cannot deny that this small group has nearly always existed. Their position presented no problem as long as their intellectual and spiritual interests were congruous with those of the class that was struggling for social supremacy. They experienced and knew the world from the same utopian perspective as that of the group or social stratum with whose interest they identified themselves. This applies as well to Thomas Münzer as to the bourgeois fighters of the French Revolution, to Hegel as well as to Karl Marx.

Their situation always becomes questionable, however, when the group with which they identify themselves arrives at a position of power, and when, as a result of this attainment of power, the utopia is released from politics, and consequently the stratum which was identified with that group on the basis of this utopia is also set free.

The intellectuals will also be released from these social bonds as soon as the most oppressed stratum of society comes to share in the domination of the social order. Only the socially unattached intellectuals will be even more than now in increasing proportions recruited from all social strata rather than merely from the most privileged ones. This intellectual section of society, which is becoming more and more separated from the rest and thrown upon its own resources, is confronted at another angle by what we have just now characterized as a total situation tending towards the complete disappearance of social tension. But since the intellectuals by no means find themselves in accord with the existing situation and so completely congruent with it that it no longer presents a problem to them, they aim also to reach out beyond that tensionless situation.

The four following alternatives are open to the intellectuals who have thus been cast up by the social process: the first group of intellectuals which is affiliated with the radical wing of the socialist-communist proletariat actually does not concern us here at all. For it, at least to that extent, there are no problems. The conflict between social and intellectual allegiance does not yet exist for it.

The second group, which was cast up by the social process at the same time that its utopia was discarded, becomes skeptical and proceeds, in the name of intellectual integrity, to destroy the ideological elements in science, in the manner described above (M. Weber, Pareto).

The third group takes refuge in the past and attempts to find there an epoch or society in which an extinct form of reality-transcendence dominated the world, and through this romantic reconstruction it seeks to spiritualize the present. The same function, from this point of view, is fulfilled by attempts to revive religious feeling, idealism, symbols, and myths.

The fourth group becomes shut off from the world and consciously renounces direct participation in the historical process. They become ecstatic like the Chiliasts, but with the difference that they no longer concern themselves with radical political movements. They take part in the great historical process of disillusionment, in which every concrete meaning of things as well as myths and beliefs are slowly cast aside. They therefore differ from the Romanticists, who aim essentially at conserving the old beliefs in a modern age. This a-historical ecstasy which had inspired both the mystic and the Chiliast, although in different ways, is now placed in all its nakedness in the very center of experience. We find one symptom of this, for example, in modern expressionistic art, in which objects have lost their original meaning and seem simply to serve as a medium for the communication of the ecstatic. Similarly in the field of philosophy, many nonacademic thinkers like Kierkegaard, in the quest for faith, discard all the concrete historical elements in religion, and are ultimately driven to a bare ecstatic "existence as such." Such a removal of the Chiliastic element from the midst of culture and politics might preserve the purity of the ecstatic spirit but it would leave the world without meaning or life. This removal will, in the end, be fatal for Chiliastic ecstasy as well, since, as we have already seen, when it turns inward and gives up its conflict with the immediate concrete world, it tends to become gentle and innocuous, or else to lose itself in pure self-edification.

It is inevitable that after such an analysis we should ask ourselves what the future holds; and the difficulty of this question lays bare the structure of historical understanding. To predict is the task of prophets, and every prophecy of necessity transforms history into a purely determinate system, depriving us thereby of the possibility of choice and decision. As a further result, the impulse to weigh and to reflect with reference to the constantly emerging sphere of new possibilities dies away.

The only form in which the future presents itself to us is that of possibility, while the imperative, the "should," tells us which of these possibilities we should choose. As regards knowledge, the future—in so far as we are not concerned with the purely organized and rationalized part of it—presents itself as an impenetrable medium, an unyielding wall. And when our attempts to see through it are repulsed, we first become aware of the necessity of willfully choosing our course and, in close connection with it, the need for an imperative (a utopia) to drive us onward. Only when we know what are the interests and imperatives involved are we in a position to inquire into the possibilities of the present situation, and thus to gain our first insight into history. Here, finally, we see why no interpretation of history can exist except in so far as it is guided by interest and purposeful striving. Of the two conflicting tendencies in the modern world—the utopian trends on the one hand, struggling against a complacent tendency to accept the present on the other hand—it is difficult to tell in advance which one will finally conquer, for the course of historical reality which will determine it still lies in the future. We could change the whole of society tomorrow if everybody could agree. The real obstacle is that every individual is bound into a system of established relationships which to a large extent hamper his will.[3] But these "established relationships" in the last analysis rest again upon uncontrolled decisions of individuals. The task, therefore, is to remove that source of difficulty by unveiling the hidden motives behind the individual's decisions, thus put-

[3] Here, too, in such ultimately decisive questions as these, the most fundamental differences in possible modes of experiencing reality are revealed. The anarchist, Landauer, may again be quoted to represent one extreme:—

"What do you understand then by the hard objective facts of human history? Certainly not the soil, houses, machines, railroad tracks, telegraph wires, and such like. If, however, you are referring thereby to tradition, custom, and complexes of relations, which are the objects of pious reverence, such as the state and similar organizations, conditions, and situations, then it is no longer possible to dismiss them by saying they are only appearances. The possibility and the necessity of the social process as it fluctuates from stability, to decay, and then to reconstruction is based on the fact that there is no organism that has grown up that stands above the individual, but rather a complex relationship of reason, love, and authority. Thus again and again there comes a time in the history of a social structure, which is a structure only as long as individuals nourish it with their vitality, when those living shy away from it as a strange ghost from the past, and create new groupings instead. Thus I have withdrawn my love, reason, obedience, and my will from that which I call the 'state'. That I am able to do this depends on my will. That you are not able to do this does not alter the decisive fact that this particular inability is inseparably bound up with your own personality and not with the nature of the state." (From a letter of Gustav Landauer to Margarete Susmann, reprinted in *Landauer, G., sein Lebensgang in Briefen,* edited by Martin Buber (1929), vol. ii, p. 122.)

At the other extreme, cf. the following citation from Hegel:—

"Since the phases of the ethical system are the conception of freedom, they are the substance of universal essence of individuals. In relation to it, individuals are merely accidental. Whether the individual exists or not is a matter of indifference to the objective ethical order, which alone is steadfast. It is the power by which the life of individuals is ruled. It has been represented by nations as eternal justice, or as deities who are absolute, in contrast with whom the striving of individuals is an empty game, like the tossing of the sea." Hegel, *Philosophy of Right*, trans. by J. W. Dyde (London, 1896), p. 156 §145, addition.

ting him in a position really to choose. Then, and only then, would his decisions *really* lie with him.

All that we have said so far in this book is meant to help the individual to disclose these hidden motives and to reveal the implications of his choice. For our own more restricted analytical purpose, however, which we may designate as a sociological history of modes of thought, it became clear that the most important changes in the intellectual structure of the epoch we have been dealing with are to be understood in the light of the transformations of the utopian element. It is possible, therefore, that in the future, in a world in which there is never anything new, in which all is finished and each moment is a repetition of the past, there can exist a condition in which thought will be utterly devoid of all ideological and utopian elements. But the complete elimination of reality-transcending elements from our world would lead us to a "matter-of-factness" which ultimately would mean the decay of the human will. Herein lies the most essential difference between these two types of reality-transcendence: whereas the decline of ideology represents a crisis only for certain strata, and the objectivity which comes from the unmasking of ideologies always takes the form of self-clarification for society as a whole, the complete disappearance of the utopian element from human thought and action would mean that human nature and human development would take on a totally new character. The disappearance of utopia brings about a static state of affairs in which man himself becomes no more than a thing. We would be faced then with the greatest paradox imaginable, namely, that man, who has achieved the highest degree of rational mastery of existence, left without any ideals, becomes a mere creature of impulses. Thus, after a long tortuous, but heroic development, just at the highest stage of awareness, when history is ceasing to be blind fate, and is becoming more and more man's own creation, with the relinquishment of utopias, man would lose his will to shape history and therewith his ability to understand it.

RAYMOND ARON

The End of
*the Ideological Age?**

It may seem rather paradoxical to envisage the end of the ideological age at a time when Senator [Joseph] McCarthy continues to play a leading role on the Washington stage, when *Les Mandarins* has just won the Prix Goncourt and the flesh-and-blood "mandarins" are making the pilgrimage to Moscow and Peking. One is not, of course, so naïve as to expect peace to blossom forth in the immediate future: the idealists disillusioned or liquidated, the bureaucrats continue to reign.

The Westerners themselves may dream of political tolerance just as, three centuries ago, they tired of futile slaughter in the name of the same God for the choice of the true religion. But they have communicated to the rest of the world their faith in a radiant future. Nowhere, in Asia or in Africa, has the Welfare State spread enough benefits to stifle the impulse towards irrational and foolish hope. The nations of Europe preceded the others on the road to industrial civilization. Now, perhaps, moved by the first glimmerings of skepticism, they are beginning to foreshadow, however prematurely, a new shape of things to come.

Let us look back and survey the centuries which have elapsed since the dawn of the philosophy of immanence and of modern science. Every one of the ideologies which, for a few years or for a few decades, has seized the imagination of the crowd or of thinking men, reveals, retrospectively, a simple structure with one or two guiding ideas.

The optimism of the Left was created and maintained by a strong feeling: admiration for the power of reason, certainty that the application of science to industry would revolutionize the order of human society and the condition of its individual members. The ancestral aspiration toward human brotherhood was united with faith in practical science in order to inspire either nationalism or socialism or both.

Freedom of enquiry asserted against Church orthodoxy, and the equality of fighting men established on the field of battle by the introduction of firearms, undermined the edifice of traditional hierarchies. The future would belong to free and equal citizens. After the storm which precipitated the collapse of the most grandiose edifice of aristocratic Europe, after the fall of the French monarchy, the revolutionary fervor, encouraged by flamboyant successes as well as bloody defeats, split into two separate channels, nationalist and socialist.

Called upon to defend the Fatherland at the risk of their lives, the servants of the throne felt entitled to demand a State which they could call their own and rulers whose language they could understand. Historians, philosophers and novelists, stressing the individuality of ethnic or cultural groups or the right of self-determination, sensitive to the unconscious workings of the centuries or to the coherence of the cities of antiquity, elaborated the various theories of the nation. Perhaps, in justifying national passions, they merely succeeded in exacerbating them, sometimes on the level of primitive tribalism, sometimes ennobled by the dream of liberty. At all events, the sort of reasonable administration accepted by several nationalities because foreign to each of them was in the long run

28

rendered anachronistic by the speed of primary education and conscription.

National sentiments are still strong on both sides of the Iron Curtain. In the people's democracies Russian domination is detested. The French are easily aroused against the American "occupation." The European Defense Community was denounced as the supreme surrender because it transferred to a supra-national organism some of the prerogatives of sovereignty. The Communist militant follows the orders which are sent from Moscow; in 1939–40 he sabotaged the war effort, in June 1941 he joined the Resistance, but the Party won recruits by the millions during the period when the interests of France coincided with those of the Soviet Union.

National feeling remains and must remain the cement of human collectivities, but the nationalist ideology is nonetheless condemned in Western Europe. An ideology presupposes an apparently systematic formalization of facts, interpretations, desires and predictions. The intellectual who wants to be *essentially* nationalist must interpret history as the permanent struggle of jungle states or prophesy peace between independent nations on a basis of mutual respect. The combination of revolutionary nationalism and Machiavellian diplomacy advocated by Charles Maurras could not survive the weakening of the European states.

By all means let the rulers defend tooth and nail the interests and rights of their country against the encroachments of strong and tactless allies. But how can one get excited about the temporal grandeur of a collectivity which is incapable of manufacturing its own arms? The American defense budget represents three-quarters of the total military expenditure of the Atlantic alliance. Isolation, neutrality, and the playing off of one bloc against the other, are sometimes possible and always legitimate, but they do not contribute toward an ideological transfiguration. In our century, a second-class nation-state is not an adequate framework for full human expression.

The United States and the Soviet Union are capable of spreading the pride of domination and the will to conquest. Their nationalism is on a different level from that of the European states tied to one soil, one culture, one language. In Russia, whether Tsarist or Soviet, and in the United States, citizenship is accorded to men of many different races, colors, and languages. Color prejudice in the United States has put a brake on the realization by the Negroes of the equality promised by the American constitution. If they have not responded to the appeal of Communism, it is to a large extent because of this promise. Externally the United States, except for a few years at the end of the last century and the beginning of this, have been innocent of imperialism in the European fashion, or of the desire for expansion and the permanent struggle with other states. American citizenship involves not so much the participation in a culture rooted in history as the acquisition of a way of life.

The Soviet Union has carried on in a new form the Tsarist tradition which allowed the ruling classes of neighboring peoples entry into the aristocracy of the imperial State. Thanks to the Communist Party, it has maintained the unity of the multi-national élite. Soviet citizenship, offered to innumerable nationalities, requires loyalty to a State and adherence to an ideology, but not the renouncing of the nationality of origin.

The Big Two, as a result of their rivalry and of the power vacuum which grew up between them after the Second World War, have been led to set up supra-national systems one against the other. NATO is dominated by the United States which provides arms for the allied divisions and which alone is powerful enough to form a counterweight to the Soviet mass. Marshal Rokossovsky is in command in Warsaw because the Soviet leaders are doubtful about the loyalty of the Poles and because several divisions of the Red Army are stationed in the heart of Germany. *Lebensraum,* one of the favorite themes of the pundits of the Third Reich, has been realized on both sides of the Iron Curtain, *but only on the military plane.*

30

One hesitates to use the word empire. There is not the slightest sign of an Atlantic patriotism and it is scarcely likely that Soviet Russian patriotism is very widespread in the satellite states, outside the Communist minorities. The supranational system, in theory unified by the triumph of a common faith, denies itself by isolating the people's democracies one from the other. It is not much easier to travel from Roumania to Poland than from Poland to France. The people's democracies, deprived of the substance of independence, have been given a sort of travesty of it; they are all shut in between their own frontiers as if each state necessary to the total plan had to be closed, even against its allies.

No less than the domination of men of other races and other languages, extreme inequalities of economic conditions seemed to be in contradiction with the spirit of the new times. The miracles of science made human misery scandalous and inexcusable. Nobody doubted that industry must soon eliminate the relics of immemorial poverty; people differed only on the choice of means. The ideal of the social community oscillated between the notion of a balance achieved by all without having been the object of a conscious will, and the notion of prosperity for all thanks to a global plan and the elimination of the exploiters.

Liberalism and socialism continue to inspire convictions and to provoke controversies, but it is becoming more and more difficult reasonably to transform such preferences into doctrines. Western "capitalist" society today comprises a multitude of socialist institutions. One can no longer count on collective ownership or planning to bring about a dramatic improvement in man's lot.

Technological progress lived up to men's expectations and has gone on increasing by leaps and bounds. Perhaps, some years or some decades hence, it will have overcome the limitations of material resources. But its price and its limits are now generally realized. Mechanized societies are not pacific; they deliver man from the servitudes of poverty and weakness, but they subject millions of workers to the logic of mass production, and they risk turning human beings into machines.

Neither the optimist who conjures up a vision of fraternity thanks to material plenty, nor the pessimist who visualizes a consummate tyranny extended over human minds with the help of the new instruments of mass communication and torture, is quite refuted by the experience of the twentieth century. The dialogue between them, begun at the time of the first factories, is still being pursued. But it does not take the form of an ideological debate, since the opposing themes are no longer connected with a particular class or party.

The last great ideology was born of the combination of three elements: the vision of a future consistent with human aspirations, the link between this future and a particular social class, and trust in human values above and beyond the victory of the working class, thanks to planning and collective ownership. Confidence in the virtues of a socio-economic technique has begun to wane and one looks in vain for this class which is supposed to bring about the radical renewal of institutions and ideas.

The theory of the class struggle, which is still current today, is falsified by a spurious analogy: the rivalry between bourgeoisie and proletariat differs in essence from the rivalry between aristocracy and bourgeoisie.

Certain nineteenth-century thinkers transfigured into a Promethean exploit the overthrow of the French monarchy and the blood-stained, terror-haunted, faction-ridden adventure of the Republic. Hegel claimed to have seen the spirit of the world passing on horseback, in the form of an officer risen from the ranks whom the god of battles had crowned. Marx and then Lenin painted dream-pictures of the Jacobins, the active minority which stirs up the stagnant pool of popular feeling, the missionary order in the service of the socialist revolution. There could be no doubt about it—the proletariat would finish the work begun by the bourgeoisie.

The ideologists of the proletariat are bourgeois intellectuals.

The bourgeoisie, whether it derived its ideas from Montesquieu, Voltaire or Jean-Jacques Rousseau, set up its own conception of human existence and the political order in opposition to the *Ancien Régime* and the Catholic vision of the world. *The proletariat has never had a conception of the world opposed to that of the bourgeoisie; there has been an ideology of what the proletariat should be or should do, an ideology whose historical ascendancy was most powerful when the number of industrial workers was smallest.* The so-called proletarian party, in the countries where it has seized power, has had peasants rather than factory workers as its troops, and intellectuals, exasperated by the traditional hierarchy or by national humiliation, as its leaders.

The values to which the working class spontaneously subscribes differ from those of the bourgeoisie. It is not impermissible to construct antitheses between the two: the sense of solidarity against the desire for possessions, participation in the community against individualism or egoism, the generosity of the penniless against the avarice of the rich, etc. In any case there is no denying the obvious fact that the system and style of living in working-class districts are very different from those of the wealthy middle classes. So-called proletarian régimes, that is régimes governed by Communist parties, owe practically nothing to authentic working-class culture, to the parties or unions whose leaders themselves belong to the working class.

Popular culture in our century has succumbed to the blows of *Pravda, France-Soir* or the *Readers' Digest.* Revolutionary syndicalist or anarchist movements cannot resist the unconscious coalition of employers' organizations which fear them, and socialist, especially communist, parties which detest them. The latter have been affected by the thought and action of the intellectuals.

It was in the hope of accomplishing fully the ambitions of the bourgeoisie—the conquest of Nature, social equality or equality of opportunity—that the ideologists handed on the torch to the proletariat. The contrast between technological progress and the misery of the workers was a crying scandal. How could one help but impute to private ownership and the anarchy of the market the survival of ancestral poverty which was in fact due to the exigencies of accumulation (capitalist or socialist), insufficient productivity and increases in population. Soft-hearted intellectuals, revolted by injustice, seized on the idea that capitalism being in itself evil, would be destroyed by its contradictions and that its victims would eventually overthrow the privileged. Marx achieved an improbable synthesis between the Hegelian metaphysic of history, the Jacobin interpretation of the Revolution, and the pessimistic theory of the market economy developed by British authors. To maintain the continuity between the French Revolution and the Russian Revolution, it was only necessary to call Marxist ideology proletarian. But one has merely to open one's eyes to be rid of the illusion.

The market economy and total planning are rival models—which no existing economy actually reproduces—not successive stages in evolution. There is no necessary link between the phases of industrial development and the predominance of one model or the other. Backward economies approximate more to the model of the planners than do advanced economies. Mixed systems are not monsters incapable of surviving, or transitional forms on the way to the pure type; they are the normal thing. In a planned system one will find most of the categories of the market economy, more or less modified. As the standard of living rises and the Soviet consumer has more freedom of choice, the benefits and the problems of Western prosperity will appear on the other side of the Iron Curtain.

The revolutions of the twentieth century have not been proletarian revolutions; they have been thought up and carried out by intellectuals. They have overthrown the traditional power, ill-adapted to the exigencies of the technological age. The prophets imagined that capitalism would precipitate a revolution comparable to the one which convulsed France at the end of the eighteenth century. Nothing of the sort happened. On the contrary, wherever the ruling classes have been unable or unwilling to reform themselves quickly enough, the dissatisfaction of the bourgeoisie, the impatience of the intellectuals and the immemorial aspirations of the peasants have provoked an explosion.

Neither Russia nor the United States ever fully experienced the struggle between the aristocracy and the bourgeoisie. Tsarism sought to borrow the technical civilization of the West while discarding its democratic ideas. It has been replaced by a power which has re-established the identification between society and the State, the administrators constituting the only privileged class.

The United States became conscious of its identity through the progressive ideas of the European eighteenth century. It sought to put them into practice on virgin soil which had to be conquered not so much in the face of the Indians, who were doomed to extinction by the gap between their tribal culture and that of the European immigrants, as in the face of recalcitrant Nature and the elements. There was no aristocracy, clinging to its privileges, to restrain the impetus of reason and industry. American religion taught moral strictness, not a creed or orthodoxy. It urged the citizens both to intransigence and conformism, but it did not unite with the State to put a brake on the movement of modern thought. No event comparable to the French Revoluiton and the secession of the proletariat came to belie the eighteenth-century optimism of the New World. The Civil War was interpreted by the historians—the spokesmen of the victors—as a triumph, proving that the world cannot live half free and half enslaved. The American workers accepted the promises of the American Idea and did not believe in the necessity of an Apocalypse.

Armed with a doctrine which condemned their enterprise in advance, the Bolsheviks were the builders of an industrial society of a kind hitherto unknown. The State took over the responsibility for distributing the collective resources, for managing the factories, for savings and investments. The Western working class in the nineteenth century rose against the employers, not directly against the State. Where the employers and the State are identical, revolt against the one would involve dissidence toward the other. The Marxist ideology offered an admirable justification for the necessities of a State economy: the proletarians owed unconditional obedience to their own collective will embodied in the Party.

Certainly, if criticism had been tolerated, the intellectuals would have denounced the misery of the slums of Leningrad and Moscow in the Russia of 1930, just as their colleagues had denounced those of Manchester or Paris a century earlier. The contrast between the growth of the means of production and the aggravation, apparent or real, of the sufferings of the people would have inspired familiar Utopian visions of progress without tears or of fecund catastrophes.

In any case, what possible program could the oppositionists offer as an alternative to the Soviet reality? They might demand political liberties, the participation of the workers in the management of industry, but not the individual appropriation of the instruments of production, except perhaps in agriculture. Under a capitalist régime the masses can at least imagine that public ownership would cure or attenuate the evils of industry, but under a collectivist régime they cannot expect the same miracle from a restoration of private ownership. The malcontents dream of a return to Leninism, of a truly proletarian State; in other words they aspire to institutions and a way of life which would be a more faithful expression of the reigning ideology.

In the United States, the proletariat does not think of itself as such. The workers' organizations demand and obtain many of the reforms which in Europe are associated with the Welfare State or socialism; the leaders of the masses are satisfied with the position accorded to them under the present régime, and the masses themselves do not aspire to a different society or different values. Unanimity on "free enterprise," on competition and the "circulation of the élites" does not mean that the American reality accords with these ideas, any more than the obligatory teaching of Marxist-Leninism ensures that Russian society conforms to the official ideology.

Thus, by different routes, either spontaneously or with the help of the police, the two great societies of our time have come to suppress the conditions of ideological debate, have integrated the workers, and imposed a unanimous adherence to the principles of the régime. The debate remains a burning one in those countries of the second rank who are not entirely at home in the ideological camp to which they belong; too proud to accept their *de facto* dependence, too arrogant to admit that the dissidence of the internal proletariat reflects a national failure rather than a decree of history, fascinated by the power which spreads terror, prisoners of the geography which tolerates criticism and abuse but which forbids escape.

By a conspicuous paradox, the diffusion of the same technological civilization throughout the globe gives a special character to the problems which confront each separate nation today. The political consciousness of our time is falsified by the failure to acknowledge these distinctions.

Whether liberal, socialist, conservative or Marxist, our ideologies are the legacy of a century in which Europe was aware of the plurality of civilizations but did not doubt the universality of its message. Today, factories, parliaments and schools are springing up in every latitude, the masses are in ferment, the intellectuals are taking over power. Europe, which has finished conquering and is already succumbing to its victory and the revolt of its slaves, hesitates to admit that its ideas have conquered the universe but have not kept the form they used to have in our own debates and controversies.

Prisoners of the Marxist-Leninist orthodoxy, the intellectuals of the East are not allowed to admit the obvious fact that industrial civilization comprises a multiplicity of forms between which neither history nor reason imposes a radical

37

choice. Those of the West sometimes hesitate before making an avowal in the opposite sense: Without freedom of enquiry, individual initiative, the pioneering spirit of the traders and industrialists, this civilization would perhaps never have arisen; but are the same virtues necessary in order to reproduce or prolong it? Strange century, in which one can travel round the globe in forty-eight hours, but in which the principal protagonists in the drama are compelled, after the fashion of the heroes of Homer, to exchange their insults from afar.

India cannot model herself either on the Europe of today or on that of 1810. Even supposing that the income per head of population and the distribution of labor were, in the India of today, what they were in Europe a century and a half ago, the phases of economic development would not be homologous. India borrows technological recipes instead of inventing them; she receives the ideas which are accepted in semi-socialist England; she applies the lessons of contemporary medicine and hygiene. The growth of the population and the development of the economy will not be harmonized in the Asia of the twentieth century as they were in the Europe of the nineteenth.

Politics are differentiated not only by the economic and demographic ages of different countries, but also by the traditions peculiar to each nation, each sphere of culture. Everywhere, in the so-called free world, assemblies deliberate side by side with blast furnaces. Everywhere, parliament, the institution which, in the West, was the crowning glory of democracy, has been adopted from the start. In Paris in the last century people legitimately demanded universal suffrage and the sovereignty of parliament; the State had been consolidated by centuries of monarchy, the nation forged by centuries of life in common. An intellectual class, trained in political debate, aspired to exercise power. The Westerners were not wrong to believe that their parliaments—Continental hemicycles or Anglo-Saxon rectangles—were destined for the same triumphal progress across the globe as motor-cars or electricity.

They would be wrong to ascribe a universal significance to the ideologies which glorify these institutions.

Political theorists must and can take into consideration the various circumstances—the strength of national unity, the intensity of the quarrels of language, religion or party, the integration or dissolution of local communities, the capacity of the political élite, etc.—which determine in each country the chances of success of the parliamentary system. The preferences expressed by political or economic doctrinaires for one method as against another are reasonable as long as the limits and uncertainties are not forgotten. The free world would be guilty of a fatal error if it thought that it possessed a unique ideology comparable to Marxist-Leninism.

The Stalinist technique, at least in the first phase, remains applicable in every country where the Party, thanks to the Russian army or the national army, has taken possession of the State. A false doctrine manages to inspire effective action because this is determined by tactical considerations based on the experience of half a century.

The falseness of the doctrine is proved by the widespread aversion to this pseudo-liberation. In Europe, outside Russia, Communist régimes have been incapable of installing themselves, and are perhaps incapable of maintaining themselves, without the help of the Red Army. As time goes on, national peculiarities will reassert themselves within the Soviet universe. The expansion of Communist power does not prove the truth of the doctrine, any more than the conquests of Mohammed proved the truth of Islam.

The Soviet world is not the victim of its errors; it is the West which is the victim. The idea of government by discussion, consent or compromise is perhaps an ideal; the practice of elections and parliamentary assemblies is one practice among others. To try to introduce it without bothering to examine the circumstances is simply to guarantee its failure. And the failure of a democratic practice cannot be camouflaged by the organization of terror and enthusiasm; it breaks out in broad daylight and leads inevitably to despotism.

No intelligentsia suffers as much as the French from the loss of universality, none clings so obstinately to its illusions, none would gain more from recognizing its country's true problems.

France belongs to the non-Communist world and could not change sides without provoking the catastrophe which she is so desperately anxious to avoid. This connection does not forbid any so-called left-wing measure, whether the nationalization of industries or reforms in North Africa. Geography precludes the adoption of the Soviet technique of government and the participation of Russian representatives in the running of the country as in the satellite States. Almost as if to guarantee their own ineffectiveness, the French intellectuals never cease to recommend the impossible, and to offer to the Communist Party a collaboration which the latter rejects or accepts, according to the circumstances, with unalterable contempt.

Hankering after a truth applicable to humanity as [a] whole, they watch and wait upon events. For some time after Yugoslavia's excommunication by Moscow, Saint-Germain-des-Prés was Titoist. Then Marshal Tito, without abandoning Communism, concluded military alliances analogous to those with which the progressives reproached the Western states, and his prestige immediately sank to zero.

Mao Tse-tung's China has now succeeded Tito's Yugoslavia in their esteem. Vaster and more mysterious than the country of the Balkan David, the Oriental colossus will at last achieve the true Communism. As no one can decipher the characters of its written language, and as visits are limited to a few towns and a few factories, there is not much risk that the enthusiasm of Western travelers might be threatened by contact with the true reality. Those who might be able to provide information about the other side of the picture—missionaries and counter-revolutionaries—will be conveniently ignored or disbelieved. The victory of Communism in China is probably the most significant fact of the twentieth century; the destruction of the family, the building of a heavy industry and a powerful army and a strong State mark the beginning of a new era in the history of Asia. But what possible model, what lessons can the régime of Mao Tse-tung offer to France?

Many of the tasks which should compel the attention and the energies of France in the middle of the twentieth century would have a significance far transcending our frontiers. To organize a genuine community between Frenchmen and Moslems in North Africa, to unite the nations of Western Europe so that they are less dependent on American power, to cure the technological backwardness of our economy—such tasks as these might well arouse a clear-sighted and practical enthusiasm. None would revolutionize the condition of men on this earth, none would make France the soldier of the ideal, none would rescue us from the tiny foreland of Asia with which our fate is indissolubly linked; none would have the glamor of metaphysical ideas, none the apparent universality of socialist or nationalist ideologies. By placing our country in its exact position in the planetary system, by acting in accordance with the teachings of social science, our intellectuals could achieve the only political universality which is accessible in our time. They might give to mechanical civilization a form attuned to the traditions and the maturity of the nation, and organize with a view to prosperity and peace the zone of the planet over which our power and our thought can still extend their influence.

To these immediate and attainable prospects, the French intellectuals seem indifferent. One has the feeling that they aspire to recapture, in a philosophy of immanence, the equivalent of the lost eternity, and that they murmur to one another: "What's the point of it all, if it isn't universal?"

The attitude of the French intellectuals is determined by national pride and nostalgia for a universal idea. This attitude has repercussions abroad which are not solely due to the talent of French writers. If the men of culture cease to believe heart and soul in a truth for all men, are they not lapsing into indifference?

An intellectual's religion, Communism recruits disciples among the intellectuals of Asia and Africa, whereas the reasonable democracy of the West, though it often wins free elections, finds scarcely any supporters ready to sacrifice all for the triumph of the cause.

"In offering to China and Japan a secularised version of our Western civilisation, we have been offering them a stone instead of bread, while the Russians, in offering them Communism as well as technology, have been offering them bread of a sort—a gritty, black bread, if you like to call it so; but that is still an edible substance that contains in it some grain of nutriment for the spiritual life without which man cannot live."*

Communism is a degraded version of the Western message. It retains its ambition to conquer nature, to improve the lot of the humble, but it sacrifices what was and must remain the heart and soul of the unending human adventure: freedom of enquiry, freedom of controversy, freedom of criticism, and the vote.

Must it be said that the Communist version succeeds because of its intellectual weakness? No true theory will suppress the uncertainties of the present; it will maintain and encourage controversy, it will offer no hope of speedy progress, it will not liberate the Asian intellectuals from their complexes. The secular religion retains the prestige and the force of the prophetism; it creates a small number of fanatics, and these in their turn mobilize and control the masses, who themselves are not so much seduced by the vision of the future as revolted by the miseries of the present.

The content of the Communist faith differs scarcely at all from the content of the other ideologies to which left-wing intellectuals everywhere adhere. For the most part the latter remain on the threshold, unamenable to the discipline of the

* Arnold Toynbee, *The World and the West*.

sect. The minority who take the final step, overcoming all their doubts and scruples, are possessed by the faith which "moves mountains." The liberals are consumed with doubts and uncertainties and sometimes feel vaguely guilty for being on the "wrong side"—the side of the Right, of Reaction, of Feudalism. The climate of the Western universities has rendered students from all over the world susceptible to the Marxist-Leninist doctrine which is not the logical fulfillment but the dogmatic hardening of the progressivist philosophy.

Communism, it is said, is the first essentially European belief to have succeeded in converting millions of Asians. The first of the new catechumens were intellectuals. They had not been converted by Christianity, which ran counter to the traditional system of values and customs, whose teachings were belied by the behavior of the invaders, and which did not accord with scientific thought, the essence of the military superiority of the imperialists. Communism attracts not because it is a Christian heresy but because it seems to be the extreme form, the definitive interpretation, of the rationalist and optimist philosophy. It gives a coherent expression to the political hopes of the West.

Simple people are susceptible to these hopes, but indifferent to the interpretative scholasticism. In allowing themselves to be mobilized by the Party they do not become true believers in the Church. The peasants do not aspire to collective ownership but to individual ownership. The workers do not visualize in advance the building up of socialism by the *Gleichschaltung* of the trade unions. It is the prophetism which confers on Communism a sort of spiritual substance.

What remains of this when the conquerors of the future have become the planners of the economy? "The deified militarist has been a flagrant scandal. Alexander, as the Tyrrhenian pirate told him to his face in the story as we have it from St. Augustine, would have been called not a god but a gangster if he had done what he did with a couple of accomplices instead of doing it with a whole army. And what about the deified policeman? Augustus, now, has made himself into a policeman by liquidating his fellow-gangsters, and we are grateful to him for that; but, when we are required to register our gratitude by worshipping this reformed gangster as a god, we cannot comply with much conviction or enthusiasm." * What could possibly be our feeling toward Stalin when he liquidates Zinoviev and Bukharin, or toward Malenkov when he liquidates Beria? Does Communism, when it is installed in power, still contain a spiritual substance?

How long will the exaltation of the builders continue to sustain the militants? How long will national grandeur continue to testify to the mandate of the historical powers-that-be? Perhaps China will find in this mandarins' religion a durable peace. Christian Europe will not. The official orthodoxy will decline into a ritual language, or else the only authentic faith, that which no temporal god can satisfy, will revolt against the secular clericalism. Perhaps men can live without adoring a God in spirit and in truth. They will not live long, after the "proletarian" victory, in the expectation of a paradise on this earth.

Is there, then, no alternative to faith in the proletariat but faith in Christ? Can the West offer a spiritual truth in opposition to Soviet materialism? We must be careful not to compromise religion in the struggles of temporal powers, to attribute to the system we defend virtues which it does not possess.

The liberal democracies do not represent a "Christian" civilization. They have developed in societies whose religion was Christian, and they have been inspired to a certain extent by the absolute value which Christianity gives to the individual soul. Neither electoral and parliamentary practices nor the mechanism of the market, as such, are either Christian or contrary to the Christian spirit. Doubtless the free play of initiative, competition between buyers and sellers, would be unthinkable if human nature had not been sullied by the Fall. The individual would give of his best in the interests of others

* Arnold Toynbee, *op. cit.*, p. 182.

44

without hope of recompense, without concern for his own interests. Man being what he is, the Church, which cannot approve unbridled competition or the unlimited desire for wealth, is not obliged to condemn the economic institutions which are characteristic of industrial civilization. The planners, too, are compelled to appeal to the appetite for money or personal glory. No régime can afford to ignore human egotism.

Communism comes into conflict with Christianity because it is atheist and totalitarian, not because it controls the economy. It arrogates to itself the sole right to educate the young. The Communist State allows religious rites to be celebrated and the sacraments to be administered; but it does not consider itself neutral, it calls religious beliefs superstitions, doomed to disappear with the progress of socialist construction. It enrolls the hierarchy in political crusades; "popes," priest, bishops and Metropolitans are invited to lead the campaign in favor of peace, to denounce the conspiracies of the Vatican.

It is not for those of us who belong to no church to recommend a choice to the believers, but it behooves us all, incorrigible liberals who tomorrow would return again to the struggle against clericalism, to fight today against this totalitarianism from which professing Christians happen to suffer as much as free-thinking scientists and artists. The tyranny we denounce is not solely directed against a faith we do not share; it is one which affects us all. The State which imposes an orthodox interprteation of day-to-day events also imposes on us an interpretation of global development and ultimately of the meaning of human existence. It seeks to subordinate all the achievements of the mind, all the activities of autonomous individuals and groups, to its pseudo-truth. In defending the freedom of religious teaching, the unbeliever defends his own freedom.

What essentially distinguishes the West from the Soviet universe is the fact that the one admits itself to be divided and the other "politicizes" the whole of existence. The least important aspect of plurality, although it is more readily cited than any other, is the party system. This is not without its disadvantages; it maintains an atmosphere of division and discord in the body politic, it blurs the sense of communal responsibilities and jeopardizes internal peace and friendship. It is tolerated, in spite of everything, as a means of limiting arbitrary power and ensuring a legal expression to discontent, and as a symbol of the lay impartiality of the State and the autonomy of the human mind.

The Westerners, especially the intellectuals, suffer from the fragmentation of their universe. Diffusion and obscurity in poetry, and abstraction in painting, isolate poets and artists from the big public which they affect to despise but which, in their heart of hearts, they long to serve. Physicists or mathematicians can extract energy from the atom but cannot extract freedom of movement, opinion and friendship from suspicious politicians, from a sensation-hungry Press, from anti-intellectualist demagogues or the secret police. Masters of nuclear fission but slaves of "security," the scientists, enclosed in their narrow community, feel that they lose all control over their discoveries as soon as they transmit their secrets to the generals and the politicians. The specialist has control over but a limited field of knowledge; present-day science seems to leave him as ignorant of the answers to the ultimate questions as a child awakening to consciousness. The astronomer can foretell an eclipse of the sun with faultless precision; neither the economist nor the sociologist knows whether humanity is progressing toward an atomic holocaust or Utopian peace.

That is where ideology comes in—the longing for a purpose, for communion with the people, for something controlled by an idea and a will. The feeling of belonging to the elect, the security provided by a closed system in which the whole of history as well as one's own person find their place and their meaning, the pride in joining the past to the future in present action—all this inspires and sustains the true believer, the man who is not repelled by the scholasticism, who is not disillusioned by the twists in the Party line, the man who lives entirely for the cause and no longer recognizes the humanity of his fellow-creatures outside the Party.

Such fanaticism is not for us. We can admire the somber grandeur of these armies of believers. We can admire their devotion, their discipline and self-sacrifice: such warrior virtues are of the kind that lead to victory. But what will remain tomorrow of the motives that led them to fight? Without a scintilla of doubt or guilt or regret, we can leave the fanatics their inevitable superiority.

Does the rejection of fanaticism encourage a reasonable faith, or merely skepticism?

One does not cease to love God when one gives up converting the pagans or the Jews and no longer reiterates: "No salvation outside the Church." Will one cease to desire a less unjust society and a less cruel lot for humanity as a whose if one refuses to subscribe to a single class, a single technique of action and a single ideological system?

True, the comparison is not unreservedly valid. Religious experience gains in authenticity as one comes to distinguish better between moral virtue and obedience to the Church. The secular religions dissolve into politico-economic opinions as soon as one abandons the dogma. Yet the man who no longer expects miraculous changes either from a revolution or an economic plan is not obliged to resign himself to the unjustifiable. It is because he likes individual human beings, participates in living communities, and respects the truth, that he refuses to surrender his soul to an abstract ideal of humanity, a tyrannical party, and an absurd scholasticism.

Perhaps it will be otherwise. Perhaps the intellectual will lose interest in politics as soon as he discovers its limitations. Let us accept joyfully this uncertain promise. Indifference will not harm us. Men, unfortunately, have not yet reached the point where they have no further occasion or motive for killing one another. If tolerance is born of doubt, let us teach everyone to doubt all the models and utopias, to challenge all the prophets of redemption and the heralds of catastrophe.

If they alone can abolish fanaticism, let us pray for the advent of the skeptics.

EDWARD SHILS

The End of Ideology? *

From the 12th to the 17th of September [1955] about one
hundred and fifty writers, politicians, journalists, university
teachers met in the austerely elegant Museo Nazionale della
Tecnica e della Scienza to expound to each other their ideas
about "The Future of Freedom."

The conference, which was convoked by the Congress for
Cultural Freedom, was painstakingly prepared with clear intention. It was not the purpose of the organizers to end with
definite conclusions, with agreed statements or with public
pronouncements. It was rather to forward the process of breaking the encrustations of liberal and socialist thought, to discover their common ground, and to push forward with the task
of formulating more realistic and more inclusive ideas on the
conditions of the free society.

There were, nevertheless, material hindrances imposed by
the ground plan of the long, relatively narrow, meeting hall,
and by the lowness of the rostrum from which speakers addressed the audience; and a general deficiency of the conference lay in the fact that there was so much so well and so
challengingly said on so many topics related to the central
themes that heads were sent into a whirl. Appetites for further
discussion were continually being aroused—first by an ava-

* Reprinted with permission of the author from *Encounter*, Vol. 5,
Nov. 1955.

lanche of papers and then by a steady stream of speakers who were allowed some five minutes in which to set forth their best ideas—and they could not be satisfied except on the occasion when it was possible to meet at lunch or dinner, by which time the scent of the idea had been somewhat dissipated. In the sessions themselves there was little such interchange—though what there was, was exceptionally spirited and to the point. Rather, each speaker commented on some aspect or issue in one of the several papers which had been laid before the conference at that particular session, and then the author of each paper at the end of the session commented on the points made by the speakers about his papers. Only when the chairman was far-sighted enough to group the commentators about a few basic themes did the procession of speakers become a parade rather than a promenade. This happened, for example, when Mr. Minoo Masani, the clear-witted author-diplomat-politician-businessman from Bombay, presided over the session devoted to the similarities and differences of "Communist" and "capitalist" economic systems; he had, it was true, the advantage of having under his chairmanship two extremely lucid and polemical papers each devoted to exactly the same theme—Soviet economic growth—and taking diametrically opposed positions. Normally, however, this was not the case; there were several in which there were four to six papers all very stimulating and on a very high intellectual level, each different from the others but no one more challenging than the others. Then the range of attention spread and the analysis was not cumulative.

For this reason it would be very difficult to summarize the results of the conference. It was like a conversation among a group of lively, well-informed, and disciplined minds which goes on for hours and hours and touches on long series of fascinating and tricky problems, refreshes them all, settles none, and passes from one to the other without either an explicit consolidation of the incipient consensus or a promulgation of the outstanding differences of opinion. Then, when the conversation breaks up, one leaves with one's head buzzing with ideas, with the feeling that this idea ought to be rethought and that that problem ought to be reconsidered, and at the same time cannot restate exactly what was said, exactly what new idea or bit of knowledge was added to one's understanding. Such conversations, without adding a single proposition to our existing stock of knowledge, heighten our sensitivities, direct our attention, open our minds and trouble them. This was the way in which the Milan Conference worked.

The papers prepared for the Milan Conference numbered more than fifty and practically none was pedestrian, fatuous, or excessively clichéd; at least four-fifths contained novel ideas or fresh formulations. Some of the papers, e.g. M. Bertrand de Jouvenel's "Some Fundamental Similarities between the Soviet and Capitalistic Economic Systems," were of striking originality; others though less original were written with such lucidity and incisiveness that it was a pleasure to read them and to hear their authors summarize their main points—here I may mention Mr. John Plamenatz's "Threats to a Free Society," Professor Ely Devon's "Changing Economic Ideologies in the United Kingdom," M. Kamal Jumblat's "Reflections on Nationalism and Free Societies," Michael Freund's "Tradition and Freedom"; others impressed by their somber clarity, particularly Professor German Arciniegas's "South America: Freedom vs. Totalitarianism" and Professor Takeyasu Kimura's "The Economic Foundations of Freedom: Some Observations in the Light of Japanese Experience"; still other papers, like Mr. R.H.S. Crossman's "Democratic Control of Foreign Policy," although not original, stimulated by the lively and bellicose tones in which they were written and presented; and there were still others, like Miss Hannah Arendt's "The Rise and Development of Totalitarianism and Authoritarian Forms of Government in the 20th Century," which intrigued by a fascinating obscurity and the rumble of profundity; finally I should mention the representatives of American sociological wisdom, sometimes turgid and seldom elegant, but bringing to the conference an insistent independence of thought and an original feeling for the reality of social life.

The papers, despite their diversity of viewpoint and subject matter, circled over a single theme. Almost every paper was in one way or another a critique of doctrinairism, of fanaticism, of ideological possession. Almost every paper at least expressed the author's idea of mankind cultivating and improving its own garden, secure against obsessional visions and phantasies, and free from the harassment of ideologists and zealots. It was the intention of the conference's organizers to move thought further around the turning-point to which we have come in the last years. This turning point might be described as the end of ideological enthusiasm.

In one of the preliminary papers written to state the theme of the conference, Professor Raymond Aron pointed out that the underpinnings of the great ideological conflicts of the first part of this century had largely been pulled out. The once unequivocal distinction between "right" and "left" had been damaged by the knowledge that combinations once alleged by extremist doctrines to be impossible—combinations like collective ownership and tyranny, progressive social policies and full employment under capitalization, large-scale governmental controls with public liberties—are actually possible. The full awareness that nationalization is no universal solution to economic problems and that British socialism has not resulted in tyranny have materially weakened the ideologies of thorough-going socialism and thorough-going neo-liberalism.

The obscuring of the once clear distinction between "left" and "right," the discovery that over the past thirty years the extremes of "right" and "left" had disclosed identities which were much more impressive than their differences, the disasters of governing societies by passionate adherence to formulae, the crimes committed in the names of sacred principles of policy in Nazi Germany and the Soviet Union, had all left a residue of skepticism among many intellectuals in most countries, and created uneasiness among others who are not yet skeptical regarding their inherited doctrines. The fact, too, that in our decade the nations which have most successfully managed their internal affairs—Great Britain, the United States, Western Germany, and the Scandinavian countries—have increasingly considered their major domestic policies without regard for the standard distinctions of "left" and "right," of socialism and laissez-faire, but in a matter-of-fact way which recognized no general principles and treated each emerging situation on its own merits, has contributed to disillusion intellectuals of these countries of the notion that one side or the other had a monopoly of the care of freedom and welfare.

This was the background of reflection in which the conference had its origin. The agenda was prepared accordingly. The first session dealt with the growing hollowness of the conventional distinctions between socialism and capitalism. The position had already been taken in an authoritative manner by Mr. Hugh Gaitskell, who held to his realist and moderate equalitarian Socialism while renouncing every cliché. Three papers by Professor J. K. Galbraith of Harvard University, Professor Devons of Manchester University, and Dr. Walter Tritsch of Ascona dealt with the vanity of the claims of simon-pure socialists and free-enterprise liberals. Professor Devons' paper was devoted to showing in detail for Great Britain, while Galbraith's and Tritsch's papers were occupied with the general argument, that it was futile to continue to argue along the old lines as if the crucial distinction in economic policy was between socialism and capitalism. What was striking in these three papers was the deliberate electricism of the authors in their attitude toward the solution of economic problems. Intellectuals were chastised for their rigidity, unwillingness to compromise, and especially for their fear of being impure.

From this preliminary sally against doctrinairism in economic policy, and its emphasis on the need to confront problems rather than to conform with the tenets of a general faith, the program went forward to distinguish the real differences between the Soviet and the Western types of economy. It was the desire of the organizers of the conference to examine the extent to which the Soviet economic system, simply by virtue of being a large-scale industrial system, was forced to meet the same conditions and to face the same problems as the capitalist economies of the West. In other words, was central planning a myth, did the Soviet economic system have to confront the same problems as a market economy in making decisions as to the types and quantities of goods to be produced, the allocation of resources, etc.? The problem was unfortunately not addressed by the speakers in this session. Mr. Peter Wiles and Mr. Colin Clark (who was very regrettably absent from the conference) treated the question of the rate of development of the Soviet economy in their papers. Professor Libero Lenti's more academic and theoretical paper was passed over in the discussion, and so, on the surface, the conference seemed to veer away from its task of discovering what solid ground was still left under the claims of our inherited ideologies. Instead, the passions of the cold war were raised by some participants who thought that Mr. Wiles' interpretation gave too favorable a picture of the achievements of the Soviet economy. Yet here, too, the pressure of the program was effective. Although there was no agreement between Mr. Wiles and the disputants, many of whom were horrified by Mr. Wiles' mischievous manner of presenting the Soviet achievements, it definitely served to prevent any complacency from settling over the conference.

One could not avoid being struck by the impression that the conferees were not on the defensive. As against Mr. Stuart Hampshire's feeling of repugnance for the idea of safeguarding or defending freedom which he thought characterized the conference, it seemed to me that the conference had in part the atmosphere of a post-victory ball. There was a very widespread feeling that there was no longer any need to justify ourselves *vis-a-vis* the Communist critique of our society. The calls for a renewal of faith or a system of beliefs which we could offer in competition with Bolshevism were very few and were either rejected or disregarded. There was, in a variety of ways, a sometimes rampant, sometimes quiet conviction that Communism had lost the battle of ideas with the West. Even the "thaw" about which there was disagreement was taken in stride, whatever the interpretation, as a vindication of the anti-ideological attitude. Mr. Wiles' paper performed the great service of putting a block in the way of complacency, and even those who were not convinced by him must surely have assimilated some restraints on a tendency to write the Communists off as not only morally and intellectually in the wrong, but as weak too.*

Whatever complacency there might have been among the Western anti-Communist participants was blown sky high in the third session. This session, devoted to economic progress in the underdeveloped countries and the rivalry of Communist and democratic methods, presented a large number of papers. Mr. Eric da Costa's paper was remarkable for the fluent optimism with which he looked on the economic future in India. Professor Arthur Lewis was optimistic too, but he was more insistent on the need for strong measures which he thought fully compatible with political liberty and representative institutions in the newly sovereign states of Asia and Africa. M. de Jouvenel's paper, a really remarkable piece of ingenious research, seemed to try to show that there was no short cut for the economically underdeveloped countries. They would have to go through an industrial revolution which, for the severity of life it inflicted on the people as consumers, would not be less painful than the industrial revolution in the West or the development of Soviet industry. His paper, which established

* This assumption should not be attributed to the organizers. Professor Polanyi's insistence on his belief that the Soviet economy had been forced to become a surreptitious market economy could be interpreted as an admission that some of Mr. Wiles' contentions regarding the magnitude of Soviet economic growth were correct.

striking parallels between the pattern of Soviet and capitalist economic development and which belonged more properly in the preceding session, disclosed one of the subsidiary intentions of the Congress: namely, the persuasion of the intellectual leaders of the free societies with underdeveloped economies that they should not think that, by renouncing the ample political liberties which they now enjoy, they will be able to make more rapid and better economic progress.

A storm burst. It would be wrong to say that the organizers of the conference had overlooked the problem of freedom and welfare in those countries of Africa and Asia which had only recently acquired sovereignty. The mere fact of the presence of so many distinguished participants from those two continents, the generous references in Mr. Gaitskell's talk on the opening day to the need for economic and political independence in the underdeveloped areas, Mr. Wiles' reference in his paper, and the provision of two full sessions were all evidence enough of this desire to reach out toward a more universal concern for liberty and not to rest content with a European-American view of the matter. Yet the bounds of provision were broken as soon as the discussion started. Speaker after speaker went to the platform, Africans, Asians, Middle Easterners: some speaking with statesmanlike judiciousness, others with sardonic defiance, some in sober academic language, others like forthright sages. They asked for aid from the more advanced countries, stressed how precarious was the situation of liberty among them, and expressed their belief that without an impressive rate of economic progress, liberty might collapse. There were grounds for disagreement here. The Westerners had in their earlier statements disavowed any sympathy for the idea that liberty rests on an economic basis. Not only were they anti-Marxist but they were opposed to the same line of thought when it emanated from the extreme liberals, who insisted that political liberty depended on a free market economy. Perhaps because they were put off by the economism of the Africans and Asians, perhaps because it was thought to be more courteous to those from outside the West to allow them to speak first, perhaps because the delegates were worn out by the strenuous and lively discussion of the morning session, the Western members of the conference did not speak until Mr. Max Beloff of Oxford went to the platform. With angry eloquence, he denied the obligation of the richer countries to provide economic aid to the poorer countries, in a voice which expressed resentment against the resentful overtones which were noticeable in the remarks of some of the Asians. This was followed shortly by another vigorous criticism of the intellectuals of underdeveloped countries for their excessive demands which generated hopes which could not be realized.

A genuine tension was generated by this session which weighed on many minds with disturbance and benefit throughout the conference. It came out even more strongly in Thursday morning's session on Nationalism, under the heading of the "Threats and Obstacles to a Free Society." Here again the distance between the African and Asian members on the one side and the Europeans and Americans on the other became tangible. For the Westerners, nationalism was an unfortunate distraction, at worst a source of great troubles springing from the passions, at best a worthy actor in the 19th century drama which was now over. For the Asiatics and Africans it was as integral a part of the concept of freedom as liberty of the press or of personal movement. This session underscored the danger of Western complacency at having weathered the storm of ideologies.

After the effort to show the baselessness of ideological pretensions, and the discovery of the persistence of nationalist sentiment as a part of the love of liberty outside the Western world, the conference went on to examine the impact of extremist ideologies on the working of democratic institutions. The paper by Professor Seymour Lipset of Columbia University, which touched in an imaginative way on the dangers to political democracy of lower-class fundamentalism and authoritarianism, and which raised the question of "McCarthyism" without the usual stereotypes, aroused not a word of comment. It is not easy to explain why the complex of irrationalities which had so exercised European and American intellectuals until very recently should have been disregarded in this conference. Of the discussants only Mr. George Kennan referred to the loyalty-security excitement in American society when replying at a later session to Mr. Daniel Bell's gratified contemplation of American life. Likewise there was little anxiety about Communist infiltration. There was not a word of comment on Professor Arthur Schlesinger, Jr.'s paper on "Freedom and Subversion." Have the Communists come to appear so preposterous to our Western intellectuals that it is no longer conceivable that they could be effectively subversive? Is it now thought that there is no longer any danger of the working classes in the advanced Western countries falling for their propaganda?

On the other hand, Mr. Crossman's bashing offensive to vindicate the good judgment of the masses in questions of foreign policy found little support and much dissent. This paper, which dominated the discussion, called forth no echoes of the older criticisms of democracy based on the incompetence of the public; Mr. Denis Healey, Mr. Max Beloff, and Mr. Stuart Hampshire were less sanguine about the capacity of the masses to understand the complex problems of foreign policy, but they did not at the same time speak ill of the ordinary man. He was not criticized for irrationality, savagery, etc. In short, the working and the lower middle classes have ceased to be the objects of ideological passions. The thesis of Walter Lippman from which Mr. Crossman took his point of departure, namely a belief in a higher law, found no support, either. The fact that the whole morning's discussion, which was one of the most energetic, drew on none of the older lines of argument about the effectiveness of democracy might be regarded as evidence that the British scholars who held the floor most of the time know little or nothing of Michels, Wallas, Ostrogorski,

Weber, Tocqueville, or that the emancipation from ideology has gone so far that the inherited objects of enthusiasm in the debate about the inner stability of democracy have lost their meaning to be best minds in the contemporary intellectual classes.

This view of the situation is reinforced by the meeting in the afternoon of the same day when the influence of the mass media and the rise of totalitarianism were discussed under the amiable chairmanship of Professor Galbraith. The views of Ortega y Gasset, Lederer, and all the quasi-aristocratic critics of the culture of the masses and of the danger which they were alleged to offer to free institutions, in consequence of apathy, ignorance, vulgarity, bestiality, frivolousness, might have expected a favorable hearing here. On the contrary, the masses were exculpated by Mr. Bell and their highbrow critics rebuffed. In a brilliant paper in the following day's session on "The Resilience of Liberty," Mr. Manes Sperber accepted with only a little regert the unideological character of the ordinary man's outlook, even though he was fully aware that indifference toward public events reduced the effectiveness of democratic institutions, and provides no bulwark against the emergence of tyranny—although once a tyranny exists it provides a limit to the expansive powers of the tyrannical authority. Only Mr. Czeslaw Milosz in his charming paper on "Belinsky and the Unicorn" was unsparing in his ideologist's criticism of the refusal of the ordinary man to live on the heroic heights of historical grandeur.

The fact that in this great assembly of intellectuals only Messrs. Kennan and Milosz took shots at the private life and trivial culture of the ordinary citizen showed how far we have moved from the ideology-ridden period when the simple philistine was exhorted to renounce his drab routine for life on the peaks, or when he was denounced for failing to do so and when the working man had a heroic ideology attributed to him.

The narrowing of the gap which separates most of the

friends of freedom was apparent also on the session on Saturday, when Professor Sidney Hook, steeped in Deweyian instrumentalism, took the lead in conceding the importance of a traditional framework of thought and sentiment for the maintenance of liberal democratic institutions.

The Milan Conference showed us how much we still have to do. For decades the proponents of freedom have been struggling against National Socialism, Fascism, and Bolshevism, on the battlefield, in the legislative chamber, and in the study. Now in America, Great Britain, Germany, and the Scandinavian countries, and to a lesser extent in Italy and France, as well as in the international arena, we have achieved some success. The work of subversion has been confined in Europe and America, or demolished. There is a standstill of an enigmatic sort in the relations of the West and the Soviet Union, and Marxism, like National Socialism and Fascism before it, has lost its appeal to the intellectuals. We no longer feel the need for a comprehensive explicit system of beliefs. We have seen not only the substantive errors of totalitarianism and extremist enthusiasm, but we have also seen the wrongfulness of the type of ideological orientation which once constituted its attraction.

There is, however, more to life, and especially intellectual life, than the detection and refutation of error. There are great tasks to be undertaken amidst the ruins of the ideologies. We must reconstruct our beliefs without yielding to the temptation —which can never die out completely among intellectuals—to construct new ideologies, as rigid, as eager for consistency and for universal observance as those which have been now transcended. The avoidance of the temptation to build a new ideology is a negative achievement, too.

The positive standards of action inherent in our present attachment to moderation in action and orderliness and stability in change have to be more clearly discerned. To get rid of heroism as a universal rule of action and to replace it by unqualified and unmeasured philistinism will not do. To get rid of rebelliousness and antinomianism and to replace it by an uncritical acceptance of tradition will not do. To get rid of the tyranny of the highbrow and to replace it by popular vulgarity will not do. If we undo every one of our older errors by running as far as we can in the opposite direction, we shall only rehabilitate the need for ideology; it will creep in through the back door, or more particularly, through a rebellious younger generation. The belief that our traditional ideals have now been exhausted because of their complete fulfillment must be avoided as much as the conviction that our virtue consists in our rejection of whatever exists. We must rediscover the permanently valid element[s] in our historical ideals— elements which must be recurrently realized without ever being definitively realizable, once and for all.

In our rejection of the ideologies we must study what can be salvaged from them, and what in them should be kept alive, how and in what measure grandiose visions and austere standards have their place. Every society needs a certain amount of these ideals just as it would be ruined by too much of them.

There is another task which Milan has imposed with great force. We must no longer think only for European or American society. Our theories of liberty, of the relation between religion and progress, tradition and intellectual independence, must be thought out and formulated in such a way that they will do justice to the situations of the new countries of Asia and Africa and South America.

It is too early to say yet just how to go about these tasks of helping the growth of a fruitful liberty in the Asiatic and African and South American countries. A few things are, however, very clear: having recently freed ourselves from ideological radicalism, we must not be affronted to see it among our Asiatic and African friends who learned it in our own universities in the West; still ourselves penetrated by strong national identifications, we must not be repelled by the greater national sensitivities of the members of nations which have only recently

61

become states. Condescension, resentment against resentment, the insistence on gratitude will avail us nothing. It will only narrow our own minds, render our own thought less fruitful than it might be, and obstruct the growth of freedom in those countries. Even if Milan had not stirred our thoughts into the direction in which they should go in the better understanding and reinforcement of our own liberties, it would have justified itself by its reminder, not always very pleasant, of the problems of maintaining and developing free societies outside the West. Mr. A. D. Gorwala, a great Indian civil servant, tireless in his own country on behalf of reason and freedom, and in Milan a powerfully impressive example of Roman dignity of bearing, reminded the conference on the last day that

"the contradictions of the free world would indeed sustain its enemies even more than their own strength. Its many units hardly seem to realize their essential unity, and make ancestral memories more potent guides to action than present needs. The strong and the weak nations, the old and the new, alike allow themselves to be affected in varying degrees in this fashion. Some of the strong have not yet grasped at all, some have grasped only in part, and only one seems to have even approached full understanding of Abraham Lincoln's magnificent saying: 'As I would not be a slave, so I would not be a master.' Slaves they will not be, but they seem not to have much compunction about remaining masters. Whence flows all that disruption of the human spirit, that stream of ill-will and anger that is connotated by the word 'colonialism.' . . . The people (of Asia and Africa) make clear by their attitudes, and when possible, by their words and actions, that in their view, government by others, even if good, is no substitute for self-government. The time for gratefulness may be later, when foreign domination has ended and the good that it did lives after it."

Professor Michael Polanyi who, with Professors Aron and Hook, and M. Nabokov, conceived the conference and guided it, expressed the new sensitivity of many Westerners. In the final session of the conference, he sought, with his customary grace, to acknowledge this new sense of the necessity of thinking of the problems of liberty in a more universal perspective. He said:

"The project of this conference was first mooted about two years ago and I can still clearly remember what we then hoped it would achieve. . . . I confess that after this meeting I can hardly recognize myself as the person who entertained these prospects. For I took it for granted at the time that the decisive problems of our age were those raised in Europe by Europeans. That we had only to resist victoriously and finally to overcome the explosive forces of Moscow's Leninism, to regain the peaceful leadership of the world which had temporarily slipped from our hands.

"But the interventions made at this meeting by Asiatic, African, and South American delegates have made me realize that this perspective was altogether distorted. The proud people of the ancient lands who are now coming into their own in Asia and Africa, are not awaiting the decision of our European conflicts. They have started their political life as indepent nations on premises of their own for which there is no precedent in Europe. We shall not begin to understand them until we accept the fact that in these new nations, born of the most ancient soil of the human race, we are facing our partners in the shaping of man's destiny on this planet. They are, of course, equal partners already by virtue of their statehood in the counsels of the United Nations. But their interventions at this Congress have revealed the power of their political thought, which on a number of occasions has commanded not merely intellectual appreciation, but the respect due to true greatness of mind.

"I confess that it was for the first time that the exhilarating perspective was opened up to me of this immense area of new companionship. Yet for all that, this encounter has brought us new cares. We were brought up against the poverty of the areas held by the new Asiatic and African nations, and the instability of their public life. And having pondered these immense problems, the conference could do little more than pass on in silence. The only result was to give us a new sense of proportion, in which our European conflicts could be seen as a fragment, rather than as a whole of the contemporary scene."

63

LEWIS S. FEUER

Beyond Ideology *

A man without an ideology is today as rare as a man without a country, and certainly as unrespectable. Modern history is a history of warring creeds, of passionate faiths, and the man without an ideology is bannerless in an age when thinking is enlisted in battalions.

But the upshot of our analysis is that free thought and action are also free from ideology. What are ideologies? They are indeed works of presumption. An ideology projects wish-fulfillments where knowledge is unavailable; it denies those realities whose existence it would repress, it enhances into ultimates what it prizes. An ideology is a world-system based on one's political and social feelings, an attempt, conscious or unconscious, to impose one's political will upon the nature of the universe. It entangles emotions, actions, and ideas into one amalgam, so that one does not know where the emotion ends and the idea begins; it regards every idea as a plan for action, and every idea as the projection of some interest. The Universe is handed a card of membership in a political party or affiliation to a religious sect; it is declared pluralistic or democratic, dialectical, or organismic.

An age of ideology may finally make men restless with an

* From *Psychoanalysis and Ethics* by Lewis S. Feuer, pp. 126–130. Reprinted with the permission of the author.

aspiration for intellectual freedom. They perceive that they have defied words and formulas. Emotions of good will, suppressed longings for friendliness, work havoc with the rigidities of ideology.

The age of religious wars was followed by an age of skepticism. The rumor spread through France that there was a king to whom men's religions didn't matter; the skeptic Montaigne was heard asking other men as he asked of himself: "What do I know?" and avowing to an "ignorance, strong and noble, which yields nothing to knowledge in honor and courage—an ignorance which requires as much knowledge to attain as knowledge does itself." The age of fanaticism in England was followed by the age of David Hume. "Enthusiasms" were distrusted, men became modest in their pretensions, and forebore from claims of knowing the universe. With their recognition of their status as men, they became reluctant to immolate themselves upon man-made creeds which were presented as divine-given truths. Men, to act as men, would acknowledge their character, their mixture of ignorance and knowledge.

The adherent to ideology believes that the making of history is its handmaiden. He demands for himself and his followers the assurance that "history is on our side." Ideology makes men believe that they are acting with the blessing, with the sanction of the Total Universe. Cromwell believed he was the servant of the Lord, and executant of His Will upon earth. The Nazi leader, Hitler, saw his political party as fortified by a *Weltanschauung;* therein was its superiority to liberalism, the weapon which would enable it to battle Marxist ideology on equal terms; ideology brought the assurance that the genocide of the Jews was "the Lord's work." [1] The communist has the guarantee of ideology that he is of the vanguard of the World Dialectic. All the modes of ideology have a common source of emotional satisfaction. They confer a father's blessing, the ap-

[1] Hitler, Adolf: *Mein Kampf.* New York, Reynal (Harcourt), 1941, pp. 582–583, 84.

proval of a superego, when one is feeling most insecure. The ideological fanatic is repressing tremendous segments of his personality; he represses doubts and fears, he inhibits his emotions of good will, he drives his affections along paths approved by party authority. Emotions of friendship in his life dissolve into nothingness, in his actions he no longer has the sense of freedom. The follower of ideology is always ambivalent toward his church or party, hating it for the way it warps his life, so that he no longer reacts as himself, freshly and spontaneously, but always as the representative, a moment, of historical forces. Cruelty as a political value is the counterpart of an extreme personal repression, and it constructs its own new conscience; the intensified motive for cruelty is internalized as the mandate of the historical superego. Ideology gives to the cruelty-dominated man the approval of a cosmic conscience; organized cruelty thus has its unchallengeable certitude of world-historical process. Ideology thus helps provide the internal energy for the repression of humane impulses and external energy for aggression against others. Ideology is the instrument whereby men repress their human responses, and shape their behavior to a political mandate.

Liberal civilization begins when the age of ideology is over. On whose side, if anyone's history is, no one can pretend to know. No one can say that history is on our side, and no one can enroll the Universe as a Whole into any political party. We can act to realize as far as we may our own, human values, but we do so without the knowledge that our embodiments and realizations are elected to withstand all time. The age of religious wars was followed by a time in which cosmopolitanism and the rational spirit were admired of men. There was an aspiration to rise above tribalism and national ethnocentrism to be a "citizen of the world." Those hopes of the eighteenth century foundered, but perhaps they will be renewed. When ideologies recede, humanity may discover for itself a common language and common values. When ideologies recede, it will be the ebb tide of human hatreds, and the energies of men, disenthralled from conflict and suppression, will know new horizons of happiness and achievement.

And, suppose it were true that human hopes will be wrecked, that the dreams of radical reform will never live but on paper, suppose it were true that humankind lacks the resources for self-liberation. Would wisdom then dictate that we should retreat into ourselves? Is social action wise only when it has the warrant of success? Is there a basic imperative that one be always on the winning side?

There is a passage in Silone's great novel, *The Seed Beneath the Snow,* when Pietro Spina, wandering revolutionary, hiding in a hut with a donkey and a halfwit, is queried by a peasant friend:

"Pietro, don't you think that human society will always be ruled by some sort of oligarchy; that there will always be unfairness and oppression?"

"No, I don't believe so, Severi. And even so, what does it matter? We shall always be on the side of the poor."

Men's values in the end need make no obeisance to power and success. If the universe finally defeats human aspirations, it still remains true that the effort to realize them brings life to its fullest and most intense liberation. William James once spoke of "the potential social self" which lives as an ideal in human action: ". . . it may be represented as barely possible. I may not hope for its realization during my lifetime. . . . Yet still the emotion that beckons me on is indubitably the pursuit of an ideal social self. . . ." [2] This "ideal social self" consists of the affectional impulses of men, which have survived their dark oppressive surroundings, and which are looking for some way to the light of knowledge and human friendship. When social groups are dominated by hatred, when actual societies and persons have abandoned humane values,

[2] James, William: *The Principles of Psychology,* Vol. I. New York, Holt, 1890, p. 315.

67

one's social feelings are directed toward man as he might be, a kingdom not of the present, but a kingdom which might be of this world. And if this hope founders, it will have given to life those moments which were free of anger and hatred, the moments which brought the fullness of joy which only love can bring.

SEYMOUR MARTIN LIPSET

The End of Ideology? *[1]

A basic premise of this book is that democracy is not only or even primarily a means through which different groups can attain their ends or seek the good society; it is the good society itself in operation. Only the give-and-take of a free society's internal struggles offers some guarantee that the products of the society will not accumulate in the hands of a few power-holders, and that men may develop and bring up their children without fear of persecution. And, as we have seen, democracy requires institutions which support conflict and disagreement

* From *Political Man* by Seymour Martin Lipset. Copyright © 1960 by Seymour Martin Lipset. Reprinted by permission of Doubleday & Company, Inc. and the author.

[1] I have taken the chapter heading from the title of Edward Shils' excellent report on a conference on "The Future of Freedom" held in Milan, Italy, in September 1955, under the auspices of the Congress for Cultural Freedom. See his "The End of Ideology?" *Encounter*, 5 (November 1955), pp. 52–58 [reprinted in this volume, pp. 48–63]; for perceptive analyses of the nature and sources of the decline of ideology see Herbert Tingsten, "Stability and Vitality in Swedish Democracy," *The Political Quarterly*, 2 (1955), pp. 140–51; and Otto Brunner, "Der Zeitalter der Ideologien," in *Neue Wege der Sozialgeschichte* (Gottingen: Van den Hoeck and Ruprecht, 1956), pp. 194–219. For a prediction that the "age of ideology" is ending see Louis S. Feuer, "Beyond Ideology," *Psychoanalysis and Ethics* (Springfield: Charles C. Thomas, 1955), pp. 126–30 [reprinted in this volume, pp. 64–68]. Many of these topics are discussed in detail by Daniel Bell in *The End of Ideology* (Glencoe: The Free Press, 1960) and by Ralf Dahrendorf in *Class and Class Conflict* (Stanford: Stanford University Press, 1959).

as well as those which sustain legitimacy and consensus. In recent years, however, democracy in the Western world has been undergoing some important changes as serious intellectual conflicts among groups representing different values have declined sharply.

The consequences of this change can perhaps be best illustrated by describing what happened at a world congress of intellectuals on "The Future of Freedom" held in Milan, Italy, in September 1955. The conference[2] was attended by 150 intellectuals and politicians from many democratic countries, and included men ranging in opinions from socialists to right-wing conservatives. Among the delegates from Great Britain, for example, were Hugh Gaitskell and Richard Crossman, socialists, and Michael Polanyi and Colin Clark, conservatives. From the United States came Sidney Hook, then the vice-chairman of the Union for Democratic Socialism, Arthur Schlesinger, Jr., of Americans for Democratic Action, and Friedrich A. Hayek, the arch-conservative economist. The French representatives included André Philip, a left-socialist leader, Raymond Aron, once active in the Gaullist movement, and Bertrand de Jouvenel, the conservative philosopher. Similar divergencies in political outlook were apparent among the delegates from Scandinavia, Germany, Italy, and other countries.

One would have thought that a conference in which so many important political and intellectual leaders of socialism, liberalism, and conservatism were represented would have stimulated intense political debate. In fact, nothing of the sort occurred. The only occasions in which debate grew warm were when someone served as a "surrogate Communist" by saying something which could be defined as being too favorable to Russia.

On the last day of the week-long conference, an interesting

[2] My original report on this conference which I attended was published as "The State of Democratic Politics," *Canadian Forum*, 35 (November 1955), pp. 170–71. It is interesting to note the similarities of the observations in it and the report by Edward Shils, *op. cit.*

event occurred. Professor Hayek, in a closing speech, attacked the delegates for preparing to bury freedom instead of saving it. He alone was disturbed by the general temper. What bothered him was the general agreement among the delegates, regardless of political belief, that the traditional issues separating the left and right had declined to comparative insignificance. In effect, all agreed that the increase in state control which had taken place in various countries would not result in a decline in democratic freedom. The socialists no longer advocated socialism; they were as concerned as the conservatives with the danger of an all-powerful state. The ideological issues dividing left and right had been reduced to a little more or a little less government ownership and economic planning. No one seemed to believe that it really made much difference which political party controlled the domestic policies of individual nations. Hayek, honestly believing that state intervention is bad and inherently totalitarian, found himself in a small minority of those who still took the cleavages within the democratic camp seriously.

A leading left-wing British intellectual, Richard Crossman, has stated that socialism is now consciously viewed by most European socialist leaders as a "Utopian myth . . . often remote from the realties of day-to-day politics." [3] Few socialist parties still want to nationalize more industry. This objective has been largely given up by the socialist parties of the more industrialized states like Scandinavia, Britain, and Germany. The Labor party premier of the Australian state of Queensland, defending the retention of socialization as an objective at the party's 1950 convention clearly acknowledged that its significance was largely ritualistic when he said:

"I point out that there are serious implications in any way altering our platform and objectives. In the first place it is a bad thing to break ground in attack if we can avoid it, and I think we should not duck around corners and pretend we do not want so-

[3] Richard Crossman, "On Political Neurosis," *Encounter* 3 (May 1954), p. 66.

cialization of industry. It is a long term objective in the Labor movement, exactly in the same way that there is a long term objective in the Christian movement. The people who espouse Christianity have been struggling for over 2,000 years and have not arrived at it." [4]

The rationale for retaining long-term objectives, even those which may not be accomplished in 2,000 years, was well stated by Richard Crossman:

A democratic party can very rarely be persuaded to give up one of its central principles, and *can never afford to scrap its central myth.* Conservatives must defend free enterprise even when they are actually introducing state planning. A Labour Government must defend as true Socialism policies which have very little to do with it. The job of party leaders is often to persuade their followers that the traditional policy is still being carried out, even when this is demonstrably not true.[5]

The fact that the differences between the left and the right in the Western democracies are no longer profound does not mean that there is no room for party controversy. But as the editor of one of the leading Swedish newspapers once said to me, "Politics is now boring. The only issues are whether the metal workers should get a nickel more an hour, the price of milk should be raised, or old-age pensions extended." These are important matters, the very stuff of the internal struggle within stable democracies, but they are hardly matters to excite

[4] Cited in T. C. Truman, *The Pressure Groups, Parties and Politics of the Australian Labor Movement* (unpublished M.A. thesis, Department of Political Science, University of Queensland, 1953), Chap. II, p. 82.

[5] Richard Crossman, *op. cit.,* p. 67. (My emphasis.) And in Sweden, Herbert Tingsten reports: "The great controversies have thus been liquidated in all instances. As a result the symbolic words and the stereotypes have changed or disappeared. . . . Liberalism in the old sense is dead, both among the Conservatives and in the Liberal party; . . . and the label of socialism on a specific proposal or a specific reform has hardly any other meaning than the fact that the proposal or reform in question is regarded as attractive. The actual words 'socialism' or 'liberalism' are tending to become mere honorifics, useful in connection with elections and political festivities." Tingsten, *op. cit.,* p. 145.

intellectuals or stimulate young people who seek in politics a way to express their dreams.

This change in Western political life reflects the fact that the fundamental political problems of the industrial revolution have been solved: the workers have achieved industrial and political citizenship; the conservatives have accepted the welfare state; and the democratic left has recognized that an increase in over-all state power carries with it more dangers to freedom than solutions for economic problems. This very triumph of the democratic social revolution in the West ends domestic politics for those intellectuals who must have ideologies or utopias to motivate them to political action.

Within Western democracy, this decline in the sources of serious political controversy has even led some to raise the question as to whether the conflicts that are so necessary to democracy will continue. Barrington Moore, Jr., a Harvard sociologist, has asked whether

. . . as we reduce economic inequalities and privileges, we may also eliminate the sources of contrast and discontent that put drive into genuine political alternatives. In the United States today, with the exception of the Negro, it is difficult to perceive any section of the population that has a vested material interest on behalf of freedom. . . . There is, I think, more than a dialectical flourish in the assertion that liberty requires the existence of an oppressed group in order to grow vigourously. Perhaps that is the tragedy as well as the glory of liberty. Once the ideal has been achieved, or is even close to realization, the driving force of discontent disappears, and a society settles down for a time to a stolid acceptance of things as they are. Something of the sort seems to have happened to the United States.[6]

And David Riesman has suggested that "the general increase of wealth and the concomitant loss of rigid distinctions make it difficult to maintain the Madisonian [economic] bases

[6] Barrington Moore, Jr., *Political Power and Social Theory* (Cambridge: Harvard University Press, 1958), p. 183.

for political diversity, or to recruit politicians who speak for the residual oppressed strata." [7] The thesis that partisan conflict based on class differences and left-right issues is ending is based on the assumption that "the economic class system is disappearing . . . that redistribution of wealth and income . . . has ended economic inequality's political significance." [8]

Yet one wonders whether these intellectuals are not mistaking the decline of ideology in the domestic politics of Western society with the ending of the class conflict which has sustained democratic controversy. As the abundant evidence on voting patterns in the United States and other countries indicates, the electorate as a whole does not see the end of the domestic class struggle envisioned by so many intellectuals. A large number of surveys of the American population made from the 1930s to the 1950s report that most people believe that the Republicans do more for the wealthy and for business and professional people and the Democrats do more for the poor and for skilled and unskilled workers.[9] Similar findings have been reported for Great Britain.

These opinions do not simply represent the arguments of partisans, since supporters of both the left and the right agree on the classes each party basically represents—which does not mean the acceptance of a bitter class struggle but rather an agreement on the representation functions of the political parties similar to the general agreement that trade-unions represent workers, and the Chamber of Commerce, businessmen. Continued class cleavage does not imply any destructive consequences for the system; as I indicated in an early chapter, a stable democracy requires consensus on the nature of the polit-

[7] David Riesman, "Introduction," to Stimson Bullitt, *To Be a Politician* (New York: Doubleday & Co., Inc., 1959), p. 20.

[8] Bullitt, *ibid.*, p. 177.

[9] See Harold Orlans, *Opinion Polls on National Leaders* (Philadelphia: Institute for Research in Human Relations, 1953), pp. 70–73. This monograph contains a detailed report on various surveys conducted by the different American polling agencies from 1935–53.

74

ical struggle, and this includes the assumption that different groups are best served by different parties.

The predictions of the end of class politics in the "affluent society" ignore the relative character of any class system. The decline of objective deprivation—low income, insecurity, malnutrition—does reduce the potential tension level of a society, as we have seen. But as long as some men are rewarded more than others by the prestige or status structure of society, men will feel *relatively* deprived. The United States is the wealthiest country in the world, and its working class lives on a scale to which most of the middle classes in the rest of the world aspire; yet a detailed report on the findings of various American opinion surveys states: "The dominant opinion on polls before, during, and after the war is that the salaries of corporation executives are too high and should be limited by the government." And this sentiment, prevalent even among prosperous people, finds increasing support as one moves down the economic ladder.[10]

The democratic class struggle will continue, but it will be a fight without ideologies, without red flags, without May Day parades. This naturally upsets many intellectuals who can participate only as ideologists or major critics of the *status quo*. The British socialist weekly, *The New Statesman*, published a series of comments through 1958–59 under the general heading "Shall We Help Mr. Gaitskell?" As the title suggests, this series was written by various British intellectuals who are troubled by the fact that the Labor party is no longer ideologically radical but simply the interest organization of the workers and the trade-unions.

The decline of political ideology in America has affected many intellectuals who, as I pointed out in Chapter X, must function as critics of the society to fulfill their self-image. And

---

[10] *Ibid.*, p. 149. The one exception is among the very poor who are somewhat less intolerant of high executive salaries than those immediately above them.

75

since domestic politics, even liberal and socialist politics, can no longer serve as the arena for serious criticism from the left, many intellectuals have turned from a basic concern with the political and economic systems to criticism of other sections of the basic culture of American society, particularly of elements which cannot be dealt with politically. They point to the seeming growth of a concern with status ("keeping up with the Joneses"), to the related increase in the influence of advertisers and mass media as the arbiters of mass taste, to the evidence that Americans are overconformist—another side of keeping up with the Joneses. Thus the critical works about American society in the past decades which have received the most attention have been sociological rather than political, such books as David Riesman's *The Lonley Crowd,* William H. Whyte's *The Organization Man,* Max Lerner's *America as a Civilization,* and Vance Packard's *The Status Seekers.*

Yet many of the disagreeable aspects of American society which are now regarded as the results of an affluent and bureaucratic society may be recurring elements inherent in an equalitarian and democratic society. Those aspects of both American and socialist ideology which have always been most thoroughly expressed in the United States make a concern with status and conformity constant features of the society.

The patterns of status distinction which Lloyd Warner, Vance Packard, and others have documented have been prevalent throughout America's history, as the reports of various nineteenth-century foreign travelers plainly show. These visitors generally believed that Americans were *more* status-conscious than Europeans, that it was easier for a *nouveau riche* individual to be accepted in nineteenth-century England than in nineteenth-century America; and they explained the greater snobbery in this country by suggesting that the very emphasis on democracy and equalitarianism in America, the lack of a well-defined deference structure, in which there is no question about social rankings, make well-to-do Americans place more emphasis on status background and symbolism than do Europeans.

It may seem a paradox to observe that a millionaire has a better and easier social career open to him in England than in America. . . . In America, if his private character be bad, if he be mean or openly immoral, or personally vulgar, or dishonest, the best society may keep its doors closed against him. In England great wealth, skillfully employed, will more readily force these doors to open. For in England great wealth can, by using the appropriate methods, practically buy rank from those who bestow it. . . . The existence of a system of artificial rank enables a stamp to be given to base metal in Europe which cannot be given in a thoroughly republican country.[11]

The great concern with family background (which generation made the money?) that many observers, from Harriet Martineau (one of the most sophisticated British commenters on American life in the 1820s) to the contemporary American sociologist Lloyd Warner, have shown to be characteristic of large parts of American society may be a reaction to the feelings of uncertainty about social position engendered in a society whose basic values deny anyone the inherent right to claim higher status than his neighbor. As the sociologist Howard Brotz has pointed out in comparing the status systems of Britain and the United States:

In a democracy snobbishness can be far more vicious than in an aristocracy. Lacking that natural confirmation of superiority which political authority alone can give, the rich and particularly the new rich, feel threatened by mere contact with their inferiors. This tendency perhaps reached its apogee in the late nineteenth

[11] James Bryce, *The American Commonwealth*. Vol. II (New York: Macmillan, 1910), p. 815. Cf. D. W. Brogan, U.S.A. (London: Oxford University Press, 1941), pp. 116 ff.; see Robert W. Smuts, *European Impressions of the American Worker* (New York: King's Crown Press, 1953), for a summary of comments by many visitors in the 1900s and the 1950s who reported that "social and economic democracy in America, far from mitigating competition for social status, intensified it" (p. 13).

century in Tuxedo Park, a select residential community composed of wealthy New York businessmen, which, not content merely to surround itself with a wire fence, posted a sentry at the gate to keep nonmembers out. Nothing could be more fantastic than this to an English lord living in the country in the midst, not of other peers, but of his tenants. His position is such that he is at ease in the presence of members of the lower classes and in associating with them in recreation. For example, farmers [that is, tenants] ride to the hounds in the hunts. It is this "democratic" attitude which, in the first instance, makes for an openness to social relations with Jews. One cannot be declassed, so to speak, by play activities.[12]

The problem of conformity which so troubles many Americans today has been noted as a major aspect of American culture from Tocqueville in the 1830s to Riesman in the 1950s. Analysts have repeatedly stressed the extent to which Americans (as compared to other peoples) are sensitive to the judgments of others. Never secure in their own status, they are concerned with "public opinion" in a way that elites in a more aristocratic and status-bound society do not have to be. As early as the nineteenth century foreign observers were struck by the "other-directedness" of Americans and accounted for it by the nature of the class system. This image of the American as "other-directed" can, as Riesman notes, be found in the writing of "Tocqueville and other curious and astonished visitors from Europe." [13] Harriet Martineau almost seems to be paraphrasing Riesman's own description of today's "other-directed" man in her picture of the early nineteenth-century American:

Americans may travel over the world, and find no society but their own which will submit [as much] to the restraint of perpetual caution, and reference to the opinions of others. They may travel over the whole world, and find no country but their own

[12] Howard Brotz, "The Position of the Jews in English Society," *The Jewish Journal of Sociology*, 1 (1959), p. 97.

[13] David Riesman, *et al., The Lonely Crowd: A Study of the Changing American Character* (New Haven: Yale University Press, 1950), pp. 19–20.

where the very children beware of getting into scrapes, and talk of the effect of actions on people's minds; where the youth of society determines in silence what opinions they shall bring forward, and what avow only in the family circle; where women write miserable letters, almost universally, because it is a settled matter that it is unsafe to commit oneself on paper; and where elderly people seem to lack almost universally that faith in principles which inspires a free expression of them at any time, and under all circumstances.[14]

It may be argued that in an open democratic society in which people are encouraged to struggle upward, but where there are no clearly defined reference points to mark their arrival, and where their success in achieving status is determined by the good opinion of others, the kind of caution and intense study of other people's opinions described by Martineau is natural. Like Riesman today, she notes that this "other-directed" type is found most commonly in urban centers in the middle and upper classes, where people live in "perpetual caution." Nowhere does there exist "so much heart-eating care [about others' judgments], so much nervous anxiety, as among the dwellers in the towns of the northern states of America." [15] Similarly, Max Weber, who visited the United States in the early 1900s, noted the high degree of "submission to fashion in America, to a degree unknown in Germany," and explained it as a natural attribute of a democratic society without inherited class status.[16]

A society which emphasizes achievement, which denies status based on ancestry or even long-past personal achievements, must necessarily be a society in which men are sensitively oriented toward others, in which, to use Riesman's analogy, they employ a radar to keep their social equilibrium. And precisely as we become more equalitarian, as the lower strata

14 Harriet Martineau, *Society in America,* Vol. II (New York: Saunders and Otley, 1837), pp. 158–59.

15 *Ibid.,* pp. 160–61.

16 Max Weber, *Essays in Sociology* (New York: Oxford University Press, 1946), p. 188.

attain citizenship, as more people are able to take part in the status race, to that extent do we, and other peoples as well, become more concerned with the opinions of others, and therefore more democratic and more American in the Tocquevillian sense.

The politics of democracy are to some extent necessarily the politics of conformity for the elite of the society. As soon as the masses have access to the society's elite, as soon as they must consider mass reaction in determining their own actions, the freedom of the elite (whether political or artistic) is limited. As Tocqueville pointed out, the "most serious reproach which can be addressed" to democratic republics is that they "extend the practice of currying favor with the many and introduce it into all classes at once," and he attributed "the small number of distinguished men in political life to the ever increasing despotism of the majority in the United States." [17]

The same point has been made in Chapter X in regard to much of the discussion about the negative consequences of mass culture. Increased access by the mass of the population to the culture market necessarily means a limitation in cultural taste as compared to a time or a country in which culture is limited to the well-to-do and the well-educated.

The current debates on education reflect the same dilemma —that many who believe in democracy and equalitarianism would also like to preserve some of the attributes of an elitist society. In England, where the integrated "comprehensive" school is seen as a progressive reform, the argument for it is

[17] Alexis de Tocqueville, *Democracy in America*, Vol. I (New York: Vintage Books, 1954), pp. 276, 277. Of course, Plato made the same points 2500 years ago when he argued that in a democracy, the father "accustoms himself to become like his child and to fear his sons, and the son in his desire for freedom becomes like his father and has no fear or reverence for his parent. . . . The school master fears and flatters his pupils . . . while the old men condescend to the young and become triumphs of versatility. . . . The main result of all these things, taken together, is that it makes the souls of the citizens . . . sensitive." *The Republic of Plato*, ed. by Ernest Rhys (London: J. M. Dent and Co., 1935), pp. 200–26.

based on the assumption that the health of the society is best served by what is best for the largest number. This argument was used in this country when liberal educators urged that special treatment for the gifted child served to perpetuate inequality and that it rewarded those from better home and class environments at the expense of those from poorer backgrounds. Educators in Britain today argue strongly that separate schools for brighter children (the so-called "grammar schools") are a source of psychic punishment for the less gifted. Many of us have forgotten that liberals in this country shared similar sentiments not too long ago; that, for example, Fiorello La Guardia, as Mayor of New York, abolished Townsend Harris High School, a special school for gifted boys in which four years of school work were completed in three, on the ground that the very existence of such a school was undemocratic, that it gave special privileges to a minority.

What I am saying is simply that we cannot have our cake and eat it too. We cannot have the advantages of an aristocratic *and* a democratic society; we cannot have segregated elite schools in a society which stresses equality; we cannot have a cultural elite which produces without regard to mass taste in a society which emphasizes the value of popular judgment. By the same token we cannot have a low divorce rate and end differentiation in sex roles, and we cannot expect to have secure adolescents in a culture which offers no definitive path from adolescence to adulthood.

I do not mean to suggest that a democratic society can do nothing about reducing conformity or increasing creativity. There is considerable evidence to suggest that higher education, greater economic security, and higher standards of living strengthen the level of culture and democratic freedom. The market for good books, good paintings, and good music is at a high point in American history.[18] There is evidence that toler-

---

[18] See Daniel Bell, "The Theory of Mass Society," *Commentary*, 22 (1956), p. 82, and Clyde Kluckhohn, "Shifts in American Values," *World Politics*, 11 (1959), pp. 250–61, for evidence concerning the

ance for ethnic minorities too is greater than in the past. More people are receiving a good education in America today than ever before, and regardless of the many weaknesses of that education, it is still true that the more of it one has, the better one's values and consumption patterns from the point of view of the liberal and culturally concerned intellectual.

There is a further point about the presumed growth of conformity and the decline in ideology which has been made by various analysts who rightly fear the inherent conformist aspects of populist democracy. They suggest that the growth of large bureaucratic organizations, an endemic aspect of modern industrial society, whether capitalist or socialist, is reducing the scope of individual freedom because "organization men" must conform to succeed. This point is sometimes linked to the decline in the intensity of political conflict, because politics is seen as changing into administration as the manager and expert take over in government as well as in business. From James Burnham's *Managerial Revolution* to more recent restatements of this thesis by Peter Drucker and others, this trend has been sometimes welcomed, but more often in recent years deplored.

The growth of large organizations may, however, actually have the more important consequences of providing new sources of continued freedom and more opportunity to innovate. Bureaucratization means (among other things) a decline of the arbitrary power of those in authority. By establishing norms of fair and equal treatment, and by reducing the unlimited power possessed by the leaders of many nonbureaucratic organizations, bureaucracy may mean less rather than greater need to conform to superiors. In spite of the emergence of security tests, I think that there is little doubt that men are much less likely to be fired from their jobs for their opinions and behavior today than there were fifty or even twenty-five years

---

growth rather than the decline of "genuine individuality in the United States."

ago. Anyone who compares the position of a worker or an executive in a family-owned corporation like the Ford Motor Company when its founder was running it to that of comparably placed people in General Motors or today's Ford Motor Company can hardly argue that bureaucratization has meant greater pressure to conform on any level of industry. Tradeunions accurately reflect their members' desires when they move in the direction of greater bureaucratization by winning, for example, seniority rules in hiring, firing, and promotion, or a stable three-year contract with detailed provisions for grievance procedures. Unionization, of both manual and whitecollar workers, increases under conditions of large-scale organization and serves to free the worker or employee from subjection to relatively uncontrolled power. Those who fear the subjection of the workers to the organizational power of unionism ignore for the most part the alternative of arbitrary management power. In many ways the employee of a large corporation who is the subject of controversy between two giant organizations—the company and the union—has a much higher degree of freedom than one not in a large organization.

Although the pressures toward conformity within democratic and bureaucratic society are an appropriate source of serious concern for Western intellectuals, my reading of the historical evidence suggests that the problem is less acute or threatening today than it has been in the past, if we limit our analysis to domestic threats to the system. There is reason to expect that stable democratic institutions in which individual political freedom is great and even increasing (as it is, say, in Britain or Sweden) will continue to characterize the mature industrialized Western societies.

The controversies about cultural creativity and conformity reflect the general trend discussed at the beginning of the chapter—the shift away from ideology toward sociology. The very growth of sociology as an intellectual force outside the academy in many Western nations is a tribute, not primarily to the power of sociological analysis but to the loss of interest in political inquiry. It may seem curious, therefore, for a sociologist to end on a note of concern about this trend. But I believe that there is still a real need for political analysis, ideology, and controversy within the world community, if not within the Western democracies. In a larger sense, the domestic controversies within the advanced democratic countries have become comparable to struggles within American party primary elections. Like all nomination contests, they are fought to determine who will lead the party, in this case the democratic camp, in the larger political struggle in the world as a whole with its marginal constituencies, the underdeveloped states. The horizon of intellectual political concerns must turn from the new version of local elections—those which determine who will run national administrations—to this larger contest.

This larger fight makes politics much more complex in the various underdeveloped countries than it appears within Western democracies. In these states there is still a need for intense political controversy and ideology. The problems of industrialization, of the place of religion, of the character of political institutions are still unsettled, and the arguments about them have become intertwined with the international struggle. The past political relations between former colonial countries and the West, between colored and white peoples, make the task even more difficult. It is necessary for us to recognize that our allies in the underdeveloped countries must be radicals, probably socialists, because only parties which promise to improve the situation of the masses through widespread reform, and which are transvaluational and equalitarian, can hope to compete with the Communists. Asian and African socialist movements, even where they are committed to political democracy (and unfortunately not all of them are, or can be even if they want to), must often express hostility to many of the economic, political, and religious institutions of the West.

Where radicals are in power—in India, Ghana, Ceylon, Burma, and other countries—they must take responsibility for the economic development of the country, and hence must

84

suffer the brunt of the resentments caused by industrialization, rapid urbanization, bad housing, and extreme poverty. The democratic leftist leader must find a scapegoat to blame for these ills—domestic capitalists, foreign investors, or the machinations of the departed imperialists. If he does not, he will lose his hold on the masses who need the hope implicit in revolutionary chilliastic doctrine—a hope the Communists are ready to supply. The socialist in power in an underdeveloped country must continue, therefore, to lead a revolutionary struggle against capitalism, the western imperialists, and, increasingly, against Christianity as the dominant remaining foreign institution. If he accepts the arguments of Western socialists that the West has changed, that complete socialism is dangerous, that Marxism is an outmoded doctrine, he becomes a conservative within his own society, a role he cannot play and still retain a popular following.

The leftist intellectual, the trade-union leader, and the socialist politician in the West have an important role to play in this political struggle. By virtue of the fact that they still represent the tradition of socialism and equalitarianism within their own countries, they can find an audience among the leaders of the non-Communist left in those nations where socialism and trade-unionism cannot be conservative or even gradualist. To demand that such leaders adapt their politics to Western images of responsible behavior is to forget that many Western unions, socialist parties, and intellectuals were similarly "irresponsible and demagogic" in the early stages of their development. Today Western leaders must communicate and work with non-Communist revolutionaries in the Orient and Africa at the same time that they accept the fact that serious ideological controversies have ended at home.

This book's concern with making explicit the conditions of the democratic order reflects my perhaps overrationalistic belief that a fuller understanding of the various conditions under which democracy has existed may help men to develop it where it does not now exist. Although we have concluded that

Aristotle's basic hypothesis of the relationship of democracy to a class structure bulging toward the middle (discussed initially in Chapter II) is still valid, this does not encourage political optimism, since it implies that political activity should be directed primarily toward assuring economic development. Yet we must not be unduly pessimistic. Democracy has existed in a variety of circumstances, even if it is most commonly sustained by a limited set of conditions. It cannot be achieved by acts of will alone, of course, but men's wills expressed in action can shape institutions and events in directions that reduce or increase the chances for democracy's development and survival. Ideology and passion may no longer be necessary to sustain the class struggle within stable and affluent democracies, but they are clearly needed in the international effort to develop free political and economic institutions in the rest of the world. It is only the ideological class struggle within the West which is ending. Ideological conflicts linked to levels and problems of economic development and of appropriate political institutions among different nations will last far beyond our lifetime, and men committed to democracy can abstain from them only at their peril. To aid men's actions in furthering democracy in then absolutist Europe was in some measure Tocqueville's purpose in studying the operation of American society in 1830. To clarify the operation of Western democracy in the mid-twentieth century may contribute to the political battle in Asia and Africa.

DANIEL BELL

*The End of Ideology in the West**

> Men commit the error of not knowing
> when to limit their hopes.
> —MACHIAVELLI

There have been few periods in history when man felt his world to be durable, suspended surely, as in Christian allegory, between chaos and heaven. In an Egyptian papyrus of more than four thousand years ago, one finds: ". . . impudence is rife . . . the country is spinning round and round like a potter's wheel . . . the masses are like timid sheep without a shepherd . . . one who yesterday was indigent is now wealthy and the sometime rich overwhelm him with adulation." The Hellenistic period as described by Gilbert Murray was one of a "failure of nerve"; there was "the rise of pessimism, a loss of self-confidence, of hope in this life and of faith in normal human effort." And the old scoundrel Talleyrand claimed that only those who lived before 1789 could have tasted life in all its sweetness.[1]

---

* Reprinted with permission of The Macmillan Company from *The End of Ideology* by Daniel Bell. © The Free Press, a Corporation 1960.

[1] Karl Jaspers has assembled a fascinating collection of laments by

This age, too, can add appropriate citations—made all the more wry and bitter by the long period of bright hope that preceded it—for the two decades between 1930 and 1950 have an intensity peculiar in written history: world-wide economic depression and sharp class struggles; the rise of fascism and racial imperialism in a country that had stood at an advanced stage of human culture; the tragic self-immolation of a revolutionary generation that had proclaimed the finer ideals of man; destructive war of a breadth and scale hitherto unknown; the bureaucratized murder of millions in concentration camps and death chambers.

For the radical intellectual who had articulated the revolutionary impulses of the past century and a half, all this has meant an end to chiliastic hopes, to millenarianism, to apocalyptic thinking—and to ideology. For ideology, which once was a road to action, has come to be a dead end.

Whatever its origins among the French *philosophes,* ideology as a way of translating ideas into action was given its sharpest phrasing by the left Hegelians, by Feuerbach and by Marx. For them, the function of philosophy was to be critical, to rid the present of the past. ("The tradition of all the dead generations weighs like a nightmare on the brain of the living," wrote Marx.) Feuerbach, the most radical of all the left Hegelians, called himself Luther II. Man would be free, he said, if we could demythologize religion. The history of all thought was a history of progressive disenchantment, and if finally, in Christianity, God had been transformed from a parochial deity to a universal abstraction, the function of criticism—using the radical tool of alienation, or self-estrangement—was to replace theology by anthropology, to substitute

philosophers of each age who see their own time as crisis and the past as a golden age. These—and the quotations from the Egyptian papyri as well as the remark of Talleyrand—can be found in his *Man in the Modern Age* (rev. ed., London, 1951), Chapter II. The quotation from Gilbert Murray is from *Five Stages of Greek Religion* (2d ed.; New York, 1930), Chapter IV.

Man for God. Philosophy was to be directed at life, man was to be liberated from the "specter of abstractions" and extricated from the bind of the supernatural. Religion was capable only of creating "false consciousness." Philosophy would reveal "true consciousness." And by placing Man, rather than God, at the center of consciousness, Feuerbach sought to bring the "infinite into the finite." [2]

If Feuerbach "descended into the world," Marx sought to transform it. And where Feuerbach proclaimed anthropology, Marx, reclaiming a root insight of Hegel, emphasized History and historical contexts. The world was not generic Man, but men; and of men, classes of man. Men differed because of their class position. And truths were class truths. All truths, thus, were masks, or partial truths, but the real truth was the revolutionary truth. And this real truth was rational.

Thus a dynamic was introduced into the analysis of ideology, and into the creation of a new ideology. By demythologizing religion, one recovered (from God and sin) the potential in man. By the unfolding of history, rationality was revealed. In the struggle of classes, true consciousness, rather than false consciousness, could be achieved. But if truth lay in action, one must act. The left Hegelians, said Marx, were only *littérateurs.* (For them a magazine was "practice.") For Marx, the only real action was in politics. But action, revolutionary action as Marx conceived it, was not mere social change. It was, in its way, the resumption of all the old millenarian, chiliastic ideas of the Anabaptists. It was, in its new vision, a new ideology.

The analysis of ideology belongs properly in the discussion of the intelligentsia. One can say that what the priest is to religion, the intellectual is to ideology. This in itself gives us a clue to the dimensions of the word and the reason for its mul-

---

[2] The citation from Marx from the celebrated opening passages of *The Eighteenth Brumaire of Louis Napoleon* has a general discussion of alienation, but I have followed here with profit the discussion by Hans Speier in his *Social Order and the Risks of War* (New York, 1952), Chapter XI.

tivariate functions. The word *ideology* was coined by the French philosopher Destutt de Tracy, at the end of the 18th century. Together with other Enlightenment philosophers, notably such materialists as Helvetius and Holbach, de Tracy was trying to define a way of discovering "truth" other than through faith and authority, the traditional methods encouraged by Church and State. And, equally, under the influence of Francis Bacon, these men were seeking some way to eliminate the accidents of bias, the distortions of prejudice, the idiosyncracies of upbringing, the interventions of self-interest or the simple will to believe, all of which, like shadows in Plato's cave, created illusions of truth.* Their aim was to "purify" ideas in order to achieve "objective" truth and "correct" thought. Some of them, Helvetius, for example, believed that one had to go back to the origin and development of ideas in order to see how distortions entered. De Tracy believed that one "purified" ideas by reducing them to sense perceptions—a belated French variant of British empiricism with a barely concealed antireligious bias—and this new science of ideas he called "ideology."

The negative connotations of the term arose with Napoleon. Having consolidated his power, he forbade the teaching of moral and political science at the Institut National and denounced the "ideologues" as irresponsible speculators who were subverting morality and patriotism. As a republican, Na-

---

* Francis Bacon in the *Novum Organum* sought to release Reason from the "imperfections of the mind" by positing different kinds of distortion. These he called *The Idols of the Tribe; The Idols of the Cave* ("everyone . . . has a cave or den of his own, which refracts and discolors the light of nature; owing . . . to his education and conversation with others; or to the reading of books, and the authority of those he esteems and admires . . ."); *The Idols of the Market-Place; and The Idols of the Theatre* ("because in my judgment all the received systems [of philosophy] are but so many stage-plays representing worlds of their own creation after an unreal and scenic fashion"). For a discussion of the history of the idea of bias in the social sciences in relation to ideology, see Reinhard Bendix's *Social Science and the Distrust of Reason* (University of California Press, 1951).

poleon had been sympathetic to the ideas of the philosophers; as Emperor, he recognized the importance of religious orthodoxy for the maintenance of the State.

But it was with Marx that the word "ideology" went through some curiously different transmutations. For Marx, as in his work *The German Ideology,* ideology was linked to philosophical idealism, or the conception that ideas are autonomous, and that ideas, independently, have the power to reveal truth and consciousness. For Marx, as a materialist, this was false since "existence determined consciousness" rather than vice versa; any attempt to draw a picture of reality from ideas alone could produce only "false consciousness." Thus, for example, in following Feuerbach—from whom Marx drew most of his analysis of ideology and alienation—he considered religion to be a false consciousness: Gods are the creation of men's minds and they only appear to exist independently and determine man's fate; religion therefore is an ideology.

But Marx went one step further. Ideologies, he said, are not only false ideas, but they mask particular interests. Ideologies claim to be truth, but reflect the needs of specific groups. In his early essays on *The Jewish Question,* one of the few places where he dealt specifically with the philosophical problems of State and Society, Marx sharply attacked the concept of "natural rights" as it appeared in the French Revolution's Declaration of the Rights of Man, and as these rights were specified in the State constitutions of Pennsylvania and New Hampshire. The presumption of "natural rights"—the freedom to worship or the freedom to own property—was that they were "absolute" or "transcendant" rights; for Marx, they were only "bourgeois rights," historically achieved, which made false claim to universal validity. The function of the State, Marx pointed out, was to create some basis for the "general will." In the "civil society" which the bourgeoisie had created, the State presumably was to be negative or neutral. Each man would pursue his own self-interest, and a social harmony would prevail. But in fact, he argued, the State was used to enforce the rights of particular groups. Thus the claim of "natural rights" simply masked the demand of the bourgeoisie to be able to use property to their own advantage. Marx believed that the individualism of "natural rights" was a false individualism, since man could only "realize" himself in community, and that true freedom was not freedom *of* property or freedom *of* religion, but freedom *from* property and freedom *from* religion—in short, from ideology. The attempt, therefore, to claim universal validity for what was in fact a class interest, was ideology.

Marx differed from Bentham, and other utilitarians, in recognizing that individuals were not always motivated by direct self-interest. (This was "vulgar hedonism.") Ideology, he said, was a meaningful force. "One must not form the narrow-minded idea," he wrote in *The Eighteenth Brumaire,* "that the petty-bourgeoisie wants on principle to enforce an egoistic class interest. It believes, rather, that the *special* conditions of its emancipation are *the general* conditions through which alone modern society can be saved and the class struggle avoided." The "unmasking" of ideology, thus, is to reveal the "objective" interest behind the idea, and to see what function the ideology serves.*

The implications of all this are quite direct. For one, a rationalistic analysis of politics alone is inadequate. What people say they believe cannot always be taken at face value, and one must search for the structure of interests beneath the ideas; one looks not at the *content* of ideas, but their *function.* A second, more radical conclusion is that if ideas mask material interests, then the "test of truth" of a doctrine is to see what class interests it serves. In short, truth is "class truth." Thus, there is no objective philosophy, but only "bourgeois philosophy" and "proletarian philosophy"; no objective sociology but only

---

* To this extent, the "unmasking of ideology" is somewhat akin to the theory of "rationalization" in the Freudian system. A rationalization hides an underlying motive. This does not mean it is necessarily false. In fact to function effectively, a rationalization has to have some "close fit" with reality. Yet an ulterior or underlying motive exists as well, and analysis seeks to point this out.

"bourgeois sociology" and "proletarian sociology." But Marxism is not, simply, a relativistic doctrine: there is an "objective" ordering of the social universe, which is revealed through "history." History, for Marx as for Hegel, is a progressive unfolding reason, in which society, through man's conquest of nature and the destruction of all mythologies and superstitions, moves on to "higher stages." The "truth" of doctrine, therefore, is to be determined by its "closeness of fit" to the development of history; and in practice, it has meant that "truth" was determined by whether or not it contributed to the advancement of revolution.

There are many difficulties to the theory of the "social determination of ideas." One is the role of science. Marx did not speak of the natural sciences as ideologies. Yet a number of Marxists, particularly in the Soviet Union in the 1930s, did claim that there was a "bourgeois science" and a "bourgeois physics" and a "proletarian science" and a "proletarian physics." Thus, the relativity theories of Albert Einstein were attacked as "idealistic." And while today in the Soviet Union, there is hardly any talk of "bourgeois physics," the theories of Sigmund Freud are officially condemned as "idealistic." Yet if science is not class-bound, is this equally true of the social sciences? The question of the autonomy of science is one that has never been satisfactorily resolved in Marxian thought.

A second difficulty is the deterministic presumption that there is a *one-to-one* correspondence between a set of ideas and some "class" purpose. Yet this is rarely the case. Empiricism is usually associated with liberal inquiry. Yet David Hume, the most "radical" empiricist, was a Tory and Edmund Burke, who had argued the most vigorously against rationalist efforts to blueprint a new society, was conservative. Hobbes, one of the most profound of materialists, was a royalist, and T. H. Green, one of the leaders of the idealist revival in Great Britain, a liberal.

And the third difficulty is the definition of class. For Marx (though class was never rigorously defined in his work) the key social divisions in society arose out of the distribution of property. Yet in a politico-technological world, property has increasingly lost its force as a determinant of power, and sometimes, even, of wealth. In almost all modern societies, technical skill becomes more important than inheritance as a determinant of occupation, and political power takes precedence over economic. What then is the meaning of class?

And yet, one cannot wholly discount the force of the proposition that "styles of thought" are related to historic class groups and their interests, or that ideas emerge as a consequence of the different world-views or perspectives, of different groups in the society. The problem is how to specify the relationships between the existential base and the "mental production." Max Weber, the sociologist, argued, for example, that there is an "elective affinity" between ideas and interests. The social origin of an idea, or of a theorist, or a revolutionist, is less relevant than the fact that certain ideas become "selected out," so to speak, by social groups that find them congenial and thus espouse them. This was the basis for the theory of the "Protestant Ethnic," in which he argued that certain features of Calvinistic thought, and the kind of personality that such a doctrine sanctioned, became necessary, and causal, in the development of capitalism, despite the other-worldly foundation of these ideas. Karl Mannheim, another sociologist, sought to divide social thought into two fundamental styles, which he called "ideological" and "utopian." He accepted the proposition, derived from Marx, that ideas are "time-bound" but insisted that Marx's ideas, as those of all socialists, came within the same stricture. Since all ideas serve interests, those which defended the existing order he called "ideological" and those which sought to change the social order he called "utopian." But was all effort, then, at objective truth hopeless? Was Bacon's quest therefore a mirage? Mannheim felt that one social group could be relatively objective—the intellectuals. Since the intelligentsia were a "floating stratum" in society, and therefore were less bound than other class groups, they could achieve multi-perspectives that transcended the parochial limits of the other social groups.

In the development of the social sciences, the problem raised by Bacon, de Tracy, Marx and others—the clarification of the role of ideas in social change—has become part of a technical field known as the "sociology of knowledge." (For a clear discussion of these issues, see the chapter by Robert K. Merton in his *Social Theory and Social Structure*.) But in popular usage the word *ideology* remains as a vague term where it seems to denote a world-view or belief-system or creeds held by a social group about the social arrangements in society, which is morally justified as being right. People then talk of the "ideology of the small businessman," or of liberalism, or fascism, as an "ideology." Or some writer will talk of "the dream-world of ideology (in which) Americans see their country as a place where every child is born to 'equality of opportunity,' where every man is essentially as good as every other man if not better." In this sense, ideology connotes a "myth" rather than just a set of values.

Clearly, such usages, by mixing together many things, create only confusion. Some distinctions, therefore, are in order.

We can, perhaps, borrow a distinction from Mannheim, and distinguish between what he called "the *particular* conception of ideology," and "the *total* conception of ideology." In the first sense, we can say that individuals who profess certain values do have interests as well, and we can better understand the meaning of these values or beliefs, or the reasons why they come forth where they have, by linking them up with the interests they have—though the interests may not always be economic; they may be status interests (such as an ethnic group that wants higher standing or social approval in a society), political interests, such as representation, and the like. It is in this sense that we can talk of the *ideology* of business, or of labor, or the like. (When Charles E. Wilson, the Secretary of Defense in the Eisenhower Administration and one-time president of General Motors, said, "What is good for the United

States is good for General Motors, and vice-versa," he was expressing ideology—i.e., the view that economic policy should be geared to the needs of the business community, since the welfare of the country depended on the health of business.) A *total* ideology is an all-inclusive system of comprehensive reality, it is a set of beliefs, infused with passion, and seeks to transform the whole of a way of life. This commitment to ideology—the yearning for a "cause," or the satisfaction of deep moral feelings—is *not* necessarily the reflection of interests in the shape of ideas. Ideology, in this sense, and in the sense that we use it here, is a secular religion.

Ideology is the conversion of ideas into social levers. Without irony, Max Lerner once entitled a book *Ideas Are Weapons.* This is the language of ideology. It is more. It is the commitment to the consequences of ideas. When Vissarion Belinsky, the father of Russian criticism, first read Hegel and became convinced of the philosophical correctness of the formula "what is, is what ought to be," he became a supporter of the Russian autocracy. But when it was shown to him that Hegel's thought contained the contrary tendency, that dialectically the "is" evolves into a different form, he became a revolutionary overnight. "Belinsky's conversion," comments Rufus W. Mathewson, Jr., "illustrates an attitude toward ideas which is both passionate and myopic, which responds to them on the basis of their immediate relevances alone, and inevitably reduces them to tools." [3]

What gives ideology its force is its passion. Abstract philosophical inquiry has always sought to eliminate passion, and the person, to rationalize all ideas. For the ideologue, truth arises in action, and meaning is given to experience by the "transforming moment." He comes alive not in contemplation, but in "the deed." One might say, in fact, that the most important, latent, function of ideology is to tap emotion. Other

[3] Rufus W. Mathewson, Jr., *The Positive Hero in Russian Literature* (New York, 1958), p. 6.

96

than religion (and war and nationalism), there have been few forms of channelizing emotional energy. Religion symbolized, drained away, dispersed emotional energy from the world onto the litany, the liturgy, the sacraments, the edifices, the arts. Ideology fuses these energies and channels them into politics.

But religion, at its most effective, was more. It was a way for people to cope with the problem of death. The fear of death—forceful and inevitable—and more, the fear of violent death, shatters the glittering, imposing, momentary dream of man's power. The fear of death, as Hobbes pointed out, is the source of conscience; the effort to avoid violent death is the source of law. When it was possible to believe, really believe, in heaven and hell, then some of the fear of death could be tempered or controlled; without such belief, there is only the total annihilation of the self.[4]

It may well be that with the decline in religious *faith* in the last century and more, this fear of death as total annihilation, unconsciously expressed, has probably increased. One may hypothesize, in fact, that here is a cause of the breakthrough of the irrational, which is such a marked feature of the changed moral temper of our time. Fanaticism, violence, and cruelty are not, of course, unique in human history. But there was a time when such frenzies and mass emotions could be displaced, symbolized, drained away, and dispersed through religious devotion and practice. Now there is only this life, and the assertion of self becomes possible—for some even necessary—in the domination over others.* One can challenge death by em-

---

[4] See Leo Strauss, *The Political Philosophy of Hobbes* (Chicago, 1952), pp. 14–29.

* The Marquis de Sade, who, more than any man, explored the limits of self-assertion, once wrote: "There is not a single man who doesn't want to be a despot when he is excited . . . he would like to be alone in the world . . . any sort of equality would destroy the despotism he enjoys then." De Sade proposed, therefore, to canalize these impulses into sexual activity by opening universal brothels which could serve to drain away these emotions. De Sade, it should be pointed out, was a bitter enemy of religion, but he understood well the latent function of religion in mobilizing emotions.

phasizing the omnipotence of a movement (as in the "inevitable" victory of communism), or overcome death (as did the "immortality" of Captain Ahab) by bending others to one's will. Both paths are taken, but politics, because it can institutionalize power, in the way that religion once did, becomes the ready avenue for domination. The modern effort to transform the world chiefly or solely through politics (as contrasted with the religious transformation of the self) has meant that all other institutional ways of mobilizing emotional energy would necessarily atrophy. In effect, sect and church became party and social movement.

A social movement can rouse people when it can do three things: simplify ideas, establish a claim to truth, and, in the union of the two, demand a commitment to action. Thus, not only does ideology transform ideas, it transforms people as well. The nineteenth-century ideologies, by emphasizing inevitability and by infusing passion into their followers, could compete with religion. By identifying inevitability with progress, they linked up with the positive values of science. But more important, these ideologies were linked, too, with the rising class of intellectuals, which was seeking to assert a place in society.

The differences between the intellectual and the scholar, without being invidious, are important to understand. The scholar has a bounded field of knowledge, a tradition, and seeks to find his place in it, adding to the accumulated, tested knowledge of the past as to a mosaic. The scholar, *qua* scholar, is less involved with his "self." The intellectual begins with *his* experience, *his* individual perceptions of the world, *his* privileges and deprivations, and judges the world by these sensibilities. Since his own status is of high value, his judgments of the society reflect the treatment accorded him. In a business civilization, the intellectual felt that the wrong values were being honored, and rejected the society. Thus there was a "built-in" compulsion for the free-floating intellectual to become political. The ideologies, therefore, which emerged from the nineteenth century had the force of the intellectuals behind them. They embarked upon what William James called "the faith ladder," which in its vision of the future cannot distinguish possibilities from probabilities, and converts the latter into certainties.

Today, these ideologies are exhausted. The events behind this important sociological change are complex and varied. Such calamities as the Moscow Trials, the Nazi-Soviet pact, the concentration camps, the suppression of the Hungarian workers, form one chain; such social changes as the modification of capitalism, the rise of the Welfare State, another. In philosophy, one can trace the decline of simplistic, rationalistic beliefs and the emergence of new stoic-theological images of man, e.g. Freud, Tillich, Jaspers, etc. This is not to say that such ideologies as communism in France and Italy do not have a political weight, or a driving momentum from other sources. But out of all this history, one simple fact emerges: for the radical intelligentsia, the old ideologies have lost their "truth" and their power to persuade.

Few serious minds believe any longer that one can set down "blueprints" and through "social engineering" bring about a new utopia of social harmony. At the same time, the older "counter-beliefs" have lost their intellectual force as well. Few "classic" liberals insist that the State should play no role in the economy, and few serious conservatives, at least in England and on the Continent, believe that the Welfare State is "the road to serfdom." In the Western world, therefore, there is today a rough consensus among intellectuals on political issues: the acceptance of a Welfare State; the desirability of decentralized power; a system of mixed economy and of political pluralism. In that sense, too, the ideological age has ended.

And yet, the extraordinary fact is that while the old nineteenth-century ideologies and intellectual debates have become exhausted, the rising states of Asia and Africa are fashioning new ideologies with a different appeal for their own people. These are the ideologies of industrialization, modernization,

Pan-Arabism, color, and nationalism. In the distinctive difference between the two kinds of ideologies lies the great political and social problems of the second half of the twentieth century. The ideologies of the nineteenth century were universalistic, humanistic, and fashioned by intellectuals. The mass ideologies of Asia and Africa are parochial, instrumental, and created by political leaders. The driving forces of the old ideologies were social equality and, in the largest sense, freedom. The impulsions of the new ideologies are economic development and national power.

And in this appeal, Russia and China have become models. The fascination these countries exert is no longer the old idea of the free society, but the new one of economic growth. And if this involves the wholesale coercion of the population and the rise of new elites to drive the people, the new repressions are justified on the ground that without such coercions economic advance cannot take place rapidly enough. And even for some of the liberals of the West, "economic development" has become a new ideology that washes away the memory of old disillusionments.

It is hard to quarrel with an appeal for rapid economic growth and modernization, and few can dispute the goal, as few could ever dispute an appeal for equality and freedom. But in this powerful surge—and its swiftness is amazing—any movement that instates such goals risks the sacrifice of the present generation for a future that may see only a new exploitation by a new elite. For the newly-risen countries, the debate is not over the merits of Communism—the content of that doctrine has long been forgotten by friends and foes alike. The question is an older one: whether new societies can grow by building democratic institutions and allowing people to make choices—and sacrifices—voluntarily, or whether the new elites, heady with power, will impose totalitarian means to transform their countries. Certainly in these traditional and old colonial societies where the masses are apathetic and easily manipulated, the answer lies with the intellectual classes and their conceptions of the future.

Thus one finds, at the end of the fifties, a disconcerting caesura. In the West, among the intellectuals, the old passions are spent. The new generation, with no meaningful memory of these old debates, and no secure tradition to build upon, finds itself seeking new purposes within a framework of political society that has rejected, intellectually speaking, the old apocalyptic and chiliastic visions. In the search for a "cause," there is a deep, desperate, almost pathetic anger. The theme runs through a remarkable book, *Convictions,* by a dozen of the sharpest young Left Wing intellectuals in Britain. They cannot define the content of the "cause" they seek, but the yearning is clear. In the U.S. too there is a restless search for a new intellectual radicalism. Richard Chase, in his thoughtful assessment of American society, *The Democratic Vista,* insists that the greatness of nineteenth-century America for the rest of the world consisted in its radical vision of man (such a vision as Whitman's), and calls for a new radical criticism today. But the problem is that the old politico-economic radicalism (preoccupied with such matters as the socialization of industry) has lost its meaning, while the stultifying aspects of contemporary culture (e.g., television) cannot be redressed in political terms. At the same time, American culture has almost completely accepted the avant-garde, particularly in art, and the older academic styles have been driven out completely. The irony, further, for those who seek "causes" is that the workers, whose grievances were once the driving energy for social change, are more satisfied with the society than the intellectuals. The workers have not achieved utopia, but their expectations were less than those of the intellectuals, and the gains correspondingly larger.

The young intellectual is unhappy because the "middle way" is for the middle-aged, not for him; it is without passion and is deadening.[5] Ideology, which by its nature is an all-or-

[5] Raymond Aron, *The Opium of the Intellectuals* (New York, 1958)

none affair, and temperamentally the thing he wants, is intellectually devitalized, and few issues can be formulated any more, intellectually, in ideological terms. The emotional energies—and needs—exist, and the question of how one mobilizes these energies is a difficult one. Politics offers little excitement. Some of the younger intellectuals have found an outlet in science or university pursuits, but often at the expense of narrowing their talent into mere technique; others have sought self-expression in the arts, but in the wasteland the lack of content has meant, too, the lack of the necessary tension that creates new forms and styles.

Whether the intellectuals in the West can find passions outside of politics is moot. Unfortunately, social reform does not have any unifying appeal, nor does it give a younger generation the outlet for "self-expression" and "self-definition" that it wants. The trajectory of enthusiasm has curved East, where, in the new ecstasies for economic utopia, the "future" is all that counts.

The end of ideology is not—should not be—the end of utopia as well. If anything, one can begin anew the discussion of utopia only by being aware of the trap of ideology. The point is that ideologists are "terrible simplifiers." Ideology makes it unnecesary for people to confront individual issues on their individual merits. One simply turns to the ideological vending machine, and out come the prepared formulae. And when these beliefs are suffused by apocalyptic fervor, ideas become weapons, and with dreadful results.

There is now, more than ever, some need for utopia, in the sense that men need—as they have always needed—some vision of their potential, some manner of fusing passion with intelligence. Yet the ladder to the City of Heaven can no

[see pp. 27–47 in this volume]; Edward Shils, "Ideology and Civility," *Sewanee Review,* Vol. LXVI, No. 3, Summer, 1958, and "The Intellectuals and the Powers," in *Comparative Studies in Society and History,* Vol. I, No. 1, October, 1958.

longer be a "faith ladder," but an empirical one: a utopia has to specify *where* one wants to go, *how* to get there, the costs of the enterprise, and some realization of, and justification for the determination of *who* is to pay.

The end of ideology closes the book, intellectually speaking, on an era, the one of easy "left" formulae for social change. But to close the book is not to turn one's back upon it. This is all the more important now when a "new Left," with few memories of the past, is emerging. This "new Left" has passion and energy, but little definition of the future. Its outriders exult that it is "on the move." But where it is going, what it means by Socialism, how to guard against bureaucratization, what one means by democratic planning or workers' control—any of the questions that require hard thought, are only answered by bravura phrases.

It is in attitudes towards Cuba and the new States in Africa that the meaning of intellectual maturity, and of the end of ideology, will be tested. For among the "new Left," there is an alarming readiness to create a *tabula rasa,* to accept the word "Revolution" as an absolution for outrages, to justify the suppression of civil rights and opposition—in short, to erase the lessons of the last forty years with an emotional alacrity that is astounding. The fact that many of these emerging social movements are justified in their demands for freedom, for the right to control their own political and economic destinies, does not mean they have a right to a blank check for everything they choose to do in the name of their emancipation. Nor does the fact that such movements take power in the name of freedom guarantee that they will not turn out to be as imperialist, as grandeur-concerned (in the name of Pan-Africanism or some other ideology), as demanding their turn on the stage of History, as the States they have displaced.

If the end of ideology has any meaning, it is to ask for the end of rhetoric, and rhetoricians, of "revolution" of the day when the young French anarchist Vaillant tossed a bomb into the Chamber of Deputies, and the literary critic Laurent

Tailhade declared in his defense: "What do a few human lives matter; it was a *beau geste.*" (A *beau geste* that ended, one might say, in a mirthless jest: two years later, Tailhade lost an eye when a bomb was thrown into a restaurant.) Today, in Cuba, as George Sherman, reporting for the *London Observer* summed it up: "The Revolution is law today although nobody has said clearly what that law is. You are expected to be simply for or against it and judge and be judged accordingly. Hatred and intolerance are wiping out whatever middle ground may have existed."

The problems which confront us at home and in the world are resistant to the old terms of ideological debate between "left" and "right," and if "ideology" by now, and with good reason is an irretrievably fallen word, it is not necessary that "utopia" suffer the same fate. But it will if those who now call loudest for new utopias begin to justify degrading *means* in the name of some utopian or revolutionary *end,* and forget the simple lessons that if the old debates are meaningless, some old verities are not—the verities of free speech, free press, the right of opposition and of free inquiry.

And if the intellectual history of the past hundred years has any meaning—and lesson—it is to reassert Jefferson's wisdom (aimed at removing the dead hand of the past, but which can serve as a warning against the heavy hand of the future as well), that "the present belongs to the living." This is the wisdom that revolutionists, old and new, who are sensitive to the fate of their fellow men, rediscover in every generation. "I will never believe," says a protagonist in a poignant dialogue written by the gallant Polish philosopher Leszek Kolakowski, "that the moral and intellectual life of mankind follows the law of economics, that is by saving today we can have more tomorrow; that we should use lives now so that truth will triumph or that we should profit by crime to pave the way for nobility."

And these words, written during the Polish "thaw," when the intellectuals had asserted, from their experience with the "future," the claims of humanism, echo the protest of the Rus-

sian writer Alexander Herzen, who, in a dialogue a hundred
years ago, reproached an earlier revolutionist who would
sacrifice the present mankind for a promised tomorrow: "Do
you truly wish to condemn all human beings alive today to the
sad role of caryatids . . . supporting a floor for others some
day to dance on? . . . This alone should serve as a warning to
people: an end that is infinitely remote is not an end, but, if you
like, a trap; an end must be nearer—it ought to be, at the
very least, the labourer's wage or pleasure in the work done.
Each age, each generation, each life has its own fullness. . . ." [6]

[6] To see history as changes in sensibilities and style or, more, how different classes or people mobilized their emotional energies and adopted
different moral postures is relatively novel; yet the history of moral temper is, I feel, one of the most important ways of understanding social
change, and particularly the irrational forces at work in men. The great
model for a cultural period is J. H. Huizinga's *The Waning of the Middle
Ages,* with its discussion of changing attitudes toward death, cruelty, and
love. Lucien Febvre, the great French historian, long ago urged the writing
of history in terms of different sensibilities, and his study of Rabelais and
the problem of covert belief (*Le problème de l'incroyance du XVIème
siècle*) is one of the great landmarks of this approach. Most historians of
social movements have been excessively "intellectualistic" in that the emphasis has been on doctrine or on organizational technique, and less on
emotional styles. Nathan Leites' *A Study of Bolshevism* may be more
important, ultimately, for its treatment of the changing moral temper of
the Russian intelligentsia than for the formal study of Bolshevik behavior.
Arthur Koestler's novels and autobiography are a brilliant mirror of the
changes in belief of the European intellectual. Herbert Leuthy's study of
the playwright Bert Brecht (*Encounter,* July, 1956) is a jewel in its
subtle analysis of the changes in moral judgment created by the acceptance
of the image of "the Bolshevik." The career of Georg Lukács, the Hungarian Marxist, is instructive regarding an intellectual who has accepted
the soldierly discipline of the Communist ethic; other than some penetrat-
ing but brief remarks by Franz Borkenau (see his *World Communism*
[New York, 1939], pp. 172–75), and the articles by Morris Watnick
(*Soviet Survey* [London, 1958], Nos. 23–25), very little has been written
about this extraordinary man. Ignazio Silone's "The Choice of Comrades"
(reprinted in *Voices of Dissent* [New York, 1959]) is a sensitive reflection of the positive experiences of radicalism. An interesting history of the
millenarian and chiliastic movements is Norman Cohn's *The Pursuit of
the Millennium.* From a Catholic viewpoint, Father Ronald Knox's study
Enthusiasm, deals with the "ecstatic" movements in Christian history.

IRVING KRISTOL

*Keeping Up With Ourselves**

The most marked characteristic of the modern world is its commitments—one can almost say its slavish subservience—to social change. It is quite a new thing, never before known to history or to political philosophy; and the more one thinks on it, the more incredible it appears. No traditional political thinker, from Plato to Rousseau, could have understood it. (Perhaps this is why the student of today has so much difficulty in understanding *them*.) We have achieved a sovereignty over nature that they would have thought truly marvelous; but we have also surrendered our sovereignty over ourselves in a way they would have thought fantastic. Classical political philosophy was duly appreciative of the fact that knowledge is power, and therefore had mixed feelings about its pursuit and diffusion. We, in contrast, have so profound and religious a faith in the ultimate goodness of this knowledge, and of the power associated with it, that we prostrate ourselves before it. One is reminded of a parable that Morris Raphael Cohen was fond of putting before his philosophy students. "Imagine," he said, "that some superhuman being appeared on earth and offered to teach mankind a magical trick that would make life more comfortable, more colorful, more convenient. In return, he demanded only the blood sacrifice of fifty thou-

* From *The Yale Review,* Vol. 49, June 1960, copyright Yale University Press. Reprinted with permission.

sand lives a year. With what indignation would this proposal be rejected! And then came the automobile. . . ."

It is very hard to articulate the premises beneath the religion of technology. The idea of progress is essential to it, of course. But it is not exactly the Enlightenment idea of progress, as expounded by Condorcet for instance. For though this assumed that, with the accumulation of knowledge, men would become superior creatures, it also assumed that this knowledge would be moral and philosophical, not merely technological. In contrast, we do not assert man's necessary goodness but locate the necessity in man's power. We are therefore opposed to any authority, moral, philosophical or political, that would set "arbitrary" limits to the way in which the increase of technological knowledge shapes our world. We are against a "closed society," for an "open" one. Open to what? Well, to perfection perhaps, but to the future certainly. The justification for modernity is to be found in the modern adventure itself.

One of the consequences, however, of living in a world where Flux is king is that it is ever more difficult to have ideas with any sort of purchase on reality. That is, probably, the reason why the modern age has also been the Age of Ideologies. Being incapable of adequate knowledge, we console ourselves with a total knowledge. If we are constantly being moved by forces outside our control, it is a blessing to be informed that they are at least encompassed in our intelligence.

The word "ideology," as we use it today, has an interesting origin. It came into existence in France at the end of the eighteenth century, to signify the study of ideas as entities derived wholly from sense impressions—a belated French variant of British empiricism, though with a barely concealed antireligious bias. Napoleon detested this approach as preparing the way for the subversion of morality, patriotism, and the police; and he heaped scorn upon "ideologues" as irresponsible speculators who were up to no good. Possibly because Napoleon used the word pejoratively, "ideology" later came to be used as a flattering synonym for idealism and the more elevated social sentiments generally. The upshot is the ambiguous term we have now, describing an intellectual enterprise that (a) attempts to give a comprehensive explanation of the past, present, and future of mankind; and (b) incorporates in this explanation an imperative of social transformation.

Ideologies are religions of a sort, but they differ from the older kinds in that they argue from information instead of, ultimately, from ignorance. They do not ask us to trust in an inscrutable Providence, but to accept a reading of events which are happening here and now, in the world about us. It is not knowledge of these events that ideology disseminates, but their "true" meaning which it renders. And therefore ideology presupposes an antecedent "enlightenment"; before it can do its special job of work, facts must be widely available, and curiosity about these facts quickened. Men must be more interested in the news of this world than in the tidings from another. The most obdurate enemy of ideology is illiteracy; which is why all ideological regimes set out to eradicate this, first of all.

The *philosophes* of the Enlightenment, whatever might be said against them did regard themselves as philosophers—Baconian rather than Aristotelian, to be sure, but philosophers nevertheless. And they looked forward to the day when all men would be philosophers; this was the radical novelty of their undertaking, and this was the root of their zeal for the promotion and circulation of knowledge. What made them, despite themselves, the first ideologists was an event they did not anticipate: the intrusion—overwhelming and transfiguring—into the lives of men and polities of modern scientific technology. This had two extraordinary consequences: (1) The prospect of indefinite material enrichment, of an earthly contentment attainable by all, heightened a quality that all men always possessed but which they had only rarely an opportunity to express. That quality was impatience. (It is the emergence of this quality as a social and political phenomenon that economists call, a bit grandly, "the revolution of rising expectations.") and (2) the world that technology made had so many more people in it, was so complicated in its organization, was above all so protean in its measure, that it was beyond anyone's comprehension. The bridge between (1) and (2) was ideology, which was simultaneously promise and explanation.

Democracy itself is, of course, a perfectly respectable, traditional political idea. But under modern conditions, it too tends to lapse into the ideological. Thus, because we have conceived of democratic government in such a way as to assume that an "informed public opinion" is something in which every citizen ought to have an equal share, we are loath to face the fact that this conception is, under present conditions, absurd. It is not merely that there is so much to know. It is also that we so often don't even know what little we think we do know, and this can hold true for areas of American life in which we are personally involved and for which we may have some kind of personal responsibility.

Daniel Bell's brilliant new book, *The End of Ideology* (Free Press), addresses itself in a comprehensive way to the problem of the modern world's sophisticated ignorance. One of its chapters is devoted to an analysis of crime statistics—how they are collected and calculated, by whom, for what purposes, etc. Reading that chapter is a chastening experience for those of us who have (and who has not?) expressed large opinions on the subject. For it turns out that the statistics are so partial and imperfect that it is impossible to say firmly whether or not crime really has increased in the United States (relative to the growth in population, that is) over the past five decades. Professor Bell's own belief is that it has not. What has happened, he suggests, is that it has only become more pervasive. Formerly restricted to the city slums, crime has "spread" as these slums have spilled over into what were once genteel neighborhoods. The memory that many people cherish today, of a period when it was safe to walk along the streets at night, is not an illusion. Those streets did exist, as for the most part they do not today. But there were other streets along which one never dreamed of walking, of whose existence one might have been unaware, over on the other side of the tracks, or of the park. One's middle-class memory naturally does not include *them*.

Now, crime is a "newsworthy" subject, and the press, radio, and TV cannot be said to have neglected it. Yet the kind of point Mr. Bell is making is not what they communicate to us. Why not? It is tempting to say accusingly that these mass media underestimate the intelligence of the public, pander to its instincts for the sensational; and there can be no doubt that the melodramatic definition of "news" which is now unassailably orthodox (it is the one that is accepted in all journalism schools) is an unmitigated curse. Yet it will not do simply to call upon the top executives of our mass media to rededicate themselves to the proposition of an "informed public opinion." For the major reason they do not tell us this sort of thing about crime in America is, quite simply, that they do not know it. How should they? True, they can now read it in Mr. Bell's book. But it is a big book (over 400 pages), there are so many books in so many fields, one's time is inevitably limited, one is called on every day to say *something,* etc., etc. In the end, one must accept these apologies as valid, and realize that people who are busy putting out newspapers do not have the time, the energy, and often the talent to find out the facts about the enormously complicated world we live in.

That reference to talent is not meant invidiously. It is true that the methods of recruiting personnel for the American press are antiquated in the extreme; that a foreign news editor of a major newspaper will in all likelihood not know a single foreign language and be unable to pass a college senior's examination in modern history; that journalistic skill in the abstract (which is the skill of the hack writer) is preferred over any specific competence. But while there is a margin for improvement in these respects, it is not so wide as some think. The ability to discover truth is so rare because the act of dis-

covery is intrinsically so difficult—it requires not merely training and intelligence, but also imagination, insight, and infinite
patience. One cannot expect these talents to be widely diffused.
Mr. Bell's book demonstrates that they do indeed exist; but his
is a rather lonely eminence.

Another chapter in *The End of Ideology* illustrates this
point. It is an account of the situation along New York's wa-
terfront. That this situation is scandalous our press, in collaboration with various Congressional committees, has made
known. But a reading of Mr. Bell's chapter makes us realize
how badly we have been informed about the roots of this
scandal—in history, in economics, in the sociology of the
ethnic groups involved. And we are reminded once again that
the process of discovering truths about our social world is
coming more and more to resemble that of discovering truths
about our physical world: it is impossible to know who is capable of disclosing them until after he has done so—because
one cannot know what the knowledge of these truths implies
and involves until after they have been made known.

The only perceptible result of a grandiloquent emphasis on
"informed public opinion" is to encourage reliance on ideology. A man with an ideology can experience the sense of being
genuinely well-informed because he reads the newspapers as a
way of confirming his beliefs; and newspapers are doubtless
useful for this purpose. Sometimes it seems that this kind of
ideological opinionatedness is actually what our society means
by an "informed public opinion." How else explain the extraordinary phenomenon of "youth forums"? At these events,
young and immature people are positively encouraged to form
and express opinions on matters they know nothing, and can
know nothing, about. They may drop or revise these opinions
as they grow older; but they are all too likely to retain the
habit of forming half-baked opinions, and to regard this as an
exercise in civic responsibility. Would it not be more desirable
to inculcate young people with the sense of the risk, of the
presumption, associated with their having opinions at all?

It is Mr. Bell's conviction that American realities have been obscured mainly because the effort has been to conceive of them in European terms. Ours, he points out, is the first society that has "built in" the principle of constant social change, has oriented all our institutions toward the predominance of this principle; whereas in older societies, change is something external and coercive that "happens" to institutions whose assumption is one of permanence, or at least duration. Mr. Bell proves his thesis with wit and vigor, particularly for those European categories that have their provenance in Marxism. But his is not an apologia for "American exceptionalism," for he is well aware that Americans are capable of manufacturing ideologies of their own.

To take one instance: the transformation of American society which we have witnessed during the past three decades is related in our textbooks in entirely mythical terms. The myth, as presented, goes something like this: with the advent of the New Deal, American society amended its individualistic, laisser-faire tradition in the direction of creating a "welfare state"; and this welfare state, by purposeful intervention in the nation's economic life, has brought the business cycle under control as well as producing a fairer (i.e., more equal) distribution of the nation's wealth. It is, understandably, liberal Democrats who are most assiduous in urging this interpretation; but it is by now a non-party affair. There is no question that American society is more prosperous today than it was thirty years ago, and anyone who casts doubt upon the standard explanation might leave the impression of begrudging it—which is the last impression any politician wants to create.

Yet, as Mr. Bell points out, the most important feature of the Big Change we have lived through since the great depression of the 30s is not the social reforms of the New Deal (there were few social reforms to speak of under the "Fair Deal" of President Truman). It is the fantastic growth of the military budget: "Of every dollar spent in 1953 by the U. S. Government, eighty-eight cents went for defense and payment of past wars; social security, health and welfare, education, and housing comprised 4 per cent of the budget." In other words, what we like to think of as the "Roosevelt Revolution" can be more accurately described as "The Revolution of World War II." The social reforms of the New Deal were long overdue, but it was not they that released America's frozen productive resources, or made for any purposeful management of the economic system. It was war, and the ensuing struggle for world leadership, which did that.

As for the more equal distribution of wealth, there is little evidence that anything of the sort has taken place. The poor have got richer; but so have the rich. It is true that the working and middle classes now have a larger share of the national income, if not of the national wealth. But this is a normal aspect of prosperity in an industrialized (maybe in any) society, and is nothing but a function of the fact that the rich are, by definition, only a tiny part of the population. The high taxes on large incomes may have some moral and political value, but they have little economic significance. The only class that would suffer if these taxes were reduced would be the tax lawyers.

There is no question that terribly important things have happened to America in recent decades; but "the end of ideology" is not one of them, and Mr. Bell's title is in that respect a little misleading. The feverish urge for material improvement and technological innovation is as prevalent as it ever was; the need for easy explanations of the tangled, incomprehensible reality is as pressing. What *has* happened is that one particular form of ideology has collapsed. By the "end of ideology," Mr. Bell appears to mean, above all, the collapse of the socialist ideal. And he is quite correct in the emphasis he puts upon this event.

It is not too much to say that the collapse of the socialist ideal is the most striking event in the history of political thought in this century. The process of its deflation has been so intermittent—an irregular series of gasps rather than one instantaneous exhalation—that it is not easy for us to grasp its full significance. Since the death of socialism has not affected our belief in progress, we are tempted to interpret its passing as merely one episode in the interminable education of the human race. Socialism was useful in its time in calling attention to certain unpleasant aspects of modern life; we have absorbed its insights while transcending its dogmatism and naïveté—that sort of thing represents the common enlightenment attitude. (The unenlightened are convinced that we *have* socialism.) But it is not so easy as that. . . .

What this view ignores is that, while we are all as strongly committed as ever to "creating a better world," it was socialism —and socialism alone—which in the past century attempted to offer a full definition of this ideal. It was socialism that proposed a system of controlling modern technology for human purposes, that sustained a vision of the good society and the good life. The socialist critique of capitalist society, cogent enough in many ways, was its least significant aspect. This critique was not a socialist prerogative, and certainly not a socialist monopoly; most of the reforms it advocated were in the end enacted by non-socialists, for non-socialist (if sometimes humane) reasons. There are many former socialists who take satisfaction in the belief that socialism expired because the capitalist parties "stole" essential parts of its program. But this is to fall into the same fallacy as do the inveterate laisser-fairistes —it is to identify the emergence of the "welfare state" (or, as it can be just as properly called, the "managerial state") with the creeping success of socialism. This is itself nothing but a flight into ideology, whether consolatory or alarmist.

Socialism did not succeed; it failed. The socialist impulse was, like all human impulses, a mixed thing. But it was—particularly in its original, pre-Marxian form, which was never quite extinguished—as much a philosophical ideal as an ideology. It set out to master man's fate, not rationalize it. It aimed at a community of virtuous men, whose dominant motive would be compassion and fellow-feeling. Whether or not this

ideal is intrinsically utopian—i.e., unsuited to man's fallen nature—is endlessly arguable. But what *is* absolutely clear is that
socialism turned out to be utterly unsuited to the nature of
modern man. For, in this nature, concupiscence is stronger
than compassion—a concupiscence that is constantly stimulated (even as it is fleetingly satisfied) by the unfolding promise of modern technology to create ever greater wealth. Socialists thought that the "abolition of poverty" would purify and
ennoble human nature, and were therefore persuaded that
technology worked ineluctably in its favor. They turned out to
be wrong. In large areas of the world today, there is wealth
enough for people to live full and contented lives in socialist
equality and fraternity—if only people wanted to. They do not.
What they want is—more. Though what they want more for,
they do not know.

Our commitment to a "better world" is intense and unconditional, but it floats uneasily in a void. The President has ap-
pointed a committee to compose a memorandum that will
define our "national goals" and "national purpose." The radical nature of this action has, surprisingly, gone unremarked:
only a couple of decades back it would have been taken for
granted that a "national purpose" was the blind sum of individual purposes. The pathetic nature of the President's action
has, on the other hand, evoked some tart comment. The goals
of life are not something constructed in committee, we know.
But we do not know much more than this.

Still, if the modern world is not yet ripe for a political philosophy that will enable it to control the energies it has set
loose, it is a good thing for it to be continually chastened by
the exposure of its ideological daydreams and nightmares. A
true knowledge of facts does not in itself, of course, lead to
knowledge of ends. But false knowledge excludes the very possibility of it. The demolition of ideologies, as executed in Bell's
work, cannot tell us where we ought to go, as Americans and
twentieth-century men. But it does at least help us to keep up
with ourselves.

DENNIS H. WRONG

꧁꧂

*Reflections on the End of Ideology**

The phrase "the end of ideology" is becoming a catchword which sums up a major tendency of our time. Daniel Bell chose it as the title for his recently published collection of essays on American politics and culture. Edward Shils in his book on McCarthyism and in several later essays contrasts the "ideological politics" which he hopes and believes to be declining in the West with what he calls "the politics of civility." Seymour Martin Lipset's book *Political Man: The Social Bases of Politics* might have been called with equal appropriateness "The End of Political Man," considering that Lipset is largely concerned with documenting the attenuation of the class struggle in Western countries and that the term "political man" unavoidably suggests a militant partisan. On the more rarefied level of political philosophy and covering a far longer historical time-span—from the Enlightenment to the present day—Judith Shklar pursues the same theme in her book *After Utopia: The Decline of Political Faith.*

All of these writers, with the partial exception of Miss Shklar, tend to favor the development they describe, although their precise attitudes differ, some taking a "tragic" view of politics and the human condition while others are complacent.

* Reprinted with permission from *Dissent,* Vol. 7, No. 3, 1960.

Their overall verdict has by now become something of a cliché, repeated endlessly by columnists, journalists, and often by politicians anxious to appear as sound moderates. It becomes necessary, therefore, to ask just what the "end of ideology" means. Does it mean the end of any important domestic political conflicts in Western industrial societies? Does it mean simply the absence of new social and political movements? Does it imply that a consciously Utopian view of human possibilities is both dangerous and irrelevant? To what degree is the judgment that the ideological conflicts of the past are not likely to recur associated with approval for a politics of compromise, of piecemeal reform and short-run goals? Rather than address myself directly to these questions, I should like to review the two related but partially independent historical developments to which the heralds of the end of ideology are reacting.

First and foremost, of course, is the experience of totalitarianism, especially of a Soviet totalitarianism that has besmirched the heritage of the Left. The Left, as Philip Toynbee has put it, now has "blood on its hands" and no amount of protestation can restore the pristine moral authority it once possessed. The Soviet experience has had a traumatic impact, creating a suspicion of politics as such and especially of any politics making far-reaching demands and inspiring even modest Utopian hopes. The intensity and authenticity of this recoil from politics is not to be dismissed by easy references to "failure of nerve" or "Cold War chauvinism." Motives of cowardice and opportunism were, to be sure, present in some cases and a number of writers made rather nasty exploitative use of the liberal-radical *mea culpa* theme during the years when attitudes toward Communism became a national obsession. Some who were once drawn to Communism, however fleetingly, have never recovered from the shock of having been wrong about the Soviet Union, while others of the old anti-Stalinist Left have succumbed to the corrupting effects of having been proven so utterly and dramatically right about a major historical issue.

Yet whatever one's relation to Stalinism may have been, a shocked withdrawal from any effort to transcend what is in the name of an exalted version of what might be was a genuine and, in light of the realities that evoked it, an understandable response. Thus had "ideology" acquired its present bad name, becoming identified with secular messianism, chiliastic millenarianism, and, ultimately, with the nihilism and power-worship of totalitarian mass movements.

Barely fifteen years ago the term lacked the ominous overtones it possesses today. One meaning, then, of the "end of ideology" is renunciation of long-range and broad political goals by aging intellectuals who are in a chastened mood after the experiences of recent history. The end of ideology means the fear of ideology, or rather of the destructive mass emotions that ideology has proved capable of unleashing. The cruelty and fanaticism of organized masses is seen as a possibility inherent in modern industrial society and all social movements are anxiously scrutinized for their vulnerability to the totalitarian spirit. A kind of political hypochondria tends to result, viewing as safe only a politics of compromise and limited goals.

But if totalitarianism is the most crushing refutation of the nineteenth century belief in progress, whether in its evolutionary or its revolutionary-apocalyptic form, the counterview of the future as nightmare is now losing its authority as well. If the Age of Apocalyptic Hope is dead, the Age of Apocalyptic Fear is also passing. Orwell's *1984,* Arendt's *The Origins of Totalitarianism,* Milosz's *The Captive Mind*—the three books which captured most fully and imaginatively the essence of totalitarianism—today seem less relevant than when they were published a decade or so ago, in part, of course, owing to the very influence they have exerted. The pall is lifting; in the West at least, the lesson appears to have been learned.

Increasingly the second development encouraging belief in

the end of ideology looms larger. In this version the end of ideology means the end of the class struggle, the modification of late capitalism by welfare legislation, redistributist taxation, the consolidation of powerful unions, and the acceptance by all political parties of Keynesian full employment policies. Economic inequalities, even extreme ones that are hard to justify, have by no means disappeared—some men are a good deal more affluent than others in the affluent society. Sources of social tension remain in the position of victimized racial minorities and marginal groups of unorganized workers and agricultural laborers. But it is impossible to believe any longer that the plight of these groups is intrinsic to "the system" in the classical Marxist sense. Even references to the "war economy" as a catch-all explanation of the failure of capitalism to exhibit internal contradictions have vanished from radical discourse in recent years, outside of the Marxist sects. The arguments and evidence mustered by sociologists like Bell and Lipset indicating that the moderation of party and class conflicts in the West is more than a temporary or cyclic phenomenon are not easily refuted. Even the struggle between the left and right wings of the British Labour Party is largely a disagreement over electoral strategy. Fierce electoral contests between parties representing the relatively privileged and the relatively deprived continue in all Western countries, as Lipset acknowledges in *Political Man*. But his book is largely a documentation of the reduced intensity of the struggle now that "the fundamental political problems of the industrial revolution have been solved: the workers have achieved industrial and political citizenship; the conservatives have accepted the welfare state; and the democratic left has recognized that an increase in over-all state power carries with it more dangers to freedom than solutions to economic problems."

At this point, however, an air of complacency begins to suffuse the argument. Moderation is approved not merely as a "lesser evil" or as the only visible alternative but for its own sake, and impatience is displayed with those who continue to find fault with society. Lipset maintains that "many liberal intellectuals in the 1950s know that they should like and defend their society, but they still have the uneasy feeling that they are betraying their obligation as intellectuals to attack and criticize." The unmistakable suggeston is that no real grounds remain for attacking and criticizing, that the continuing dissidence of intellectuals represents a neurotic fixation on an anachronistic role.

Now Lipset and Bell are both aware of the degree to which complaints about the boredom, moral emptiness, and cultural mediocrity of contemporary life have tended to replace a truly political radicalism. They point out that mass culture, unlike economic exploitation or racial discrimination, is not obviously susceptible to correction by political means so that campaigns against it are hardly continuous with the older radicalism. Moreover, critics of mass culture borrow many of their themes from European aristocratic and romantic reactionaries. Ideas, of course, are not invalidated by the politics of their creators and many of the European theorists of mass society and culture are challenging figures who cannot be easily categorized. Nevertheless there *is* something a bit anomalous about egalitarian socialists drawing so liberally on thinkers whom they would have been—and in some cases were—roundly condemning not so very long ago.

In short, Bell and Lipset are right in contending that much contemporary cultural criticism is ambiguous in its political implications and has its origin in intellectual traditions remote from the political and economic radicalism that it often claims to be extending. But to point this out, while it may be a good polemical gambit, is not to eliminate the genuine problem which is at issue. Both writers often give the impression of thinking that because addiction to television is possible only where high living standards prevail, critics of mass culture ought to shut up unless they are prepared to embrace T. S. Eliot's political as well as his cultural opinions. And both of them finally try to reconcile the tension between the claims of cultural excellence and social justice by resorting to flagrant apologetics on behalf of American culture.

In a curious sense Bell and Lipset remain too Marxist, too determinedly "political men" themselves. This is especially true of Lipset who, as in the remark cited above about intellectuals, seems to be saying "the class struggle is over, the contradictions of capitalism have been resolved, so why do these people keep on bitching?" In a much discussed essay, he even argues that the special "class interests" of intellectuals are well taken care of, now that grants and jobs are lavished on them and their typical occupations are highly esteemed by the public. But "intellectual" and "professor" or even "artist" are not necessarily synonymous categories. And there is something a bit philistine about Lipset's supposition that the intellectuals' lack of enthusiasm for life in the United States stems from nothing more substantial than the alleged American habit of tapping heads instead of tipping hats when confronted with men of learning and cultivation. His elaborate demonstration that Americans are becoming more respectful of intellect when it is properly labeled and bottled and that, unlike Europeans, they are disinclined to show deference to anyone, bankers, statesmen, bureaucrats, or professors, is not as relevant as he thinks.

Yet whatever the tone of voice—self-satisfied, nostalgic, full of foreboding—with which it is asserted, it is undeniable that intellectuals no longer believe in apocalyptic social transformations, in "total" solutions to be achieved by political action in the traditional sense. It is also clear that we are moving into a post-bourgeois, though not post-capitalist, era in which the class struggle is ceasing to be the major source of social change and the most enduring and central issue in the political life of Western nations. This being the case, there seems to me to be little advantage or merit, in America especially, in retaining the label "socialism" to describe the outlook of those whom, for want of a better term, must be called secular radicals. Socialism is too closely linked, both as idea and movement, to the historical objectives of the working class in the century following the Industrial Revolution; specifically, to the issues of economic equality and security posed by the unregulated capitalism of the past. Unlike many *Dissent* contributors and editors, I do not believe the term can sustain the entire weight of humanist protest against the alternately terrifying and stupefying trends of modern society. I prefer Judith Shklar's insistence on the need for a return to the spirit of the Enlightenment, the original source of our ethos, to its freshness, questing vigor, and bold sense of possibility.

The threat of nuclear war, the population explosion, and the rise of the peoples of the world's underdeveloped regions pose the most immediate and truly monumental problems, dangers, and opportunities of our time. But these too are resistant to the old terms of ideological debate between left and right. Though not wishing to appear to deny their urgency (how could one?), I would insist that the implications of the end of ideology as a development in the internal politics of the West must be examined independently.

Considering party politics in the narrowest sense, it needs to be emphasized that the celebrated virtues of moderation and compromise cannot become manifest unless, to begin with, there are conflicting political demands to be moderated and compromised. Otherwise, politics becomes a dull if intricate game played by professionals. The extravagant admiration bestowed by much of the press on such ordinary political operators as [Richard] Nixon and Lyndon Johnson is a sign of how widely accepted such a conception of politics has become in recent years. But what if politics is in fact reduced to debate over minor adjustments among interest groups under conditions where no major group is disenfranchised either literally or figuratively and all are broadly satisfied with the status quo? Can we not then afford to leave things to the technicians, specialists in the arts of legislative and administrative bargaining, and settle back to applaud the end of ideology? Even if we assume, falsely, that the United States has reached such a happy, or at least somnolent, state, moderation will "work" only if *everyone* plays the game, if no group with any bargaining power stands firm on behalf of a principle or goal opposed by others. And this is manifestly not the case in America today. By elevating compromise and "realism" into the cardinal political virtues, the anti-theology of moderation plays into the hands of Southern segregationists and Republican right-wingers who remain less impressed with these virtues than many liberals. The view of the former come to represent one of the extremes to be compromised, while the other "extreme" goes by default to—the NAACP and Senator [Hubert] Humphrey.

The point is not that these worthies are so deficient. Nor even that they can scarcely be called radical—almost by definition we do not expect to find radicals sharing social power and political representation with conservatives and reactionaries. But the total absence of any influential body of radical opinion in the country has the effect of narrowing the spectrum of opinion to the point where "moderation" becomes simple stand-pattism. When intellectuals begin to look at politics through the eyes of the professional politicians, they are failing to perform their role as unattached critics and visionaries.

If "ideology" is by now, and perhaps with good reason, an irretrievably fallen word, is it necessary that "Utopia" suffer the same fate? Is it to be equated permanently with the drawing up of abstract blueprints of the future to which the present must be ruthlessly sacrificed? Or with the empty myth that validates the "organizational weapon" of the totalitarian party?

Utopia is "nowhere," located neither in space nor in time— it is not the future "struggling to be born." But Utopia is not for that reason an incredible dream, a fantasy violating the limits of the possible. On the contrary it is the vision of a *possible* society, a vision that must deeply penetrate human consciousness before the question of how it might be fulfilled is seriously considered—and by that time we will already have advanced a long way towards its fulfillment. To convert Utopia immediately into a chiliastic political goal or to envisage it as the inevitable or even the probable end of history or to use it manipulatively to legitimize the day-by-day objectives and tactics of an organization—these are corruptions of the Utopian imagination.

In justification of "piecemeal technology" (Karl Popper's phrase), Daniel Bell exclaims "but look where the eschatological visions have led!" Piecemeal technology is indeed necessary and important, but in the very same chapter, a valuable and sympathetic examination of the thought of the young Marx, Bell observes that Marx, Lenin, and their followers "sought to win millions of people for the idea of a new society without the slightest thought about the shape of that future society and its problems." In other words, there is a sense in which the Marxists were not visionary enough: they were too caught up in the upheavals of their time, too overwhelmed by the urgencies of social crisis. True, one understands the world in order to change it. But to see the acquisition of supreme political power as the sole means of changing it is to take too narrowly instrumental a view of history, a view, moreover, which is easily corruptible as we have learned to our pain.

The very fact that the possibility of transforming crises and conflicts has vanished frees the Utopian imagination from the terrible urgencies of economic class struggle and political collapse. But this is not an unqualified blessing, for the end of ideology also brings with the danger of a placid acceptance of the given, of the loss, in Stuart Hughes' words, of "any notion of transcendence in social and cultural pursuits." Already we can see this happening to mass publics in Western society. The residues of Marxist "realism" about the facts of power and the built-in determinism, however benign in spirit, of contemporary sociological thought encourage intellectuals to follow in the same direction. It is neither vanity nor nostalgia for the past to resist these tendencies in the name of what man might yet become.

C. WRIGHT MILLS

*Letter to the New Left**

When I settle down to write to you, I feel somehow "freer" than usual. The reason, I suppose, is that most of the time I am writing for people whose ambiguities and values I imagine to be rather different from mine; but with you, I feel enough in common to allow us "to get on with it" in more positive ways. Reading your book, *Out of Apathy,* prompts me to write to you about several problems I think we now face. On none of these can I hope to be definitive; I only want to raise a few questions.

It is no exaggeration to say that since the end of World War II in Britain and the United States smug conservatives, tired liberals and disillusioned radicals have carried on a weary discourse in which issues are blurred and potential debate muted; the sickness of complacency has prevailed, the bi-partisan banality flourished. There is no need—after your book—to explain again why all this has come about among "people in general" in the NATO countries; but it may be worthwhile to examine one style of cultural work that is in effect an intellectual celebration of apathy.

Many intellectual fashions, of course, do just that; they stand in the way of a release of the imagination—about the cold war, the Soviet bloc, the politics of peace, about any new beginnings at home and abroad. But the fashion I have in

* From *New Left Review,* No. 5, 1960. Reprinted by permission.

mind is the weariness of many NATO intellectuals with what they call "ideology" and their proclamation of "the end of ideology." So far as I know, this began in the mid-fifties, mainly in intellectual circles more or less associated with the Congress for Cultural Freedom and the magazine *Encounter*. Reports on the Milan Conference of 1955 heralded it; since then, many cultural gossips have taken it up as a posture and an unexamined slogan. Does it amount to anything?

Its common denominator is not liberalism as a political philosophy, but the liberal rhetoric, become formal and sophisticated and used as an uncriticized weapon with which to attack Marxism. In the approved style, various of the elements of this rhetoric appear simply as snobbish assumption. Its sophistication is one of tone rather than of ideas; in it, the *New Yorker* style of reportage has become politically triumphant. The disclosure of fact—set forth in a bright-faced or in a dead-pan manner—is the rule. The facts are duly weighed, carefully balanced, always hedged. Their power to outrage, their power truly to enlighten in a political way, their power to aid decision, even their power to clarify some situation—all that is blunted or destroyed.

So reasoning collapses into reasonableness. By the more naïve and snobbish celebrants of complacency, arguments and facts of a displeasing kind are simply ignored; by the more knowing, they are duly recognized, but they are neither connected with one another nor related to any general view. Acknowledged in a scattered way, they are never put together: to do so is to risk being called, curiously enough, "one-sided."

This refusal to relate isolated facts and fragmentary comment with the changing institutions of society makes it impossible to understand the structural realities which these facts might reveal; the longer-run trends of which they might be tokens. In brief, fact and idea are isolated, so the real questions are not even raised, analysis of the meanings of fact not even begun.

Practitioners of the no-more-ideology school do of course

127

smuggle in general ideas under the guise of reportage, by intellectual gossip, and by their selection of the notions they handle. Ultimately, the end-of-ideology is based upon a disillusionment with any real commitment to socialism in any recognizable form. *That* is the only "ideology" that has really ended for these writers. But with its ending, *all* ideology, they think, has ended. *That* ideology they talk about; their own ideological assumptions, they do not.

Underneath this style of observation and comment there is the assumption that in the West there are no more real issues or even problems of great seriousness. The mixed economy plus the welfare state plus prosperity—that is the formula. U.S. capitalism will continue to be workable; the welfare state will continue along the road to ever greater justice. In the meantime, things everywhere are very complex, let us not be careless, there are great risks. . . .

This posture—one of "false consciousness" if there ever was one—stands in the way, I think, of considering with any chances of success what may be happening in the world.

First and above all, it does rest upon a simple provincialism. If the phrase "the end of ideology" has any meaning at all, it pertains to self-selected circles of intellectuals in the richer countries. It is in fact merely their own self-image. The total population of these countries is a fraction of mankind; the period during which such a posture has been assumed is very short indeed. To speak in such terms of much of Latin America, Africa, Asia, the Soviet bloc is merely ludicrous. Anyone who stands in front of audiences—intellectual or mass —in any of these places and talks in such terms will merely be shrugged off (if the audience is polite) or laughed at out loud (if the audience is more candid and knowledgeable). The end-of-ideology is a slogan of complacency, circulating among the prematurely middle-aged, centered in the present, and in the rich Western societies. In the final analysis, it also rests upon a disbelief in the shaping by men of their own futures—as history and as biography. It is a consensus of a few provincials about their own immediate and provincial position.

Second, the end-of-ideology is of course itself an ideology—· a fragmentary one, to be sure, and perhaps more a mood. The end-of-ideology is in reality the ideology of an ending; the ending of political reflection itself as a public fact. It is a weary know-it-all justification—by tone of voice rather than by explicit argument—of the cultural and political default of the NATO intellectuals.

All this is just the sort of thing that I at least have always objected to, and do object to, in the "socialist realism" of the Soviet Union.

There too, criticism of milieux are of course permitted—but they are not to be connected with criticism of the structure itself; one may not question "the system." There are no "antagonistic contradictions."

There too, in novels and plays, criticisms of characters, even of party members, are permitted—but they must be displayed as "shocking exceptions"; they must be seen as survivals from the old order, not as systematic products of the new.

There too, pessimism is permitted—but only episodically and only within the context of the big optimism: the tendency is to confuse any systematic or structural criticism with pessimism itself. So they admit criticisms, first of this and then of that; but engulf them all by the long-run historical optimism about the system as a whole and the goals proclaimed by its leaders.

I neither want nor need to overstress the parallel, yet in a recent series of interviews in the Soviet Union concerning socialist realism I was very much struck by it. In Uzbekistan and Georgia as well as in Russia I kept writing notes to myself, at the end of recorded interviews: "This man talks in a style just like Arthur Schlesinger, Jr." "Surely this fellow's the counterpart of Daniel Bell, except not so—what shall I say?—so gossipy; and certainly neither so petty nor so vulgar as the more envious status-climbers. Perhaps this is because here they are not thrown into such a competitive status panic about the ancient and obfuscating British models of prestige." The would-be enders of ideology, I kept thinking, "Are they not the self-coordinated, or better the fashion-coordinated, socialist realists of the NATO world?" And: "Check this carefully with the files of *Encounter* and *The Reporter*." I have now done so; it's the same kind of . . . thing.

Certainly there are many differences—above all, the fact that socialist realism is part of an official line; the end of ideology is self-managed. But the differences one knows. It is more useful to stress the parallels—and the generic fact that both of these postures stand opposed to radical criticisms of their respective societies.

In the Soviet Union, only political authorities at the top—or securely on their way up there—can seriously tamper with structural questions and ideological lines. These authorities, of course, are much more likely to be intellectuals (in one or another sense of the word—say a man who actually writes his own speeches) than are American politicians (about the British, you would know better than I). Moreover, such Soviet authorities, since the death of Stalin, *have* begun to tamper quite seriously with structural questions and basic ideology—although for reasons peculiar to the tight and official joining of cultures and politics in their set-up, they must try to disguise this fact.

The end-of-ideology is very largely a mechanical reaction—not a creative response—to the ideology of Stalinism. As such it takes from its opponent something of its inner quality. What does it all mean? That these people have become aware of the uselessness of Vulgar Marxism, but not yet aware of the uselessness of the liberal rhetoric.

But the most immediately important thing about the "end of ideology" is that it *is* merely a fashion, and fashions change.

Already this one is on its way out. Even a few Diehard Anti-Stalinists are showing signs of a reappraisal of their own past views; some are even beginning to recognize publicly that Stalin himself no longer runs the Soviet party and state. They begin to see the power of their comfortable ideas as they come to confront Khrushchev's Russia.

We who have been consistently radical in the moral terms of our work throughout the postwar period are often amused nowadays that various writers—sensing another shift in fashion—begin to call upon intellectuals to work once more in ways that are politically explicit. But we shouldn't be merely amused—we ought to try to make their shift more than a fashion change.

The end-of-ideology is on the way out because it stands for the refusal to work out an explicit political philosophy. And alert men everywhere today do feel the need of such a philosophy. What we should do is to continue directly to confront this need. In doing so, it may be useful to keep in mind that to have a working political philosophy means to have a philosophy that enables you to work. And for that, at least four kinds of work are needed, each of them at once intellectual and political.

In these terms, think—for a moment longer—of the end-of-ideology:

(1) It is a kindergarten fact that any political reflection that is of possible public significance is *ideological:* in its terms policies, institutions, men of power are criticized or approved. In this respect, the end-of-ideology stands negatively, for the attempt to withdraw oneself and one's work from political relevance; positively, it is an ideology of political complacency which seems the only way now open for many writers to acquiesce in or to justify the *status quo.*

(2) so far as orienting *theories* of society and of history are concerned, the end-of-ideology stands for, and presumably stands upon, a fetishism of empiricism; more academically, upon a pretentious methodology used to state trivialities about

131

unimportant social areas; more essayistically, upon a naïve journalistic empiricism—which I have already characterized above—and upon a cultural gossip in which "answers" to the vital and pivotal issues are merely assumed. Thus political bias masquerades as epistomological excellence, and there are no orienting theories.

(3) So far as the *historic agency of change* is concerned, the end-of-ideology stands upon the identification of such agencies with going institutions; perhaps upon their piecemeal reform, but never upon the search for agencies that might be used or that might themselves make for a structural change of society. The problem of agency is never posed as a problem to solve, as our problem. Instead there is talk of the need to be pragmatic, flexible, open. Surely all this has already been adequately dealt with: such a view makes sense politically only if the blind drift of human affairs is in general beneficent.

(4) So far as political and human *ideals* are concerned, the end-of-ideology stands for a denial of their relevance—except as abstract ikons. Merely to hold such ideals seriously is in this view "utopian."

But enough. Where do *we* stand on each of these four aspects of political philosophy? Various of us are of course at work on each of them, and all of us are generally aware of our needs in regard to each. As for the articulation of ideals: there I think your magazines have done their best work so far. That is *your* meaning—is it not?—of the emphasis upon cultural affairs. As for ideological analysis, and the rhetoric with which to carry it out: I don't think any of us is nearly good enough, but that will come with further advance on the two fronts where we are weakest: theories of society, history, human nature; and the major problem—ideas about the historical agencies of structural change.

We have frequently been told by an assorted variety of dead-end people that the meanings of Left and of Right are now liquidated, by history and by reason, I think we should answer them in some such way as this:

The Right, among other things, means—what you are doing, celebrating society as it is, a going concern. Left means, or ought to mean, just the opposite. It means: structural criticism and reportage and theories of society, which at some point or another are focused politically as demands and programs. These criticisms, demands, theories, programs are guided morally by the humanist and secular ideals of Western civilization —above all, reason and freedom and justice. To be "Left" means to connect up cultural with political criticism, and both with demands and programs. And it means all this inside *every* country of the world.

Only one more point of definition: absence of public issues there may well be, but this is not due to any absence of problems or of contradictions, antagonistic and otherwise. Impersonal and structural changes have not eliminated problems or issues. Their absence from many discussions—that is an ideological condition, regulated in the first place by whether or not intellectuals detect and state problems as potential *issues* for probable publics, and as *troubles* for a variety of individuals. One indispensible means of such work on these central tasks is what can only be described as ideological analysis. To be actively Left, among other things, is to carry on just such analysis.

To take seriously the problem of the need for a political orientation is not of course to seek for A Fanatical and Apocalyptical Vision, for An Infallible and Monolithic Level of Change, for Dogmatic Ideology, for A Startling New Rhetoric, for Treacherous Abstractions—and all the other bogeymen of the dead-enders. These are of course "the extremes," the straw men, the red herrings, used by our political enemies as the polar opposite of where they think they stand.

They tell us, for example, that ordinary men can't always be political "heroes." Who said they could? But keep looking around you; and why not search out the conditions of such heroism as men do and might display? They tell us we are too "impatient," that our "pretentious" theories are not well enough grounded. That is true but neither are they trivial; why don't they get to work, refuting or grounding them? They tell us we "don't really understand" Russia—and China— today. That is true; we don't; neither do they; we are studying it. They tell us we are "ominous" in our formulations. That is true: we do have enough imagination to be frightened—and we don't have to hide it: we are not afraid we'll panic. They tell us we "are grinding axes." Of course we are: we do have, among other points of view, morally grounded ones; and we are aware of them. They tell us, in their wisdom, we don't understand that The Struggle is Without End. True: we want to change its form, its focus, its object.

We are frequently accused of being "utopian"—in our criticisms and in our proposals; and along with this, of basing our hopes for a New Left *politics* "merely on reason," or more concretely, upon the intelligentsia in its broadest sense.

There is truth in these charges. But must we not ask: what now is really meant by utopian? And: Is not our utopianism a major source of our strength? "Utopian" nowadays I think refers to any criticism or proposal that transcends the up-close milieux of a scatter of individuals: the milieux which men and women can understand directly and which they can reasonably hope directly to change. In this exact sense, our theoretical work is indeed utopian in my own case, at least, deliberately so. What needs to be understood, and what needs to be changed, is not merely first this and then that detail of some institution or policy. If there is to be a politics of a New Left, what needs to be analysed is the *structure* of institutions, the *foundation* of policies. In this sense, both in its criticisms and in its proposals, our work is necessarily structural—and so, *for us,* just now— utopian.

Which brings us face to face with the most important issue of political reflection—and of political action—in our time:

the problem of the historical agency of change, of the social
and institutional means of structural change. There are several
points about this problem I would like to put to you.

First, the historic agencies of change for liberals of the capitalist societies have been an array of voluntary associations,
coming to a political climax in a parliamentary or congressional system. For socialists of almost all varieties, the historic
agency has been the working class—and later the peasantry;
also parties and unions variously composed of members of the
working class or (to blur, for now, a great problem) of political parties acting in its name—"representing its interests."
I cannot avoid the view that in both cases, the historic
agency (in the advanced capitalist countries) has either collapsed or become most ambiguous: so far as structural change
is concerned, *these* don't seem to be at once available and effective as *our* agency any more. I know this is a debatable point
among us, and among many others as well; I am by no means
certain about it. But surely the fact of it—if it be that—ought
not to be taken as an excuse for moaning and withdrawal (as
it is by some of those who have become involved with the end-
of-ideology); it ought not to be bypassed (as it is by many
Soviet scholars and publicists, who in their reflections upon the
course of advanced capitalist societies simply refuse to admit
the political condition and attitudes of the working class).
Is anything more certain than that in 1970—indeed this
time next year—our situation will be quite different, and—the
chances are high—decisively so? But of course, that isn't saying much. The seeming collapse of our historic agencies of
change ought to be taken as a problem, an issue, a trouble—in
fact, as *the* political problem which *we* must turn into issue
and trouble.
Second, is it not obvious that when we talk about the collapse of agencies of change, we cannot seriously mean that
such agencies do not exist. On the contrary, the means of history-making—of decision and of the enforcement of deci-

sion—have never in world history been so enlarged and so available to such small circles of men on both sides of The Curtains as they now are. My own conception of the shape of power—the theory of the power elite—I feel no need to argue here. This theory has been fortunate in its critics, from the most diverse points of political view, and I have learned from several of these critics. But I have not seen, as of this date, any analysis of the idea that causes me to modify any of its essential features.

The point that is immediately relevant does seem obvious: what is utopian for us is not at all utopian for the presidium of the Central Committee in Moscow, or the higher circles of the Presidency in Washington, or—recent events make evident— for the men of SAC and CIA. The historic agencies of change that have collapsed are those which were at least thought to be open to *the left* inside the advanced Western nations: those who have wished for structural changes of these societies. Many things follow from this obvious fact; of many of them, I am sure, we are not yet adequately aware.

Third, what I do not quite understand about some New Left writers is why they cling so mightily to "the working class" of the advanced capitalist societies as *the* historic or even as the most important agency, in the face of the really impressive historical evidence that now stands against this expectation.

Such a labor metaphysic, I think, is a legacy from Victorian Marxism that is now quite unrealistic.

It is an historically specific idea that has been turned into an a-historical and unspecific hope.

The social and historical conditions under which industrial workers tend to become a-class-for-themselves, and a decisive political force, must be fully and precisely elaborated. There have been, there are, there will be such conditions; of course these conditions vary according to national social structure and the exact phase of their economic and political development. Of course we can't "write off the working class." But we must *study* all that, and freshly. Where labor exists as an agency, of course we must work with it, but we must not treat it as The Necessary Level—as nice old Labor Gentlemen in your country and elsewhere tend to do.

Although I have not yet completed my own comparative studies of working classes, generally it would seem that only at certain (earlier) stages of industrialization, and in a political context of autocracy, etc., do wage-workers tend to become a class-for-themselves, etc. The "etc." means that I can hereby raise the question.

It is with this problem of agency in mind that I have been studying, for several years now, the cultural apparatus, the intellectuals—as a possible, immediate, radical agency of change. For a long time, I was not much happier with this idea than were many of you; but it turns out now, in the spring of 1960, that it may be a very relevant idea indeed.

In the first place, is it not clear that if we try to be realistic in our utopianism—and that is no fruitless contradiction—a writer in our countries on the Left today *must* begin there? For that is what we are, that is where we stand.

In the second place, the problem of the intelligentsia is an extremely complicated set of problems on which rather little factual work has been done. In doing this work, we must—above all—not confuse the problems of the intellectuals of West Europe and North America with those of the Soviet Bloc or with those of the under-developed worlds. In each of the three major components of the world's social structure today, the character and the role of the intelligentsia is distinct and historically specific. Only by detailed comparative studies of them in all their human variety can we hope to understand any one of them.

In the third place, who is it that is getting fed up? Who is it that is getting disgusted with what Marx called "all the old crap?" Who is it that is thinking and acting in radical ways? All over the world—in the bloc, outside the bloc and in between—the answer's the same: it is the young intelligentsia.

I cannot resist copying out for you, with a few changes, some materials I've just prepared for a 1960 paperback edition of a book of mine on war:

"In the spring and early summer of 1960—more of the returns from the American decision and default are coming in. In Turkey, after student riots, a military junta takes over the state, of late run by Communist Container Menderes. In South Korea too, students and others knock over the corrupt American-puppet regime of Syngman Rhee. In Cuba, a genuinely left-wing revolution begins full-scale economic reorganization—without the domination of U.S. corporations. Average age of its leaders: about 30—and certainly a revolution without any Labour as Agency. On Taiwan, the eight million Taiwanese under the American imposed dictatorship of Chiang Kai-shek, with his two million Chinese, grow increasingly restive. On Okinawa—a U.S. military base—the people get their first chance since World War II ended to demonstrate against U.S. seizure of their island: and some students take that chance, snake-dancing and chanting angrily to the visiting President: "Go home, go home—take away your missiles." (Don't worry, 12,000 U.S. troops easily handled the generally grateful crowds; also the President was "spirited out the rear end of the United States compound"—and so by helicopter to the airport.) In Great Britain, from Aldermaston to London, young—but you were there. In Japan, weeks of student rioting succeed in rejecting the President's visit, jeopardise a new treaty with the U.S.A., displace the big-business, pro-American Prime-Minister, Kishi. And even in our own pleasant Southland, Negro and white students are—but let us keep that quiet; it really *is* disgraceful.

"That is by no means the complete list; that was yesterday: see today's newspaper. Tomorrow, in varying degree, the returns will be more evident. Will they be evident enough? They will have to be very obvious to attract real American attention: sweet complaints and the voice of reason—these are not enough. In the slum countries of the world today, what are they saying? The rich Americans, they pay attention only to violence—and to money. You don't care what they say, American? Good for you. Still, they may insist: things are no longer under the old control; you're not getting it straight, American: your country—it would seem—may well become the target of a world hatred the like of which the easy-going Americans have never dreamed. Neutralists and Pacifists and Unilateralists and that confusing variety of Leftists around the world—all those tens of millions of people, of course they are misguided, absolutely controlled by small conspiratorial groups of troublemakers, under direct orders straight from Moscow and Peking. Diabolically omnipotent, it is *they* who create all this messy unrest. It is *they* who have given the tens of millions the absurd idea that they shouldn't want to remain, or to become, the seat of American nuclear bases—those gay little outposts of American civilization. So now they don't want U-2's on their territory; so now they want to contract out of the American military machine; they want to be neutral among the crazy big antagonists. And they don't want their own societies to be militarized.

"But take heart, American; you won't have time to get really bored with your friends abroad: they won't be your friends much longer. You don't need *them;* it will all go away; don't let it confuse you."

Add to that: In the Soviet bloc, who is it that has been breaking out of apathy? It has been students and young professors and writers; it has been the young intelligentsia of Poland and Hungary, and of Russia too. Never mind that they've not won; never mind that there are other social and moral types among them. First of all it has been these types. But the point is clear—isn't it?

That's why we've got to study these new generations of intellectuals around the world as real live agencies of historic change. Forget Victorian Marxism, except whenever you need it; and read Lenin again (be careful)—Rosa Luxemburg, too.

"But it's just some kind of moral upsurge, isn't it?" Correct. But under it: no apathy. Much of it is direct nonviolent action, and it seems to be working, here and there. Now we must learn from their practice and work out with them new forms of action.

"But it's all so ambiguous. Turkey, for instance. Cuba, for instance." Of course it is; history-making is always ambiguous; wait a bit; in the meantime, *help* them to focus their moral upsurge in less ambiguous political ways; work out with them the ideologies, the theories, the strategies that will help them consolidate their efforts: new theories of structural changes of and by human societies in our epoch.

"But it's utopian, after all, isn't it?" No—not in the sense you mean. Whatever else it may be, it's not that; tell it to the students of Japan.

Isn't all this, isn't it something of what we are trying to mean by the phrase, "The New Left?" Let the old men ask sourly, "Out of Apathy—into what?" The Age of Complacency is ending. Let the old women complain wisely about "the end of ideology." We are beginning to move again.

Yours truly,
C. Wright Mills

KENNETH K. KROGH

Needed: New Political Labels*

Of all the political ideas that have gone into shaping our modern world, none has gained wider usage or wielded greater influence than the left-right concept of political relationships. This is the concept that visualizes our political world as a spectrum stretching between two polar extremes, the extreme left denoting revolutionary radicalism, and the extreme right denoting revolutionary reactionism. The various political schools of thought are ranged in between like the colors of a spectrum according to the intensity of their respective tendencies.

This concept of political relationships stands as the common denominator of political thought throughout the modern world. The terms "left-wing" and "right-wing," derived from this concept, are the most common of all political labels. They reflect the scale by which we evaluate the political thinking of ourselves and others. They also reflect the attitudes with which we look upon change, whether in regard to laws, customs, ideals, cultures, economic arrangements, class structures, educational systems, religious institutions and creeds, or any of the other relations of man to man. In short, it is this left-right

* Reprinted by permission of author and publisher from *Saturday Review*, Dec. 3, 1960.

concept of political relationships that provides the sense of political direction by which men steer themselves in the troubled waters of our world.

But what if the sense of political direction it imparts is wrong? What if it confuses and distorts, so that man is directed into the very conflicts and pitfalls he wants most to avoid? What if our whole system of political relationships can be realistically explained only on the basis of a very different concept?

Despite its wide acceptance, the left-right concept is vague and ill-defined. No complete agreement exists as to the number of categories to be included in the spectrum. Furthermore, the division between any two categories is not a precise line but an imperceptible gradation. And people generally do not fall neatly into one category so much as they are mixed between them in their various views. The spectrum as outlined below, however, would seem to represent the most widely held view of the concept.

The left is generally understood to include those parties and movements that demand wider popular participation in government, push actively for reform, and draw particular support from the disinherited, dislocated, and disgruntled. The right is generally understood to include those parties and movements that are skeptical of popular government, oppose the bright plans of reformers and do-gooders, and draw particular support from men with a sizable stake in the established order.

This general concept provides the master frame of reference in which is cast the bulk of all our thinking about political phenomena, both past and present. But is it accurate? Is it realistic? Does it truly represent our world of political relationships?

The major premise of the concept is the existence of two political extremes which are thought to be a world apart in their fundamental principles. Thus Communism on the left and fascism on the right are thought to be opposites—the most divergent of all political beliefs. Yet we know from the experiences of recent decades that they actually share important features. Their commitment to the totalitarian state structure, the single party, the leader, the secret police; their image of the political world as a struggle between morally irreconcilable forces; their belief that all their opponents are secretly leagued against them; their own aspirations for concentrated and total power; their common recognition of war as a tool in their growth and development—all of these show that the two "extremes" are more like each other than they are like anything that is found in between.

Indeed, Communism and fascism are so much alike that most people are unable to observe any real differences between them. There is a general awareness that they have different names, fly different flags, and use abusive language toward each other, but beyond this most people are unable to recognize distinguishing features. The more discerning may point out that under Communism the means of production belong to the people while under fascism they belong to wealthy capitalists. But this distinction pales in significance beside the fact that in both cases the means of production are in reality under the control of an unchallengeable dictatorship wielding unlimited power. And it is this primary similarity rather than the secondary distinction that most significantly characterizes the relationships between the two.

Thus, although the concept says they are complete opposites, reality tells us they are much like twins. And the result is an explosion of the left-right concept as a reliable guide to political relationships. We cannot accept it except by pretending that vast differences exist between fascism and Communism which, in fact, do not exist at all.

The error of the two "opposites" is of no less magnitude than Ptolemy's error of an earth-centered universe. And just as Ptolemy's concept required a series of assumed epicycles to make it work, so does the left-right concept require certain assumed trends to make it work. If the concept is to hold together and make sense, for example, it must be assumed that any trend in the direction of liberalism and socialism will lead toward Communism. But what is the reality of the situation?

The reality is that no nation which has achieved a liberal or socialist government has ever become Communist of its own volition. Instead, it is precisely those nations that are the most advanced along the line of liberal and socialist policies (notably England and the Scandinavian countries) which stand among the strongest and most effective opponents of Communism. The strongest evidence of fact thus indicates that, if anything, a move toward liberalism and socialism really is a move *away* from Communism.

A companion assumption, which also must be believed if the left-right concept is to work, is that any trend in the directions of conservatism and reactionism will lead *away* from Communism. But reality tells us that Communism has come to power as an indigenous movement only in those countries that have been characterized by reactionary governments (notably Czarist Russia and Nationalist China). And today Communism enjoys its most powerful following in precisely those countries which are still laboring under the effects of conservative and reactionary rule. The strongest evidence of fact therefore indicates that, if anything, a move to conservatism and reactionism really is a move *toward* Communism.

The error in assumed trends thus adds further to the explosion of the left-right theory as a reliable guide to political relationships. Further, there is the fact that the left-right concept is forever shifting its ground. As political and economic conditions change, the left-wing position of yesterday tends to become the right-wing position of today. Thus, as early as the French Revolution, the left of the National Assembly became the right of the Legislative Assembly and the left of the Legislative Assembly became the right of the National Convention, and so on down to the present day, when "right-wing" politicians are to be found embracing as moral certitudes the very measures their predecessors denounced as the epitome of wickedness.

Inevitably, the question arises: How can a world that has attained such fantastic precision in the physical sciences continue to fumble along with such inaccuracies in political science?

How did it come to believe in a system of political relationships which is clearly shot through with error and which shifts ground with every passing decade?

To understand this situation we need to go back to the very origins of the left-right concept.

The terms "left" and "right" as used in the political sense appear to have originated during the French Revolution. In the National Assembly, which met in the summer of 1789, three parties were represented. One party was of a conservative type, opposed to any changes in the powers of the monarchy or the privileges of the nobility. A second was of a more liberal type, favoring limited reforms which would have introduced some form of representative government without unleashing the fury of the oppressed people at the expense of the nobility. The third was viewed as a radical party which, although at first not opposed to the monarchy as such, demanded a constitution to limit and regulate the powers of the monarch and insisted on such other reforms as equal taxation, freedom of speech and press, trial by jury, and abolition of feudal dues. The meeting place for the assembly in Paris was a large hall with a horseshoe-shaped amphitheater. The conservatives sat to the right of the speaker, the radicals to the left, and the liberals in the center, and it was this seating arrangement that is said to have given rise to the use of directional terms in politics.

The French Revolution, however, was only one part of the growing democratic movement. The British Bill of Rights and the American Revolution had preceded the French Revolution, and all three developments served to give impetus to the belief in the inevitability of democracy and progress. Here Western civilization saw itself progressing out of the tyrannies and oppressive traditions of old along a path which pointed in the direction of democracy and expanded human freedom.

At this stage of the democratic movement, the left-right concept was adequate to the political complexities of the day. The right simply stood for those who wished to preserve the existing order, while the left stood for those who wished to change it in the direction of expanded democratic freedoms.

But then something happened which has left its imprint on man's political thinking to this day.

Looking back from a perspective of more than a century and a half, we can see that two diverging lines of political development emerged from these early beginnings. In England and the United States, the democratic movement followed a way of progress in liberal constitutional democracy. In France, however, the movement veered off along what Walter Lippmann has described as "a morbid course of development into totalitarian conditions."

If we follow the political development of England we see, as did de Tocqueville, that the English aristocracy had a way of accommodating itself to the pressures and demands of the growing democratic movement. As a result, the aristocracy retained its place in the government, and the government and its constitution continued to grow ever more representative of the people as a whole and ever more responsive to their needs. Here was "government by discussion," following a course which was steadily to broaden the base of decision-making power among the English people. A similar tradition was developing in the United States.

In France, however, the reverse was true. The nobility of France proved unable to merge and mix with other social groups. On the eve of the revolution, the nobility closed ranks and resisted every attempt toward reform. The result was a virtual impasse which led to the formation of the Jacobin Clubs and a clamor for the head of the king. The Jacobins, who eventually came to power, believed that the principle of the revolution itself was at stake and proceded to guillotine not only Louis XVI but all others suspected of conspiring or wishing to conspire against the revolution and the new republic. The Jacobin policy of Terror was to claim the lives of thousands from all ranks of life. Even the head of Robespierre, key instigator of the Terror, was to fall under the guillotine before a reaction to the slaughter set in. And so great was the reaction that many Frenchmen turned about to favor a restoration of the monarchy.

Here a movement toward government by discussion had turned into government by terror. A movement toward government by assimilation had turned into government by liquidation. A historic issue of *progress* had turned back upon itself to become a historic issue of *excess*. And the stain of excess was to be indelibly imprinted on the left-right concept.

What is significant here is that the left-right concept did not evolve from the sucessful movement toward democratic progress in England and the United States, but from the unsuccessful attempt in France. Thus the left retained the distinction of its democratic aspirations, but it tended to take on the coloration of excess as experienced in France. And the issuance of the "Communist Manifesto" in 1848 was to give further impetus to this tendency.

With the issuance of the "Manifesto" there was need for accommodating the Communist approach to politics within the left-right system. But this posed a dilemma. In theory, the Communists were committed to the high goals of the withering away of the state and the liberation of individuals—goals in keeping with the democratic ideals of leftists everywhere. But in practice, Marx and Engels used the same formula as the Jacobins had used a half-century earlier. They championed liquidation of the ruling class through force and violence and committed themselves to a concentration of decision-making power in the hands of a dictatorship. Significantly, the elements of force and violence and the concentration of decision-making power in the hands of a single individual were precisely the characteristics of power exercised by European monarchs from feudal times. Thus the Communists, like the Jacobins before them, sought to fight fire with fire. But fire is fire, and force is force, and tyranny is tyranny, no matter what other labels they bear. In their practical approach to politics, therefore, the Communists committed themselves to a position on the political right. But in the end, theory won out over practice. With their Utopian goals, the Communists did not *seem* to belong to the right or center. So they were given a position on the far left, solidifying the belief that the democratic movement is inherently addicted to excesses of the most objectionable sort.

In 1925 Hitler issued his *Mein Kampf,* and there was need for accommodating the fascist approach to politics. The fascists were hardly conservative, since they did not wish to preserve the existing order. They were revolutionaries in every sense of the word, purposefully planning to transform the existing order into an all-absorbing authoritarianism that would overcome the frustrations of modern industrialism. Yet their totalitarian ideal did not fit the left's Utopian goals of freedom, so they were given the position on the far right.

Thus we have the left-right concept in its present form. It is a concept that started out to mirror the outlines of the world's democratic movement. But when the movement split into two diverging lines, the left-right concept stuck with its parent body, the French Revolution. As a result, the concept reflects the logic of the French Revolution and insists that pursuit of the democratic ideal leads to and requires government by terror and measures of class *liquidation.* It utterly fails to reflect the logic of the English and American experiments, which prove that pursuit of the democratic ideal through "government by discussion" leads to measures of class *assimilation* in which all classes gain representation and a voice in the decision-making power.

The tragedy of political thinking over the past century and a half is the fact that the devotees of class assimilation have never put the devotees of class liquidation in their proper place. Instead of developing a concept that could comprehend the success of assimilation and the futility of liquidation, the entire democratic movement has succumbed to and suffered from the left-right concept.

Consider the devastating effects of the catastrophic default on the fortunes of the democratic movement. Conceptually, its first effect was to trap the democratic movement between two forms of dictatorship. Gone was the promising democratic horizon and its new vistas of "verifiable progress" which beckoned to Bagehot and other advocates of "government by discussion." Astride the path stood a new political specter, Communism, which spat on "government by discussion" as a decadent "bourgeois" institution and which championed instead a "dictatorship of the proletariat" as extreme as any known to history. To the rear, in league with all the tyrannies of old, stood the other modern specter of dictatorship, fascism.

Outflanked by the arbitrary placement of Communism in the left-right concept, the freedom movement split asunder. Part of it tried to come to terms with Communism, with the tortured results now becoming evident in the writings of those who have emerged, shaken to the very core, from their involvement in "dictatorship of the proletariat." Another segment, composed of the traditional socialists, has tried to go ahead as if Communism might not be an inevitable end to the freedom movement after all. But it has itself been confused in part by the Communist apparition on the far left and has been dogged at every step by fusillades of opposition from fore and aft. The relentless tenets of the left-right concept have allowed the Communists to brand them as "running dogs of capitalism" and as "capitalist lackeys," while the conservatives and reactionaries have responded to the confusion in the socialist ranks by throwing charges of "fellow travelers," "pinks," and "Communist-fronters" at the group as a whole. A third segment, the liberal group, has all but halted and turned back upon itself to join a large segment of the world's body politic in a desperate attempt to find new facets of the middle-of-the-road approach which might solve the world dilemma.

Thus we see that what started out as a clearheaded approach to progress through the enlargement of human freedom has today become a splintered, dazed, demoralized effort characterized by indecision and defeatism. Beset from left and right, and yet finding the center position intolerable in the face of world conditions, the democratic movement has no place to go.

In the midst of these developments, man has become increasingly preoccupied with a different basic question. With the advent of the left-right concept he has gradually switched from "What is progressive?" to "What is excessive?" as his chief political concern. And it is this basic question which now grips the political thinking of the world. With despotism prevailing at either end of the political spectrum, the center and *status quo* have been glorified as the only safe realm of political life. Conformity has become the ruling consideration, and departures from traditions have become the greatest causes of political heat. "What is excessive?" is the characteristic question of the left-right concept and the age which it dominates.

Our intellectual world is thus in a state of crisis today over the meaning and possibility of human progress for the very reason that its basic concept of politics does not admit of progress. The left-right concept is an anti-progress concept. The full import of its logic is to discourage new approaches of any kind. What progress may be made toward greater freedoms in our modern world must be made on the basis of a blind faith in human nature so moving as to override the influences of this villain concept.

Can the situation yet be saved?

Can we replace the left-right concept with a more realistic theory of political relationships, one that can comprehend the opportunities and promises of the democratic movement as well as its failures?

Voltaire has underlined the urgency of our need for such a concept with his dictum that "men will continue to commit atrocities so long as they believe absurdities." Fortunately, the clues to a new concept are already at hand as a result of the accumulated knowledge of recent decades. The next forward step in political theory will be to piece these clues together in a meaningful fashion and relate them to the chaotic situation in which we now find ourselves.

SEYMOUR MARTIN LIPSET

*My View From Our Left**

The act of writing is inevitably one of selection. When writing, an author, consciously or not, has some audience in mind. And one does not want to bore his readers by stating facts or concepts that are obvious. The height of intellectual achievement is to be original. This is as true in the social sciences as in the arts of the natural sciences.

But what may be well known to many of an author's prospective readers will be quite unknown to others. The writings of a social scientist or political analyst are inevitably and necessarily subject to criticism for having ignored matters which he is well aware of, and may, in fact, have written about in other places. It is for some such reason, I believe, that in reviewing my book called *Political Man,* published in 1960, a number of politically involved critics took me to task for my presumed "conservatism." The evidence for this alleged tendency rests, in the eyes of these leftist reviewers, primarily in my failure to address myself to the analysis of economic power or the punitive character of social and economic inequality. A number of these critics, notably in Europe, said that *Political Man* exemplified not only my own conservative bias but the way in which the particular theoretical basis of American po-

* Reprinted from The Columbia University *Forum,* Fall 1962, Vol. V, No. 4. Copyright 1962 by the Trustees of Columbia University in the City of New York.

litical sociology leads to conservative conclusions—"whatever is is right," in this case, Western political democracy, the principal subject of my book.

Indeed, I confess that in reading reviews of *Political Man* I have been unable at times to believe that they were all about the same book, or to recognize views credited to me as my own, a common enough experience among authors, I suppose. One critic who has examined various reviews remarked that "the reviews of *Political Man* in the American magazines of liberal opinion (such as *The New Republic* and *The Nation*) were generally favorable, and spoke approvingly of the way Lipset destroyed 'out-worn slogans' and the 'myths' of liberalism. The British liberal reviewers in the *New Statesman* and the *Guardian* were—predictably—far more hostile, accusing the author in effect of complacency, indifference, an opposition to democracy, and a host of other sins normally imputed to 'bourgeois intellectuals.'"

Now the fact is, I consider myself a man of the Left. But confusing or not, I must add that I think of the United States as a nation in which *Leftist values* predominate. I also think that the truth of this is worth exploring.

My own politics derive from the belief that while differences in the distribution of status, income, and power (stratification) are inherent in the nature of any complex social system, such inequality is punitive and unfair. The lower strata in all societies are punished psychically, and often physically, for being in an inferior position. They and their children have less opportunity to achieve the good things available in the society than those of equal ability who enter the system through a higher class. Stratification advantages or disadvantages cumulate in a self-sustaining cycle. And since I feel that inequality, though inevitable, is *immoral,* I support all measures which would bring the utopian "equality of status and of opportunity" closer to realization.

My commitment to democracy as a political system does not rest solely on the belief that free debate and institutionalized conflict among opposing interest groups are the best ways for society to progress intellectually as well as materially; it also rests on the assumption that only a politically democratic society can reduce the pressures—endemic in social systems—to increase the punitive and discriminatory effects of stratification. I believe with Marx that all privileged classes seek to maintain and *enhance* their advantages against the desire of the underprivileged to reduce them. I agree with Plato that the family necessarily fosters inequality, that parents and others tied by the affective values of kinship must seek to give to their children and others to whom they are tied by family sentiments all the advantages they possibly can. And consequently, ruling strata under *all* economic and social systems will try to institutionalize their superiority so that their kin may inherit it. This tendency is as true for the Soviet Union as it is for the United States, as strong in China as in France or Japan.

If it is true, as I assume, that pressures toward inequality are basic to human society, then it follows that those who would reduce the effects of such pressures as much as possible must look for institutionalized means of restraining them. And I know of no means to do this which are superior to, or even approach, the efficacy or conflict. The only group which has an "interest" in modifying inequality is the underprivileged. But the underprivileged can only impress their concerns on the social system in a polity in which they are free to organize in unions, parties, cooperatives, and the like. *The only effective restraint on the power of the dominant class is counter-power.* The primary strengths of the lower strata, of the exploited classes, are the ability to organize, to strike, to demonstrate, and to vote rulers out of office. In any given society at any given time in history, the lower classes may not use these weapons effectively, they may not recognize their interests, but there is no other way.

Hence a society which denies the masses such rights not only is undemocratic politically, it also fosters the privileges of the ruling groups. As Milovan Djilas and many others have shown, Communist dictatorship has meant the creation of a "new class" more exploitative than the ruling classes of Western capitalism. The distribution of good things in the Soviet Union is radically unequal compared with distribution in most other industrialized nations. And it is primarily the fear of the potentially revolutionary masses which has, since 1953, led the rulers of the Eastern European states to make concessions to improve the standard of living of workers and peasants.

Now, the fact that the dominant political ideology of the United States is a Leftist one stems, of course, from the history of the United States as a former colony which made a successful revolution against its imperial master. And few foreigners realize how thorough this revolution was. The values of liberty and equality became institutionalized within America to a greater extent than in any other nation. Anyone reading the writings of foreign travelers to the United States sees how the phenomenon of social equality has impressed them. It does not, of course, severely limit income or power differences; obviously, the variations between the wealthy and the poor in America are great, as are the differences in status or authority, and Americans have never denied the existence of such inequalities. But as Tocqueville and others have noted, Americans act as if they believed that such differences are accidental, not essential; that among men of equal worth it is not good taste to publicly emphasize accidental and perhaps temporary distinctions.

The concern with equality of status has fostered or supported the objective of equal opportunity, of "achievement for all." The first Workingmen's Parties in the world were founded in the United States in the 1820s and were greatly concerned with securing universal free education, with reducing the steep advantage of the children of the well-to-do. The Workingmen's Party of New York even proposed that *all* children be required to attend state boarding schools from the age of six, so that the cultural advantages of the offspring of all classes might be equalized. That this concern for opportunity and education is basic to America, and not simply a reflection of great wealth, may be seen in the fact that the United States' two former colonies, the Philippines and Puerto Rico, are the second and third leading nations in the proportions of their populations attending university. A larger ratio of their youth (12 to 14 per cent) are in institutions of higher learning than any country in Asia or Europe including the Soviet Union. One could say that while the European and Japanese Leftist parties have concentrated on protecting the underprivileged through social security, state medicine, government ownership and planning, the American Left has attempted to widen access to economic and cultural opportunities through the more even spread of educational opportunities. (It is true, however, that since the 1930s, American liberals and Leftists, among whom I number myself, have attempted to extend the welfare and planning function of government in much the same way as the democratic Left has done in other countries; and the domestic issues which divide the Left from the Right in contemporary America are much the same as those which differentiate politics abroad.)

The image that exists abroad of the United States as a conservative nation rests on the twin facts that it has no significant socialist movement and that it is the wealthiest capitalist nation. Perhaps the most interesting explanation of the absence of a socialist tradition in America, one suggested by the socialist writer Leon Samson, is that *the values of socialism and Americanism are similar*. Samson found that when he contrasted the writings and speeches of conservative American politicians and leading capitalists—Herbert Hoover, Andrew Carnegie, John D. Rockefeller, and others—with the writings of Marx, Engels and Lenin, putting economic system apart, they advocated the same set of social relations among men. In his book *Towards a United Front,* Samson shows that it is almost impossible to tell which of the utterances he reproduces are by a Marxist and which by a conservative American. Both see the ideal society as one which emphasizes social equality, opportunity, and abundance through hard work. He argues, in effect, that socialism has appeared to Americans as that which they already have, or which their existing political parties are working to achieve. Neither I nor Samson argues that America is socialist. What I am suggesting is that most Americans still see themselves as a radically democratic people and the Soviet Union as a reactionary state; reaction, to Americans, consists in re-creating the monolithic imperialist state which their ancestors fought.

Americans, are, however, remarkably naïve about the relation of economic to political power. And they have been remarkably unsophisticated about the realities of economic imperialism. But anyone who seeks to understand American foreign policy must recognize that in the main it has rested on the commitment of the United States to extend democracy and to oppose political imperialism ever since it overthrew its own colonial rulers. Even during World War II, the political leaders of the United States continued to view Churchill and Britain as imperialists whose machinations to preserve their empire had to be defeated. But while the United States sought to end Western rule in Asia and Africa, it ignored to a considerable extent the extension of Soviet power in Europe and Asia. America pressed the English to leave their colonies; it intervened against the Dutch in Indonesia, it backed the Algerian uprising against France. Much to Stalin's surprise, it did little to help Chiang Kai-shek retain power on the mainland, since most Americans who dealt with him, including a number of conservatives, were convinced he was a reactionary and corrupt dictator. Stalin had been absolutely convinced that capitalist America would never allow the Communists to take over China. The fact that it did undoubtedly contributed to his willingness to unleash the Korean war; it must have seemed obvious that a nation which would not fight for China in 1948–49 would hardly intervene for South Korea in 1950. Today, most Americans view the struggle against Communism as a fight with a reactionary and oppressive tyranny seeking to subjugate peoples to imperialist domination, *not* as a campaign in defense of capitalism. Alliances with Right-wing regimes in different parts of the world are seen by the politically aware as a regrettable lesser evil made necessary by the aggressive power of the Communist bloc, *not* as something which is good.

Now one cannot deny that American conservatives and businessmen oppose Communism and socialism because they see these as threats to their interests. And American business has had considerable power and influence in the forming of government policy. But I would argue that such power would be ineffective were it not for the fact that Communism appears as an evil also to the American Left, to unions, intellectuals, and others, because it is an expanding totalitarian imperialism. Today in Italy, American policy supports "the opening to the left," the admission of the Nenni Socialists to the governing coalition, even though this means that major Italian industries (electric power is one) will be nationalized. The stability of Italian democracy is more important to those who hold office in the United States than the issue of who owns industry. America has given much more aid per capita to Yugoslavia or Poland than Russia has given to China, but it has set fewer conditions on this aid than the Soviet Union has done with China. It was Stalin, not Truman, who insisted in 1948 that the nations of eastern Europe be barred from participation in the Marshall Plan program. The United States strongly supports the growth of the European Community as an economic and political entity, though one consequence of the Community's success is to weaken the economic position of the United States.

It should never be forgotten that during the period in which the United States was the only power in the world possessing atom bombs it rejected the advice of men like Bertrand Russell and Winston Churchill, who urged that it use its bomb monopoly to force the Soviet Union to accept controls over its nuclear arms potential. Russell, in fact, stated in 1948 that the

United States should threaten Russia with use of the bomb, that the alternative to such an American policy was permitting Russia to become a power quite able to carry out its objective of reducing western Europe to the status of a Soviet colony. This refusal of the United States to force the Soviet Union into international control and inspection during the period of its bomb monopoly followed directly upon its unwillingness during World War II to use its military superiority to prevent the Soviet Union from absorbing parts of eastern Europe. Thus, the United States vetoed Churchill's demand that the western Allies invade the Balkans, a plan which would have retained at least some portion of the area for the West. And Dwight Eisenhower himself made the decision to permit the Russians to occupy Berlin, though American troops could have gotten there first. The Left-wing British socialist, Richard Crossman, then on Eisenhower's staff, urged a different policy, and now reports:

"I was nearly dismissed from my job for challenging the wisdom of a Supreme Commander who was content to halt on the Elbe and see the Russians take Berlin, "because they will treat the Germans toughly, as they deserve, whereas we would be soft to them."

The underlying desire to avoid war which characterizes democratic regimes, and which contributed to the appeasement policy of the Western powers in dealing with Nazi Germany, continued even under the conservative administration of Eisenhower. Thus, during the East German uprising in June, 1953, American policy was chiefly concerned with preventing any clash between the Communists and West Germans rather than with finding ways to aid the East Germans. I was teaching at the Free University of Berlin at the time, and I witnessed American military police being stationed blocks from the zonal borders *to hold West Berliners back.* The American military commandant in West Berlin ordered the Social Democratic Party *not* to hold a mass meeting in solidarity with their brethren in the eastern part on the city. In Poland during the revolt against the Stalinist regime in October, 1956, American Embassy personnel devoted themselves to advising leaders of the movement, both within and outside the Communist Party, that they could expect no help from the West, that they should endeavor to come to terms with the Russians. One high-ranking official of the Workers' (Communist) Party told me that after the revolt was over, a top officer in our Embassy, who had advised him to be moderate, called to congratulate him on his role in restraining the uprising.

And can anyone who sees the United States as a warmongering imperialist power explain why she joined with the Soviet Union in 1956 to force the French, British, and Israelis out of Egypt, at the same time that she did nothing to aid the government of Hungary against an invasion by the Russian army? The Republican Eisenhower regime helped the neutralist, "socialist" Nasser against three of its best allies, while it refused to aid the revolutionary democratic government of Hungary. In the first case, of course, there was no danger that American intervention would lead to war; in the second, as in East Germany and Poland, the State Department was chiefly concerned to avoid giving the slightest excuse to the Soviet Union for starting an international conflict.

I will be told that the relationship of the United States to Cuba belies the argument that Americans see themselves primarily as democratic opponents to foreign rule and tyranny. It is not so. True, the United States worked with Batista before he was overthrown, as did the Cuban Communist Party. But Castro's rise was made possible by American help and sympathy. *The New York Times,* the paper with closest connections to the State Department, was the first to bring Castro's struggle to the attention of the American people and world public opinion in a highly sympathetic series of articles published at a time when Castro's armed supporters numbered in the few hundreds. Although the American military cooperated with Batista until his fall, Castro was able to secure arms from America; the State Department clearly opposed Batista and demanded he hold genuinely free elections and give up office long before he finally left Cuba. Right-wing Senators and organs of opinion in the United States have, in fact, blamed State Department policy for Castro's rise to power. American officials, including then Vice-President Nixon, have reported that they sought to discuss financial aid with Castro during his first tour of the United States, but that he simply refused, a contention that has been confirmed by Castro's former finance minister and others then in his entourage. In 1962, the Kennedy Administration has offered economic assistance to the Marxist and pro-Communist regime in British Guiana, asking only that it remain formally neutral in international affairs.

It is the fact that the plans to assist Cuban refugees to overthrow Castro began only after Castro had indicated his sympathies with the Soviet Union and after many democratic Leftist leaders of his revolution had defected and fled to the United States. And it should be noted that the disastrous "invasion" effort at the Bay of Pigs consisted in landing 1,500 Cuban émigrés *without air support* or heavy equipment—with much less aid, in fact, than Communist regimes have given to the Pathet Lao in Laos or the Viet Cong in Viet Nam. In spite of its conviction that Cuba was in the hands of a Communist regime, the United States did not organize a foreign invasion, rather it assisted an extremely stupid and ill-planned effort by exiles to begin an uprising in their country. To place this event on a par with the Russian invasion of Hungary with many divisions of Soviet troops, the Chinese conquest of Tibet, or the suppression of the East German uprising by Russian forces in 1953 would be equivalent to equating the Nazi murder of six million Jews and current anti-Semitic policies within the Soviet Union.

Most recently, the Left socialist *New Statesman,* a journal not noted for its friendly interpretations of American foreign policy, has suggested the blame for the increased anxiety in the United States concerning Cuba rests in some large part with the Soviet Union:

> Mr. Khrushchev's decision to send massive shipments of arms and technicians to Cuba was a provocative gesture of the worst sort. . . . Cuban policy in the US has been on dead center since the disastrous invasion of last year. . . . Indeed, Cuban exiles . . . have been complaining bitterly that they have been unable to get US support for sabotage forays into Cuba or for clandestine movements on the island. . . .
>
> For a proper parallel, one must ask what would happen if Finland elected a belligerently pro-Western regime that immediately imported arms and technicians from the US—for "defensive" purposes only, of course. The US in such a case would be properly condemned for irresponsible brinksmanship.

Until the Russians placed atomic missiles on Cuba, the United States had not attempted a serious effort to overthrow Fidel Castro by force largely because the American political tradition finds such behavior repugnant. It is of course also true that certain groups in the military and the Central Intelligence Agency engaged in secret operations that nearly violated these assumptions. But the very fact these were pursued in secret pays tribute to the political morality of most Americans; and it should be noted that, excepting the case of Guatemala, accusations by foreign or domestic critics of such efforts to overthrow anti-Western regimes have brought out American failures (as in Laos) rather than successes. "Secret" intervention is necessarily minimal and weak as compared to the open intervention of Communist states.

But the moralism which affects American foreign policy is not an unmixed blessing. It leads Americans to perceive other states as Good or Evil, and if a state is defined as an enemy, it is the very locus of evil; compromise with it becomes difficult if not impossible. The World War II demand for unconditional surrenders, as well as the adoption of the Morgenthau Plan designed to reduce Germany to an agrarian state, are dismally apt illustrations. And currently, popular attitudes to Communism as a monolithic and unchanging evil inhibit the Administration's freedom to deal with Communist China, or to engage in unilateral initiatives which might serve both to show up the falsity of the Soviet clamor to resolve international tensions, and to encourage those within the Communist leadership who support international comity. A Swiss journalist has recently argued that foreigners must understand the essential concern with morality that underlies American action abroad, must stop treating the United States as if it were a cynical materialist power, or it will be pressed into an isolationist "fortress America" policy:

Whoever interprets American foreign policy in terms of economic interest or imperial power does not understand that it springs from sincere convictions rooted in the Puritan inheritance. Anyone who takes the trouble to investigate will find that this is the view of most Americans and that more or less consciously, it permeates all social classes. . . . The idealistic approach to foreign policy of a people who are assumed to be hard-minded businessmen is one of the most important reasons for serious misunderstanding between Europe and America.

Democracy and equality, then, are not simply ideological propaganda phrases for Americans. Economic well-being for the masses is much more likely to flow from a concern with democracy and equality than vice versa. And consequently, all interest in the conditions which foster and maintain democracy is a concern for the good society in all its aspects, economic, social, cultural, and political. Democracy, as I suggested in the final chapter of *Political Man,* is not simply a means to the end of the good society, it is itself the only society in which the social tendencies which press man to exploit man may be restrained.

This does not mean that any democratic society is a good society. All of them retain enormous room for behavior which men of good will must denounce as evil. In the United States, discrimination against Negroes continues to make a mockery of all our claims to be egalitarian. The American South is neither democratic nor egalitarian; it had to be defeated in battle before it formally freed its slaves, and it has only remained in the Union because of inferior economic and military power. In spite of her great wealth, there is much poverty in America. The state may provide more adequately for education than any other country in the world; it performs much less well in caring for the tribulations of its citizens which arise from illness and old age. Slums continue in broad areas in all our large cities. According to the 1960 US Census, 25 per cent of all family units in the country had an income of *less* than $2,500 a year.

There is much to be done. But, as in other free societies, men may and do struggle to end these and other ills—the Negro is doing so, the labor unions are doing so, in nameable instances. And this is a struggle which has its continuing victories as well as its defeats. Currently, in fact, American Right-wingers and businessmen feel themselves weak and isolated. Anyone who reads the conservative and business press in the United States will find that those writing for it see themselves as spokesmen for politically inferior groups, not for those running the country. The Right-wing leaders speak of "the liberal Establishment," that is, they see the ruling circles of the United States as the liberals, not the conservatives. A recent poll of 30,000 American businessmen reported that 86 per cent of them believed that the Kennedy Administration was opposed to business. But businessmen are not persecuted in America; profits are still high even if their authority is subject to restriction by government and unions.

Some European commentators who are themselves deeply committed to ideological politics have questioned assertions, by me and by other American writers, of the decline of ideology —have suggested that I, for one, reflect a typical American attitude in repudiating ideological belief and behavior. I trust that it is clear that I do not favor a decline in political interest or in reform movements. I simply believe in the actuality of the event, and would hazard the prediction that another decade or two of political democracy and economic growth will find "welfare democracy" in other nations than my own—in France, Italy, and Japan—where the extremists of the Right and the Left will also find little support. Such developments have their bad side, of course, since all nations, no matter how "affluent," retain many sources of human misery that men of good will should seek to eliminate. Non-ideological welfare democracies face the problem that they may no longer possess the internal Leftist vigor to counter the forces endemic in all stratified societies which cumulate advantages for the "have" groups. The fact that the satisfied classes in these countries now include a majority in numerical terms, the middle classes and the skilled and well-organized trade-unionists, makes the tasks of further reform that much more difficult. Perhaps the one "have" group which is sensitive to the injustices of stratification, and which retains the means to whip up opposition to them, is the intellectuals. Since many of these remain motivated to be "political men" even after the "end of ideology," they bear a heavy responsibility to keep democracy representative as well as free.

When contemporary democratic socialists and other Leftists and liberals reject certain measures of state intervention because recent history in various totalitarian states suggests these policies are incompatible with the goal of freedom, they are acting in the direct tradition of the nineteenth-century democratic Left. Those men and those political parties which seek to extend democracy *and* to reduce the punitive aspects of stratification are the contemporary legitimate heirs of the democratic and socialist revolutionaries of the last century.

IRVING LOUIS HOROWITZ

✦

*Another View From Our Left**

> All events are linked up in this best of
> all possible worlds; for, if you had not
> been expelled from the noble castle by
> hard kicks in your backside for love of
> Mademoiselle Cunegonde, if you had
> not been clamped into the Inquisition,
> if you had not wandered about Amer-
> ica on foot, if you had not stuck your
> sword into the Baron, if you had not
> lost all your sheep from the land of
> Eldorado, you would not be eating
> candied citrons and pistachios here.
> —PANGLOSS' CONCLUDING
> REMARK TO CANDIDE

OURS IS AN AGE OF PESSIMISM. Camus, in fact, once declared that the only properly twentieth-century posture is cynicism. And indeed any survey of the century which takes into
account the totalitarianisms of Hitlerism and Stalinism (and
let us not forget the lesser tyranny of McCarthyism), the sav-
age bombings of Hiroshima and Nagasaki, the slaughter of
twenty million innocents in gas chambers, and the constant
threat of all-out thermonuclear warfare, cannot lightly dismiss
Camus' sentiment. After all, this cynicism is not simply an an-
ticipation of what may occur, but is based in good measure on

* Reprinted with permission from *New Politics,* Winter 1963.

what has happened. The Freudian "destruction fantasy" has become externalized as part of the real world. Fantasy has become reality, dreams have become nightmares, and utopias have turned sour.

Of course, there is a way to escape—simply by avoiding newspapers, that is, by withdrawal as the psychologists say, and by privatization as the sociologists say. But such a means is unbecoming to intellectual prophets. They must resort to Orwellian double-think. Only in the case of our sociological Leibnizians, so supremely represented by Seymour Martin Lipset (see his "My View from Our Left," *Columbia University Forum.* Vol. 5, No. 4, Fall 1962) [reprinted in this volume, pp. 152–165],* Right must become Left, fear must become morality, and confusion must become democracy.

It would be uncharitable to take off after Mr. Lipset by making references to other of his writings which offer a less Panglossian view of American life and values. But it does seem that he is going all out to make amends for any past transgressions on Establishmentarian toes. How does our "leftist" go about proving that the "leftist reviewers" of *Political Man* were operating under grave misapprehensions when they accused him of a "conservative bias"? This is really quite simple: take the current liberal rhetoric and combine with the writings of such great American Marxists as Herbert Hoover, Andrew Carnegie, John D. Rockefeller, and you turn up the only conclusion possible—to wit, that the values of socialism and Americanism are similar. Now the troubled may rest content in the knowledge that our support for Spanish dictators, Korean militarists and Brazilian latifundists is in the best tradition of left-wing socialism (or in the pithy though impenetrable phrase used by Lipset—"non-ideological welfare democracy"). To soothe the intellectuals there is special advice: to accept a special mission of keeping democracy representative, linking socialism with sociology, leftism and Americanism. And the price

* A condensed version of the introduction to the paperback (Doubleday-Anchor) edition of *Political Man.*

of this? None beyond that of remaining watchdogs over what we have—providing one is not too touchy over the general moral descent in the nation's political and cultural apparatus.

This is all poppycock of course. Verbal debris arranged to prove that not only flowers can put us in a state of euphoria. Let us focus a little more closely on this view from the left (or dead-center).

While differences in the distribution of status, income and power stratifications are inherent in the nature of any complex social system, such inequality is punitive and unfair. . . . I feel that inequality, though inevitable, is *immoral,* I support all measures which would serve to reduce its extent, or which would bring the utopian "equality of status and opportunity" closer to realization.

A decade ago, there was a raging debate in sociological circles on this question of stratification *versus* equalization. In the form presented by Kingsley Davis and Melvin Tumin (among others) this was a legitimate debate. But as Lipset has done for everything from de Tocqueville and Marx to conflict and consensus, he sees only global resolutions which recognize inequality as inevitable and yet morally reprehensible. Why should one work for the reduction of what is "inherent in the nature of any complex social system"? How can equality be declared "utopian" and yet something which can be brought to fructification? What kind of morality is it which pre-ordains the defeat of what is being fought for? While the Marxists undoubtedly exaggerated the extent to which ethics is anti-historically bound; and the Nietzschians have likewise exaggerated the extent to which ethics is anti-historical—neither would be so ingenuous as to suggest that it is the height of being a "political man" to struggle to gain an end declared to be impossible. Indeed, if Lipset were more forthright he could uphold the honor of morality *against* polity—as many European socialists have come to do. But since politics is declared to be the elephantine resting place of leftism in America, this our author cannot do. Who would be left to utilize his moral expertise if not politicians?

. . . ruling strata under *all* economic and social systems will try to institutionalize their superiority so that their kin may inherit it. This tendency is as true for the Soviet Union as it is for the United States, as strong in China as in France or Japan.

This statement is quite true. But why has Lipset nothing to say about reducing differences in this area? Does he say with Marx (with whom he abstractly identifies) that the family, based as it is on private gain, ought to be eliminated? Does he urge that "the bourgeois clap-trap about the family and education" be replaced by the intervention of society to equalize matters? Not at all. The socialism of Andrew Carnegie has its limits. It is simpler to talk of counter-power as a potential "restraint" on the power of the dominant class. *Is it not the case that the extension of class stratification and differentiation in the Soviet bloc defines how far the Russians are from socialism and not how close the Americans are to socialism?*

The fact that the dominant political ideology of the United States is a Leftist one stems, of course, from the history of the United States as a former colony which made a successful revolution against its imperial master. And few foreigners realize how thorough this revolution was. The values of liberty and equality became institutionalized within America to a greater extent than in any other nation. . . . It does not, of course, severely limit income or power differences.

Here again we find ourselves in the best of all possible worlds. In the first place, values of liberty and equality are quite different. And it is precisely on the differences of such values that the American nation was formed. The federalist papers, the writings of Madison, Hamilton and Jay, are indeed concerned with liberty—but the traditional definition of liberty was explicit throughout their writings—namely liberty for those whose knowledge makes possible the exercise of free choice. The "leveling tendencies" implicit in the more radical figures of the American Revolutionary movement were everywhere outflanked and outvoted. It does not require a Beardian view of the American Revolution to recognize the simple fact that the Constitution is a conservative document, more fearful of surrendering traditionalist parochial values than in ensuring progressive national values. The amendments to the Constitution, one through ten and thirteen through fifteen, bear strong witness to the fact that the simple colonial status of the revolutionary period did not ensure a "leftist" America. One might just as well argue that the Magna Carta so ingrained the idea of liberty in Englishmen that it was unthinkable that they should spend the next centuries as a colonial power. Did the fact that the Bolsheviks made a thorough revolution against an unpopular and despotic Czarist regime "institutionalize" the values of liberty in Russians? Of course not. The most damaging remark to Lipset's thesis of a Leftist United States is the assertion (really, from the "socialist" viewpoint, an admission), that this faith in the values of liberty and equality does *not* severely limit income or power differences. If socialism is not to be viewed as an absurd hoax, just how and in what sense can America be said to be Leftist and at the same time intensify social stratification? Is it possible that Lipset, in his anxiety to identify the going course of American history with the strange course of one man's strange Leftism, has simply attributed to the nation qualities which he possesses as an individual? Strange as it is to attribute such an egomania to Lipset, he himself confesses as much when early in his essay he notes that "now the fact is, I consider myself a man of the Left. But confusing or not, I must add that I think of the United States as a nation in which *Leftist values* predominate." It must be exhilarating to identify with nation and *patria* and at the same time uphold oneself as a man of science and a man of morality. It would seem that there is nothing left to do but rally 'round the flag, sing the *Internationale,* and in good clenched-fist style, curse those who dare to speak of our socialist fatherland in terms of power elites.

That the concern for opportunity and education is basic to America, and not simply a reflection of great wealth, may be seen in the fact that the United States' two former colonies, the Philippines and Puerto Rico, are the second and third leading nations in the proportions of their populations attending univerity.

It has always been the classic liberal notion that education and opportunity are one and the same. In fact, they are quite distinct. High educational achievements do not necessarily lead to high opportunity. Indeed, the key to revolutionary sentiment among the youth of South America, Asia and parts of Africa, is not so much the lack of education, but the lack of opportunity following education. The great worry is what to do with an education once acquired. This is common knowledge to even a casual visitor to these "underdeveloped" areas. In fact, the dichotemization of education and opportunity is a good part of what is meant by underdevelopment. (This and the concomitant factor of miseducation, i.e., 1,000 lawyers for every agronomist in Brazil.) Then again it must be frankly noted that a concern for education is the common property of all industrially advanced societies—whether capitalist or socialist, right-wing, centrist, or left-wing. It can hardly be employed to show that the United States is a democracy, any more than the fact that there are more students in schools of higher learning in the Soviet Union than in England necessarily demonstrates that the former is more democratic than the latter. In addition to this faulty logical reasoning, Lipset's examples are particularly inappropriate. The Philippines remains a poor country, a debtor nation on the world market, still badly bound to its export of raw materials for any wealth it has. Puerto Rico might be a better case to use, if the United States could extend its democratic generosity so far as to allow and encourage the children to learn the course work in their native

Spanish rather than in English. Leftist values, if they have any general meaning, are linked to planned economic rationalization, technological advancement and stressing of criticism of the *status quo*. Attendance at universities remains a neutral fact until related to these qualities as aims or reflect leftist values.

Perhaps the most interesting explanation of the absence of a socialist tradition in America . . . *is that the values of socialism and Americanism are similar.* . . . Putting economic systems apart, they (conservative American politicians and Marx, Engels and Lenin) advocated the same set of social relations among men.

Even Mr. Lipset must have his bad moments reflecting on this canard—preferring as he does to share his opinions with "the socialist writer Leon Samson." Now there is always something especially appealing about crackpot formulations such as this one. It does indeed prevent an author from being a "bore to his readers" as Lipset mentions at the outset. Unless the statement, Andrew Carnegie and Vladimir Lenin are both men, and both men of power, and therefore share in certain attributes common to the species *homo sapiens* is meant, I can see no other meaning to the Lipset-Samson assertion. Private enterprise is not public ownership is a logical truism without originality. And what else could this assertion mean, once Lipset himself adds the qualifying phrase, "putting economic systems aside." What else is left of any sound definition of either capitalism or communism once the economic system is laid aside? To talk about "values" and to identify Americanism with socialism by consciously ruling out economic difference is simply not serious either as science or as general commentary. And given Lipset's overweaning desire to identify intellectual achievement with originality—rather than with the more prosaic identification of intellect with integrity (and in all likelihood the more boring identification) one can only suggest that he return to the "classics" of capitalist and socialist economics for a refutation of such amateurish nonsense.

And before moving on to the next point let us not ignore a plain mistake in fact. The fact is that America has a long-standing socialist tradition. The reasons for its present weakness do not have to be sought in any exotic theory of socialism as Americanism. In the first place, capitalism has done very well in this country. One cannot expect the social protest activities of the socialist movement to flourish in a state of relative affluence. In the second place, socialism in America has been schismatic and factional; dissipating whatever vigor it had in factional battles and debates between the years 1900 and 1920 reflecting the rift between the "foreign" and "indigenous" varieties of socialist thinking; and after that between "right" socialism and "left" socialism. In the third place the inertia bred by two-party politics has made third-force politics very difficult, especially so for socialist candidates subject to repression. What Lipset clearly can't stand is the idea that socialism is a minority idea, in a country which has made majority acquiescence and political victory as the only principle.

Now one cannot deny that American conservatives and business men oppose communism and socialism because they see these as threats to their interests. . . . But I would argue that such power would be ineffective were it not for the fact that Communism appears as an evil also to the American left, to unions, intellectuals, and others, because it is an expanding totalitarian imperialism.

The problem here is that Lipset has now shifted his terms to a considerable degree. For here we are presented with a "classic" model of left and right—with business men contrasted with union men. Now, concern on the part of all sectors for welfare and prosperity is understandably a neutral value until there occurs a rift over questions of the sources of injustice and the remedial measures needed to overcome them. It is in this rift that left and right values are separated out. Furthermore, a context is the only basis for making the discussion meaningful. Except for a right-wing fascism gone utterly mad it is as conceivable for left and right to embrace notions of governmental responsibility for mass welfare, the former on "social contract" and the latter on élitist grounds. The debate rages over how, to what degree, determinations to be made by whom, the margin allowed for criticism. America is as conservative in its addiction to the values of the small businessman of early Protestantism as it is leftist in its growing tolerance of collectivist-bureaucratic organization. They both texture American life and questions to right and left do not separate political loyalty sufficiently to operate as a criterion. Therefore action on the basis of interest must serve to delineate. Here we see that the business community has behaved well within the limits of its "class interests." It is the business community which acts for itself and not the labor unions. It is true that all power sectors in American life see Communism as an evil; but it is no less true that they have joined in a chorus of anti-socialist values as such. The sharp decline in an independent socialist movement rests squarely on the abandonment of leftist principles on the part of unions and intellectuals. It is precisely the sought-after solutions to injustice and economic irrationality of a left character from which they have become disabused and disenchanted and not general opposition to totalitarian imperialism.

The stability of Italian democracy is more important to those who hold office in the United States than the issue of who owns industry.

This statement is made in the context of showing that the United States supports democracy around the world, and further proof of this statement is federal support for aid to Yugoslavia and Poland. Now it is quite true that the United States has a flexible aid policy in relation not only to the regimes mentioned but to others as well, e.g., the MNR movement in Bolivia. But aside from the obvious fact that the United States has often thrown its support against democratic movements when such a policy was feasible, there is the added fact that in a total world-wide struggle between the United States and the Soviet Union, one employs weapons not always of one's own choosing. Thus, it was no sign of Soviet love of Egyptian nationalism that led it to support the Aswan dam project—simply good politics (following the United States' rejection of this same project). Likewise, the potential "loss" of Bolivia to communism were we not to support the radical socialists, or the loss of Italy were there not an "opening" to the Nenni left socialists, outweighs the congenital dislike for openly socialist regimes. The aid to Yugoslavia and Poland likewise makes good sense in the effort to neutralize the outer perimeter of the Warsaw Pact nations. It does not require any exaggerated theories of a socialist-oriented America to lead one to see the wisdom in such a flexible policy. Would Lipset consider the United States fascistic because it supports the Franco regime? Of course not. Neither should it be termed leftist or socialist because of its foreign-aid programs.

It should never be forgotten that during the period in which the United States was the only power in the world possessing atom bombs it rejected the advice of men like Bertrand Russell and Winston Churchill, who urged that it use its bomb monopoly to force the Soviet Union to accept controls over its nuclear arms potential.

Several elements entered into the decision not to act in a bellicose fashion. One, the United States and the Soviet Union were still not "enemies" in the sense that they were to become so during the fifties. Two, as P. M. S. Blackett noted in 1948, in *Fear, War and the Bomb,* the atomic bomb was not considered an "ultimate weapon" either by the United States or the Soviet Union. The Russians had an overwhelming superiority in conventional weaponry at the time, which then may have proven more than adequate compensation for the lack of atomic weapons. Three, while the Soviets did not have atomic weapons they did have bacteriological and chemical weapons which might have been used to answer an atomic strike. Four, is the moral climate of the time. The fact is that the United States was the first and is still the only power to have used atomic weapons, and it was not only the Japanese who had this in the forefront of their collective conscience. The common sense of the situation in 1948, as in 1962, was not to "cross the atomic line." And if Lipset wanted to defend U.S. rationality he would be on firm ground, but to argue for its leftist values is an "outrageous hypothesis" in the bad sense of the term.

The underlying desire to avoid war which characterizes democratic regimes, and which contributed to the appeasement policy of the Western powers in dealing with Nazi Germany, continued even under the conservative administration of Eisenhower.

Even if we grant that the avoidance of warfare is a democratic trait, a thesis that is highly dubious given the present fear of thermonuclear weaponry as reason enough in any political context, Lipset's statement is more imaginary than imaginative. Any reading of Walter Millis' *Road to War* will reveal that alternating currents of militarism and pacifism have existed throughout the twentieth-century U.S. policy-making. Indeed, the martial spirit of the U.S. is nowhere better revealed than in its continued demands for "unconditioned surrender" in both World Wars—a policy with no military necessity but based on "morality." Then again, a good deal of the anti-military posture in American history, as I have tried to show in my work on *The War Game,* is characteristic of right-wing, conservative, isolationist elements. Indeed, the isolationist movement prior to World War II drew its strength from a paranoic anti-communism and anti-socialism, which held with Hitler that the struggle against Russian Bolshevism was worth any price—even that of freedom and democracy in the West. Hence Lipset's equation of pacificism and democracy is, however well-intentioned, mechanical, and violates basic facts of American history.

Castro's rise was made possible by American help and sympathy. . . . It is the fact that the plans to assist Cuban refugees to overthrow Castro began only after Castro had indicated his sympathies

176

with the Soviet Union and after many democratic Leftist leaders of his revolution had defected and fled to the United States. . . . In spite of its conviction that Cuba was in the hands of a Communist regime, the United States did not organize a foreign invasion, rather it assisted an extremely stupid and ill-planned effort by exiles to begin an uprising in their country. . . . Until the Russians placed atomic missiles on Cuba, the United States had not attempted a serious effort to overthrow Fidel Castro by force largely because the American political tradition finds such behavior repugnant.

To deal with the Cuban problem in so brief a space as Lipset does is only to offer in effect counter-statements. But whatever the facts of the Cuban situation are, they have nothing in common with Lipset's myth-making about how the United States' attitudes were in a state of suspended animation until the "democratic left" deserted Castro. The facts are, of course, that the United States first tried 30 years of paternalism with the infamous Platt Amendment which made of Cuba a virtual U.S. colony in domestic matters and an absolute colony in regard to world trade and world politics. We sent Harry F. Guggenheim to Cuba as ambassador to ride horses while the infamous Machado regime ran roughshod over the peasants. And as for the Fulgencio Batista regime, which we supported to the last, we can only mention Hubert Herring's characterization of that regime as being "marked by growing repression, terrorism by the police, and violent reprisals from angry citizens. As for Lipset's alleged evidence for American support of the Castro regime in the early period, we need only recall these events: May, 1959; Drilling by Cuban counter-revolutionaries protected by local Florida authorities. Air raids by planes from Florida against Cuba. July 25, 1959; Capture of plane proceeding from Florida, with Rafael del Pino, wanted by the Cuban police. July 26, 1959; Incendiary bombs dropped on sugar fields in Pinar del Rio. October 18, 1959; Aerial attack on Camaguey. October 21, 1959; Bombs over Havana from two planes based in the U.S. October 28, 1959; Second bombing of central Niagara region. Based in Southern Florida. Throughout 1960, relations between the United States and Cuba deteriorated badly. Castro was indeed guilty of kangaroo trials, undervaluation of its technical and middle-class intelligentsia, too rapid agrarian reform, unreceptiveness and unwarranted fear of U.S. offers of economic aid, and other such errors. The United States for its part remained only half-hearted in its attempts to negotiate differences. The explanation offered of the "stupid" invasion attempt at the Bay of Pigs in 1961 cannot be attributed to American morality so much as to American ambivalence—of which, to be sure, morality was a part.

It is therefore a long-standing crisis in conscience as well as policy that accounts for the ambivalence of the United States toward Cuban affairs. The removal of the Soviet offensive missile weapons only accentuates the fact that the main struggle was, and continues to be, one between the United States and Cuba, and not between the United States and the Soviet Union. Of course, there were desertions from Castro's ranks; and of course such desertions are highest in number among the intelligentsia which has a traditional animus for revolutions whose blueprint is marred by realities. But to hold that United States policies in any way reflect our *leftism* is simply to replace the long history of United States' policy iniquities toward Latin America with cheap political sentiment.

As for why we continue to "tolerate" a Communist Cuba, there are any number of sound policy reasons for this (and our "socialist" leanings is not among them). (a) There is the fear that an invasion attempt employing conventional military weaponry would mean heavy costs in human life on both sides. (b) Such an invasion would not have the support of the Latin American states, and it would open up other violations of international law. (c) Such an invasion might well cost us a decade of political violence and anti-American revolutions throughout the rest of Latin America. (d) There is a growing feeling that Castro—both as *el maximo lider* and as an ideology—can best be overcome through the intrinsic economic and political shortcomings of the Cuban regime. (e) Lastly, it must be kept in mind that the dangers of total nuclear annihilation have not been obviated by the removal of offensive Soviet missiles. The backdown of the Soviets on this issue does not necessarily lessen the chance of its intervention in the events of an all-out United States attack upon the Cuban mainland. And prudence dictates that we do not try to win a skirmish that may result in complete destruction.

All of this indicates that whatever the actual status of American-Cuban-Soviet relations, the policy decisions taken or contemplated have little to do with America being socialist. Indeed, the degree of secrecy in United States military decisions with respect to Cuban affairs would indicate how little concerned our new civilian militarists are with even liberal sentiments, much less the imaginary strength of the American left. Indeed, where did the labor unions and the intellectuals stand on the Cuban situation? How many were willing to criticize United States policy during the Batista regime (how many even knew or cared)? And how many were willing to decry the Bay of Pigs landing on any "moral" grounds. The only thing liberals seemed irked about was the way the CIA "bungled" the job, and lost "face" for the United States. Few and far between were those who denounced the invasion on anything even approximating legalist, much less socialist, grounds. Lipset's position is thus as cowardly as it is ingenuous. Unwilling to support socialism elsewhere, he instead uses the Cuban situation for a denunciation of a socialist regime—in the name of socialism no less! What is at stake is not the ethics of American-Cuban relations, but the lack of ethics of a person who uses the pretext of socialist defectors to justify American foreign policy. Conservatives and liberals may have misevaluated the Cuban scene, but at least they are not guilty of rank hypocrisy.

Perhaps the one "have" group which is sensitive to the injustices of stratification, and which retains the means to whip up opposition to them, is the intellectuals. Since many of these remain motivated to be "political men" even after the "end of ideology," they bear a heavy responsibility to keep democracy representative as well as free.

Apparently, to the note of ingenuity is to be added a motif of piety. It is one thing to make a general platitudinous call for intellectuals to keep democracy representative and free, it is quite another to say one word on how this is to be achieved. Does Lipset see the intellectual as a watchdog over what we already have, or as a force battling for what we do not have and ought to? If the former, how does the intellectual differ in his task from any other sector of society, and if the latter, just what does he have in mind? Indeed, the only concrete thing set forth is the traditionalist notion that "state intervention" may be "incompatible with the goal of freedom." But surely, everyone from Lord Acton to Irving Babbitt has made similar proposals. It is utterly ludicrous to claim that those who take this view are "legitimate heirs of democratic and socialist revolutionaries of the last century."

The plain truth is that Mr. Lipset, despite his socialist camouflage and leftist phraseology, is indeed, as his English critics have already noted, a tried and tested (or is it tired and testy) conservative. Now there is nothing horrible in being a conservative. There is something wrong with hypocritical cant which attempts to pose as radical, while at the same time going down the line for the Establishment. Lipset is correct to note the "heavy responsibility" shouldered by the intellectuals. It is just about time that he began pointing the way. Perhaps as a starter he should start by overthrowing the ballast of weasel words and conscience-soothing phraseology. After that, he might go on to indicate where he stands on the vital issues of the present: thermonuclear war, disarmament and deterrence, U.S.-Soviet relations, American attitude toward our hemispheric neighbors. One clear breeze would do much to dispel the widespread fear that intellectuals make treacherous "political men"—precisely because they have neither ideology nor morality, neither a sense of commitment nor the courage to be.

Lipset offers us a surrealistic dialectic, brought to an abrupt halt in the final synthesis of the "non-ideological" Welfare State shimmering in the radiance of a non-committed scientism. Lipset offers us neither sociology nor morality, but a philosophy of history.

And like most philosophies of history, his celebrates the present. The present becomes the touchstone for measuring the past as well as the future. Instead of the better being the critic of the good, we are assured that the good is already here. Iron out the kinks in leftist America—such is the proper mission of the intellectual as Lipset sees him. To this we need only a single-line reply. In the words of Marx: "Impotence expresses itself in a single proposition—the maintenance of the *status quo.*"

ROBERT A. HABER

The End of Ideology
as Ideology*

Introduction

Since the mid-1930s, a sociological literature has developed
analyzing or forecasting "the end of ideology" in the West.
Major statements of this theory have been: Daniel Bell, *The
End of Ideology;* Seymour Lipset, *Political Man;* and Edward
Shils, "Ideology and Civility: on the Politics of the Intellec-
tual."

While some left-wing intellectuals have taken issue with
the theory, in general, its pronouncement was welcomed as an
important air-clearing statement of the self-evident.

The "end of ideology" theory states that political theory and
practice which aims at radical social transformation has ended,
at least in the West. The reasons for this are: first, the disillusionment of the last forty years with mass movements, with
revolution and with the socialist-classless utopia projected by
Marxism. Second, Marxism-Leninism which has been the main

*From Frank V. Lindenfeld: *Reader in Political Sociology,* Funk and
Wagnalls, 1968. A portion of the original article, which was written in
1962, has been omitted. Reprinted with permission of the author.

carrier of ideology has been discredited as an intellectual-political system. Third, the class conflicts and system-wide problems which give rise to ideology have generally been solved, so no longer is there an objective base for such a social analysis. Further, the problems which are pressing for the society are of high complexity, do not have clear solutions, and political methods don't appear the most fruitful means of treatment. Finally, the social and economic theories, on which ideology has been based, have been disproved or brought into serious question, so the intellectual underpinnings for ideological politics is removed.

In addition to this contention about reality, the "end of ideology" theorists make a value assertion. They see the end of ideology as a desirable development. In its place they describe a different kind of politics—the politics of "civility," or as it will be called in this paper, reformism.

There are several key problems in analyzing this theory:

1. "Ideology" has passed through many meanings. The theorists use it vaguely. Can the concept be given a rigorous definition?
2. There is an empirical problem of verification. Has "it" ended? And, if so, are the causes those suggested by the theorists?
3. The theory is both descriptive and evaluative. It describes a change and holds that the change is *good*. Does the value judgment influence the empirical analysis?

This paper will attempt to give a precise statement of the theory and to subject it to critical analysis. It will give particular attention to the social conditions alleged to underlie the end of ideology, as contrasted with those leading to ideology.

What Is Meant by the "End of Ideology"?

The writers give numerous examples of ideology. They include older views like Nazism, McCarthyism, Bolshevism, and contemporary passions like nationalism, Pan-Africanism and economic development. However, they are quite imprecise in defining ideology, in specifying the applicability of the theory, or in making clear the key variables responsible for the change they describe.

For instance, they attribute a number of characteristics to ideology: the discontinuity of good and evil, the secularization of religious fervor, the ease with which rhetoric replaces reason, passion substitutes for analysis, and double standards and distortion displace objective criteria of evaluation. But they do not include in their theory status quo ideology like the American Way of Life and Anti-Communism, even though these exhibit many of the same characteristics.

Also, they disclaim the applicability of the theory to the newly developed countries—where it is acknowledged, and lamented, that ideology *is* the basis of politics. However, they fail to specify the institutional or other characteristics which differentiate the "West" from the non-West for the purpose of indicating the decline or ascendence of ideology.

They do not analyze the radical right in America as a mass political movement having ideological bases, nor do they deal with the scope, social basis and ideological character of the "New Conservatism" such as represented by the *National Review,* the Chicago economists, and related intellectual centers. Nor do they deal with the neo-fascistic movements in western Europe and Japan. Often they seem to equate ideology with Marxism, and hence with a materialist analysis of society, a social dynamic built on class struggle, and a dialectic of history leading inevitably, though convulsively, to the "good society."

Yet they do not identify the critical conditions which lead to the decline of the left while invigorating the right.

Several points can give specification of the object of their analysis:

First, the "end of ideology" is meant to be historically specific. It refers to the end since the last war of a kind of *idea system* held by intellectuals. It does not mean a rejection of the intellectual theory that ideas are socially determined or that they mask and rationalize economic or social relations.

Second, the theory concerns what Mannheim would call *utopian* thinking—ideas which transcend reality and themselves enter the dialectic as instruments of change. It is not referring to the relatively stable set of ideas with which a society justifies and mythologizes itself.

Third, the theory is almost wholly concerned with *"left"* ideology, that is, with utopian ideas oriented around equalitarian, democratic values, and critical of the existing order.

Fourth, their use of ideology refers to politics, the set of ideas underlying a political movement which seeks radical social transformation. The "end of ideology" theory is really an "end of ideological politics" theory.

Ideology and Ideological Politics

The writers identify a number of values and attitudes alleged to define ideology. They stress its projection of a utopia, qualitatively different from present society, its belief in revolution or apocalyptic change, its willingness to sacrifice the present for the future, its rejection of the existing institutions of change and above all, its passionate, irrational, and millenarian conviction in the truth and ultimate triumph of its position.

This description fundamentally confuses the problem. In

the first place, it is highly value-laden, reflecting the anti-ideology position of the theorists. A theorist's values should be clear in his writings, and research should have explicit policy motivation. But clarity of values does not excuse the requirement of scholarly rigor in defining independent and dependent variables.

More importantly, the theory fails to differentiate ideology —the set of ideas underlying a political movement—from the emotional bonds which fire and sustain the movement on a mass basis. The neglect of this crucial distinction derives from the failure to distinguish ideology from ideological politics.

Such a distinction is important. Ideology is an intellectual production describing the society. In understanding ideology the social position of the intellectual is crucial. Politics is an attempt to influence the allocation of rewards in the society. In understanding politics, the institutional context of the political action is crucial.

Ideology as an intellectual production has several elements: 1) a set of moral values, taken as absolute, 2) an outline of the "good society" in which those values would be realized, 3) a systematic criticism (or, in the case of status quo ideology, affirmation) of the present social arrangements and an analysis of their dynamics, 4) a strategic plan of getting from the present to the future (or, in the case of status quo ideology, how continued progress is built into the existing system).

For ideology to be linked to a political movement and for that movement to develop a mass following certain requisites must be met: 1) the ideas must be easily communicated, which usually involves their simplification and sloganization, 2) they must establish a claim to truth, and 3) they must demand a commitment to action.

In this process the ideology as an intellectual production is altered. A basis of authority—divine, institutional or charismatic—is invoked to establish and maintain the claim to truth and the focus of the idea system is shifted to intermediate goals and instrumental actions.

Appeal may be pointed to the direct psychological experience of prospective recruits with society, rather than to the theoretical abstractions of that experience. The "passions of the mass" are attached to the movement by having it serve each individual as a vehicle for his own self-realization and as a release for his particular frustrations, aggressions and fears. The individual becomes psychologically dependent on the movement and sees society through its medium. Thus, many of the bonds on which the solidarity of the political movement is built may be quite irrelevant (and even contrary) to the ideals in the ideology behind that movement. As a consequence there is a wide range of both intellectual and psychological commitment to the movement.

The goal in this process for a left or opposition movement is to create a language and a common frame of reference which, on the one hand, separates the adherents of the movement from the dominant or status quo ideology of the society, and on the other, breaks the hold of that ideology on their thinking and unifies them behind a program of political opposition, leading ultimately to the overthrow of the dominant ideology and the interests it represents.

There is an implicit rejection of the socially sanctioned institutions of change, holding that they function to maintain social equilibrium within the fixed assumptions and power relations of the status quo.

An opposition movement based on ideology, however, need not be doctrinaire, it need not be demagogic; it need not be dehumanizing of either its members or its antagonists. It need not advocate violent revolution or sacrificing of the present for the future. Such conditions are historically specific, depending on the values of the movement, its leadership, the nature of the conflict it engages and the social experience of its adherents. For instance, none of these attributes apply to the nonviolent civil-rights movements in the United States, yet they possess in varying degrees all the defining features of ideology and ideological politics.

187

Further, millenarian or chiliastic expectations are associated not with ideological movements in general, but with movements involving groups from the lowest social stratum whose possibilities for mobility within the existing system are substantially blocked. And when these tendencies exist, as they do in parts of the Negro movement, they are not necessarily associated with the doctrinaire and dehumanizing qualities which the "end of ideology" theorists ascribe to all ideology.

The "End of Ideology" Hypothesis

In its most limited form, the theory states that the mass socialist movements of the 1930s have declined and that the vulgar Marxism which provided a base for those movements has been abandoned.

This is obvious, and hardly profound. One would expect political opposition to alter its form and its analysis on the basis of its own experience (and failures) and in response to the massive changes in the society as a whole. Even so, organizational remnants of the "old Left" continue to exist and to recruit new members. Furthermore, the hypothesis begs the question of how *mass* any of these old ideological movements were, even at their height.

However, the "end of ideology" theorists are making more general and serious assertions. They are saying:

1. Radical movements of all sorts have ceased to exist in the West, and
2. The ideas which intellectuals contribute to political movements have changed in quality. They are no longer ideological.

Both these hypothesis have an obvious range of truth; but also both have evident exceptions. The Communist Party has a mass base in Italy and France. The left wing of the Social Democratic Party is vigorous, if suppressed, in Germany and is even ascendent in England. In America, the civil-rights and peace movements, while not having explicit political structure, do have radical ideological currents.

And an intellectual community, loosely known in the United States, Canada, and Europe as the "New Left," is clearly ideological in its orientation. Outside of the United States materialism and various forms of economic determinism remain legitimate intellectual positions. The existence of exceptions suggests the hypotheses need closer examination.

What Has Happened to Left Political Movements?

The lack of oppositional political movements from the Left is attributed to the ending of class conflict and the decline of the objective deprivations on which class conflict was based. It is undoubtedly correct that welfare capitalism has remedied many of the injustices of its *laissez-faire* predecessor. But it is highly oversimplified to see the decline of political opposition solely in these terms.

Conflict can decrease because there is increased harmony and real consensus among the various interests in the society. And it can decrease because it is suppressed, overtly through coercion and intimidation, or covertly through manipulation, the building of false consciousness and the structuring of the institutions and processes which are necessary for "conflict resolution." The "end of ideology" theorists put great emphasis on the decrease in conflict because of consensus; they virtually ignore the *more important* suppression of conflict.

There have been a number of major developments, particularly in the United States but having their parallels in the

West generally, which have substantially altered the *context* in which political opposition can be expressed.

1. *Radical opposition is not possible within the political system.* An opposition (third) party cannot operate in the United States because of election laws, lack of money and organizational resources necessary to operate in each state, anti-subversion laws, issue-raiding by the major parties, etc. And a radical faction cannot function within the two major parties, not only because they represent converging economic and social interests, but also because they are personality—rather than issue—oriented and there are no continuing deliberative bodies in which a factional (minority) caucus could operate. Consequently, it is not possible to organize and maintain a formal political constituency committed to a radical program.

2. *Revolutionary opposition has ceased to be possible.* The means of violence have reached a degree of sophistication and efficiency that their control by the state cannot be broken or challenged by extra-legal, private groups. To overthrow the government is no longer a realistic strategic goal; change must be in the context of an "evolutionary" process.

3. *The public is excluded from political responsibility.* A process of "concurrent consensus" maintains harmony among representatives of competing interests. This consensus is not necessarily static—but the decisions which lead to change are not made publicly nor publicly accountable. The information and alternatives of choice made directly available to the people are sharply limited. The press and mass media are virtually closed. An opposition must orient to the managerial elites rather than to constituents of those elites who have any functioning democratic control. Consequently, opposition organization is forced into an elite pattern and its primary strategic problem is gaining access to and influence in centers of power, rather than building a base of independent power through mass organization.

4. *Conflict is managed.* The state or the dominant institutions sharing in the status quo consensus have sufficient control

of social resources to ameliorate any grievance which is used as a basis of generalized political opposition. The mechanism of "reform" is sensitive to the magnitude of the pressure for change. It operates to satisfy those whose psychological and intellectual commitment to the generalized movement is weakest. It thereby serves to divide the radical organization on short-run goals and to undermine the mass base of its leaders. The existence of a plurality of "intermediate groups" serves further as a cushion to absorb disruptive conflict, to divide its focus, and to siphon off the loyalties of dissidents by a variety of material and non-material enticements.

5. *The "foreign threat" is used to discredit any action which rests on generalized criticism of the domestic system.* "Anti-communism" is a basis to provide system integration as well as to specifically undermine any conceptual formulation which has Marxist or "pro-communist" implications. The post-war "red-purges" in the trade unions, in universities, in journalism and entertainment, in politics, the professions, and liberal voluntary organizations were the specific historical means by which dissent from the Left was isolated, destroyed or forced to conform to a non-ideological mold within the great American consensus.

These five aspects of the contemporary political system seem decisive in undercutting the generalization of social conflict and the limitation of mass political activity. Changes in the institutional context of politics have combined with direct and sustained attack on the individuals and organizations which were the vehicles of radical dissent. This suggests an end to politics, not an end to ideology.

The decisive factor in the decline of ideological politics is the end of a revolutionary alternate. Revolution has consistently been the basic framework of radical ideology. This is for good reason.

The defining characteristic of any social system is not the distribution of rewards—material, status, safety, etc.—but the *process* by which they are allocated. The "power structure" is not defined by its share of the wealth, but by the means through which it controls the allocation of wealth. (Of course, it also gets the lion's share.)

It is able to incorporate potentially disruptive movements by reallocating resources, thus meeting material, immediate demands.

As already described, any political opposition movement consists of two (not discontinuous) types: 1) people with an integrated critique of society, ideologies committed to opposition of basic structural characteristics of the going social order, and 2) people with an immediate discontent who join and support the movement because it promises to relieve their grievances.

The second group is the larger, but in terms of radical goals it is politically impotent. If it becomes politically dangerous because a radical leadership gives it certain organization and articulated objectives, then it can be separated from the leadership (or the leadership bought off to forestall such separation) by the offer of concessions. These "reforms" meet immediate demands and they establish a constitutional (i.e., controlled) process of working for continued change.

The "power structure" thus neutralizes the radical potential of a movement through its control of the allocation decisions. This means 1) that the constituents of the opposition movement become beholden to established power interests for progress achieved, and 2) that the opposition leadership is pressured by the constituents to seek further benefits or concessions from the "power structure," that is to seek influence in the allocation process and consequently not to threaten the interests of any group presently dominant in that process.

The power structure has the advantage, because they have power: they are able to *deliver*. Leaders of the opposition are able only to motivate demands and promise rewards. A concession by the system solidifies an individual's commitment to the system. It weakens the vital "separating function" of radical ideology.

Radicals have recognized this situation. In its ideological formulation, they hold that the economic-political system functions as an integrated whole. Adjustments or reforms cannot fundamentally re-orient it to public, democratic values and away from exploitative, manipulative and anti-democratic ones. The magnitude of change does not determine its political quality. There can be tremendous changes in Gross National Product, standard of living, education, leisure, health, all without altering the exploitative character of the system. There may be incrimental improvements in living standards, care of marginal people, security, social justice and equality before the law, etc., without there being any alteration in the political control of the society or change in the goals to which social resources are directed, or without there being any improvement in the non-material aspects of social existence.

In its political formulation, the revolutionary objective has generally been the response to this situation. This means the opposition seeks power rather than influence. Its goal is to replace the existing power structure: to overthrow it by killing or jailing its personnel, and by seizing the vital means of its functioning—the communication media, the police power, and the legislative authority. This means that they can organize on the basis of and build primary commitment to the utopia consequent on the social restructuring to be accomplished by the revolution. The promise of the utopia cannot be delivered, or even seriously challenged by the existing system. So there is no danger of the revolutionary organization being driven by minor reforms or concessions.

This revolutionary objective has *not* been adopted in the United States. The *political reasons* for this, as already noted, are that the established system is too decentralized, has too strong a control of the means of violence and facilities of organization for revolution either to be organized or to succeed. But there are also *ideological reasons* based on the political experience of this century: a revolutionary leadership won't give up elite power any more than the previous elite would. *If the central issue of the "revolution" is more democratic control, as it is for the contemporary radicals, then anti-democratic organization can hardly insure it. Furthermore, the idea of non-violence develops tremendous moral force for people horrified by the wars of our century and seeking freedom from the oppression of state or private power.*

The non-violent strategy involves several untested, and even unlikely assumptions:

1. That the political process is sufficiently disjunctive from the economic so that the former can be used to gain control of and to change the latter; i.e., it is possible to gain political power without having economic power.

2. That the economic system can be attacked directly and in a way to highlight those points at which constitutionally superior political power must intervene.

3. That change can be made and sustained in terms of new values in small sections of social relations, while most relations are left intact and still reflect old values.

4. That sucessive demands for change in the allocation of resources can reach a point beyond which the system cannot adjust—that there are structural limitations on the ability of the system to satisfy the kind of immediate demands on which disadvantaged people can be organized—and when pushed to those limits, the system itself will be open to fundamental change.

5. That people can be organized in terms of a common interest beyond immediate gain, that they can see the enemy as those who profit from the status quo and not those who are in the same exploited position as themselves within the system competing for its scarce resources: that reason can prevail over immediate perceived necessity.

Within a revolutionary strategy, none of these assumptions is necessary. But now, a political movement must build in terms of *all* of them. The ground is uncharted; since the organizational experience of previous movements has generally been within the revolutionary framework, it is not now directly applicable. If any of these assumptions proves false, that is, fails in practice, then the possibility for radical change in the organization and allocation of resources is highly unlikely.

Has Ideology Ended?

The existence of a "New Left" struggling with the intellectual and organizational problems of non-revolutionary radicalism indicates that ideology has not ended. That it has changed, and must necessarily have changed, should be obvious from what has already been said about the altered conditions in which ideology is transformed into political action. The major changes are:

1. *Values:* No longer is there a complete rejection of the system. Many of the equalitarian values mythologized (but barely realized) by contemporary society are embraced by New-Left intellectuals. The points of attack are more the processes by which minority economic interests dominate formally democratic institutions and misallocate public resources for selfish ends.

2. *Utopia:* The oppositional emphasis is modified by a much greater uncertainty about the institutional structure of the good society. Concrete slogans such as nationalization, workers' control, state planning and socialism are replaced by more complicated and speculative formulations of the market economy, decentralized planning and participatory democracy. The experiences and failures of the "socialist" countries have not yet been incorporated in a new utopian synthesis.

3. *Critique:* The aspects of contemporary society that are criticized include more than economic and political components. Increasing concern is given, for instance, to cultural and educational problems. How to extend the freeing potentiality of material abundance to the masses without losing the quality

of high culture developed in the context of aristocratic or bohemian leisure.

4. *Strategy:* As noted, revolution and the crude Marxian dynamics of the class struggle are rejected or highly modified as a basis of historical analysis and as political strategy.

In spite of these changes in content and emphasis, the thinking of the "New Left" retains a basic ideological character. It begins from moral values which are held as absolute. It develops an image of utopia and a systematic critique of the present. While it doesn't see change as apocalyptic, it does hold a fundamental discontinuity: the good society will look and function very differently from this one.

The necessary conditions for ideological thinking must be analyzed in order to understand this change. By hypothesis these conditions are:

1. an independent intellectual class or group
2. the existence of real conflict
3. the existence of institutions which can develop and carry ideology
4. a language in which it can formulate its critique
5. the possibility of change.

That these conditions exist much less now than earlier in this century or in the nineteenth century suggests that ideological thinking should be decreased in amount and ideologists should be a rarer breed of intellectual. The way in which these conditions are realized, to the extent they are, suggests some of the particular aspects of contemporary ideology.

1. *An independent intellectual class.* If the intellectual is beholden to the system, he cannot separate himself from its values and assumptions, and hence, cannot create or embrace a total analysis of it. In part or whole he is committed to the ideology of the system, since his socially supported roles and rewards are rationalized and given importance in terms of that ideology.

The intellectual is not now independent. No longer is he

denied status or material rewards; no longer is he limited in his location to the relatively segregated academic communities. He is employed as a consulting technician (where other people set the policy goals) by all the mainstream institutions—corporations, unions, government professional societies, foundations, churches, etc. He can get research money for work that is rationalized in terms of general social benefit. He can publish, and indeed, his advancement is largely conditional on publication that meets the scrutiny (i.e., conforms to the broad value framework) of his colleagues. The academic community is actively hostile to ideological formulations. In all these things, his advancement draws him into the thinking and values of the society. Whereas, intellectual independence requires either being cut off from or consciously rejecting the sanctioned or available social rewards.

Furthermore, ideological thinking is wholistic. To the degree that numerous opportunities and alternatives exist within the system, as they do for contemporary intellectuals, the approach to planning and conceptualization is more likely to be piecemeal than organic. This is reinforced by increasing professional specialization.

2. *The existence of real conflict.* Ideology is formulated in terms of conflicts of interests, the blocking of values by the holders of power. When conflict does not exist, or when contending interests are not directly laid bare, then there is no existential basis for ideology.

There is now very little visible conflict, except in the area of Negro rights. A plurality of governmental and voluntary institutions create bureaucratic channels of remedy which segregate issues. The most exploited groups are without the political facilities of self-expression. The ethic of service seeks to aid the welfare of the oppressed without providing trusts or building their sovereignty. Lingering Social Darwinism combines with the conservative ethic of individual initiative to undermine the psychological basis of an assertion by the oppressed of a claim against society.

Expressed conflict is channeled into forms which obscure the underlying causes of the conflict and the real centers of power which govern the reward allocation and are responsible for the oppression complained of. Intermediate institutions are made visible and become targets of attack, while masking the decisive economic interests responsible both for the oppression and the maintenance of the intermediate buffer.

Not only is conflict suppressed, atomized and misdirected; but intellectuals are isolated from the places of conflict and its passion. The university is the place where the intellectual has the greatest freedom (compared with technical and consulting roles in government and other organizations) but it is an isolated institution providing a self-contained, highly artificial and modulated environment.

Furthermore, not only is freedom bought at the price of isolation, but it is anesthetized by a "professional standard" which prescribes that things be studied without reference to the observer's values—lest biasing commitment becloud "objectivity."

3. *The existence of institutions which can develop and carry the ideology.* An essential aspect of ideology is strategic. There must be the interplay between the experience of political action and the intellectual formulation. The action component of an ideological development must have organization form; it must be able to communicate and to organize people.

No institutions exist on a national scale which are sufficiently independent to be a vehicle for ideology. The labor unions to which leftists have traditionally looked, are legally, intellectually, and psychologically part of the system. Many universities are semi-independent, but as noted, the university is isolated from community power structure. In some areas, the church has the requisite independence, but it directs emotional energy to religious rather than political goals. There is no mass distribution opposition newspaper or opposition political party. The monopolization of financial and organizational resources by the status quo—supported by the direct coercive power of the state—prevents the creation of such an independent vehicle of mass communication and action.

4. *A language in which its critique can be formulated.* The main currents of left ideology have been broken by the discrediting of the Soviet translation of Marxist ideology and by the attack of social science methods and values. The old utopia has been shattered and not yet rebuilt.

The system has monopolized much of the language. Freedom, democracy, social justice, equality, and individualism are values which exist in the traditions of the society and are used to rationalize the institutions. It is difficult to use them also as points of appeal against the traditions.

5. *The possibility of change.* Another condition for ideology is a possibility of success. If intellectuals see no chance to alter the present they will retreat to apathy, privatism, and cynicism, and express their political energy within the established institutions for piecemeal reform. Passion will attach only to a cause that is real.

The degree to which these conditions do not now exist explains some of the features of contemporary ideological thinking.

1. The people who are doing it are often young. They are independent because they have yet to undertake family and social commitments. They are dissociated from the main academic currents of their discipline and they associate themselves with independent publications, institutes, or organizations.

2. They are likely to have some involvement in a non-traditional sort of political action. Where direct conflict does exist there is likely to be a greater degree of ideological thinking.

3. The lack of avowed institutions leads to a preoccupation with questions of "agents of social change." The labor movement, the universities, the civil-rights movement, the Democratic Party, a third party are all exhaustively evaluated as to whether they can carry ideology and an ideological movement.

4. The monopolization of language has led to an elaborate

rhetoric of participatory democracy, a shying from the traditional language of Marxism and socialism, and an overworking of some of the less tarnished ideas like alienation.

5. The realistic doubt that anything is possible leads to a preoccupation with strategy. Debates abound on realignment versus a labor party, university reform, violence *versus* nonviolence.

The "End of Ideology" as Ideology

A substantial number of those left intellectuals who, twenty or thirty years ago, were ideologists have since changed their position. They now represent a mode of political thought which might be called "reformist." In this group would fall the "end of ideology" theorists.

The "end of ideology" theorists present a fairly consistent set of values, which might be called "transitional values," in terms of which they justify a rejection of ideology as a basis for politics.

1. History is unknowable. The persecutions, manipulation, and suffering of people in the present cannot be morally justified as necessary conditions in the building of a future utopia.

2. The evils of the present are not so bad as the evils *inherent* in revolutionary or disruptive change.

3. The dangers inherent in mass action are greater than the evils of injustice more slowly ameliorated through parliamentary process.

4. No class or elite, once it gains privilege, will voluntarily give it up, hence no political strategy can "level" a present elite which is to serve as the vehicle for equalitarian transformation.

5. The values of free expression, association, and political organization are fundamental, both in the present and in any

future. There is no conceivable ground on which they can be abrogated.

These values held in conjunction fairly well commit one's political energies to working within the system. Ideology is certainly a dangerous business and its end is much to be desired. The crucial elements however are Number 2 and Number 3. The others, particularly the civil-liberties emphasis, are all compatible with an ideological approach to politics (though they are certainly not characteristic of all ideologies). Numbers 2 and 3, however, disallow or at least treat with great suspicion the value of social dislocation and of change which is not mediated through established parliamentary institutions. They are values which essentially ratify the present social order.

The origin of these values, according to the "end of ideology" theorists, is in the reflection on the horrors of Nazism, the atrocities and failures of Communists and the shattered hopes of the democratic left in the face of mass psychology and totalitarian attack.

It should be granted that catastrophic events can have a permanent effect on the ideas of a generation—independent of any shift in the social or economic position of the people involved. However, the reformist position reflects a fundamentally different perspective on the society, and, by hypothesis, a fundamentally altered social location of the reformist intellectual.

The essential points of the reformist position are:

1. A positive commitment to the values of the present, historically specific system of Welfare Capitalism. The system embraces his values—democracy, equality, and individual freedom. And the system is highly successful.

He celebrates the high level of material abundance, the progressive lessening of inequality and the progressive remedying of specific deprivations. He notes the wide degree of personal freedom from arbitrary authority: for production workers, guaranteed by trade unions; for the white-collar worker, afforded by the impersonalization of bureaucratic roles; for the political dissenter, guaranteed by civil liberties. He sees remarkable advance in education, science, and culture. And most important, he sees the general acceptance of welfare goals by all interests in the society and thereby the assurances of continued progress.

His perspective is on how far we have come. He has participated in the struggles for change and identifies himself with their successes. What was sound in the old ideologies has been realized, and what was unsound has been disproved and properly rejected.

He believes that the good society is defined by the *process* through which conflict is mediated and progress achieved, rather than by a new *structural* ordering of power, social relations and resources. American democracy, of course, reflects (or closely approximates) that ideal process.

2. A belief that no issues of generalized conflict exist. There are limited situations of conflict—like the race issue, or poverty, or unemployment—but these are essentially discontinuous and the product of specialized anomalous conditions. They can be dealt with in isolation; they do not derive from fundamental contradictions or weakness in the system. Mechanisms within the system are fully adequate for their solution—such as constitutional legislation, public education, welfare programs, increased production, etc. There is no need to see solutions in the perspective of (or conditional on) total social reorganization.

3. The problems that do exist—like those of mass culture and mass education—are too complex to be conceptualized in solely political terms. And the value questions, as to what is desirable, are too indeterminant to allow coherent political solution. Issues must be dealt with in a pragmatic piecemeal way. Action should follow only when the goal is precise and its consequences understood and desirable. The interplay of differing interests and perspectives *over time,* within a libertarian

constitutional framework, will yield the *best* solution, with the least danger of grave error.

4. The interests of all groups are to mediate and compose these conflicting interests. No group can be deprived of its rights or subjected to arbitrary authority in the name of some abstract value. Constitutional process is the only guarantee against the abuse of authority or extra-legal power. The side of justice is never so clean as to warrant an abridgment of the formal processes by which justice is publicly determined—for in that process the interests of all are assured a fair hearing and equitable treatment. This is essentially a position of moral relativism—that each group whatever its objective position contributes to the common good and that every group is important in making up the composite.

5. The realities of world politics do not permit ideological nonalignment. Whatever one's views on domestic politics, the issues of the international scene must take precedence. It is necessary to oppose communist expansion and to provide democratic influence in the "Third World" and in non-communist revolutions. This requires an orientation to and support of national authority internationally.

These values—the acceptance of the present, discontinuity of conflict, complexity of issues, legitimacy of all interests, and separation of domestic and international issues—are exactly opposite of the values inherent in ideology. They suggest a number of hypotheses about social position of those intellectuals who hold them. Again, exactly contrary hypotheses would be suggested for ideologists.

1. They do not have an independent perspective on the social system. They have a wide variety of alternatives and possibilities within the system.

2. Conflict is not salient to them, in terms either of being involved in social conflict or of perceiving their own interests as directly at stake, or of a high identification and involvement with groups whose interests are so at stake.

3. Their approach to problems is in terms of specialization; formal criteria of method and validity, and scientific "objectivity," rather than speculation and wholistic or value-oriented analysis.

4. They are defensive of their status; every action must be defensive in the face of expected criticism.

5. They have experience with and are in relations of interdependency with a wide variety of groups in society.

6. They identify with national authority as an object of loyalty and patriotism.

A good deal of ideological thinking would come from youth and particularly students for several reasons. They have little established connection with the reward system of the society. They are often subsidized and enjoy a variety of immunities from social demands and obligations. Potentially, they have greater "independence" than any other group.

Their lack of responsibilities gives them greater possibility of geographical mobility and hence direct access to conflict situations. Their own incomplete socialization can give increased emotional saliency to conflict by transference of psychological and familial tensions.

They lack specialized skills and attachment to a professional discipline, so reflection on social issues is much more apt to take a wholistic form. And as students they are exposed to a variety of ideological and political positions as objects of study and as adjuncts to non-academic (extra-curricular) activities.

They have experienced little vertical mobility and have no recognized social status. Rather than being defensive, they are more apt to be assertive in an effort to define their own identity in the society.

Conclusion

One of the major problems in the sociology of knowledge is to demonstrate the linkage between "mental productions" and the existent base. The foregoing analysis of the "end of ideology" thesis has been developed with the view of providing the opportunity for an empirical test of some of these relationships.

The analysis has:

1. distinguished two types of political thinking, ideological and reformist, each characterized by a set of specific and mutually exclusive attributes;

2. hypothesized a number of social conditions necessary for ideological thinking;

3. hypothesized a number of values (called transitional values) held characteristically by those intellectuals who in the course of their lives have shifted from ideological to reformist thinking;

4. developed a number of hypotheses designed to differentiate ideological from reformist intellectuals on such dimensions as social position, past experience, status, self-image, approach to work, and attitude to national authority.

It should be possible to test the relationships suggested in these hypotheses. A sample of intellectuals would be divided on the basis of ideological *versus* reformist (as determined by questionnaire, interview or content analysis of their writing). Correlations would then be sought with the social conditions.

The outcome of such an empirical study would, I believe, confirm that the "end of ideology" is a status quo ideological formulation designed to rationalize the incorporation of intellectuals into the American way of life.

STEPHEN W. ROUSSEAS
AND
JAMES FARGANIS

American Politics and the End of Ideology[*]

I

In a collection of essays written over a ten-year period, Daniel Bell[1] hails the end of ideology. In a similar volume of previously published essays, Seymour Martin Lipset[2] joins Bell in the apotheosis of a non-committed scientism, or what amounts to pragmatism leached of all its passion for meaningful social reform. This growing litany in the United States, on the European Continent, and in England, in praise of the *status quo* continues to remain, in its own image, inherently liberal. It is convinced that democracy today has solved all the major prob-

---

[*] From *British Journal of Sociology*, Vol. 14, No. 4, 1963. Reprinted by permission of Routledge & Kegan Paul Ltd.

[1] *The End of Ideology: On the Exhaustion of Political Ideas in the Fifties* (Collier Books, rev. ed., 1961).

[2] *Political Man* (Doubleday, 1960).

lems of industrial society, and that those which do remain are of a second order magnitude involving merely technical adjustments within a now prevailing *consensus gentium*. If modern liberalism has thus been recast into a less critical mold, it is because of its conviction that modern democracy *is* the good society. Lipset makes this very clear in the epilogue to his book. "Democracy," he writes, "is not only or even primarily a means through which different groups can attain their ends or seek the good society; it is the good *society* itself in *operation*." [3]

More explicitly, we are told by Lipset that within the Western democracies "serious intellectual conflicts among groups representing different values have declined sharply"; that "the ideological issues dividing left and right [have] been reduced to a little more or a little less government ownership and economic planning;" and that it really makes little difference "which political party controls the domestic policies of individual nations." All this, according to Lipset, "reflects the fact that the fundamental political problems of the industrial revolution have been solved: the workers have achieved industrial and political citizenship; the conservatives have accepted the welfare state; and the democratic left has recognized that an

[3] Page 403 [p. 69 in this volume], italics supplied. In response to criticisms of *Political Man*, Lipset has somewhat modified this statement and has sought to restate his liberalism ("My View From Our Left," *Columbia University* Forum, Fall, 1962) [reprinted in this volume, pp. 152–165]. "Democracy," now, "is not simply a means to the end of the good society, it is itself the only society in which social tendencies which press man to exploit man may be restrained." This rather negative approach to democracy and the good society is further confirmed by his statement that his espousal of democracy "rest on the assumption that only a politically democratic society can reduce the pressures—endemic in social systems—to increase the punitive and discriminatory effects of stratification." For it is the democratic freedom of the underprivileged classes to organize which gives rise to an effective and leveling "counter-power" operating within the rules-of-the-game of institutionalized conflict. The similarity of this to John Kenneth Galbraith's theory of "countervailing power" is obvious, and is subject to the same limitations. Lipset's ideal is the non-ideological welfare state toward which, he believes, the United States is moving.

increase in over-all state power carries with it more dangers to freedom than solutions for economic problems." [4]

In this milieu intellectuals functioning as critics of society have become disaffected, according to Lipset, because "domestic politics, even liberal or sicialist politics, can no longer serve as the arena for serious criticism from the left" (p. 408 [pp. 75, 76 in this volume]). Disorganized, at a loss for a cause, and unable to fulfill their self-image, the liberal intellectuals "have turned from a basic concern with political and economic systems to criticism of other sections of the basic culture of society, particularly of elements which cannot be dealt with politically" (p. 409 [p. 76 in this volume]). Or, in Bell: "Some of the younger intellectuals have found an outlet in science or university pursuits, but often at the expense of narrowing their talent into mere technique" (p. 404 [p. 102 in this volume]).

[4] Pages 403–6 [pp. 70–73 in this volume]. In addition Lipset cites, with apparent approval a comment made to him by the editor of a leading Swedish newspaper: "Politics is now boring. The only issues are whether the metal workers should get a nickel more an hour, the price of milk should be raised, or old-age pensions extended." Similarly in Bell we have: "In the Western world . . . there is today a rough consensus among intellectuals on political issues: the acceptance of the Welfare State; the desirability of decentralized power; a system of mixed economy and of political pluralism . . . [And] the workers whose grievances were once the driving energy for social change, are more satisfied with the society than the intellectuals" (pp. 402–4) [pp. 99–101 in this volume].

For other views reflecting the end of ideology the following recent works should be consulted: John Strachey, *Contemporary Capitalism* (Random House, 1956); C. A. R. Crosland, *The Future of Socialism* (Macmillan, 1957); John Kenneth Galbraith, *American Capitalism* (Houghton Mifflin, rev. ed., 1956), and *The Affluent Society* (Houghton Mifflin, 1958); Henry Wallich, *The Cost of Freedom* (Harper & Bros., 1960); and the debate going on in England between the neo-revisionists and the fundamentalists in the pages of *Encounter, New Left Review,* and the *New Statesman,* particularly during 1960–1. Limitations of space preclude any examination of these various approaches. With the exception of the English "fundamentalists," they all reflect the view, in greater or lesser degree, that the major problems of industrial society have been solved and that the remaining problems are basically technical and easily within our grasp. Perhaps the most unabashed statement of this position is to be found in Arthur Schlesinger, Jr., "Where Does the Liberal Go From Here?" (*New York Times Magazine Section,* August 4, 1957).

II

The full import of the Bell-Lipset thesis can be derived principally from a misinterpretation of Max Weber; a misinterpretation which leads Bell to consider Machiavelli and Weber in
the same light, and to quote them at the head of the two key
chapters of his study.[5] In keeping with his own interpretation
of Weber, Bell distinguishes between the normative "ought"
and the empirical "is" of politics and the "ineluctable tension"
between the two. Ethics is concerned with justice whereas concrete politics involves "a power struggle between organized
groups to determine the allocation of privilege" (p. 279).
Concrete politics, in other words, is not concerned with the
realization of an ideal, but, following Lord Acton, with the
reaping of particular advantages within the limits of a given
ethic—an ethic which sets out clearly the rules of the game
governing the political jockeying for position and privilege.
Thus, modern, mature democracies representing the end of
ideology have, in effect, separated ethics from politics; and ideology, in so far as it continues to exist as a force in modern
society, is nothing more than a cynical propaganda cover for
the specific self-interest of competing groups. Modern politics,
therefore, becomes amenable to analysis in terms of the mixed
strategies of game theory (though neither Bell nor Lipset have
done so). The game is to be played, however, according to the
generally accepted constitutional limits of a Weberian "ethic
of responsibility." It implies, above all, the flat rejection of the
radical commitment required by an "ethic of conscience"
which "creates 'true believers' who burn with pure, unquench-

[5] Ch. 12, and "The End of Ideology in the West: An Epilogue." The
quotations used by Bell are: "He who seeks the salvation of souls, his own
as well as others, should not seek it along the aveune of politics"
(Weber); and "Men commit the error of not knowing when to limit their
hopes" (Machiavelli).

able flame and can accept no compromise with faith." The ethic of responsibility is, in sum, "the pragmatic view which seeks reconciliation as its goal" (pp. 279–80). Modern liberals, willing as they are to accept their progress piecemeal and within the rules of the game are, therefore, to be distinguished from genuine ideologues who are seemingly unaware that the good society has already been achieved.

The basic distinction between the modern liberal and the idealogue revolves around the notion of commitment. If the ideologue, in Bell's terms, is committed to the consequences of ideas and is governed by passion, then, in contradistinction, the non-ideological liberal is uncommitted and free of any chiliastic vision of the transforming moment. The ideologue seeks political success, according to Bell, by organizing and arousing the masses into a social movement, and the function of ideology, therefore, is to fuse the energies of the great unwashed and ignite their passions into a mighty river of fire. But in order to do so, ideology must "simplify ideas, establish a claim to truth, and, in the union of the two, demand a commitment to action" (p. 401 [p. 98 in this volume]).

The *end* of ideology is therefore linked to its inability nowadays to arouse the masses. And this inability, as we have seen, is the direct consequence of modern society's having solved the basic problems of the industrial order. In this kind of Panglossian society there is no room for ideologues who, standing on the upper rungs of the faith ladder, have become politically destabilizing factors. They are, if anything, a direct threat to the continuation of the good society. The modern politician qua politician is the man who understands how to manipulate and how to operate in a Machiavellian world which divorces ethics from politics. Modern democracy becomes, in this view, transformed into a system of technique *sans telos*. And democratic politics is reduced to a constellation of self-seeking pressure groups peaceably engaged in a power struggle to determine the allocation of privilege and particular advantage. Compromise and evolution are to be the means for achieving in the context of this struggle, the few second order social goals which continue to remain in an otherwise near perfect society. It is in this limited sense that the end of ideology clings desperately to its self-imposed label of enlightened, non-ideological, non-committed liberalism. And the status quo it defends in the name of democracy is a fundamental one—the already achieved good society.

All this is carefully nailed onto Max Weber's door by Bell. Had he, instead, opened the door and looked in, he would have found that Weber's primary concern was with the *fusion* of the "ethic of responsibility" and "the ethic of absolute ends." Contrary to Bell's easy interpretation, Weber was in no sense advocating a politics without passion. Passion without responsibility, and politics without commitment were equally unacceptable to Weber. "Passion," "a feeling of responsibility," and a "sense of proportion" were for Weber the three pre-eminent qualities which are decisive for the politician. For Weber, the problem was the forging of "a warm passion and a cool sense of proportion . . . in one and the same soul." [6] In so far as the politician plays the game of politics without any sense of purpose, his actions are without meaning. In Weber's words, "The mere 'power politician' may get strong effects, but actually his work leads nowhere and is senseless."

In Weber, the "ethic of responsibility" and the "ethic of ultimate ends" were not to be regarded as absolute contrasts. They were, instead, to be thought of as supplements reinforcing each other within the mind of the true politician who was to act as the agent of social progress. In failing to take into account the consequences of his actions, and in refusing to admit the condition of human frailty, the chiliast was irresponsible and ineffective. But equally vacuous, in Weber's opinion, was the politician who sought to enhance his own power without any vision in mind. "Certainly all historical experience,"

[6] For Weber's position and the quotations used, see H. H. Gerth and C. Wright Mills, eds., *From Max Weber* (Oxford, 1946), pp. 115–16, 127–28.

wrote Weber, "confirms the truth—that man would not have attained the possible unless time and again he had reached out for the impossible."

III

Despite Bell's misinterpretation of Weber, there can be little doubt that his and Lipset's arguments on the decline, if not the end, of ideology as an operative force in the Western world are based largely on fact. But whether or not this represents a desirable state of affairs is quite another matter. The favorable interpretation given to this development by Bell and Lipset has been generally accepted, if not applauded, by most observers. Yet, there may be a great deal of potential confusion over the meaning of "ideology" and "ideological thought" if care is not taken to use these terms consistently. The most exhaustive analysis of the concept appears in Karl Mannheim's well-known *Ideology and Utopia*.[7] In Mannheim, *ideology* is taken to mean the ideas and thought-patterns of the interest-bound ruling groups which explain, justify and rationalize the status quo, while *utopia* is the intellectual stimulus provided by the oppressed groups who challenge the established order and seek to transform it into the good society. When Bell and Lipset speak of the "end of ideology," what they mean is the "end of utopian thought," for they are both clearly referring to the decline of socialist or Marxian ideas within the context of an affluent Western society. Lipset, however, pushes his argument further (and more explicitly than Bell) when he declares, contrary to the judgment of many of the most profound minds of Western political thought that democracy "is the good society itself in operation." The classical distinction between "na-

[7] International Library of Psychology, Philosophy and Scientific Method, 1936. Reprinted as a paperback by Harcourt, Brace.

ture" and "convention" is thus obliterated, and the traditional role of the intellectual as social critic is no longer logically possible. For if "what ought to be" already is, then the intellectual has no other function than to describe and to celebrate the arrival of a utopia. Yet much of the intellectual output of today in film, on the stage, and in art reveals a profound discontent with things as they are. Lipset and Bell recognize this intellectual alienation but conclude that it is not political. It is only by narrowly defining politics as concerned with "voting behavior" or with "welfare measures," that they can come to such a conclusion. But if the traditional idea of political philosophy is maintained, there is yet some small contribution that intellectuals can make, which will be something other than a justification, tacit or overt, for whatever is.

"Liberals such as Lipset," writes one political scientist, "are proud of the progress which has been made in the Western world, but it is curious that they never acknowledge the fact that we have gotten as far as we have precisely because of the ideologies which stirred men to action." And if the end of ideology is, in fact, the case, "then we have the best explanation of why we in the West are standing still." [8]

But the most bitterly forceful comments have come from another source. C. Wright Mills and Bell-Lipset have been each other's severest critics[9] and C. Wright Mills, defining the

[8]Andrew Hacker, in an otherwise favourable review of Lipset's book (*Commentary,* June 1961). A further criticism made by Hacker concerns the limitations of a purely empirical approach to the problems of modern society. If the myths of left-wing ideology have in fact declined, this does not necessarily imply that we have matured, politically, in the sense of being willing not only to face, but to live with the facts. In the words of Hacker: "Lipset hopes to supplant myth with fact. Empiricism, like it or not, forces one to concentrate on things as they are or as they have been. A description of how things might be were we to embark on changing the social order is bound to be speculative, not factual. . . . The visions of ideologues, then, coupled with their mythologies about the world of reality, should be evaluated not on empirical but on strategic grounds."

[9] To Bell and Lipset, C. Wright Mills was an annoying gadfly and a bad scholar. To many others he was, above all, a great social critic who, unlike most good scholars, had something meaningful to say. For an in-

end of ideology as "an intellectual celebration of apathy" which has collapsed reasoning into reasonableness, attacks the Bell-Lipset emphasis on strictly factual analysis: [10]

The disclosure of fact . . . is the rule. The facts are duly weighed, carefully balanced, always hedged. Their power to outrage, their power truly to enlighten in a political way, their power to aid decision, even their power to clarify some situation—all that is blunted and destroyed.

Facts, of course, do not in themselves have the power to outrage, enlighten or clarify. And perhaps, for this reason, C. Wright Mills' argument is in need of some elaboration. A brute empiricist, devoid of any "passion," is no more capable of describing the world *as it is* than is an ideologue who views the world around him solely through the lens of his ideological *weltanschauung.* The hope, or the belief, that the end of the ideological caste of mind will permit us to view the real world uncolored by any value judgments, is nothing but the delusion of an unsophisticated positivism; which is, in essence, a flight from moral responsibility. For facts are themselves the product of our viewing "reality" through our theoretical preconceptions which, in turn, are conditioned by the problems confronting us. And the theoretical precepts which determine the relevant facts of a particular view of "reality" are not themselves entirely value free. Social theories, in short, are the result of our concern with specific problems. And social problems, at bottom, are concerned with ethical goals. Social theorists, furthermore, differ in their value judgments and thus differ in their theoretical constructions of "reality." They differ, that is, in the problems they see, or, what amounts to the same thing,

---

credibly nasty reference to the late C. Wright Mills, see Seymour Martin Lipset and Neil Smelser, "Change and Controversy in Recent American Sociology," *The British Journal of Sociology,* March, 1961, reprinted by the *Institute of Industrial Relations,* Reprint No. 164, Berkeley, 1961, no. 12, pp. 50–51.

[10] "Letter to the New Left," *New Left Review,* September-October 1960 [reprinted in this volume].

they see a given problem in different ways. Consequently, they differ as to the facts relevant to a given problem. There is, in other words, a selectivity of facts in the anaylsis of social problems. Some facts included in one approach are excluded in another; and even those held in common may, and usually do, differ in the weight given to them and in their theoretical and causal interrelations.

All this, of course, raises the following possibilities: that the theory of verification in the social sciences is of a different order from that found in the other sciences; that the moral preconceptions of social theorists unavoidably determine the shape of their theories, the classification systems they employ, and their concepts and hypotheses; and that objective criteria of relevance for the evaluation of competing constructions of social reality, therefore, may not exist. Perhaps the best we can hope for is some form of objective relativism. But however that may be, it is clear that those who would suggest that sociological analysis is a pure science objectively concerned with pure "facts" are indulging in an ideological positivism uniquely their own; a *wertlos*[11] positivism which amounts to nothing more than an unthinking apologia for whatever is. And their value judgments, because of their implicit subconsciousness, are all the more inflexible and rigid. Their pronouncements, moreover, do not admit of compromise and take on an *ex cathedra* quality found only in those who believe they have somehow secured *the* truth—or *the* good society. In this respect they parallel the more extreme ideologues of their analysis.

Along these lines, C. Wright Mills would have agreed that the end of ideology makes a fetish of empiricism and entails an ideology of its own—an ideology of political complacency for the justification of things as they are, and the celebration of

[11] Max Weber distinguishes between science as *wertfrei* and *wertlos*. *Wertfrei* is defined as being free from prevailing passion and prejudice; free, that is, to create its own values. *Wertlos*, on the other hand, is applied to the falsely objective or "scientistic" approach to social problems.

modern society as a going concern. Utopian thought, or left-wing criticism, according to Mills, is concerned with a "structural criticism" of the institutions of society and with the formulation of programs for reform and fundamental change. It need not entail an apocalyptic or dogmatic vision. The choice is not between the wild-eyed fanatic and the cool, uncommitted pragmatist who is willing to take his progress piecemeal, if at all. Ideology need not, as Bell sometimes tends to do, be equated with chiliastic fanaticism. Its major function is to apply intelligence—the fusion of passion and critical reason—to the problems of the modern world. An intelligence can never lie down with itself in a passionate embrace of self-love. It must be concerned with the human condition and its betterment in an always imperfect world. Its justification for being is, in a word, progress.

Whether or not it is true that progress in the past has been exclusively the result of ideological conflict it is nevertheless true that progress, as distinct from mere change, can be defined meaningfully only in terms of some "vision." For progress, as Santayana has observed, "is relative to an ideal which reflection creates." And it is here that, perhaps, the most serious criticism of the end of ideology can be made.

The modern politician is viewed, appreciatively by Bell and Lipset, as a non-committed individual skilled in the art of compromise. The ideologue, on the other hand, is committed to some pattern of institutional change which, in terms of his values, becomes transformed into social progress. It is irrelevant whether one agrees with the vision of a particular ideology. The important point is that freedom, in the philosophical sense, and a social commitment which transcends the status quo, are interrelated and interdependent.

Rejecting the notion of man tied to a merciless fate which robs him of his future, we are left to regard him free and immersed in the process of becoming. Man is, in other words, a potential, and his willingness or ability to seize life by the throat, as it were, and force it to serve his needs, is a measure of

his freedom. Freedom, in short, excludes a complacency which
rests on past or present achievements, or which nurtures the
illusion of having already achieved the best of all possible
worlds where progress, in any meaningful sense is, by definition, no longer possible. If man, living as he does in a grossly
imperfect world, is not uniquely determined by his past and is
nothing but a potential in terms of his impending future, then
the act of commitment is a prior requirement for the realization of his freedom and thus his future. And if modern democracy is predicated on the end of ideology, that is, on the end of
commitment, then it negates itself and becomes the very denial
of freedom. If it has any commitment at all, it is the false
commitment to itself—to the narcissistic approval of itself as it
is—with the net result that it has retreated from the problems
of the world about it.

IV

Another objection to the end of ideology lies in its inability to
make the fundamental distinction between what it considers to
be the good society and a social theory which has become obsolete as a result of the changing values and problems of suc-
ceeding generations. Confusing the two and still obsessed and
blinded by the orientations of the 1930s, it looks at the current
situation and declares that the problems of the Great Depression have been, by and large, satisfactorily resolved.

Bell's book was accurately subtitled *On the Exhaustion of
Political Ideas in the Fifties.* Indeed, we have been, and continue to be, faced with a bankruptcy of political ideas at a time
when certain critical developments have been taking place in
the United States—developments for which the end of ideology is in large measure responsible. On the international front
there is the tendency to apply a splintering empiricism to our

international problems, and on the domestic front there is inability to cope with, let alone admit, the economic malaise that has seized the American economy since the end of the Korean War.

Concerning international matters, Hans J. Morgenthau writes of our "surrendering piecemeal to the facts of foreign policy . . . of thinking and acting as though there were nothing else to foreign policy but this [or that] particular set of empirical facts" concerning this or that foreign policy problem.[12] The latter-day pragmatists, in Morgenthau's opinion, are basically anti-theoretical, anti-utopian empiricists who pride themselves on having "no illusions about the facts as they are nor any grand design for changing them." Indeed, their crowning achievement, in their own view, is their "courage to look the facts in the face and . . . deal with each issue on its own terms." Underlying their entire approach is their profound belief that "the problems of the social world [will] yield to a series of piecemeal empirical attacks, unencumbered by preconceived notions and comprehensive planning." As a result foreign policy lacks an overall cohesiveness and has degenerated into a series of unrelated operations not always consistent with each other, and often far removed from the realities of the situation which the facts, of their own accord, are supposed to make clear. Thus, according to Morgenthau, in trying to escape the Scylla of utopianism we are foundering on the Charybdis of empiricism. In the name of "facts" we are reduced to approaching the major problems of our existence as though they were mere matters of technical manipulation. What is obviously needed is an ideology to interpret the "facts" of a social situation and to suggest meaningful solutions in terms of a particular reading of these self-same "facts."[13]

[12] "The Perils of Political Empiricism," *Commentary*, July, 1962.
[13] Hans Morgenthau denies the existence of unalloyed facts as follows: "Facts have no social meaning in themselves. It is the significance we attribute to certain facts of our sensory experience—in terms of our hopes and fears, our memories, inventions, and expectations—that creates them

In a similar vein, others deny that there is anything substantively wrong with the American economy. It is their unwillingness to engage in any form of structural criticism, and their tendency to look upon those who do as vestigial appendages of modern democratic society, that compels them to regard the existing tools as adequate for the correction of what they consider to be a temporary and fleeting imbalance. They deny the necessity for any structural reorganization of society and insist that it is all a matter of mere technical adjustment within the existing canons of responsibility. This ability of the end-of-ideology approach to blur understanding and lead to inaction is magnified out of all sensible proportions by the internal economic problems of the United States since 1953. The phenomenon of the business cycle has not disappeared from the American scene. Since the end of World War II the American economy has continued to experience alternating periods of expansion and contraction. The postwar boom of 1946–8 involved a huge spending spree by households and business firms for long denied consumers' and producers' durable goods. And the liquid assets accumulated by both groups during the war provided the means for financing the boom. The 1948–9 recession which followed was quickly reversed by the outbreak of the Korean War, and with the cessation of hostilities in Korea the American economy dipped into the trough of 1953–54. These two initial postwar booms are easily understood. What is not so easy to understand is the grossly inadequate performance of the economy since the end of the Korean War.

---

as social facts. The social world itself, then, is but an artifact of man's mind, the reflection of his thoughts and the creation of his actions. Every social act (and even our awareness of empirical data as social facts) presupposes a theory of society, however unacknowledged, inchoate, and fragmentary. It is not given to us to choose between a social philosophy and an unconditional surrender to the facts as they are. Rather we must choose between a philosophy consistent with itself and founded on experience which can serve as a guide to understanding and an instrument for successful actions, and an implicit and untested philosophy which is likely to blur understanding and mislead action."

Since 1953 the number of quarters from trough to cyclical peak has steadily declined. And while these post-Korean recoveries have become progressively abortive and of shorter duration, the rate of unemployment has virtually doubled as we have moved from one cyclical *peak* to another—from 2.7 per cent of the civilian labor force during the second quarter peak of 1953 to 5.2 per cent for the latest cyclical peak of 1960–2. It is not surprising, therefore, that in our successive peaks of economic activity both the average duration of unemployment and the amount of long-term unemployment have increased. A corollary to this rise of chronic unemployment is the slowing down of the annual growth rate (computed on a peak to peak basis) from 4.8 per cent for the period 1948–53, to 2.5 per cent for 1953–60—a drop well below the long-term historical rate (1890–1959) of 3.2

An alternate method of illustrating the seriousness as well as the magnitude of the problem currently facing the American economy is to compute the difference between what the economy could have produced at a given point in time, assuming a full employment use of its resources, and what it actually did produce. This can be done by adopting the technique of the President's Council of Economic Advisers. Assuming a longtime potential growth rate of 3.5 per cent (comprised roughly of a 1.5 per cent increase in the labor force and a 2.0 per cent increase in the productivity of labor) and an unemployment rate of roughly 4 per cent (assumed, on the basis of mid-1955, to be compatible with relative price level stability), the gap between potential and actual output amounted to approximately $34 billion for the third quarter of 1962 on an annual basis and in constant 1954 dollars. If we accept the President's call for a higher growth rate of 4.5 per cent, the gap increases to $70 billion. And if we set a 2.4 per cent unemployment rate as our definition of full employment, then at the increased growth rate of 4.5 per cent the gap jumps to over $100 billion of output lost irretrievably.

It seems reasonable to conclude on the face of this evidence that the American economy is suffering from a non-cyclical slack of chronic proportions—despite arms expenditure which pumps into the economy an average of $50 billion a year. To argue that in spite of these developments things are not as bad as they were in the 1930s is to judge and compare business cycles solely in terms of their statistical differences, rather than the potential consequences which would follow from a protracted failure to maintain an adequate growth rate. Undue emphasis on non-ideological, "factual" analysis and statistical comparisons can breed an unthinking empiricism which ignores the context of the data and hence their meaning. It becomes unhistorical and short-sighted.

Stripped to its bare essentials the crisis facing the United States in the 1960s involves two gaps—the *internal* gap between the actual and potential output of the American economy, and the *external* gap between the growth rates of the United States, the Common Market and the Soviet Union. The closing of the internal gap and the narrowing of the external gap is of paramount importance if the United States is to survive as a major power in the long run. It should be made clear, however, that the closing of the internal gap does not necessarily imply a closing of the external gap. A closing of the internal gap would require a significantly larger increase in the short-term growth rate than we have been experiencing in the last decade. But once closed the economy would then proceed along its now inadequate long-term growth rate of 3.2 per cent. It is, therefore, of importance that, aside from the internal policies needed to close the internal gap, as measured by the Council of Economic Advisers, additional measures be undertaken to increase the long-term rate of economic growth; which would then require a still larger increase in the short-term rate.

What is desperately needed is a marked change in the American public's assessment of the role of government in a democratically oriented society. If we are to meet the joint problem of the two gaps, long-range planning on a governmental level is imperative and the present division between the private and public sectors of the economy must be looked upon as unrealistic. We must not engage, as has the Council of Economic Advisers, in historical extrapolations from the past which supposedly show that nothing has changed and that our old tools are as good as new. Nor does this necessarily imply the adoption of socialist planning. It is rather a question of what changes are needed to make the capitalist system viable in a power world. The internal gap, for example, may be a structural rather than merely a technical problem in cyclical instability. If so, then the indirect Keynesian controls of monetary and fiscal policy may no longer be fully adequate. For one thing, it must be kept in mind that business cycles and wars induce, however subtly, irreversible changes in the underlying institutional structure of a modern society. And our theoretical constructions of reality, if they are to have any meaning at all, must absorb these changes over time. In so far as existing social theories do not take these structural developments into account, they become obsolete and hence invalidated.

One of the problems of the post-war period has been the emergence of inflationary depressions attributable to the relative mildness of the periodic American recessions and to the emergence of oligopolistic concentrations of market power in both commodity and factor markets. With the economic pressures thus emanating from the supply side, more so than from the demand side, serious doubt has been cast on the ability of monetary and fiscal policy to achieve a full employment use of resources, even at an inadequate long-term growth rate based on a 4 per cent unemployment rate. And it is a bit ludicrous to suppose that, by riding things out with inadequate policies derived from inadequate theories, it is only the timetable and not the path of an economy which will be affected. It may be that no changes exist, under these circumstances, which would make American capitalism, as we know it, viable. But it is at least incumbent upon us to determine if this is so and not slide into a doctrinal rigidity which would assure its defeat. The

problem facing the United States may not be a purely technical one. We need to determine this and if the traditional tools
are found to be inadequate, then what will be needed is a re-
evaluation of the institutional framework and the value premises upon which it is based. It is time, therefore, that the graduate departments of major universities become rather more than
just places where competent technicians are trained.

V

It has been agreed that Bell's and Lipset's account of the end of
ideology in the West is, in large part, accurate. There is, nevertheless, a judgment to be made apart from the accuracy of their
account. Bell and Lipset regard the end of ideology as good.
Our point here is that it must be judged contextually, and that
under the *present* conditions it borders on the disastrous. This
can be illustrated by comparing the two supreme technicians
of American politics—Franklin D. Roosevelt and John F.
Kennedy. Both are supreme examples of the non-committed,
non-ideological politician acting out of political expediency.
Both placed the highest value on political success at the polls
and regarded such success as the *sine qua non* of their experience. And neither had any fixed vision of the good society. Yet
though they are similar in all these and other respects, the consequences of their common and purely "political approach" to
politics are not the same. The 1960s are, obviously, not the
1930s. And it is in the context of each of these two periods of
crisis that the end of ideology common to both Roosevelt and
Kennedy must be judged.

The crisis of the 1930s gave rise, through the New Dealers,
to a new wave of hope, and to the conviction that by social
engineering things could be put aright. The flood of social legislation in the early days of the New Deal was an extraordi-

nary attempt to bring about the needed institutional changes. This passion for pragmatic social experimentation was rooted deeply in the belief that human nature was highly, if not infinitely plastic. It was, in other words, basically optimistic and full of hope in a time of crisis. It was, above all, an age of critical thought, of regeneration, of faith in man's power to change the institutional complex within which he lived. It engaged, unstintingly, in a fundamental criticism of man and the institutional melange within which he had entrapped himself. Society, in short, was to be reconstructed in the image and in the interests of the so-called common man. But there was no overall blueprints. It was an empirical approach to democracy. If there was no ideological cohesion, there was at least general agreement that something had to be done and a clear understanding of the problem in personal terms. It was there, staring at them—the breadlines, the hunger, the Hoovervilles, the closed factories, the ugly tear in the social fabric of a once prosperous society. The crisis of the 1930s was readily understood by the man in the street. It was a part of his everyday experience and affected or was a direct and frightening threat to his continued well-being. And it was on this stage that the end of ideology entered in the form of President Roosevelt. The political coloration and social innovations of the New Deal were largely the result of political expediency in a country where political success counts for all. The tune of the New Deal was played by ear and the end of ideology in the guise of a charismatic president served to make the vast power of the presidency responsible to the public will.

The 1960s are an entirely different matter. The current situation is not immediately understandable in direct, personal terms by the ubiquitous man-in-the-street. The threat of nuclear annihilation numbs his sense of credulity and is so vast as to be beyond his conceptual capacity. The problem of disarmament is also much too complicated to be fully comprehended. Despite the poor performance of the economy since 1953 and the growth of unemployment, the affluent society continues to maintain its image unimpaired. There are no breadlines, as in the 1930s, and the economic problem has not yet pierced the individual's consciousness since, for most people, it is not yet a direct threat. And if one major aspect of the economic problem is the long-run power threat implied by the disparate rates of economic growth between the United States and the Soviet Union, then surely this is the most remote of his immediate concerns. In short, the problems of the 1960s are much too abstract for the limited social vision of the common man.

It is in this totally different context that a non-ideological man like President Kennedy operated. It is not the kind of crisis which confronts the individual with understandable, let alone meaningful problems to which he can respond politically. So when President Kennedy wet his finger and held it up to the political winds, he found them blowing simultaneously in all directions. There is no coherence; no well thought out sense of purpose, as Hans Morgenthau has pointed out, in foreign policy, and as is even more obvious with respect to domestic policy. Above all, and unlike the 1930s, there is no general consensus in the body politic to which the President can respond out of sheer political expediency, in a clear and consistent manner. In short, there is no limiting frame of reference within which to innovate, and lacking one of his own, he flounders, compromises and tries to be all things to all men. Indeed, like Lipset, he rationalized the emptiness of modern society and declared that it *is* the good society and that all the problems which do remain are purely technical. Two of Kennedy's recent talks more than amply demonstrate this. In his remarks before the Economic Conference held in Washington on May 21, 1962, the President distinguished between myth and reality in these words.

I would like to say a word about the difference between myth and reality. Most of us are conditioned for many years to have a political viewpoint, Republican or Democrat—liberal, conservative, moderate. The fact of the matter is that most of the problems, or at least many of them that we now face, are technical problems, are administrative problems. They are very sophisticated judgments which do not lend themselves to the great sort of "passionate movements" which have stirred this country so often in the past. Now they deal with questions which are beyond the comprehension of most men.

A month later at his 1962 commencement address at Yale University, the late President further elaborated on this theme.

Today . . . the central domestic problems of our time are more subtle and less simple. They do not relate to basic clashes of philosophy and ideology, but to ways and means of reaching common goals—to reserach for sophisticated solutions to complex and obstinate issues.

What is at stake in our economic decisions today is not some grand warfare of rival ideologies which will sweep the country with passion but the practical management of a modern economy. What we need are not labels and clichés but more basic discussion of the sophisticated and technical questions involved in keeping a great economic machinery moving ahead.

. . . political labels and ideological approaches are irrelevant to the solutions.

. . . the problems of . . . the Sixties as opposed to the kinds of problems we faced in the Thirties demand subtle challenges for which technical answers—not political answers—must be provided.

Though we do not agree with this position, it must be admitted that the President had the good sense to limit it to domestic issues. At no point would the President, or any other sensible person, have argued that our differences with the Russians were purely technical. Neither have Bell and Lipset.

VI

Bell and Lipset are of one mind. Whereas the old ideologies of the West have become exhausted by the march of Western progress, new ideologies have arisen in Asia and Africa—the ideologies, according to Bell, of industrialization, modernization, Pan-Arabism, color, and nationalism. The new ideologies, unlike the old, are not being fashioned by the intellectuals along universal or humanistic lines. Rather, they are instrumentally parochial and employed by political leaders who have created them for purposes of rapid development and national power. And the disoriented Western liberals have desperately embraced the new ideology of economic development to "wash away the memory of old disillusionments" (pp. 403–8 [pp. 99–105 in this volume]). In this sense, Lipset believes there is "still a real need for political analysis, ideology, and controversy, *within the world community,* if not within the Western democracies," and the Western ideologue, stripped of issues in his own back yard must now focus his attention on this new area. Though ideology and passion are no longer necessary in the affluent and advanced democracies of the West, they are very much needed in the less affluent countries of the world. In the underdeveloped countries, we should encourage the radical and socialist politicians because, according to Lipset, "only parties which promise to improve the situation of the masses through widespread reform . . . can hope to compete with the communists" (p. 416 [p. 84 in this volume]). Therefore, the disaffected liberals of the West, the unreconstructed intellectuals, the trade union leaders (at least those who are still liberal), and the socialists have a positive role to play—abroad; where their vision and their need to criticize can be put to good use in developing free political and economic institutions.

This is, indeed, a remarkable argument. The Lipset and Bell position is that the end of ideology exists only in the West, but that ideology has still an important role to play in the under-developed countries if only like some Sorelian myth, to meet the three conditions and purposes of ideology as set down by Bell, *viz.* (1) to simplify ideas, (2) to establish a claim to truth, no matter how specious, and (3) to demand a commitment to action. Furthermore, the displaced ideologues of the West, those disenchanted intellectuals in need of a vision to sustain them, can be used to further and to speed up the role of ideology in the underdeveloped countries, and thus forestall a takeover of these areas by the Communists.

In time, if we are successful, the underdeveloped countries will become developed and as they, too, solve all their pressing political, social and economic problems, ideology will wither on their vines. Then peace will break out in an enlarged West and international relations and disputes will, like purely internal problems, be governed by an *international* ethic of responsibility.

Lipset and Bell are, in effect, arguing that the nations of the world are all racing toward a static state of equilibrium. Only, some countries have had a head start. A few have already achieved the good society. Others are fast approaching it. And still others, the underdeveloped countries, have only just begun their ascent. In time, all will have arrived, but until such time it will be the responsibility of those already at the pinnacle to reach down and help the others up. In all this, it would seem, dynamic change is a transitory phenomenon and all of human history, in all its turmoil and in all its travail, has been moving, inexorably, toward this supreme goal of universal peace. At bottom, what Bell and Lipset are giving us is a philosophy of history—if not of the past, then certainly of the future.

HENRY DAVID AIKEN

The Revolt Against
Ideology*

Can it any longer be doubted that, on all sides of the Iron
Curtain, the age of Leviathan is upon us? And for serious men
does there remain any significant form of activity that is politically indifferent? We still profess loyalty to the ideal of "free
inquiry," but the fact is that, directly or indirectly, governments supply the major resources, and politics most of the in-
centives, for our scientific research. And if some fortunate
scientists of eminence are still encouraged to do "pure" or
"basic" research, according to their interest, the primary reason
is not that such studies exemplify one of man's essential intrinsic goods, but that the state cannot survive without them. Indeed, our universities and governments, along with our great
industrial complexes, look increasingly like the interlocking
arms of a great, if also headless, political establishment. Free
enterprise (who doubts it?) is everywhere a dead issue save in
the mythology of fundamentalist Republicanism, and whether
our political leaders favor state capitalism or corporate socialism, the welfare state is accepted by all as an irremovable reality. Politics provide the primary themes of our literature, and

* Reprinted from *Commentary* (April 1964) by permission; Copyright
© 1964 by The American Jewish Committee.

when the critics charge a novelist or poet with "retreating from life," what they mean by "life" does not need to be construed. "Aesthetics" signifies merely enfeeblement and irrelevance; the "pure" artist, like the pure scientist, is a dying species, and none will mourn him save perhaps a few old "new critics" who, be it added, well understood the political meaning of their own dandified aestheticism. Our most exigent moral perplexities are overwhelmingly political, and our gods, such as they are, seem wholly preoccupied with affairs of state.

I must admit, however, that there still exists one quiet place where a man may go if he is nauseated by problems of politics and hence of power, and one course of study which he may still pursue without fear of political encroachment: he may go, that is, to the graduate school of any great university and take up the subject known there as "philosophy." Among the intellectuals, to my knowledge, we philosophers alone are politically inert. The meaning of the concept of political obligation fascinates some few of my colleagues, but I have rarely heard them, in congress assembled, discuss their political obligations. And if any were asked to offer their opinions concerning the ends, or limits, of government they would probably either decline to answer or regard the question as philosophically improper.

In order to prove the rule, there remain a few notorious exceptions such as Bertrand Russell, Jean-Paul Sartre, and Professor Sidney Hook. But we have Russell's own word for it that his politics, like his ethics, and his philosophy have nothing in common except that both were hatched under the same head of hair, and both Sartre and Hook are frequently dismissed by their more academic colleagues as publicists who have deserted philosophy for careers as ideologists and politicians. Recalling the greatest names in the history of philosophy from Socrates to Aquinas and from Hobbes to Mill, one may wonder momentarily how such a state of affairs could have come to pass. But when one remembers what men have done, and in many parts of the world are still prepared to do, in the name of a political philosophy, the answer seems evident: from a "pragmatic" point of view, political philosophy is a monster, and wherever it has been taken seriously, the consequence, almost invariably, has been revolution, war, and eventually, the police state. Russell himself once wrote an essay entitled, "The Harm that Good Men Do." Many would regard this as an appropriate subtitle for any honest and realistic history of political philosophy. With Socrates, political philosophy became a gadfly; in Plato, a monstrous dream; in Rousseau, Fichte, Hegel, Marx, and the rest, it has become a scourge and an obscenity.

Such is the prevailing view. And if Peter Laslett, the editor of a recent volume of essays *on* political philosophy, is correct in saying that "for the moment, anyway, political philosophy is dead," then none mourn its passing less than the philosophers themselves. Those few who, as philosophers, still suppose that they have a useful political role to play, discover it to be only that of unmasking the pretensions of other political philosophers.

Just what is wrong with political philosophy as a genre nonetheless remains obscure. Of course many political philosophies from Plato to Aquinas, and from Hobbes and Rousseau to Hegel and Marx, have been tied to the kites of theological or metaphysical systems. And for some, no doubt, this fact suffices to put them beyond the pale. But roundhouse objections to "metaphysics" are less fashionable than they were some years ago. In fact, under pressure from the philosophers of ordinary language, philosophical analysts are increasingly reluctant to proscribe as meaningless any established form of discourse on principle, as the positivists used to do with the propositions, not only of metaphysics and theology, but also of ethics. In this respect, recent analytical philosophy has steadily moved in the direction of pragmatism or, I had better say, the direction in which pragmatism has tended to move since the days of William James. Any form of utterance, so it is now argued, is to be interpreted and judged only in the light of its own characteristic "practical bearings." Thus, for example, if

231

political philosophers in their own terms are given to general moral evaluations of political activities and institutions, the question is only whether such appraisals, all things considered, are acceptable as value judgments: that is to say, do they express commitments to which, on sober second thought and in view of the historical record, we should be ready to give our own conscientious assent? Do the lines of social action which they commend appear on the whole to be worth the trouble it would take to realize them? Above all, would we in conscience be able to give our blessings to the sort of "representative man" who might emerge if such lines of action were resolutely pursued?

Questions of this sort, which I take more seriously, have produced another round of objections which, although they do not rule out political philosophy on supposedly semantical or logical grounds, do nonetheless seem to condemn it virtually as a genre. These objections are all the more telling and all the more significant since they come from a quarter in which there has been no general animus against metaphysics and no self-denying ordinance which would exclude from the purview of philosophy any problem that is not purely a conceptual problem about the "logic" of expressions.

To my knowledge the most powerful attack upon political philosophy from this quarter (which for convenience may be called "existential") is to be found in Albert Camus's arresting work, *The Rebel*. Camus's indictment is easily misunderstood. To be sure, it is profoundly antirationalistic, but it is by no means based upon a romantic or nihilistic disillusionment with human reason or with the value of its exercise. Quite the contrary, reasonableness, in the more classical sense of the term, is Camus's forte. What he condemns, rather, are the crimes incited by the political philosophers in the name of Reason or of Reason's God. All men, say the philosophers, are created equal; *ergo,* let them be restored at once to their pristine estate, whatever the cost. All men are by nature free, yet everywhere they are in chains; *ergo,* Reason demands that they immedi-

232

ately be released, though ten thousand jailers perish in the process. Man is, above all, the rational animal, but because of the blinders which the ancient regime places before his mind, he cannot freely exercise his reason; then destroy the regime, let reason, or its self-appointed representatives, reign, and the devil take those who stand in the way. No doubt the political philosophers never meant to be quite so simple or so brutal as these caricatures suggest. But what of their followers, those who take them, or try to take them, at their word? Can the political philosophers altogether disclaim responsibility for their crimes? Is there not an ingrained metaphysical or moral pride, a fatal lack of continence in the very attempt of political philosophers to set forth, whether in the name of reason or of nature or of humanity, the absolute ends of government and the supposedly invariant forms of the just society?

But Camus's criticisms are by no means directed exclusively to the 18th-century *philosophes* and their descendants. They are extended also to the Hegelians and the Marxists who attempt to formulate a universal law, or dialectic, of historical development which is then made to double in brass as an immanent principle of justification for their own incitive prophecies about man's social destiny. Whether such prophecies proclaim a future of unlimited freedom, of absolute justice and equality, or of perpetual peace, in each case they too represent that criminal pride of reason which destroys the sense of limitation which for Camus is the beginning of political, as of every other form of, wisdom.

From these remarks it would be easy enough to conclude that Camus's indictment of traditional political philosophy is actually an indictment of philosophy itself. And so in a way it is, at least as philosophy has been conceived and executed in the dominant Western tradition. Yet Camus is not just another literary counter-philosopher. Nor is his indictment of rationalistic political philosophy a condemnation of political philosophy *per se*. For it is plain that, as Sir Herbert Read points out in his discerning preface to the English translation of *The*

Rebel, Camus himself has a philosophy of politics. But it is, at any rate, a philosophy of politics radically different from those of his predecessors. For Camus makes no attempt to define *the* function or the end of government or to state *the* rightful basis of political authority. Nor does he propose any universal principle of political action save one of self-limitation or restraint. It is also characteristic of Camus that although he repudiates any and all forms of unlimited revolution, he accepts the necessity, on occasion, of rebellion or civil disobedience.

Despite many differences both in philosophical background and in literary style, there are striking parallels between Camus's existentialist critique of modern political philosophy and those to be found in the writings of the pragmatist, John Dewey. In Dewey one finds the same hatred of essentialism and apriorism, the same antipathy to utopianism, and the same distrust both of radical individualism and of radical collectivism. There is a similar emphasis upon the concrete "problematic situations" (as Dewey calls them) which alone he takes it to be the business of "creative intelligence" to resolve. And there is the same underlying humanism which opposes the sacrifice of living men to principles and to ideals realizable, if at all, only in an abstract and indefinite future. For obvious reasons, Dewey was more confident than Camus of the efficacy of democratic procedures, at least in "developed" societies. Yet he was by no means prepared to demand the immediate institution of such procedures in all countries and circumstances; nor did he, like more romantic majoritarians, regard the will of the many as an absolute source of rightful political authority. Democracy for Dewey is a method rather than an end. Or if, in certain writings, democracy also tends to become an end, then it is in a looser sense of the term which now begins to take on meanings more strictly associated with the concepts of community, fraternity, and social equality.

Dewey's pragmatic criticisms of earlier political philosophy are usually regarded as methodological rather than moral—although in his case, as in that of all pragmatists, it is always a question where problems of method leave off and problems of ethics (and politics) begin. Thus, whereas Camus ascribes the primordial fault of the political philosophers to their incontinent passion for absolute transcendence of the finite conditions of man's historical social existence, Dewey ascribes it to the illusory "quest for certainty" which, according to his reading, dominated virtually the whole history of philosophy before the 20th century. Yet in Dewey's case also, one senses that the more radical evil lies not in the illusion itself but in its attendant waste and destructiveness. The quest for certainty begins in hope and ends in skepticism and despair. In promising us an unlimited intellectual and moral security, it brings us by stages to the war of all against all. Dewey's more unfriendly critics have often charged him with advocacy of the gospel of human perfectibility. No criticism could be more perverse. Man, as Dewey conceives him, is, once for all, a mortal creature who lives and has his being within the orders of nature and of history. Indeed, this is the governing metaphysical principle underlying his logic, his theory of knowledge, and his moral philosophy. Uncertainty, and hence imperfection, are ingrained in the very texture of human existence. And no method, including the methods of science, can extricate us from them.

In other spheres, philosophical forgetfulness of this fact has been unfortunate; in politics, as in ethics, it has proved a calamity. This is not to deny that Dewey has a philosophy of politics, but like Camus's it is of a sort quite different from the major political philosophies of the tradition. He is sometimes criticized for offering us no explicit general theory of governmental authority, no principled statement of the grounds or proper limits of political obligation—above all, no settled position toward the most vexatious of modern political problems, namely, revolution. But Dewey's vagueness on these scores is quite intentional. In politics as in ethics, Dewey repudiates any and all fixed principles for the institution of the good society or for the establishment and maintenance of good government. His preoccupation as a political philosopher is solely with the controlling attitudes which men bring to their political deliberations.

II. Marxism and Ideology: The First Revolt

Impressive as they are, the foregoing criticisms of political philosophy are largely matters of individual judgment. And if the professional philosophers now decline to do political philosophy, it may be argued that this is owing to their own disillusionment with the achievements of their predecessors rather than to any inherent fault in political philosophy as a genre. It remains to ask whether there may be, after all, some deeplying confusion of mind, some pervasive logical fault or category mistake, which really does afflict political philosophy as a form of discourse.

As a way of confronting this question, it may prove useful to examine certain aspects of the widespread attack against the modern offspring of and successor to political philosophy, namely, ideology. Most of the "anti-ideologists," as I shall call them, share certain attitudes in common with the existentialists; indeed, it is my impression that some of them owe more to the latter, and particularly to Camus, than they have as yet acknowledged. They owe something also to the pragmatists; in fact, most American anti-ideologists fancy their own point of view as essentially "pragmatic." But (generally speaking) they go beyond the existentialists and the pragmatists in contending that ideological thinking is the function of certain features of the social situation in which intellectuals as a group find themselves in an era of exact science, advanced technology, and the welfare state. In predicting the end of ideology, they thus imply that the social and intellectual conditions which have been conducive to ideological thinking are now disappearing. Their own role, in effect, is to make certain that the prediction will come true.

Now the primary target of our contemporary Western anti-ideologists is, of course, Marxism. And in prophesying the end of ideology, it is the end of Marxism of which they mainly dream. It is worth remembering, therefore, that: (a) Marx was the first great critic of political philosophy; and (b) he was also the first great prophet of the end of the ideological age.

According to Marx, ideology always involves a conception of reality which systematically "inverts" the whole relation of thought to being.* As a form of thought, therefore, ideology is inherently confused; it stands to science, in Marx's words, as an inverted image in a "camera obscura" stands to a veridical perception. This inversion, of which Hegel's "objective" idealism is a prime philosophical example, results directly or indirectly from that process of "alienation" whereby human artifacts, including "ideas," are invested with a power and a reality that are supposedly independent both of their producers and of the material conditions and operations involved in their production. Such an investment, which philosophers call "reification," is also necessarily accompanied by "mystification," i.e., by an obscuring of the interests and relationships that actually determine social behavior. For example, in imputing an independent reality and power to their reified ideas and principles, their

* In this section I have been aided by Stanley W. Moore's *The Critique of Capitalist Democracy, An Introduction to the Theory of the State in Marx, Engels, and Lenin,* Paine-Whitman Publishers, New York, 1957. Moore's fourth chapter, "Ideology and Alienation," pp. 114–137, is highly compressed and schematic, but I know of no other discussion of the subject which, within its limits, is so clear and so accurate. I have also benefited from Norman Birnbaum's *The Sociological Study of Ideology* (1940–60), *Current Sociology,* Vol. IX, No. 2, 1960, Basil Blackwell, Oxford England. Birnbaum's essay, which he subtitles "A Trend Report," is a masterly survey of current literature on the subject of ideology, including Marxist ideological theory. It also contains an invaluable critical bibliography.

rights and duties, their ends and "reasons," men thereby conceal from themselves the fact that it is they, the creators of such entities, whose underlying actions and whose work alone give them whatever significance they may have.

Except for genuinely empirical science, the whole cultural "superstructure" of hitherto existing societies is permeated by the same process of alienation and ideological inversion. For this reason it would be a radical mistake to conceive of ideology as limited to political philosophy; on the contrary, ideology also includes, among other things, religion, ethics, art, metaphysics, and the "dismal science" of economics. Properly understood, political philosophies are merely special applications of far-flung ideological patterns that invest them with their own magical "authority" and "justification." Furthermore, since alienation is a social process, ideologies, whether as wholes or as parts, are to be understood as expressions, not of the interests of isolated individuals, but of the conflicting concerns—or better, tendencies—of social classes. It is thus only by relating political ideologies to their objective social conditions and causes that we can begin to interpret their true objective meaning (i.e., what they signify or portend within the order of nature), and hence, by stages, to correct the inverted images of reality which they present to the ideologists themselves. One of the primary functions of Marxism, in fact, is precisely to provide the intellectual, including the social-theoretical, tools for such interpretations and corrections, and thus for the first time to enable us, in principle, to demythologize ideology.

But it is one thing to explain ideology and another to overcome it. Mankind as a whole can permanently overcome ideological thought (and action) not by any process of purely conceptual analysis on the part of individual philosophers, but only by removing the material causes of alienation which, according to Marx, are rooted in the institution of private property. And it is for this reason, and this reason alone, that Marx's historical prophecy of the coming of world socialism amounts at the same time to a prophecy of the end of the ideological ages.

III. Disillusionment in the West: The Second Revolt against Ideology

Marx's view of ideology underlies the thinking of most of our own anti-ideologists. However, they go beyond Marx in extending the pejorative associations of the term to the role of ideology in ordering human attitudes. Thus, they not only regard ideological doctrines as wrong-headed; they also object to their employment as vehicles for the formation, guidance, and control of social behavior. But they go Marx one better in another way, for they also regard Marxism itself as a prime example of ideology.

The first non-Marxist writer, so far as I know, explicitly to inquire whether we might be approaching the end of the ideological age was Raymond Aron in his book *The Opium of the Intellectuals*. The prevailing temper of Aron's book is not unlike that of Camus's *The Rebel*. There are also a number of striking parallels between Aron's point of view and that of Karl Popper, as developed in the latter's *The Open Society and its Enemies*. For example, there is the same constitutional distrust of large-scale social planning, the same insistence upon the impossibility of large-scale historical predictions of social behavior, and the same celebration of the virtues of "the open society." Above all, there is the same castigation of any attempt to determine the drift and meaning of human history as a whole and hence of the attempt to formulate universal and necessary laws of historical development.

"The last great ideology," says Aron, "was born of the combination of three elements: the vision of a future consistent with human aspiration, the link between this future and a particular social class, and trust in human values above and beyond the victory of the working class, thanks to planning and collective ownership." Aron believes that at the present time the hope aroused by that ideology is gone beyond peradventure. One main reason for this disillusionment, so he argues, is that "Confidence in the virtues of a socio-technique has begun to wane." Furthermore, on this side of the Iron Curtain, no one believes any longer in the reality of a social class that will carry us, under the leadership of the socio-economic engineers, to the frontiers of the classless society. Like Camus and Popper, Aron cannot bring himself flatly to renounce the values of the Enlightenment; but in practice he is no more able than they to take them with absolute seriousness as governing ideals for the reconstruction of society in the 20th century. In his own terms, he no longer fully believes in the vision of a future consistent with "human aspirations." And it is this fact perhaps that accounts for the vein of pessimism and the self-division which run through his writing.

In any case, it is plain that for Aron the approaching end of the age of ideology represents also a crisis of faith and of hope for mankind. On the penultimate page of his book, Aron asks, "Does the rejection of fanaticism encourage a reasonable faith, or merely skepticism?" His analogical answer is that "one does not cease to love God when one gives up converting pagans or the Jews and no longer reiterates 'No salvation outside the Church.'" Coming as late as it does in Aron's book, this has something like the effect of an unprepared major cadence at the end of a funeral march. What is its basis? No matter how personal one's religion may be, it is hard to see how it could fail to be attenuated by a radical renunciation of one's belief that it should prevail. If one really gives up trying to convert the "pagans," does this not entail reservations about the value as well as the possibility of converting them? If so, does this not also suggest that one has ceased completely to love God or else that only a gesture toward the love of Him remains? Making due allowance for the analogy, I cannot, as a pragmatist, see how one can be said actively to seek a less cruel lot for humanity if one can trust no technique and no plan for its amelioration. To will the end is to will the means, and to reject the means is, in practice, to renounce the end. Like Peirce in another connection, one is minded to say to the political as well as to the epistemological moralists: "Dismiss make-believe!" This means also, so far as I can see, "Dismiss professions of 'reasonable faith' if you do not believe in the *power* of reason; and do not talk about abolishing 'fanaticism,' unless you believe that there is a way (or 'technique') of abolishing it." Like all anti-ideologists, Aron is opposed to the expectation of "miraculous changes" either from a revolution or an economic plan. Very well. The question is whether he gives us any reason to expect unmiraculous changes from any sort of concerted human action. "If tolerance is born of doubt, let us teach everyone to doubt all the models and utopias, to challenge all the prophets of redemption and the heralds of catastrophe." And, "If they alone can abolish fanaticism, let us pray for the advent of the skeptics." The rhetoric is appealing. But it smacks of ideology, in Aron's own sense. For toleration is also a principle and a method. And it too has its dangers.

These comments are not made in a spirit of mockery. My purpose is rather to make clear what may be implied in the prophecy that we are living at the end of the ideological age, the age, in Mr. Aron's own apt words, in which men still actively search "for a purpose, for communion with the people, for something controlled by *an idea and a will*" (my italics). As he points out, we Westerners have suffered an increasing fragmentation of our universe; our poetry becomes more and more obscure and diffuse, and our poets are isolated from one another as well as from "the big public" which "in their heart of hearts, they long to serve"; our scientists have ideas aplenty but no control over their use or indeed any consistent belief in the possibility of their control; our scholars control limited areas of specialized knowledge, but present-day science "seems

to leave . . . [them] as ignorant of the answers to the ultimate questions as a child awakening to consciousness"; and
our economists and sociologists, for all their facts and statistics,
their jargon and their lore, have not the vaguest notion
whether "humanity is progressing toward an atomic holocaust
or Utopian peace." This process of fragmentation and dissocia-
tion, moreover, is not new; it has been going on at an ever
more rapid pace, at least since the Renaissance. But here precisely, as Aron admits, "is where ideology comes in. . . ." For
ideology represents the insistent demand for a coherent *way* of
individual and social life, an orientation toward the world and
toward the human predicament, controlled as he says both by
an idea and by a will, or, rather, by a will infused with an idea
and an idea animated by will. Ideology, as Aron tacitly acknowledges, is a creature of alienation, to bring it down to
bearable human proportions. It also represents the belief that
alienation may be reduced through collective human endeav-
ors. Thus, by his own account, an end to the age of ideology
would amount to this extent to a virtual skepticism about the
possibility of reducing alienation through corporate planning
and action (ideas infused with will). And this means that man
has no choice but to live with alienation. Here, however, one
faces precisely one of those metaphysical and historical "necessities" against which the anti-ideologists themselves rail when
they find them in the writings of other ideologists. Here, too, it
seems, we are faced with a "simplified" idea of man's fate
which, as in the case of the Stoicism it is plainly a variant of,
forms the basis of still another ideology, an idea that in this
instance is, if I may say so, fused with inaction.

IV. The Sociological Critique of Ideology

Aron's analysis of ideology, although suggestive, does not take
us very far. Let us therefore cross the ocean to the heartland of

contemporary anti-ideology. In the United States perhaps the leading anti-ideologist is the sociologist and social critic, Professor Daniel Bell. Bell, who knows his Marx, is also a good strategist. Already in the introduction to his book, *The End of Ideology,* he moves beyond Aron, for, unlike the latter, he proposes to make a positive virtue of alienation. "Alienation," he tells us flatly, "is not nihilism but a positive role, a detachment, which guards one against being submerged in any cause, or accepting any particular embodiment of community as final. Nor is alienation deracination, a denial of one's roots or country." This persuasive definition has its points. It is also an interesting instance of the notion of an idea fused with will which Bell, like Aron, tends to identify with ideology.

As befits a sociologist, Bell is concerned not just with the content of ideas but with their social origins, causes, and roles. Thus, in an attempt to locate the sources of ideological thinking, he begins his analysis with a characterological division of the intelligentsia into two main types: (a) the "scholars"; and (b) the "intellectuals." The scholar, as Bell conceives him, "has a bounded field of knowledge, a tradition, and seeks to find his place in it, adding to the accumulated, tested knowledge of the past as to a mosaic." He is, so to say, a "pro" for whom "the show must go on," however and whatever he himself may feel about it. Accepting the scholarly tradition within which he has found a place, he is able to judge himself, or at least his scholarly performance, by impersonal and objective standards. And if he performs with a modicum of efficiency and does not stray beyond the limits of his scholarly "competence," he is entitled to a modicum of self-respect. Indeed, his self-respect, like his role-governed conception of himself, is a function of his assurance of the respect of his peers and, more indirectly, of the society of which his discipline is an established part.

The intellectual, on the other hand, has no such responsibility or security. Lacking a scholarly discipline, perhaps lacking the talent for achievement within such a discipline, which can hold him continuously responsible to "objective" methods and to "facts" wholly independent of himself, his only recourse is an endless dialectic and critique of general ideas. And because he is without a legitimate social role to play within society, he perforce finds himself alienated from its institutions and is left to manipulate his "ideas" in a mood of unrequited and un-focused resentment. He doesn't so much think with his ideas as feel through them. In the discourses of an intellectual, therefore, the thing to look to is not his argument, which, where it exists, is merely a vehicle for his resentments, but rather to the effect which it is meant to induce. He presents his readers not with information but with a goad and with an out-let for their own repressed emotions of estrangement or vio-lence. He may, in the process, tell them something, but it is doing something to them that is his real, if unavowed, aim. For him, the beginning and end of a process of reflection is not a specific problem about objective processes and events; as Pro-fessor Bell charges, he begins always with "*his* experience, *his* perceptions of the world, his privileges and deprivations, and judges the world by these sensibilities." For him, the "world" is not a thing in itself, but rather his will and his idea, and if there is something *there,* in itself, he acknowledges it only as something which he is up against and which exists only in so far as he is up against it. His business, in Marx's words, is not to understand the world, but to change, or better, to over-come it. And if he can't change it in any other way, he may at least reject it, and thus, by an obvious inversion, still show his superiority to it.

In this way, every statement and every discussion becomes for the intellectual an implicitly political move in an endless game of power. Of course he fancies his own moves really to be in the interest (*n. b.*) of "justice" or "freedom," while those of his "opponents," whether they invoke the names of "legiti-macy" or of "law and order," are actually made in the interest of business as usual which it is the function of the established order to protect and to promote. The sad fact remains, however, that the intellectual's power *is* severely limited by the existing system. Hence, in order to maintain the illusion of his freedom or of his power to realize it, he is obliged, as Bell puts it, to embark "upon what William James called 'the faith ladder,' which in its vision of the future cannot distinguish possibilities from probabilities, and converts the latter into certainties."

What is the nature of the conceptual tools with which the "free-floating" and unscholarly intellectual does his work? In order to answer this question, Bell is obliged to move from sociology to logic and semantics. Thus he speaks repeatedly, in terms which I find merely more explicit than Aron's, of ideology as being somehow a "fusion" of thought with emotion or passion which at one and the same time does the trick of "simplify[ing] ideas, establish[ing] a claim to truth, and, in the union of the two, demand[ing] a commitment to action." The result—and it is this which Bell most seriously objects to—is not just a "transformation" of ideas, but also a transformation of people. The typical effect of any ideological argument is, then, a kind of conversion. The road by which the ideologist comes to Damascus doesn't matter; what matters is that he is made to see the light. Says Bell: "Ideology is the conversion of ideas into social levers. Without irony, Max Lerner once entitled a book *Ideas Are Weapons*. This is the language of ideology. It is the commitment to the consequences of ideas."

Bell is rarely more analytical than this, but toward the end of his study he does say one further thing which is at least symptomatic of the point of view which he represents: "If the end of ideology has any meaning, it [sic] is to ask for the end of rhetoric, and rhetoricians, of 'revolution,' of the day when the young French anarchist Vaillant tossed a bomb into the Chamber of Deputies, and the literary critic Laurent Tailhade declared in his defense: 'What do a few human lives matter; it was a *beau geste*.'" The general idea that concerns us here is not the tacit identification of ideology with revolutionary activity, especially of the more bizarre and feckless sort, but rather its identification with rhetoric.

If by "rhetoric" Bell means the use of language in order to persuade or influence others—and many things he says suggest that this is his meaning—then his vision of the end of ideology as an end to rhetoric is a utopian fantasy. Worse, it is an evil fantasy, for it implies a conception of human relations which would deprive us of the right to address one another except for the purpose of comparing notes about matters of fact. Consider what would happen were such a fantasy to come true. In any ordinary sense, it would mean a virtual end to discourse, to communication, and to argument. For it would mean an end to any speech-act addressed to others with a view to their guidance, their instruction, their edification, or their pleasure, with a view, in short, to changing their minds. Indeed, the image of man implicit in Bell's dream of the end of ideology is precisely one of an academic grind or functionary to which he himself, as a counter-ideologist and counter-rhetorician, is fortunately unable to conform.*

* What Bell does not sufficiently emphasize is that the intellectuals' "faith ladders" have indeed converted possibilities into certainties. Otherwise it is hard to see why he and his fellow anti-ideologists make such a hullabaloo about ideology and why they are enthralled with the thought that we have reached the end of the age of ideology. The simple fact is that ever since the French Revolution the intellectuals, with the help of their ideologies, have been moving mountains. And if *their* ideologies are exhausted, as Bell contends, this does not necessarily entail the end of ideology as such. No doubt the old ideologies of the right and the left have lost much of their power to persuade, and no doubt, all over the world, radicalism and intellectualism in our time must inevitably take new forms. But they will persist, by Bell's own analysis, until every intellectual has become a scholar (or worker) and until every scholar becomes a scholar (or worker) merely; that is, until there are no full- or part-time "out-groups" (to employ a fashionable term of sociological analysis) and no general ideas for them to think with. At this point one begins to have visions of an academic utopia within which there are no "free-floating" intellectuals, no alienated, critical minds, such as Professor Bell's, that are not wholly committed to their vocations and that possess an over-plus of energy and passions that is not expended in the conduct of their own "researches." In such a utopia (if I may speak metaphorically) there

The American anti-ideologists, Bell included, regard themselves as pragmatists. However, we should remind ourselves that it is the great pragmatists who have insisted, time out of mind, that ideas have consequences and that, indeed, their operative meaning can only be construed in consequential terms. Rhetoric, from this point of view, is not necessarily a bad or degenerate form of expression; rather it is a dimension of any form of speech which is addressed to others. Furthermore, pragmatism is also a formative theory which asks us to evaluate any form of speech, and hence of rhetoric, in terms of its consequences. The question, therefore, is not whether a discourse persuades or influences other minds and other hearts but how it does so and with what effect. Not every rhetorician is a demagogue. Plato's Socrates professed to despise the Sophists because they were rhetoricians, and this Socrates, I surmise, is the grandfather of all the countless anti-rhetoricians and anti-ideologists from his day to Bell's. But it should not be forgotten that Socrates himself was a master rhetorician and that his admirers ignore the fact because they believe his cause was just. Moreover, Socrates was not only a lover of truth; he was also, politically, a reactionary whose hatred of the Sophists was directed not only to their rhetoric but also to their liberal, democratic, and plebeian political and social attitudes. In saying this, I do not mean to attack our latter-day anti-ideologists by innuendo. I do mean to say that the plain effect of *their* rhetoric is to reinforce acceptance of our own institutional status quo and to declass those "intellectuals" who seek to modify in any radical way the fundamental structures of "Western" political life.

---

would be no New York and no Concord, but only a series of semi-urban centers for semi-advanced study for semi-advanced scholars who would sternly deny themselves the use of any concept or the affirmation of any statement whose "practical bearings" cannot be shown to lie wholly within the range of their legitimate scholarly activity or work. Such a utopia, I fancy, would have no place even for counter-ideologists like Professor Bell whose own "restless vanity" (the phrase is his) is evidently not sated by the rewards that accrue from the performance of his scholarly labors.

There remains a secondary sense of the term "rhetoric" which Bell may also have in mind. In this sense, rhetoric means eloquence. So conceived, the demand for an end to rhetoric is tantamount to a request for plain talk and, so to say, for an age of prose. So far so good. But there may be more to it than this. Elsewhere Bell harps upon the theme that "Throughout their history, Americans have had an extraordinary talent for compromise in politics and extremism in morality." It is plain that Bell is repelled by "this moralism," though, I gather, not so much because it is hypocritical but rather because, as moral, it is uncompromising. "The saving grace, so to speak, of American politics, as that all sorts of groups were tolerated, and the system of the 'deal' became the pragmatic counterpart of the philosophic principle of toleration. But in matters of manners, morals, and conduct—particularly in the small towns—there has been a ferocity of blue-nosed attitudes unmatched by other countries." And again, "It has been one of the glories of the United States that politics has always been a pragmatic give-and-take rather than a series of wars-to-the-death." Of course this last is *not* true. Among our national "glories" have been a war for independence and a civil war, both of them (among other things) wars of principle. Our periods of "give-and-take" have usually also been periods of drift and complacency which have ended in orgies of political corruption and degradation. In one domain, however, Bell believes that our underlying political "postures" have not been "pragmatic." "One of the unique aspects of American politics is that . . . foreign policy has always been phrased in moralistic terms. Perhaps the very nature of our emergence as an independent country forced us to constantly adopt a moral posture in regard to the rest of the world; perhaps being distant from the real centers of interest conflict allowed us to employ pieties, rather than face realities. But since foreign policy has usually been within the frame of moral rather than pragmatic discourse, the debate in the fifties became centered in moral terms."

These passages are typical. In asking for an end to rhetoric, what Bell appears to be calling for is, among other things, an end to *moral* discourse and a beginning of consistent "pragmatic discourse" in every sphere of political life. What does this mean? So far as I can make out, it means an end to judgment and to principle, to praise and to blame, in the political domain and a beginning of plain, unvarnished "politicking" in the name of our "realistic" national, social, or individual "interests." It means, in effect, that in political discourse two and only *two* forms of expression are to be regarded as legitimate: (a) realistic, verifiable statements of fact; and (b) bald, undisguised expressions of first-personal (singular or plural) interest. On such a view, one would be permitted to say, "I don't like segregation and I will try—without, however, upsetting the apple cart—to do what I can to limit segregationalist practices," but not "Segregation as an affront to the humanity of the Negro people," or, "Those who practice segregation are unfair and unjust." What is wrong with moral, as distinct from "pragmatic," discourse? It is not to be doubted that moral discourse is more eloquent and more incitive, and in this sense more rhetorical, than the "pragmatic" forms of speech which Bell prefers. But what is wrong with eloquence *per se?* No doubt it should not be used to cloud an issue, to obscure relevant facts, or to promote unreason. But this is no more a necessary consequence of moral discourse than of any other form of eloquence. Without eloquence, especially in times of crisis, few great political movements would succeed. In fact, eloquence, including the eloquence of moral judgment, is native to the language of politics, and particularly so, as Bell himself admits, in democratic societies where persuasion of the great masses is a condition of success. Thus to put an end to eloquence would be to put an end, not only to "moralism" (which is usually nothing more than the morality of those with whom we disagree) and to "ideology," but also to any form of politics in which great issues are stated or argued in terms of human rights and responsibilities and in which it is essential to gain the approval of the people, or their representatives, before any fundamental change in governmental policy is made. Perhaps a tightly knit, self-interested, and all-powerful elite might get along (among its members) with "pragmatic discourse" alone. But despite Bell, democratic politics does not just mean "bargaining between legitimate groups and the search for consensus." It means also a form of politics in which men are governed by, and hence with reference to, principles and ideals—in a word, to morals and to ideology.

But now a word of caution: It is no part of my intention to suggest, much less admit, that ideology and morality *are* rhetoric; the equation is Bell's, not mine. I contend only that if, as is true, ideological discourses are full of rhetoric (in the above senses), there is no reason to deplore the fact. Quite the contrary.

Webster also mentions a third sense (or senses) of "rhetoric" which for our purposes is perhaps the most interesting of all. In this sense, "rhetoric" means "ostentatious or artificial speech." That some ideologists and moralists are ostentatious need not be denied. My own impression, however, is that academic scholars, particularly in some of the more immature sciences of man, are at least as prone to ostentatious speech (and thought) as other intellectuals. Sociology, indeed, might also be defined as the ostentatious science. But except in beautiful women, ostentation is surely a minor vice, and only a fool would write off a whole field of study or an entire form of expression because some of its practitioners, like Molière's learned ladies, tend to give themselves airs.

Artificiality is another matter, which will merit closer scrutiny. Now "artificiality" often connotes a way of doing things which, although not necessarily ostentatious, is mannered, contrived, studied, and "unnatural." On occasion, a rhetoric which is artificial in this sense can be very powerful, as for example, in the poetry of Milton or in the prose of Burke and Macaulay. Among moralists and men of letters one associates it with the conservative wits of the 18th century and with the elaborate courtesy and the elegant banter of Matthew Arnold and his disciples. For obvious reasons, it is not a rhetoric characteristic of revolutionary disciples. In our time one runs into it only occasionally among writers of the right or the right-center. In England, Michael Oakeshott employs it with some effect, as (in another way) do T. S. Eliot and his followers. In this country, some of the so-called southern agrarians, such as Allen Tate, are minor masters of this rhetoric. But I fancy that Tate, at least, is well aware that he is fighting in a lost cause, and his style, like a ruffled cuff, is intended to give us a heightened sense of the fact. To my unaccustomed ears, the Encyclicals of Leo XIII, which are among the modern masterpieces of Catholic ideology, are also effective examples of a rhetoric of this sort. Indeed, it is precisely the impervious, anachronistic artificiality of Leo's prose which makes one realize how remote, for better or worse, is the concessive modernity of his social thought from the radical liberalism of a Bentham or a Mill.

But "artificiality" has another connotation in this context that is more central to our theme. In this sense, I take it, rhetoric is to be contrasted with literal statement. Here I must limit my remarks mainly to political ideology, but what will be said holds also of all ideologies, including those we normally think of as religious or metaphysical. Now political ideology is nothing but political discourse (as distinct from political science) on its most general formative level. It is, that is to say, political discourse insofar as the latter addresses itself, not just to specific, piecemeal reforms, but to the guiding principles, practices, and aspirations by which politically organized societies absolutely or else in certain typical situations, ought to be governed. This being so, political ideologies inevitably include, among their leading articles, statements of general principle or method and expressions of basic attitude, orientation, and concern which, as they stand, are so highly abstract as to appear to many minds preoccupied with day-to-day problems of "practical politics" virtually meaningless. Such statements are of course habitually formulated in terms like "general welfare," "common good," "justice," "equality," "democracy," "security," and the rest.

But these very terms, so natural or even essential, when one is defining and appraising political practices or systems, also tend through over-use to become mere counters which elicit from us the tired, stock response that leaves us, and hence the practices themselves, unchanged. Or worse, because our responses are dull and routine, and hence *practically* of no political importance, we may conclude that all general philosophical discussions of politics are pointless and that one political ideology is just as good—or bad—as any other. What does matter, so we feel, is not what we say or think about "the system," but only what we do within it. And so, by stages, we are led to the conservative conclusion that political manifestoes, declarations of independence, and constitutions (with their embarrassing ideological preambles) make no difference to society as a going concern. In short, so far as we are concerned, ideology is useless verbiage. On the other side, unfortunately, we discover to our dismay that other peoples, politically and intellectually less "advanced" than ourselves, are enflamed, sometimes to the point of revolution, by ideological discourses, fresher and more affecting, in part because less literal and less abstract, than those to which we are accustomed. And to our contempt for our own ineffectual ideological abstractions we now add a positive hatred (or fear) of an ideological rhetoric which suddenly endows those same abstractions with a new life that disturbs our own.

It should be observed, however, that our very hatred is itself a backhanded tribute to the power of ideology. And if, out of a misplaced loyalty to "reason," we merely limit ourselves to "exposing" it, we stand in danger of losing our world. Most of us, realizing that the world is *never* well lost, find ourselves drawn back inescapably into the ideological struggle which, if we are to win it for ends that are right and just, requires that we produce a counter-rhetoric more imaginative, more distinguished, and more durable than that of our opponents. But if, as literalists of the imagination, we still decline to go the whole hog, resorting now only to formal reaffirmation of the old abstract "principles" which no later than yesterday we professed to find meaningless, who will believe us? Why should they? They have heard the same golden words mouthed a thousand times on the party platforms by hacks who have no notion of their meaning. And, if it comes to that, what *do* they mean?

In science it normally suffices to state a fact, and one man may do this as well and as accurately as another. But in the sphere of conduct much more is involved. For here we have to do with matters of attitude and intention and with problems of authenticity, legitimacy, and authority. Here words must not only predict what will be but determine what shall be; they must not only inform but also prepare and initiate lines of action. And what *is* it that is being determined, prepared, and initiated? This, so I contend, can be fully revealed only through the "poetry" which the ideologist may afford us.

Since Plato, rationalists have ever been afraid of poetry. And even those who profess not to be so worried lest "the people" confuse the true poet with the counterfeit. But just as true poetry, known and loved, is the only real protection against the malefactions of pseudo-poets, so also its ideological analogue is the only guarantee against the factitious "myths" of a Rosenberg, a Hitler, or a Mussolini. Our worry, in America, should be not that the false rhetoric of "foreign" ideologies may divert our people from their loyalties to our establishment, but that we do so little to replenish the fund of ideological poetry with which the founding fathers, along with Lincoln and a few others, have provided us. Our contemporary ideology is, or seems to be, all ghost-written. The voice sounds as reedy and hollow as are the men who contrive it. But if we should lose the power both to create and passionately to respond to a great ideological rhetroic, we would also lose the power to tell the difference between the phony and the real thing.

Further, figurative and hence rhetorical language enables, or

compels, men to perform in advance of experience those crucial symbolic actions and imaginative experiments upon
which, as Dewey has persuasively argued, genuinely rational
judgments of practice and of value entirely depend. Know the
truth, and the truth will set you free: how dangerous and how
misleading is this half-truth. How, in a moral and practical
sense, *are* we to know it? I can assent to the proposition that
on the first day of an atomic war every major city in the United
States would be destroyed, without in the least *realizing,* in
human terms, what the statement really means. In order that I
may even remotely grasp such an idea, in absence of the event,
I must somehow try symbolically to live through the horror
and the agony of such a calamity. But this is precisely what the
cold, literal, objective statement of fact does not require me to
do. To this end, therefore, it is essential that I find a way of
thinking and talking about the fact which will make me realize from a practical, and even, if you please, from a metaphysical point of view, what it comes to. For most of us, this can be
done only through the artificial linguistic devices, known to
every reader of fiction and of poetry, which enable us to perform "in imagination," as we say, those symbolic actions in
which alone the "reality" of *literary* art exists. To disdain
"rhetoric," therefore, is to disdain the very condition through
which full practical understanding and judgment is possible.
And to deny oneself its use is not to guarantee the preservation
of scientific "objectivity" but to preclude the possibility of
really being objective in trying to decide, in political terms,
what one's way of life is to be.

It remains to say a word about "simplism," that final bogey
of the anti-ideological mentality. Through rhetoric, according
to Bell, ideology infuses ideas with passion, thus, as might be
expected, winning friends and influencing people. But the
principal underhanded intellectual (or is it, too, rhetorical?)
trick of the ideologists is to "simplify ideas." It therefore seems
necessary to remind the anti-ideologist that simplification, so

far from being a fault peculiar to ideology, is, as William
James well knew, a large part of the saving virtue of rationality itself. To oppose simplism on principle, in politics as in
every other sphere of activity, is not to make a legitimate demand for recognition of the complexities and diversities of political life, but, in effect, to ask for an abandonment of policy
and a fatal acquiescence in the drift of events. For simplification is an essential feature of any rational initiation of action.
To refuse to simplify when one confronts a problem is in effect
to reject the obligation to reach a solution; it is to make a
game of possibilities and hence to move automatically outside
the context of agency and choice. Every procedure that helps
us to make decisions does so precisely by reducing the range of
possibilities which we may reasonably be expected to consider.
And every method, in setting a limit to the considerations that
ought to be taken into account, thereby secures our deliberations against an endless spread of doubts.

On this score particularly, Professor Bell seems merely dis-
ingenuous when he tells us—incidentally letting a fair-sized
ideological cat out of his own elastic bag—that although
"There is now more than ever some need for utopia, in the
sense that men need—as they have always needed—some vision of their potential, some manner of fusing passion with
intelligence. . . . The ladder to the City of Heaven can no
longer be a 'faith ladder,' but an empirical one; a utopia has to
specify *where* one wants to go, *how* to get there, the costs of
the enterprise, and some realization of, and justification for the
determination of *who* is to pay." There is a rather terrible
irony in the fact that Bell, who in other contexts is so prone to
rail against those who think in terms of all or none, should
find it so hard at this point to think in terms of degree. Were
one seriously to try, in detail and at the outset, to meet all his
requirements for a "good" utopia, the magnitude and complexity of the task would paralyze thought. The "good" utopian,
like the unholy ideologist, must settle for considerably less if
he is ever to bring his deliberations to a conclusion. And if he

eventually does reach a conclusion, then no matter how long he reflects and however precise his calculations, it will have been conceived in sin. For it will always reflect a radical simplification of the possibilities and the alternatives which a more scrupulous utopian would think it obligatory to consider.

But Bell's advocacy of even his "good" utopia is, at best, half-hearted. For he really has no faith in any long-range scheme aimed at the amelioration of society as a whole. "Ideology," he tells us, "makes it unnecessary for people to confront individual issues on their individual merits." But in one sense this is true of any rule, any procedure, and any plan, including the plans of piecemeal social engineers like Bell and Popper. What would be the point of any such scheme, however limited in its scope, unless it relieved us of the necessity of confronting every blessed individual issue on its (otherwise) individual merits? And if it comes to that, what is an "individual issue," and what is it to confront one on its "individual merits"? Is the issue of desegregation, for example, one such issue or is it many? Indeed, is the issue of desegregating one individual classroom in one individual school in one God-forsaken county of the state of Mississippi an individual issue? And if it is, what, pray, are *its* individual merits? How far do these extend?

One of the overwhelming advantages of a bill of human rights (which is nothing but a schedule of enforced ideological commitments), is that it drastically reduces the number of "issues" over which men in societies must continue to quarrel. In this way it reduces the terrible wear and tear of political life which, even in the best-run societies, is nearly unendurable. Bell and his allies, following Popper (and at a distance Bergson), are admirers of the "open society." But of course a completely open society, if such ever existed, would be not a society, but a chaos. If an "open society" is one in which each individual issue is decided, *ad hoc,* on its own peculiar merits, then who wants an "open society"? And if a "closed society" is one in which, owing to the presence of a prevailing ideology (or constitution), many issues are, in any practical sense, dead issues, why then let us by all means continue to have a closed society. Were we Americans seriously to invoke the principle that individual cases should be settled exclusively on their (otherwise) individual merits, we would have to repudiate our Declaration of Independence and to dismantle our whole constitutional system and the characteristic rule of law which it provides.

Is this what the anti-ideologists want? The question is by no means merely "rhetorical." Consider, for example, what that most determined and most consistent of anti-ideologists, Professor Michael Oakeshott, has to say about the Declaration of Independence. It is, he tells us, "A characteristic product of the *saeculum rationalisticum*. It represents the politics of the felt need interpreted with the aid of an ideology. And it is not surprising that it should have become one of the sacred documents of the politics of Rationalism, and, together with the similar documents of the French Revolution, the inspiration and pattern of many later adventures in the rationalistic reconstruction of Society." Whatever else may be true of Professor Oakeshott, he at least knows an ideology when he sees one and is candid enough to say so. It would clear the air if his fellow anti-ideologists on this side of the Atlantic would speak as clearly and unequivocally.

Let us no longer mince words. Our own anti-ideological foxes are no more "empirical" and no less rhetorical than their leonine opponents; they are, on broad issues, merely more indecisive and more eclectic. As it stands, their point of view is so lacking both in consistency and in clarity that, as I have discovered at some cost, it is virtually impossible to argue with them without fear of doing them some frightful injustice. Still, out of a sophisticated but paralyzing fear of over-simplification, they have managed to fashion a kind of counter-ideology, or fetish, of complexity, difficulty, and uniqueness. They tell us that "the present belongs to the living" and that we should lift from our shoulders "the heavy hand of the future" as well as "the dead hand of the past." Yet they evidently have not the courage to say that the preamble to the American Constitution, which speaks among other things of securing the "Blessings of Liberty to ourselves *and our Posterity,*" is so much wicked ideological flourish and moonshine. Their "pluralism" has become a kind of mania which, when pressed to its own counter-ideological extremes, leads inescapably (as William James long ago perceived) to anarchism and, at last, to nihilism. Were their political and social attitudes generally to prevail in the West—and it is primarily of the West that they speak in talking of the end of ideology—the result would be a pessimistic *carpe diem* philosophy which would render us helpless in the world struggle against the ideology of Communism. At home, in the political parties, in the Congress, and in the courts, it continually weakens what remains of our national commitment to the ideological principles that animate our constitutional system; in the Presidency, it provides merely the covering excuses for a spate of uncorrelated, "piecemeal" moves which, however admirable from a tactical point of view and however skillful as "pragmatic" politics, result in an ever increasing loss of basic political control and social direction. Curiously, the over-all picture is one of Hegelian "gray on gray." The only difference is that unlike our anti-ideologists Hegel knew that gray on gray is the color of barrenness, of late autumn and approaching winter.

DANIEL BELL
AND
HENRY DAVID AIKEN

Ideology—a Debate*

DANIEL BELL: Define your terms, the philosophers enjoin us. One of the difficulties with Henry David Aiken's essay, "The Revolt Against Ideology," is the multiplicity of senses in which he uses the word "ideology," as well as the ambiguity of his prescriptions. He begins by citing with approval the Marxian conception that ideologies are "inverted images of reality" —ideas falsely divorced from the material conditions that produce them—and that the function of social analysis is to "de-mythologize ideology"; and he concludes—no longer mincing words!—by saying that persons like myself, who talk of the "end of ideology," would "render us helpless in the world struggle against the ideology of Communism" and weaken "what remains of our national commitment to the ideological principles that animate our constitutional system."

Now, since I accept a Marxian conception of ideology as the starting point for analysis, and since I call myself a pragmatist (as does Mr. Aiken), I am puzzled by the transitions through which I end up as subversive of my own ideals, if not of my

* Reprinted from *Commentary* (October 1964) by permission; Copyright © 1964 by The American Jewish Committee.

country's. Let me therefore indicate what I mean by the "end of ideology," and later confront Mr. Aiken himself directly.

The Marxian discussion of ideology flows from the concern with alienation. But the context is as broad as the "human condition" itself. The root of it all is in man's unhappy awareness of a divided consciousness, and his yearning or search for an Absolute. In Christian terms, man is separated from God and searches for re-unification through the figure of Christ. For Hegel, religious alienation is but one aspect of a cosmic drama in which everything is rent by duality—spirit and matter, nature and history, God and man—and the "realization," or the "end of philosophy," will occur when all dualities are overcome, when man no longer is both subject and object, or lives between society and State.

Marx's great vision provided a naturalistic foundation for the Hegelian drama. The source of man's duality, he said, lay not in thought but in the division of labor and in the social classes. The "realization" of philosophy, in other words, lay in economics, and the agency of human fulfillment was not the Idea but the Proletariat. The unity of "thought and being," the union of appearance and reality, and the end of all ideology (a phrase, as Lewis Feuer reminds us that was first used by Engels in his essay on Feuerbach) would come, said Marx, when man finally conquered material necessity and began living in a purposeful, self-directed community.

Marxism itself, however, became an ideology with the assumption, to be found in Marx's later work as well as in the vulgarization of his thoughts by Engels, that there was a single key to the "realization" of philosophy—the abolition of private property. Abolish private property, and all exploitation would disappear. As Communist apologists later put in, there could be no classes and exploitation in the Soviet Union because there was no private property in Soviet society.

It is necessary to emphasize some distinctions in order to focus the questions that divide us. Originally, "ideology" simply meant sense impression; in opposition to the rationalists, the ideologues sought to "purify" ideas by accepting only those which come through the senses. For Marx, "ideology" referred to beliefs which masked private interests; thus, such doctrines as natural rights, with their claim to a universal transcendental validity, were really constructed to justify the needs of the bourgeoisie. Among the specific examples of ideology that Marx gives (in the essays on *The Jewish Question*) are the guarantees of property rights in the various state constitutions of the United States. In the 20th century, "ideology" acquired a broader and more impassioned meaning. As the political struggles of the age took on the intensity of the earlier religious wars, the word came to denote in politics what the terms "creed" or "faith" had meant in religion.

During its crusading Bolshevik phase, Marxism became a *total* ideology. As I used the term: "A *total* ideology is an all-inclusive system of comprehensive reality, it is a set of beliefs, infused with passion, and seeks to transform the whole of a way of life. This commitment to ideology—the yearning for a 'cause' or the satisfaction of deep moral feelings—is *not* necessarily the reflection of interests in the shape of ideas. Ideology . . . in the sense used here is a secular religion."

Those of us who speak of the "end of ideology" mainly mean to reject this mode of commitment, which had such a disastrous effect on the thoughts and politics of the radical and utopian movements of the past two generations. As developed by such writers as Raymond Aron, Edward Shils, C.A.R. Crosland, and S.M. Lipset, the theme of the "end of ideology" has become a call for an end to apocalyptic beliefs that refuse to specify the costs and consequences of the changes they envision. The "end-of-ideology" school (if a school it is) is skeptical of rationalistic schemes that assume they can blueprint the entire life of a society; it argues that the existing political tags "conservative" and "liberal" have lost their intellectual clarity; it is critical of existing institutions, but it does not accept the assumption that social change is *necessarily* an improvement.

In short, it is pragmatic in the triple sense in which Dewey used the term: it defines the consequence of an action as a constitutive element of the truth of a proposition; it assumes the inextricable relation of ends and means; and it believes that values, like any empirical proposition, can be tested on the basis of their claims.

Now the curious thing is that none of this history—either of the term "ideology" or of the background of radicalism—is reflected in Mr. Aiken's discussion of ideology. He does not say whether these judgments on the past were wrong or right. He treats the word "ideology" only as a formal problem for analysis. The reason, perhaps, is that he is out to make a case—a lawyer's case, not a philosopher's case—and he goes at it in the best lawyer's manner.

The central point in his discussion of my own contribution to the theme is his analysis of the word "rhetoric." I wrote: "If the 'end of ideology' has any meaning, it is to ask for the end of rhetoric, and rhetoricians, or 'revolution,' of the day when the young French anarchist Vaillant tossed a bomb into the Chamber of Deputies and the literary critic Laurent Tailhade declared in his defense: 'What do a few human lives matter; it was a *beau geste!*' "

After quoting this passage, Mr. Aiken comments: "If by 'rhetoric' Bell means the use of language in order to persuade or influence others—and many things suggest that this is his meaning—then his vision of the end of ideology as an end to rhetoric is a utopian fantasy. Worse, it is an evil fantasy, for it implies a conception of human relations which would deprive us of the right to address one another except for the purposes of comparing notes about matters of fact."

I submit that the two paragraphs have nothing to do with each other. I was calling attention to the *distortion* of the discourse of persuasion—after all, what is a bomb?—rather than its classical use. The "end of rhetoric," in the context I gave it, plainly means an end to a way of thinking and acting which substitutes the worship of the Word—the verbal faith of Revolution—for a moral analysis of consequences. If the fetishism of commodities is the "secret" of capitalism, is not the fetishism of rhetoric—the reliance on political slogans—the "secret" of radicalism? *

Next: I wrote that American life has suffered from an excess of "moralism." My examples were the small-town fundamentalist restrictions on personal conduct; McCarthyism—an extension of such moralizing in politics; and the formulation of foreign policy from one administration to the next in moralistic terms. (And, one can now say, the political rhetoric of Barry Goldwater.)

Writes Mr. Aiken: "In asking for an end to rhetoric, what Bell appears to be calling for is, among other things, an end to *moral* discourse and a beginning of consistent 'pragmatic discourse' in every sphere of political life. What does this mean? So far as I can make out, it means *an end to judgment and to principle* [my italics], to praise and to blame, in the political domain and a beginning of plain, unvarnished 'politicking' in the name of our 'realistic' national, social, or individual 'interests.' "

Again I call foul, this time at the shift from *moralistic* to *moral*. Moralizing, or being moralistic, is a distortion of the moral code. It is the "ideological" use of morality for the sake of a hidden purpose.

As it happens, I do believe in "pragmatic discourse"; but is pragmatic discourse without principle? Isn't Locke's *Letter on Toleration* a form of pragmatic discourse? Isn't Kant's distinction between public and private—one the realm of agreed-upon procedure, the other the realm of conscience—a pragmatic one in its context? Pragmatic discourse in politics emphasizes the search for a reasoned consensus, rather than treating political issues as a war-to-the-death. It involves an "ethic of respon-

* Even sillier is Mr. Aiken's next comment: "There remains a second sense of the term 'rhetoric' which Bell *may also have in mind*. [Italics mine.] In this sense, rhetoric means eloquence. So conceived, the demand for an end to rhetoric is tantamount to a request for plain talk, and, so to say, for the age of prose." Now really!

sibility," but as Richard McKeon has pointed out, "responsibility is determined by the reciprocities in the actions of men." Where there is no reciprocity, conflict may—and at times should—develop. Between a racist and myself there is no reciprocity; between a Nazi and myself there is no reciprocity; between a Communist and myself there is no reciprocity. But where there is, or can be, an acceptance of the rules of the game—of the process of open discourse and reciprocity—there *should be* social compromise. Is this not judgment—and principle?

What is the lawyer's case that Mr. Aiken is seeking to make? On the one hand, it is a cumbersome theoretical formulation; on the other, a simplified political point.

Mr. Aiken writes: "Now political ideology is nothing but political discourse . . . on its most general formative level. It is, that is to say, political discourse insofar as the latter addresses itself, not just to specific, piecemeal reforms, but to the guiding principles, practices, and aspirations by which politically organized societies, absolutely or else in certain typical situations, ought to be governed. . . . Here words must not only predict what will be but determine what shall be; they must not only inform but also prepare and initiate lines of action. And what *is* it that is being determined, prepared, and initiated? This, so I contend, can be fully revealed only through the 'poetry' which the ideologist may afford us."

Here Mr. Aiken completely muddies the waters. For he has simply taken an old-fashioned definition of *political philosophy* and arbitrarily called it—despite the tortuous history of the word—*political ideology*. In fact a number of writers today —usually conservative ones who ask for a return to first principles, have decried the absence of political philosophy in the schools, charging modern political theory with "scientism." By calling for political ideology, Mr. Aiken has given us a stylish way of posing the problem. But otherwise the only gain is confusion.

His political barb is more pointed: "I do not mean to attack our latterday anti-ideologists by innuendo. I do mean to say that the plain effect of *their* rhetoric is to reinforce acceptance of our institutional status quo, and to declass those 'intellectuals' who seek to modify in any radical way the fundamental structures of 'Western' political life."

If you set up a straw man, it will burn brightly when you put a match to it. As in so much of Mr. Aiken's essay, there is a fine resonance but an astonishing lack of specificity in these statements. I don't know what Mr. Aiken regards as the "fundamental structures of 'Western' political life." To my mind, the fundamental structure is the democratic process, and this I do not want to change. To speak further for myself, since the question of political identification is at issue, I am a democratic socialist, and have been for almost all of my politically conscious years. As such, I wish to see a change in the fundamental structures of our economic life. I deplore the social and economic power of the corporation. I detest the cult of efficiency which sacrifices the worker to the norms of productivity. I favor national planning in the economy. I want to see more public enterprise. And I want to introduce other criteria than those of the market or the private profit motive as means of allocating resources in the society. I have guiding general principles, rooted in conceptions about the nature of work and community which shape these views. But I also have a test which guides the introduction of these changes; and I think the differences between Mr. Aiken and me on this question are the nub of the issue.

I wrote: "There is now more than ever some need for utopia, in the sense that men need—as they have always needed—some vision of their potential, some manner of fusing passion with intelligence. . . . The ladder to the City of Heaven can no longer be a 'faith ladder,' but an empirical one; a utopia has to specify *where* one wants to go, *how* to get there, the costs of the enterprise, and some realization of, and justification for, the determination of *who* is to pay."

To this, Mr. Aiken retorts: "Were one seriously to try, in detail and at the outset, to meet all his requirements for a 'good' utopia, the magnitude and complexity of the task would paralyze thought."

I find it hard to understand these remarks. The context of my discussion was quite clear. I pointed out that Lenin instigated the Russian Revolution with no idea at all of the meaning of planning or socialization (other than the simple-minded notion, expressed in *State and Revolution,* that the entire economy would be run like a single enterprise), and that the lives of millions of people were thus committed on the basis of an abstract promise. Or, to take another example: when Stalin decided in 1929 on the ruthless collectivization of agriculture in line with the ideological premise that individual peasant property should be eliminated, was not the question of costs and consequences relevant? Or again to bring the issue closer to home: if an urban renewal program bulldozes a neighborhood in response to the liberals' ideological image of "slum clearance," should one not apply tests of the consequence of this action for community life?

Does Mr. Aiken want to build a bridge to the future without any tests of costs and consequences? His fear is that such a demand would inhibit all change. But why? Is it really so difficult? Have we no resources at all in sociological and economic knowledge to assess the social costs of change? Surely we know enough by now about the effects of social change—the devastation in the depressed areas, the school dropouts, the manifold impact of automation—to understand what our *failure* to plan has cost.

But all this is bootless, for I am asking Mr. Aiken to be concrete, and he is relentlessly abstract. Yet if the debate is to have any meaning, if Mr. Aiken wants to be radical, let him state in detail what he wants to be radical about. Then we can argue about whether it is desirable or not, and what criteria we should use. But is it not the mark of the ideologue that he is usually so general and vague?

From past experience as well as from this exchange, I feel that what is really involved here is not a conflict of intellectual positions but a conflict of contrasting temperaments. Once upon a time there was a primary and meaningful tension between the orthodox and the antinomians. The orthodox, whether priests, clerks, or scholars, believed in a ritual or a tradition, a set of "right" beliefs, which were enforced in varying degrees on the society. The antinomians—gnostics, vagabonds, bohemians, rebels—resisted institutional authority, were defiant of tradition, law, and system, and sought to guide their lives by esoteric standards of conduct.

Such divisions used to be clear. But the history of the past several hundred years has seen the absorption, or containment, of heresy. Religious antinomianism and "enthusiastic" movements became orthodoxies after the Reformation. The aesthetic rebellion that emerged after 1885 was largely drained into politics in the 1920s and 1930s, as seen most markedly in the movement of the Dadaist leaders—Aragon, Tzara, and Iluard—into the Communist party. And the most subterranean of traditions, which runs from de Sade through Lautréamont to Genet and Burroughs, is today publicly acclaimed by the chic avant-garde and its camp-followers.

The point of all this is that the currently fashionable talk about Establishments and anti-Establishments, of cultural radicalism and the official academy, is substantially meaningless. What is one to make of the state of cultural criticism when Harold Rosenberg attacks F.R. Leavis as a cultural fascist in the columns of the *New Yorker* and Richard Poirier defends Leavis in the pages of *The New York Review of Books?* In *Playboy* sexual radicalism is "philosophically" intertwined with economic free enterprise; in the *Herald Tribune,* Leslie Fiedler explains the avant-garde to the stockbrokers. The notion that Mr. Aiken is a critic of society and that I am not, that Norman

Podhoretz is a radical and Lionel Trilling a "revisionist liberal," makes no sense. Today our entire society is committed to change, and in a direction which was first pointed out by the Left. In the realm of "culture" the ramparts have been manned, and each is at the station perhaps appropriate to his distinction: Harold Rosenberg is at the *New Yorker,* Norman Mailer and Dwight Macdonald at *Esquire,* Alfred Chester at *Book Week,* Seymour Krim at *Nugget,* Nicholas Calas at the *Village Voice;* and Paul Goodman is almost in the academy. Everyone is happily playing the heretic in the fields of official clover and busily exposing the nakedness of everyone else.

The shock of change, though, is real enough: the realization that escapes no one is that the egalitarian and socially mobile society which the "free-floating intellectuals" associated with the Marxist tradition have been calling for during the last hundred years has finally emerged in the form of our cumbersome, bureaucratic mass society, and has in turn engulfed the heretics. With this realization begins the process of disengagement. But it is not generally a process of responsible social thought and self-scrutiny, not an attempt to find out what kind of institutional structures in a large-scale society will best accommodate the older visions of community and individual freedom and self-determination. One simply labels oneself a radical, calls for (but rarely produces) utopian thought, and argues that the great need is to be "critical." Such disengagement is, quite simply, an escape from intellectual responsibility. Mr. Aiken's essay, with its abstract talk of moral discourse, provides a lovely cover for such an escape.

But if the old division of political temperaments into orthodox and antinomian has apparently broken down, there is still perhaps some usefulness in a three-part classification: the ideologues, the moralists, and the skeptics.

Ideologies, as organized systems of belief with ready formulas for the manipulation of the masses, are, in effect, new orthodoxies. The yearning for an ideology, the hunger for a cause, the craving for belief often mask the conformist's desire for power or the rebel's unconscious need to submit to authority. Such a reductive analysis, of course, risks the traducing of individuals who may be genuinely motivated to serve mankind selflessly or to search for new means of implementing their ideals. However, the judgment itself is not of persons but of the nature of ideologies, and of the way in which the "functional necessities" of organizing and implementing ideologies traduce all idealism.

To go back to Marx's original sense of the term, an ideology is an illusion, a false consciousness. Or, as Philip Rieff has recently remarked, "only an illusory history, or an illusory religion, or an illusory politics, could lead humans to the therapy of commitment." The yearning for a cause, for some transcendent purpose, is, of course, one of the deepest impulses of the sentient human being. The danger, always, is that this impulse will be manipulated in ways that betray its idealism. Such seductions are rarely overt or crude. It is usually the apocalyptic element, the call for a last act of violence in order to end violence, of a final deed of murder to eliminate murder, which is the agency of the ideologue's betrayal. In the dialectic of betrayal, means become ends and justifications of themselves.

Then there are those often lonely protestants who have stood outside the corridors of ideology or the pathways of power, and have spoken as moralists. In the tradition of prophecy, the moralists, on the basis of conscience, call injustice to account. In his tone and in his wrath, Mr. Aiken strikes me as a quondam moralist—which makes me all the more puzzled by his present effort to patch shreds of ideology into an intellectual argument. He does so, as I have pointed out, only by tearing the word "ideology" from its historical and sociological context, and by arbitrarily identifying it with political philosophy and moral discourse.

But why not speak directly in the language of morals and

ethics? I can account for this failure only by the fact that the religious tradition—which has been the foundation of prophecy—has itself been undermined, and that the moralist has consequently lost much of his basis of judgment. Jeremiah and Deutero-Isaiah could call for a return to tradition, a departure from the merely ritualistic observance of the law; but what can Mr. Aiken ask us to return to? The modern moralist can become either an existentialist or an ideologue, and the option now seems to be running in the latter direction.

Most skeptics, I suppose, are lapsed ideologues. This, in turn, may explain why the theme of the "end of ideology" has so often had a negative side. It began as a recoil from the easy optimism of "illusory politics" and found its texts in such documents of disillusionment as John Milton's *Ready and Easy Way* and Alexander Herzen's *Letters from the Other Shore*. Skepticism does have its dangers—it can lead to cynicism, quietism, or despair.

Where the theme of the "end of ideology" is currently most relevant is in Eastern Europe, among the intellectuals who have experienced at first hand the deadening effects of an official ideology, and among the young generation for whom ideology is simply flatulent rhetoric. (It is curious that Mr. Aiken seems to assume that ideology is always nascent and passionate, and neglects its more pervasive role as a coercive, official force.) In a recent issue of *Survey,* a Czech writer describes the calloused attitude to politics of those who have grown up in an ideological regime: "A strange, frightening breed, this new generation, these men and women born during the last war or even later, who never knew any other social order and who are the products of our society. Purposeful, tough, smart, resourceful in handling their own affairs, down-to-earth, uncommunicative outside their own group, full of obvious pity for their fathers and their ridiculous manoeuvers, full of energy to get the best out of life now and for themselves.

"To them, ideology and politics and, indeed, any form of

public activity are a lot of bunk, just hollow words with little relation to reality. Not that they are anti-Communists, a meaningless term in their ears: they just could not care less. They were born into socialism and they live in socialism and what they see around *is* socialism. Pretty dull and shabby, and certainly nothing much to write home about. . . .

"If there is still to come the final ignominy of a burial of Marxism-Leninism as we understand it today, it will be effortlessly carried out by these generations already born into socialism. And so it should be! For I believe that these young people, these young socialists will at last realize, because of what we did, that there is no socialism without freedom and that life is far more important than ideology."

The intention, then, of the "revolt against ideology" is not to make one insensitive to injustice or to the need for a transcendent moral vision. It is, rather, to make one wary of the easy solution and to deny that any embodiment of community is final. I once wrote that one of the tragedies of Marxism was that Marx, having provided a naturalistic explanation of the meaning of alienation, then narrowed the concept by locating its source entirely in the rule of private property. As we know now, to our sorrow, there are other, more debasing forms of degradation and dehumanization—the systems of totalitarianism—than economic exploitation.

However, the thinking connected with the "end of ideology" is not directed against Marxism or any other radical creed; nor does it involve a quarrel with utopianism and its visions. What it does is give us a perspective on modern history which emphasizes that the achievement of freedom and the defense of the individual constitute a permanent revolution; and it tells us that this revolution resists any final definition. It is for the sake of individual freedom that the claims of doubt must always take precedence over the claims of faith, and that the commitment to action must proceed from the ethic of responsibility.

HENRY DAVID AIKEN: On the whole Mr. Bell's reply confirms my earlier impression of the essential intellectual and spiritual confusion of the anti-ideology movement, the poverty of its ideas, and its total lack of a coherent, substantive social and political philosophy that goes a step beyond reaffirmation of shibboleths about which both of our major political parties (at least until Goldwater's ascendancy) have been in all-too-complete agreement for a generation.

There is, to be sure, one small part that doesn't quite jibe with this impression, but it is so curiously, almost touchingly, inconsistent with the remainder that I can only wonder about the degree of Mr. Bell's self-awareness in mentioning it. Specifically, he says that he has been a "democratic socialist for almost all of [his] . . . politically conscious years." Can he be serious? In other writings, including *The End of Ideology,* he has opted emphatically and without qualification for "the mixed economy"—which, of course, no socialist could accept save as a temporary stop-gap.

Socialism, I take it, is above all the position that at least the control and operation of the means of production, distribution, and exchange should be in the hands of society as a whole rather than of private individuals, groups, or corporations. Actively to take steps to bring about socialism in the United States would at once involve Mr. Bell (or anyone else) in a very sharp and deep disensus, both politically and ideologically, with the great majority of the American people, including virtually the whole industrial-business-governmental-scholarly establishment. In this country the existing democracy, or republic, is for practical purposes incompatible with socialism. And just for that reason, as S. M. Lipset, Mr. Bell's ally, has pointed out, socialism is here politically and ideologically a dead issue. Mr. Bell knows this. He must realize therefore that being a socialist in America is, for most men, rather like being a Christian; it is entirely safe to be one because socialism, for all but a revolutionary few, is outside the bounds of political possibility. In short, Mr. Bell's "socialism," the wishful and wistful sincerity of which we need not question, is, in Marx's sense, entirely utopian, and hence practically and functionally meaningless. Mr. Bell often has written perceptively and relevantly about sources of alienation among American workers. But what has he to offer, as a *socialist,* toward its drastic alleviation? I submit: nothing, or next to nothing. Here is precisely the sort of ideological schizophrenia which, in part, my essay was designed to expose.

But let me at once remove a possible source of misconception. Mr. Bell has spoken for himself; as for me, I am not a Marxist, vestigial revisionist, or otherwise. My fundamental intellectual and moral antecedents are British American, and Jewish. And although I mean always to speak of Marx *and* Engels with respect, I find it hard to understand how Mr. Bell could have gained the impression that my "citing" [*sic*] of the Marxist conception of ideology as "inverted images of reality" was meant to be approving.

However this may be, let me say for the record that I consider the Marxist (and hence Bellean) theory of ideology itself as at once vague, confused, programatic, and useful nowadays only for purposes of popular polemicizing. On this score, Lenin's theory of ideology is surprisingly better, since it freely acknowledges Marxism to be an ideology, and since it perceives that, in general, ideology can be properly conceived, not in aprioristic, metaphysically pejorative terms, but functionally and dynamically as a form of thought which, for better or for worse, is meant to focus, guide, and energize the minds (and bodies) of men in society. As Lenin saw, it is the role, not the content, which determines whether a theory or doctrine is working ideologically. Thus, in the context of social action, scientific theories, philosophical doctrines, religious creeds, and even sociological statistics, may all serve an ideological role, just as well, or better, than ideas that are or are supposed to be, "inverted images of reality." And let me add, finally, lest again I be misunderstood, that I am not remotely a Leninst either—

although, in justice, I am bound to say that, after Marx himself, Lenin remains the most interesting and suggestive among Marxist thinkers. Lenin is, above all, an institutionalist in his approach to the problems and tasks of socialism, which is precisely what Bell is not. Alas, it was my reading of Lenin that, ironically, convinced me that world socialism is probably a utopian dream.

Mr. Bell's own variations on a theme by Marx are, from my point of view, conceptually and historically regressive, polemically misleading, and ultimately (when taken seriously) debilitating so far as the causes of the alienated, the disenfranchised, and the disinherited are concerned. Moreover, they leave our "confrontation," as Mr. Bell calls it, quite unaffected —except insofar as they inadvertently help to show (what I myself earlier pointed out) that the anti-ideologists, and especially Mr. Bell, are in effect merely quasi-Marxian conservatives who have done little or nothing to advance the master's theory of ideology, but on the contrary have merely applied his ideas rather mechanically and obviously to Communism itself in defense of the primary political and social status quo in the "free world." My contention was—and is—that the anti-ideologists leave us at once morally, intellectually, and, if I may say so, metaphysically helpless in "our" confrontation not only with the Communist world, but also with the great "neutralist" movements that are emerging all over the globe, and especially in the ex-colonial areas where neither socialism nor (political) democracy appears to stand a chance of realization. Now is a time, if there ever was one, for creative and constructive social and political thought. In such a situation what are the anti-ideologists doing, really, but warning us against the dangers of the faith ladder? Well, maybe we just do need a bit of faith in the future of humanity.

Mr. Bell says that pragmatism, at least in Dewey's version, defines "the consequences of an action as a constitutive element of the truth of a proposition." This, I would say, is rather the way Dewey must look under water. I myself think that

Dewey's doctrine of the continuum of means and ends is a notable contribution to moral philosophy. But Mr. Bell makes no genuine use of it; he merely *says* he does. Marx, I may add, was implicitly employing this methodological principle in his own attacks upon utopianism, and especially utopian socialism. Mr. Bell and his "socialist" friends do not employ it; quite the contrary, theirs is a merely ideal, sentimental socialism, untouched by the slightest hesitation about what socialist aspirations can mean in a historical context in which no determinate program exists for realizing it. As for the thesis that "values, like any empirical proposition [*sic*], can be tested on the basis of their claims," it is one of the weirdest attempts at redaction of the Dewey-Hook theory regarding the empirical, or even scientific, verifiability of value judgments that I have yet seen.*

Mr. Bell claims that I treat the word "ideology" only as a formal problem for analysis, and that the reason for this is that I am out to make a lawyer's rather than a philosopher's case. How odd. Well, I did mean to make a case, the best I knew how to make. And it is all the same to me how Mr. Bell chooses to classify it, so long as it is, as he allows, "the best" of its kind. As a means to a moral and ideological end, I was and am interested in the "formal" problem which the word "ideology" presents to the logical analyst, although Mr. Bell at the outset appears to deny this when he complains that I do not "define" ideology. It was not my purpose to define it but to study and to characterize what other people, including Mr. Bell, seem to think about it. I tried to determine what Mr. Bell might be taken to mean and then to show that, once *his* rhetoric was stripped to its fighting weight, even his notions of ideology did not commit him, or us, to an across-the-board attack upon ideology as such. Again, I suggested that all ideolo-

---

* Anyone interested in why I consider this theory indefensible can find the reason in my essays on Hook and Dewey, *Commentary,* February and October, 1962. An earlier, more detailed version of the same position may be found in my book, *Reason and Conduct.*

gies should be judged, not *en bloc,* but in the light of their own respective practices and envisageable consequences. And it was precisely in these terms that I attempted to appraise the merits of Mr. Bell's own anti-ideological ideology. He doesn't reply to my specific contentions—including in particular the charge that the anti-ideological school has fallen into a weary, disillusioned *carpe diem* philosophy which may be suitable for self-centered valetudinarians but is certainly unsuitable for determined, untired, radical liberals who believe that the free world has a real future if it moves boldly and creatively and immediately on its own terrible problems of poverty, inequality, prejudice, and fear. In short, my aim has been to employ the study of a word in use, in order to expose, and if possible, transcend, a point of view which in the past I myself have found all too tempting.

Eventually, Mr. Bell gets around to quoting a passage from my essay in which, after the preparation I thought I needed, I state what in my judgment a political ideology, if not a total ideology, really comes to. By extrapolation it would be easy to derive from this my views about "total ideology," were these not already available in my little book, *The Age of Ideology.* So the charge that I don't provide a "definition" of political ideology (at the outset?) strikes me as somewhat perverse. As for the point that the "definition" of political ideology which I offer is merely a misleading definition of political philosophy, let me reply that if Mr. Bell can bring himself to take another look at my essay, he will find that I myself actually lead off by asking why so many people declare political philosophy to be dead. I turn later to a consideration of ideology precisely in order to find an answer to that question. And in fact I was led in the first instance into a discussion of the end-of-ideology school through an attempt to discover what, at bottom, people now object to in political philosophy. If my "definition" of political ideology turns out to be nothing but a "stylish" redaction of "the old-fashioned definition of political philosophy," so be it. For then in refurbishing ideology, I shall have done, as I meant to, two jobs at once.

On this score, there remains only to be added that in my opinion the ideologists often have treated the problems of political philosophy more imaginatively and in greater depth than their more classical predecessors. And the reason for this is that they nearly always see the necessity of viewing a political philosophy (or ideology) not only in the perspective of a system of moral principles, but also within the context of a philosophy of history, a metaphysical *Weltanschauung,* and, if one can be found, a theology. It is this context, largely lacking except in negative terms in the works of the anti-ideologists, which gives depth and range and power to a political ideology. And, indeed, if one knows where to look for it, the greatest classical political philosophies, such as Plato's and Aquinas's, have always provided it.

Mr. Bell's cry of "foul" in response to my charge, or informed guess, that the anti-ideologists are not only antimoralistic but also anti-moralists who really mean to go altogether beyond "good and evil," is premature. My advice to him here is to re-read, not my words, but his own. In the passage about total ideology which he quotes from his own book, there is this sentence: "This commitment to ideology—the yearning for a cause, the satisfaction of deep *moral* feelings—is not . . ." etc. [my italics]. Here, plainly, is not the obvious pejorative adjective "moralistic" but the now pejorated adjective "moral" itself. There are other analogous passages in Mr. Bell's writings, as well as a good many that might be quoted to advantage from the writings of his allies. I stand my ground: Mr. Bell's attack is not directed merely against "moralism"— which, of course, is nothing but the other chap's morals—but against morality as a form of discourse, a form of policy, a way of deciding what is to be done (and said).

Mr. Bell asks me, as I hoped he might, to be concrete. Very well (although it should be emphasized that there is nothing wrong with being abstract when the problems at issue are abstract and general, as they are to a degree in the present context). I believe in the necessity of constant, incessant pressure from the Left upon the Establishment and the status quo in order to rectify grave social wrongs; injustices, inequalities, and other miseries that are removable through collective social action. I believe, furthermore, in a never-ending "resistance" and spiritual rebelliousness. In our time, I think that the first order of business is a continuing, stop-at-nothing effort to obtain, not merely a nuclear test ban, but a progressive, ultimately total, dismantling of our entire machinery for nuclear warfare, lest some benighted Goldwater, unacquainted with the theory of games, should not merely threaten to use it, but use it. I believe in the necessity of a foreign policy for America which is predicated on the principle that any sort of brinksmanship, in whatever cause, is deeply immoral, a test not of courage but of inhumanity or madness or both. I seek, further, an approach to the problems of "underdeveloped" regions and nations which is radically non-military and which is completely indifferent to questions of ideology, race, color, or previous condition of servitude. I want us to pursue a realistic policy in regard to China, one which recognizes that China is a permanent, or semi-permanent, political and social reality which cannot be dealt with by the methods employed by the American government during the past decade. Whether we "like" the Chinese government is quite irrelevant. It belongs in the UN if Spain and Russia and Egypt belong. But this is merely emblematic. It is the "either-or" mentality exemplified by the anti-ideologists in their thinking about the confrontation between the Communist worlds and the "free" worlds which seems to me so inhuman, so dangerous, so suicidal.

Domestically, I applaud a hard, tough, *uncompromising* effort to bring the Negro people up to scratch, legally, politically, economically, humanly. People deplore the riots. What they should deplore are the causes of the riots: and what they should do about them is to remove those causes. *This can be done,* particularly if we divert a third or half of the money and effort spent on building the military establishment, moon shots, and all the rest of it, into imaginative public-works projects, educational developments, medical programs, and humanistic social activities in which all classes and colors of Americans participate together. Harlem (and "Harlem" works a bit like "Goldwater" as a type-word) is a national, not a regional, problem, and it can't wait a generation for a solution. There is also the immense aesthetic and even religious problem of saving America and the world from total permanent disfigurement. Much of New York, for example, is now so hideous that one wonders how human beings can endure it. But it is a dream city by comparison with Detroit and Chicago. The countryside is in ruins. The air stinks. The water, what there is of it, is undrinkable. And so on. A world as ugly, as fearful, as uncertain of itself as ours needs sympathy, but it needs continual action—bold, determined, and radical. Nothing else will suffice.

In part the differences between Mr. Bell's party and my own are doctrinal. But there are indeed basic differences of attitude or posture toward the whole conduct of life of men in societies. This becomes apparent in our respective conceptions of the democratic process itself. For Mr. Bell, it seems, democracy virtually means compromise. For me, compromise is as compromise does; some compromises are desirable; some necessary; others are dishonorable. Where questions of civil liberty, economic equality, and social justice are concerned, I consider compromise with the "interests," with prejudice, with indifference to be dishonorable, and I do not commend it. All too often, even in a democracy, compromise suggests, not sweet reasonableness and good will, but inaction, vacillation, collaboration, timidity. For me democracy is, minimally, a device for checking the accumulation of political power; maximally, it is a mode of participation in the communal life and a sharing of fundamental responsibilities toward the common good. What lies between seems to me, often, less admirable.

More broadly still, for Mr. Bell it appears that problems of politics generally are to be viewed, first, as problems of calculation and, secondly, as problems of adjustment (or compromise). For me, they involve much more, as is evident in my views about the role of rhetoric in political thought and discourse. To my mind, therefore, the end of ideology is, in a sense, almost tantamount to the end of politics itself. Beneath all, the anti-ideologists are men of doubt; their temperament, in the language of William James, is that of the "tough-minded." All too often, sadly, the same is true of me, but I do not glory in the fact. Pessimism is a fact of life; optimism in our time at least, almost a matter of grace. Thought, analysis, inquiry—and the itch of doubt which animates inquiry—are *of course* indispensable conditions of rational life. But aspiration, passion, hope, volition, and choice also belong inalienably to the life of the mind and the spirit. Without them, in the heat of the day, we languish, we perish. We must not allow ourselves to be paralyzed by thought; rather we must *use* it. We must not let it divert us from the necessity of action. We *dare* not forever stand and wait; we *dare* not continue to temporize. It is late, and there is a world at stake.

RAYMOND E. RIES

*Social Science and Ideology**

Modern social science traces its origin to the break-up of traditional society and the rise of the modern industrial state. Traditional society maintained a fairly stable system of social relationships over time and a fixed center of belief. In contrast, industrial society exhibits a pattern of social mobility within a changing class structure and a horizontal movement of people from one residential location to another. In the place of a fixed center of belief, modern society develops a network of central administrative agencies. It is a situation of change in which the adaptations of thought and custom give way to ever newer forms.

But such changes are not experienced by all men in the same way. The structure of society and the varying sensitivity among men filter the impact of change, so that some in varying degrees are sheltered from it and others exposed to it unmercifully. For many of the intellectuals of the past century the problem of the significance of these changes in terms of historical development was of paramount concern.

Auguste Comte, the French philosopher of Positivism, was reflecting on this situation in the early nineteenth century when he wrote: "We find ourselves living in a period of confusion, without any general view of the past, or sound appreciation of the future, to enlighten us for the crises prepared by

* Reprinted by permission from *Social Research,* Summer 1964.

the whole progress yet achieved. We find ourselves, after half a century of tentative confusion, oscillating between an invincible aversion to the old system and a vague impulsion toward some kind of reorganization." Comte sought an historical orientation, and an end to the uncertainties of the future and the disorganization of the present. He found his solution in adopting the methods of the natural sciences to these tasks; methods which had proved so fruitful in the exploration and control of nature. It was he who coined the term "Sociology," as representing a new discipline in the study of man and society. This new discipline would abandon the theological and metaphysical approaches to the study of society, and utilize the "positive" methods of observation and experiment.

Contained in Comte's program were two themes which, however much he felt them united, were nevertheless in tension with each other. On the one hand Comte wished to establish a program for the scientific study of human society, and on the other hand he wished this same program to become the basis of nothing less than the total reorganization of human society. Not only would sociology provide for an empirical study of man, it would also provide the means for the redemption of society from the chaos and disorganization in which he found it. It is one thing to expect some practical consequence from the science of society, but it is quite another thing to expect it to provide the means of salvation.

This combination of themes has had its exponents among Marxists and positivists alike. For Marx the validity of theory required that it have an active effect on the life of man. A few years ago George Lundberg wrote a book entitled *Can Science Save Us?* He was concerned with the political and economic problems of our time, and the answer to his question, although methodologically more sophisticated than Comte's, was in essence the same. At the end of his book he wrote, "To those who are still skeptical and unimpressed with the promise of social science, we may address this question: What alternatives do you propose that hold greater promise? If we do not place our faith in social science, to what shall we look for social salvation?" As with Comte, Lundberg ties salvation to society and human history, and offers the promise of achieving salvation through the science of society. The use of the terms "faith" and "salvation" are indicative of the basically religious nature of his concern.

In its more active form, the insistence that knowledge of society must act as an instrument of social change is known by the term "ideology." The force of ideology is the force of passion and commitment to an idea. An ideology provides its possessor with self-justification and with a claim to action. It is something to believe in and to give orientation to one's life and experience. Ideology has a function analogous to religious commitment. The commitment effects a transformation in the life of the individual and as a consequence in the lives of those about him.

The method of science, however, requires detachment. Not that science has no passion and commitment, for indeed it has. How else could one devote his life to such an enterprise as science? But it is a vocational commitment—not a commitment to the content of information which the scientist may help to add to the accumulative store of scientific knowledge. Indeed, the scientist must reckon with the fact that the bit of information which he adds through the energies of his lifetime may well be cancelled or discarded at some later time.

The ideologist is committed to an idea which transcends the present reality. His aim is to transform existing life, and his knowledge has a "meaning" for him in a personal sense. The scientist is committed to the observation of present reality. His knowledge will consist in the rational, empirical observation of the life of society about him, and personal "meaning" for him is not provided by the content of his tested observations. For this reason the science of society, insofar as it maintains a strictly scientific attitude, can only record the defeat of ideological or religious intention. No matter what the belief, or what the commitment, science can only reveal those everyday realities in the life of men holding such belief and commitment. It may record that such and such ideological or religious attitudes are present, but that these attitudes are contradicted by the realities of current social life. In the place of the "meaning" which the ideologist finds, science will find only the realities of class, status or psychosocial processes. Thus, for example, denominationalism among Protestants appears as a reflection of differences in status and class; the populist movement in the "Age of Reform" appears to be generated by status anxiety and discontent; and authoritarian personality structures appear to be associated with certain political attitudes and movements. By the adoption of its methods, science can neither transcend society nor find its "meaning." Although a science of society may have consequences for the transformation of human history it cannot require that transformation, nor determine its direction.

As William Graham Sumner pointed out long ago in *Folkways,* the behavior of men in society involves the acceptance of rules of meaning, some of which have the additional sanction of being sacred. That is to say, they are not open to question or trespass. Even such a simple form of social behavior as a college pep rally involves an assortment of sacred meanings, only partly conscious, and mostly inarticulate, but without which the behavior could not continue. Imagine, if you will, a visiting anthropologist describing this custom among the natives of a college campus. He would record the bodily movements, the words of the chant and songs, the course of the whole affair. He might even indicate the magical potency attributed by the natives to this activity in the winning of football games. And he might try to describe the outward manifestation of the demon or "spirit" invoked on these occasions. Using his comparative knowledge of culture he might find an activity similar in function among the Arunta of Australia, or the Crow Indians of the last century. But in all this he would neither feel nor share the meanings which affect the participants. And his final scientific description of the pep rally will provide not one

iota of substance for the value and meaning which the participants find in it.

In this manner the science of society appears to "unmask"
human behavior, to discover hidden realities, or the "illusions"
by means of which people interpret their own behavior. And
this is so because to the scientific observer these values have
the status of "facts," and as facts they are merely one element
among others which will be taken into account in analysis of
behavior. Science is not at war with ideology; it is simply incapable of supporting it.

The final separation of these two themes which positivists
and Marxists alike shared was stated unequivocally by Max
Weber toward the end of his career. "Science today is a 'vocation' organized in special disciplines in the service of self-
clarification and knowledge of interrelated facts. It is not the
gift of grace of seers and prophets dispensing sacred values and
revelations, nor does it partake of the contemplation of sages
and philosophers about the meaning of the universe." ("Science as a Vocation," *From Max Weber: Essays in Sociology,*
ed. and tr. by H. H. Gerth and C. W. Mills, New York: Oxford
University Press, 1946, p. 152) Weber made clear that the
occupation of science was not a sign of grace, and that science
had no authority to assess the meaning of life. To the question:
How shall I live my life, and what shall I do? science must
perforce remain silent.

This viewpoint, now so much a part of modern social science, had its echo in a remark attributed to the economist, J. M.
Keynes, in a conversation with President Franklin Roosevelt.
Roosevelt is said to have asked Keynes to tell him as an economist whether the United States should remain on or go off the
gold standard. And Keynes is said to have replied that as an
economist he might be able to say what might happen if we
remained on the gold standard, and what might happen if we
went off, but that, as an economist, he could not say whether
we should or should not.

Social science, at least in the West, has developed into an

empirical, rational form of the self-observation of society. As a source of critical information about the society, social science finds its uses in the administration of the modern state and the other corporate agencies of society. And in this respect it produces what might be called policy-related information. We are accustomed to having available organized forms of information about the society we live in—be it in the form of divorce rates, rates of national growth, or surveys of opinion. Consider for example a simple decision by a local school board regarding classroom needs for the next ten years, and consider the various forms of information it would find available in defining and estimating these needs. But we may not realize that such kinds of information about society were not available even a scant hundred years ago. What we know of population or birth rates of, say, seventeenth-century England is largely based on estimates of modern scholars, because no one living at that time had such information. Indeed, we today probably know more in a statistical way about the seventeenth century than anyone living at that time. The task of modern social science has been the development and interpretation of information about society. In this it aids in the achieving of clarity in thinking about our objectives and alternatives, and it may indicate possible consequences of action. And in this manner social science may inform decisions, but it does not in so doing provide the framework of value within which those decisions are finally made.

Whatever the causes, the postwar generation of intellectuals has become disengaged from ideology. The author recalls reading a statement by Dwight Macdonald written shortly after World War II that politics no longer interested him. The decline of ideology among many intellectuals in the West has been marked by apathy in regard to the search for meaning. It is true that the vague ideas associated with economic development exert an ideological claim on some, and certainly the concept of the Peace Corps rests on such ideas associated with the economic improvement of underdeveloped nations. It is hard to predict the future in these matters. Millennial hopes have had a strong grip on the pattern of western social thought. Perhaps the waiting for the living will become too hard, and the next generation will find a new way to force the "end of days." But for the present at least it would seem that social science has moved beyond ideology. But what is beyond ideology?

First of all it must be recognized that we no longer need to make a virtue of necessity. The self-observation of society in the form of a policy-related social science is a necessity under the present conditions of social organization. This is even more true of the democratically organized industrial state than the totalitarian. Without a dominating ideology, the democratic state requires information about itself as a means of social control.

Nor need one make an evil of the same necessity. The charge that social science will create the means of manipulation for a regimented society is largely misdirected. A recent account of motivational research seemed to suggest just that. But several things are overlooked here: In the first place, whatever the symptoms or motivations that social science may discover, those symptoms and motivations are still chosen by men. Secondly, human beings can and often do alter the rules of their own behavior. And finally, social science has not yet discovered that there are two kinds of people, namely those who are unconsciously motivated and those who are not.

Social science, then, performs a necessary function in our society. It is the practical consequence of this function for the life of society, however, with which we need to concern ourselves. For it is the insistence or the demand that the study of man should have some practical political consequence that we have described as the basis of ideology. Insofar as social science is concerned, beyond ideology means that social science no longer claims to deliver man from the salient predicament of his existence: namely, that he does not fit into his own environment. If the solution to that problem is to come in human history, then the solution will have to come from some other agency than social science.

Social science cannot provide the "solution" for the problems of crime, poverty, or juvenile delinquency. Social science can only clarify our understanding of these problems, indicate means of solution and their cost. All these problems involve the responsibilities of men in their capacity as self-determining agents, and social science cannot absolve man from taking responsibility for what he does.

Yet the demand for a solution, for an orientation, is still with us as it was in the time of Comte. Let me quote from a recent work of the late C. Wright Mills:

The very shaping of history now outpaces the ability of men to orient themselves in accordance with cherished values. And which values? Even when they do not panic, men often sense that the old ways of thinking and feeling have collapsed and that the newer beginnings are ambiguous to the point of moral stasis. Is it any wonder that ordinary men feel that they cannot cope with the larger worlds with which they are so suddenly confronted? That they cannot understand the meaning of their epoch for their own lives? . . . What they need, and what they feel they need, is a quality of mind that will help them to use information and to develop reason in order to achieve lucid summations of what is going on in the world and of what may be happening within themselves. (*The Sociological Imagination,* New York: Oxford University Press, 1959, pp. 4–5.)

It is instructive that the same sense of disorientation which activated Auguste Comte should appear well over a hundred years later in the writings of C. Wright Mills. At a much earlier time, it was, I believe, this same sense of disorientation that led men to the expectation of the coming of the Messiah. In fact, at various times in western history this expectation has become so intense that false Messiahs have arisen to fulfill the demands of the time. Perhaps in our age, so organized by corporate activities, this same demand leads men to seek the Messiah in the corporate body: be it a political party, the institution of science, or even a business organization. But if the concept of the Messiah and His coming means anything at all it means at least that He will come in His own time. In the past there were men who have refused to play the role of Messiah even though the demand upon them was great. And I think that social science needs also to refuse to promise the deliverance of man even though the demand made upon it may be equally great.

What then can social science offer in an age when men seek the comfort of an orientation, an image? There is little in the way of consolation which the scientific study of man can give except consciousness. It is a consciousness of the values men have pursued, the roles men have played, and the images they have forged. It is a critical consciousness of the social agencies and forces operative in contemporary life. But someone will say, "All very well and good, but I wish something more than this."

This may be answered by an analogy. The book of Isaiah describes how a person cuts a tree, and with part of its wood builds the fire to warm himself, and with another part builds a fire to cook his roast. Then warmed and fed, with the remaining wood he carves an image to which he bows down, and asks deliverance. The scientific knowledge of society, like the wood of the tree, has its uses. It is written in books, communicated to students, it is used in the lives of individuals and policy makers to clarify and organize the alternatives to action, it is used by individuals to inform and gain understanding of what they have been doing as well as what they may do. But apart from this what would you make out of the knowledge of society? Into what would you carve it? Would you make it into a redeemer? Would you make it into an instrument of propaganda? Would you make it stand in the place of a man?

The injunction against graven images is not simply a matter of bowing down before false gods nor of breaking the First Commandment. The injunction is against giving the authority of a thing to its image or its likeness. An image of man is a likeness but the authority for what a man is, is man, not an image of him. The knowledge of man, even the scientific knowledge of man, cannot take the place of authority for what a man is, for that place belongs to man. We may see this more clearly if we consider the repugnance we may feel, say, toward the image of Soviet man. The problem here is the relation between the image and the Soviet people. And the question is who is the authority for what that people shall be, the image or the people themselves.

In the end the ideologist and the maker of graven images want the same thing. The ideologists cares only that his idea have some active expression in the life of man and society. The image maker cares only that his image have some bodily expression in the wood which he carves. The image maker, unlike the artist, has no respect for the material in which he carves. It makes no difference to him what the quality of the wood may be, or whether he shapes wood, brass or stone, so long as the image stands apart from him and he can bow down to it. The ideologist in the end cares neither for the men nor the society which is to serve as the bodily expression of his idea. Men may be crushed and society torn asunder so long as this gives evidence of being effected by the force of an idea. Both image maker and ideologist seek deliverance by giving the authority of a thing to its likeness, the one through an image of God, the other through an image of man. The one carves in wood, the other carves his fellow man.

If social science moves beyond ideology, it may make us conscious of the images and the false authorities in the history of man. There is always the hope, of course, that this consciousness of society will make a difference. But what difference it shall make and how it shall make it we cannot ourselves say. The objective, interpretative study of society may entertain the hope of liberating man from some of his idols. But this is a hope and not a promise.

WILLIAM DELANY

The Role of Ideology: A Summation*

The aims of this paper are twofold: (1) to put the controversy about the so-called end of ideology in the societies of contemporary western civilization into the broader context of the sociology of ideologies; and, (2) to summarize and interpret the country trend studies we have just heard by interweaving their problems and findings into this same broader intellectual context. As I understand it, the hope is that discussion of the country studies will benefit both by a summary of their major points and by tying them to broader issues, problems, and knowledge. You will agree, I think, this is a large expectation and my task here a difficult one.

Consequently, I want to begin by sounding some notes of caution. The cautions are four. First, the sociology of ideologies is not a well developed field of sociology and I can't operate here from a base of accumulated and accepted knowledge at all comparable with this in, say, the fields of social stratification or complex organizations.[1]

* Prepared for delivery at the 1964 Annual Meeting of The American Political Science Association, Chicago, Illinois, September, 1964. By permission of the author.

[1] American sociology has shown little interest in the theoretical aspects of the field, but has contributed substantially to the empirical literature, though under such labels as mass communication, class, political sociology

WILLIAM DELANY

Secondly, general and uninhibited discussion on the role of ideology, a concept with rich connotations going back to the French Enlightenment and Marx, seems continuously capable of stimulating powerful, latent intellectual and moral tensions in the social sciences and social scientists. These include: Marxist vs. structural-functionalist theoretical orientations; intellectualist vs. more emotionalist assumptions about human conduct; cultural vs. various structural determinist approaches to comparative or historical studies; positivist vs. humanist preconceptions regarding the present achievements and future prospects of the social sciences; and, finally, nominalist conceptions of the beliefs, goals and morals of ordinary men and women as so many myths, illusions, rationalizations and false idols vs. realist conceptions of the symbolic worlds of the ordinary man as far closer both to reality and morality than are the vaporous utopias of intellectual mavericks, innovators, and critics.[2] All these and other tensions within and among social

---

and collective behavior. For example, the field is not represented as such and the word ideology does not appear in the index of Robert K. Merton, Leonard Broom and Leonard S. Cattrell, Jr. (eds.) *Sociology Today: Problems and Prospects* (Basic Books, Inc., New York, 1959). This volume is a collection of papers from the 1957 meeting of the American Sociological Society which was organized by a prestigious committee of five to "examine problems for investigation that developments in the major branches of sociology have thrust into prominence" (p. v).

[2] The nominalist vs. realist issue is illustrated by the following response of a British reviewer to a recent volume entitled *Political Thought Since World War II* (W. J. Stankiewicz (ed.), Collier Macmillan, 1964): "The interest in and commitment to Marxism varies: yet one senses throughout the book, even among the rare non-socialists . . . the same unavowed belief revealed by the addiction to (the word) "ideology" —a belief in the Marxist dichotomy between "science", based on observations of the practical activities of men yielding truth, and "ideology", which is merely ideas, rationalization and an illusion. What has happened since the thirties, if these writers are any indication, is not a repudiation of the Marxist universe, but a willingness to accept the influence of illusion on human behavior, while cherishing a nostalgic hope that ultimately man will be able to live exclusively by scientific truth." *The Economist,* August 8, 1964, p. 563.

Incidentally, this review supports Professor Christoph's observation that the word ideology continues to have low status in Britain (James B.

scientists seem to come to a head whenever the concept ideology is seriously and broadly discussed.[3]

Moreover, thirdly, you hardly need to be reminded that the word ideology is not just a social science term with various definitions but, like the words bureaucracy or totalitarianism, an epithet used variously in active political discourse for almost two centuries.[4]

Fourth, and finally, to deal, as our speakers have, with ideological trends in the full blooming confusion of the present as history is especially difficult. For me to evaluate four analyses of this sort for nations complex and varied as are Italy, France, West Germany and Great Britain greatly risks pretentiousness.

The phrase "role of ideology" in the title assigned me is, I take it, a shorthand way of referring to the problems of understanding the nature of political ideologies and of predicting their relations with a political system under varying conditions of society. I also take it that understanding and predicting nec-

---

Christoph, *British Political Ideology Today: Consensus and Cleavage*, p. 1).

[3] "The sociological study of ideology raises, in acute form, some of the most pressing problems of contemporary sociology. It entails a confrontation of Marxism, in its several versions, and bourgeois sociology . . . it is at the intersection of the empirical and philosophical components of our discipline . . . (it raises) a number of questions to which no answers of a conclusive sort have yet been found: in particular, the question of the precise relationship (and interrelationship) of ideas and social structure, and the vexed concept of interests . . .

"The curious course of discussions of ideological components of social science . . . seem to have a shock effect on many of our colleagues. Those who respond to the challenge cannot do so dispassionately: the usually complacent tone of scholarly discourse suddenly disappears—to become strident and discordant. The intellectual and moral tensions implicit in these questions seem to inhibit many others from participating in the discussion." Norman Birnbaum, "The Sociological Study of Ideology (1940-60): A Trend Report and Bibliography," *Current Sociology*, Vol. 9, no. 2 (1960), pp. 91, 116.

[4] A history of the concept ideology in Western Culture to 1930 is contained in Karl Mannheim, *Ideology and Utopia: Translated by L. Wirth and E. Shils (London, 1936), 53 ff. There are more recent accounts by Barth, Birnbaum, Eisermann and others, but I am not familiar with them.

essarily involves theoretical, empirical and evaluative modes of discourse.

With the intent of countering the tendencies in the sociology of ideologies both to separate theory and research and to attach science to polemics or vice versa,[5] I will organize my remarks as follows. The end-of-ideology theory and panel papers will be considered in relation: *one,* to the problem of the nature of ideology; *two,* to ideological trends; and, *three,* to the "determinants" and "consequences" of these trends. I postpone to the end of the paper consideration of more purely evaluative, polemical matters when I make some comments on the end-of-ideology writings *not* as theory but, which they also are, as ideology.

Though I will try to detach political argument from the more social scientific aspects of the problem, this does not mean I am assuming a positivist position on the role of values in social science. That is not my position. Values are inevitable and desirable in social science. It is not *that* they enter, but *how* they enter social scientific work that is crucial.

However, to avoid pretending to a false objectivity I should say at the outset that my stance will be generally, though not entirely, in opposition to the end-of-ideology writers. Although, in my judgment, their theoretical framework is inadequate, their empirical foundation impressionistic and their forecasts largely likely to be wrong, they have focused the attention of social scientists upon important problems and described certain limited trends in political ideologies of western countries. In addition, the political wisdom of the American writers, at least, is not very impressive to me.

[5] Birnbaum, *op. cit.,* 115–117.

II
The End of Ideology Theory
and the Nature of Ideology

Although we will agree that wide professional consensus on some neat and clear definition of ideology is not the same as understanding their nature, it is important to note that all of our speakers have had to wrestle hard with the problem of definition. It is important because an adequate notion of ideology is a continuing problem for all students in the field, not just our panel.[6] It is important, moreover, because one's research focus and findings will depend upon the definition adopted. This can be seen clearly in several of the country research studies reported here. Our speakers have responded variously to the choice of either accepting or rejecting the definition of ideology as "absolute utopias" used by the end of ideology writers.[7] LaPalombara rejects the notion of absoluteness in their definition, focuses upon the importance of utopias in Italian politics and government policy, and reports his findings in these terms. Christoph rejects the definition entirely as inapplicable to British political culture, substitutes a concept of liberal "attitude structure," and compares Britain to the Continent in these terms.[8] Secher also rejects the definition,

[6] ibid.

[7] Albert Camus' phrase "absolute utopias" seems to me the best brief way to epitomize the concept of these writers. Quoted in Roy Pierce, *Ideological Politics: French Theory and Practice* (mimeo, p. 2). Of course, as Professor Pierce points out, the end-of-ideology writers, for example Lipset, may use the term in several senses, sometimes within the same work.

[8] Professor Christoph's definitional departures and focus on comparative rather than trend statements make it impossible to relate his paper to most aspects of the end-of-ideology theory. I see his paper mainly as a critique of these writers' thesis that "pragmatic" political ideologies are a

substitutes the more critical concept of absolute ideology and reports on the persistence of certain conservative myths in West Germany. Pierce, though critical of the concept, is apparently sympathetic enough to use it, and his trend findings for France are clearly relevant to the end-of-ideology theory even though they don't particularly support it.

Why have our panelists responded to their choice of definition in these ways? I don't know. But I suspect that they realize there is a theoretical framework and polemical stance built into the end-of-ideology writer's definition which they do not share. In any case, this would be a most important topic for further discussion.

One criticism of the definition of ideology used by Camus, Bell and others, which was not made by any of our speakers, is that it contains a kind of inner theoretical contradiction. On the one hand, these writers say utopias have long become less absolute in western politics (which is true); but then they define ideology as an ideal-type, perfectly absolute utopia. This is simply a way of eliminating the concept of utopia from the lexicon of western political science, of ending utopias by definition even though, to a large degree, they continue empirically.

However, Professor LaPalombara makes what seems to me the central criticism of the definition of ideology used by these writers. He defines ideology not as an ideal-type, perfectly integrated, dogmatic, world view requiring passionate commitment, but in such a way as to include as ideologies symbol systems that vary widely in such properties as dogmatism, probability of realization, rationality, integration and rhetorical passion. Professor Christoph's attempt to distinguish between "world view" and "attitude structure" uses these variables for the purpose of differentiation as well as others such as comprehensiveness of the belief system and hostility to unbe-

---

consequent of state of economic development rather than general cultural and historic factors as Professor Christoph persuasively argues.

lievers. Change in any of these properties of ideologies over time in the direction hypothesized by end-of-ideology writers would be seen as a change in the nature of ideologies, not their end—and least up to some state of the variables when we might have something we now call "social science." But when we get ideology out of social science it will be time to worry about getting the ideology out of ideologies.

The social science of ideologies would benefit, it seems to me, from moving from an ideal-type to a more dynamic-variable type analysis. And this, in turn, raises the problem of deriving properties of ideologies that make them more or less effective. For example, what properties of ideologies make them more effective in the political process or in stimulating or preventing economic development? Professor LaPalombara's paper also contains some beginnings in this direction. His major criteria for the erosion, persistence or rise of political ideologies are not internal properties like flexibility but their effectiveness in defining political values, goals, and means in the decision-making process and in mobilizing popular support. Despite, or as seems better to me, because political ideologies in present-day Italy are more flexible he expects their effect upon decision making is rising. He also suggests that a property of ideologies ignored by the end-of-ideology writers, emotional appeal to masses of people, is important to the effectiveness of ideologies. I agree. In any case, it is by resting hypotheses like these that the study of political ideologies may advance beyond its present unsatisfactory state.

Professor LaPalombara's definition of ideology, if one adds the notion that it is more deliberately created by specialized intellectuals than political cultures, seems to me a workable definition of political ideology.[9] As Professor Christoph's paper suggests, it is important to distinguish the political, religious, economic, and familial aspects of "general belief systems" if only because then one may analyze the relations of the

[9] Joseph LaPalombara, *Decline of Ideology: Myth, Reality or Selective Perception* (mimeo, p. 2).

political to the other aspects in the way Christoph does for Britain and, to some degree, Secher does for West Germany. This, of course, is Max Weber's approach in showing ideological affinities between the protestant ethic and capitalism.[10] It is also that of *The Authoritarian Personality* studies in showing affinities among political, social, familial and characterological aspects of Nazi ideology.[11] Tracing such ideological affinities is immensely useful in locating the structural conditions and consequences of ideological patterns.

This raises another problem touched upon in Professor Christoph's paper, the problem of whether or not the beliefs and values in a political ideology form what the psychologists call a syndrome. You will recall, for example, that among U.S. subjects, *The Authoritarian Personality* studies found a low correlation between political conservatism and other aspects of Nazi ideology such as cultural ethnocentrism. On the other hand, the beliefs and attitudes forming both the political conservatism and cultural ethnocentrism aspects of the ideology were each internally more integrated and, as many other studies about the same time showed, scaled quite nicely. (The finding, by the way, has important political implications indicating as it does that paths to the political expression of certain social attitudes have not been formed.)

The lack of perfect integration with ideologies viewed behaviorally raises problems that seem to have bedeviled Professor Christoph in preparing his paper. Older, scholarly ideal-type descriptions of general belief systems like British individualism or a political ideology like liberalism assumed them to be highly comprehensive and integrated. Closer behavioral

[10] Max Weber, *The Protestant Ethic and the Spirit of Capitalism*, translated by Talcott Parsons (London, 1930). A more recent example is an attempt to show the relation of the modern decline of political faith in the west and such other non-political factors as Christian fatalism and existentialism. See J. N. Shklar, *After Utopia: the decline of political faith* (Princeton, 1957).

[11] T. W. Adorno, E. Frenkel-Brunswick, D. J. Levinson, R. N. Sanford, *The Authoritarian Personality* (New York, 1950).

analysis in particular recent places and times suggests this is often not the case. Among other implications, this raises the question whether in trend analysis theses suggesting the greater flexibility and less comprehensive and consistent character of contemporary ideologies is not, in part at least, an artifact of our more precise contemporary research techniques. But, again, we move in this way from problems of defining ideologies to discovery of their nature.

Another problem raised by Professor Christoph's paper, but with significance for all students of ideology, is whether the operational definition and methods used in the empirical studies he cites such as those by Almond and Verba, Abrams and the Keele University study are really appropriate for determining the degree of comprehensiveness and integration of ideologies.

I think that too great reliance on polling data leads one to underestimate the degree of integration of ideologies just as older, scholarly methods undoubtedly lead one to overestimate these. Let me indicate some reasons for thinking this. Polling data, and even the Keele University studies of routine petitions, votes and motions in parliament and parties, focus on changing issues and events of the day and, thus, necessarily upon more flexible surface opinions rather than upon what Floyd Allport called the "genetic groundwork" of opinion which is certainly more integrated and less flexible.[12] Polling data also focus on the distribution of opinion among individuals, not the organization of ideologically revelant beliefs, values and attitudes within either each individual taken one at a time or within real norm setting and enforcing groups. To "get at" the behavioral integration of ideology I think more clearly focused, methodologically varied and intensive studies of the sort represented by *The Authoritarian Personality* or the study by Brewster, Bruner and White which Professor Chris-

[12] Floyd H. Allport, "Toward a Science of Public Opinion," in Daniel Katz, D. Cartwright, S. Eldersveld, and A. M. Lee (eds.), *Public Opinion and Propaganda* (New York, 1954) p. 58.

toph cites are needed.[13] Finally, Christoph's discussion of the meaning of "pragmatism" in British political ideology, apparently more a matter of deep traditionalism than rational flexibility, makes one wonder about the high flexibility of party opinions, the tolerance of political opponents and the cooperativeness shown by these surveys. These more surface ideological phenomena, as has often been observed, may be made possible and, in part, may be explained by a more highly comprehensive, consistent, closed and emotional "genetic groundwork" of liberal ideology. Bernard Crick notwithstanding, an ideology of freedom is *not* a contradiction in terms—witness [Barry] Goldwater.[14]

III

End of Ideology Theory
and Political Ideological Trends

The theory of the end-of-ideology writers focuses our attention upon trends in political ideology and upon the determinants and consequences of these trends. The highly industrialized, affluent countries of western civilization are the major concern of these writers, but the developing countries of Asia and Africa also receive a share of attention, especially from Shils.[15] The time periods referred to by different writers vary widely. There are propositions about very long-run trends, two or

[13] M. Brewster, Jerome Bruner and Robert W. White, *Opinions and Personality* (New York, 1956).

[14] For two recent scholarly descriptions of American Liberalism as a for Comparative Analysis," *Comparative Studies in Social History*, Vol. 1, (New York, 1955); and Clinton Rossiter, *Conservatism in America* (New no. 1 (1958) pp. 5–22.

[15] Edward Shils, "The Intellectuals and the Powers: Some Perspectives for Comparative Analysis," *Comparative Studies in Social History*, Vol. 1, no. 1 (1958), pp. 5–22.

three centuries of western history, about short-run trends, for example, the period since World War II; and about various intermediate lengths of time. Given the highly precise conceptual, operational and observational requirements of trend analyses and the aforementioned present limitations of these tools for the study of ideologies, the theory has the intriguing intellectual and polemical quality of being always difficult, and often impossible, to check against the crucial facts.

What specific trends are hypothesized? I can distinguish four different but related hypotheses: (1) a decline of belief in and support of Marxist socialist ideologies in Western countries since about 1940 while, for roughly the same period, they increase their supporters in developing, non-Western countries; (2) a growth of belief in and support of absolute political utopias in early periods of modernization in Western countries, a decline in later periods; (3) a secular trend in the West for all utopias and ideologies to become less "absolute" in nature (an assertion we will have to specify in more detail in a moment); and (4) a decline in later periods of modernization in the West of the impact of political utopias upon political action and decision making on all political levels from government and party elites to ordinary voters.

Now, as you know, the theory also includes a set of determinant variables and a rationale which is implied by the unfortunately rather vague term "modernization." The particular determinant variables invoked vary, as LaPalombara has pointed out, from author to author and, in addition, depending somewhat on which of the four trends or which period is under discussion. We will discuss this aspect of the theory later. Quite obviously, however, if the particular hypothesized trend is not in fact a valid one (either in general or in any particular case), the set of determinants and the rationale of the theory simply fall to ground as irrelevant. So my first order of business will be to examine the evidence regarding the trends hypothesized. And I can do this in the time allotted only if I rather summarily dismiss some of these hypotheses as not at issue, as not capable of presentation here in any convincing way, or as irrelevant to our panel papers. Let me proceed now to do that.

I think you will agree that it is the third and fourth hypotheses, at least for certain delimited time periods and countries, that are most relevant for our work here. The whole purpose of this panel, as I sense it, is to bring this soaring bird of speculation, the end-of-ideology theory, down to the harder ground of a few Western countries and a specific time period, namely from about World War II to the present. However, a few words about hypotheses one and two may give perspective and clarify our consideration of the more delimited and immediately relevant ones.

The decline of belief and commitment to Marxist, socialist and communist ideologies in the West from World War II to at least 1960 is generally conceded by all sides and is not at issue.[16] The evidence regarding the disillusionment and despair of Marxist intellectuals, the decline of voter support and failures to take power etc. is widely known and convincing. So is evidence for the growth of the symbol "socialism" in developing non-Western countries though, of course, the real meaning of the symbol for elites and ordinary people in these countries is often far from Marxist or socialist in a Western European sense. The issues are whether, as Bell, Lipset and Shils maintain, a long-run secular decline is inevitable and due to "modernization" or, as socialists might argue, a transitional phenomenon due largely to such political-ideological factors as the cold war, American political-diplomatic intervention and, especially, to remediable shortcoming of socialist leadership and ideology. If the latter position is correct, there is hope for the political left; if the former, none. Personally I agree with the socialists, but as a matter of political opinion, not of sociological knowledge. Life belongs to the living. If specialists pour

[16] For example, see Stephen W. Rousseas and James Farganiz, "American Politics and the End of Ideology," *British Journal of Sociology,* Vol. 14, no. 4 (1963) pp. 347–362 [reprinted in this volume, pp. 206–228].

fresh new wine in the old bottles, and some are doing just that, they may yet shape the future.

The second trend hypothesized, that political utopias and radical movements grow in early phases of modernization only to wane later, is much too large to be handled here in any convincing way. However, I have had occasion to examine with care the considerable statistical and case-study literature[17] relevant to this hypothesis in a course I taught at Cornell University during the past four years and I would like to make a comment or two. Although the evidence for this trend is certainly not conclusive, it is generally convincing to me with some qualifications. The qualifications are: (a) the correlation with early modernization applies better to left utopias than right utopias; (b) there are important exceptions of various sorts, notably Nazi Germany, Meiji Japan and Peron's Argentina; (c) the theory tells us about the past and cannot simply be extrapolated to the present and future of either the industrialized or industrializing countries; (d) the determinants are not finely developed and as usually stated certainly overemphasize economic, class and social anomie factors at the expense of political factors like leadership, effectiveness of the political system, war and the climate of international relations.[18] But, enough, let me turn now to trends more directly relevant to the work of the panel.

The third hypothesis of these writers, I have said, is of a secular trend in the West toward less "absolute" utopias and ideologies. Less absolute usually refers to a tendency to become less millennial, less emotional and more cognitive, to involve lengthened time perspectives and broader, more detached and instrumental attitudes toward social arrangements and man himself. By secular trend here I mean one which is asserted to carry on continuously into the present since about the Renais-

[17] A reasonably representative bibliography will be found in William Kornhauser, *The Politics of Mass Society* (Glencoe, Illinois, 1959), pp. 239–249.

[18] A very good critique of this shortcoming of the theory may be found in Gabriel A. Almond, *The Appeals of Communism* (Princeton, 1954).

sance and Reformation, though with many ups and downs and many variations in particular Western countries. This is a big idea. What is the evidence? To answer this question I must distinguish between the evidence for the long-run trend, which I must and wish to pretty much ignore here, and the contemporary short-run trend which is our interest in this panel.

Let me say, however, that the evidence for the long-run trend for utopias certainly includes Karl Mannheim's justly famous chapter on "The Utopian Mentality" [19] Fredericko M. Watkins' recent volume which Christoph has summarized,[20] and a wide scholarly literature. That continuous rationalization, demythicization and associated disillusionment are characteristic of Western religious institutions, capitalism, music, bureaucracy and political ideologies is, of course, the major theme in the life work of "the sage of Heidelburg," Max Weber, and also involves an immense literature. Obviously, to comment at all here on the validity of this assertion of a long-run trend to rationalization would be absurd.

However, you may understand better why I mention this aspect at all when you consider that Professor Shils was co-translator of Mannheim's *Ideology and Utopia* and of a good part of Weber and that Lipset cut his professional eye teeth on Mannheim and Weber. Even without a single case study of ideological trends in Europe, which LaPalombara justly notes they have not made, this theoretical legacy would be used to order contemporary impressions. Moreover, finally, almost every detail in the end-of-ideology theory can be found in Mannheim, including a harsh message to German intellectuals in 1929 to sublimate their Messianic complexes, be calm, tolerant and not rock the Weimar boat. In *almost* every detail, the differences are instructive because, as I will indicate in the final part of this paper, they quickly highlight some of the central *ideological* aspects of the end-of-ideology theory.

[19] *Op. cit.,* Chapter IV, pp. 173–236.
[20] *The Age of Ideology: Political Thought, 1750 to the Present* (New Jersey, 1964).

Do the country studies reported on this panel support or fail to support the hypothesis that all political ideologies are tending to become less absolute in the highly modernized Western countries? Subjective interpretation is necessary in trying to answer this question because the studies are not strictly comparable in their conception of ideology, hypotheses or empirical focus.[21] However, I would conclude that in the sense of a quantitative shift the hypothesis is definitely supported in the period since World War II in Italy and in Germany, and, more uncertainly, in France. (Christoph's is a comparative rather than trend analysis and, consequently I lack the relevant information for Britain.) However, all the studies make clear that there is no end to inflexible, passionately aggressive ideological commitment in these countries. For example, Pierce documents rigidities in the French communist and socialist parties and regarding nationalism and planning. Secher does the same for German Catholicism, the military and public bureaucracy while agreeing that the parties and voters have become more flexible. It is clear that the phrase "end of ideology" is, ironically enough, pure rhetoric—a propaganda slogan.

I wish to illustrate this by reminding you of a few concrete facts just presented and choose the case of Italy for two reasons. First, because of our interest in the "opening to the left" as a possible reversal of the declining impact of ideology upon political decision. Secondly, because Professor LaPalombara has not himself emphasized this conclusion from his analysis. So, more specifically, the ideological changes documented by

[21] Pierce and Secher conceive of ideologies similarly as "absolute utopias," but Secher does not supply data on the decline of absoluteness but rather its persistence. LaPalombara focuses on the impact of ideology, phrases his conclusions in this framework but does supply adequate evidence for the present hypothesis as well. Christoph uses "ideology" more in the sense of political culture, and does not supply trend data. In addition, there are comparability problems regarding *whose* ideas are changing. LaPalombara focuses upon political party leaders giving little information about voters. Pierce and Christoph supply information on both. Secher pretty much ignores the party system and focuses upon the bureaucracy, Catholic Church, and military.

LaPalombara for the Italian communist and socialist parties since about 1956, for the Christian Democracy earlier in the 1950s, and associated changes in electoral support seem clearly to point to less absolute utopias. The ideological symbols of these party leaders become more flexible, less rhetorical, more cognitive in taking into consideration the complex, changing social realities of Italian life and more instrumental and cooperative in shaping party policies, power strategies and ideology to conform to these realities.[22]

As for the hypothesized decline in the impact of utopias upon the exercise of political power, only LaPalombara's paper provides us with an explicit, relevant analysis and conclusion.[23] His conclusion, namely, that the impact of ideology on Italian government policy has neither declined nor merely persisted but increased in recent years, is, of course, a complete reversal of the trend hypothesized by the end-of-ideology theory. If we grant Professor Pierce his point that the Gaullist regime in France represents a managerial ideology despite propagandizing the "end-of-ideology" rhetoric (and I would), then it must be said that ideological politics has waxed in France as well during this period. Although it is only a guess, I gather from minimal cues that our specialists on Britain and West Germany would judge these cases as pretty stable interest-group politics over recent years with little immediate prospect of change. If this guess is correct, it would mean that none of the four European cases considered here shows an eroding impact of political ideology upon power.

[22] For a study which shows that a large proportion of the communist electoral support was not militant, see Hadley Cantril, *The Politics of Despair* (New York, 1958).

[23] Again, Christoph's is not a trend analysis and, in addition, does not explicitly link party leader-follower ideologies with the exercise of power in Britain. Secher's paper focuses on the question only by implication. He seems to me to be saying that the opportunistic, interest-group politics under Adenauer continue stable under Erhard; that any immediate possibility of change to a more ideological policy comes from the authoritarian right not from the S.P.D. or the liberal wing of the C.D.U. This may be a misinterpretation on my part, however.

It is important to note before concluding this section on trends a tendency in the end-of-ideology theory to focus one's research attention upon change-oriented political belief systems (whether of left or right) as ideologies. Professor Christoph notes this and focuses his paper on non-utopian symbols which maintain the political system in a state of balance and are thought of by structural-functionalists as "political culture." Professor Secher also questions whether the opportunistic, interest-group politics of West Germany after World War II does not presuppose a political ideology.[24] Certainly identifying ideology with desire for change reverses with Marxian use of the term. Doesn't the use of the term ideology by these writers imply judgments about the sanity and morality of conformists vs. extremists?[25] Involve a static structural-functional conception of modern Western societies? Assume a rather simple cultural relativity and that there is no such thing as human nature? I think so.

[24] ". . . ideology can appear anywhere in the service of many varied purposes, not merely as a rallying cry of extremist elements but equally as a guide to the use of power for respectable, prosperous social groups. . . . Ideology in highly advanced urban-industrial societies has become primarily a defense by mainly middle-class elements who cling to imaginatively distorted thought in the hope that it will shield them from the dangers of common sense realities." H. P. Secher, *Current Ideological Emphasis in the Federal Republic of Germany* (mimeo, p. 2, also p. 20).

[25] For a survey of the social psychological literature specifically to criticize the view that radicals are psychologically more irrational than moderates, see Thelma H. McCormack, "The Motivation of Radicals," in Ralph H. Turner and Lewis M. Killian, *Collective Behavior* (New Jersey, 1957), pp. 433–440.

IV
The End of Ideology:
Determinants and Consequences

The end-of-ideology writers, by focusing their theory on long- and short-term historical changes in ideology, face the social scientist with a problem for which there is as yet no real solution. Instead a number of theoretical and disciplinary points of view contend. In general, these writers assume ideology is a dependent variable in relations with economic and social factors. Yet it is apparent that Sweden, England and the U.S.S.R. are about equally developed economically and socially but have very different political ideologies. And one doesn't have to read much history to find that political revolutions and the ideologies of their leaders have often shaped economic and social institutions. So it must be that it is only certain abstract aspects of political ideology which are dependent variables, namely, the absoluteness, utopianism and impact on power of these symbol systems.

The end-of-ideology writers use various factors to explain the declining utopianism, absolutism and impact on power of ideology in the West. I have tried to suggest that these hypothesized trends are partly true, partly false. Enough is true so that their rationale does not fall to the ground. It must be considered seriously. Enough is false to justify a critical attitude toward the rationale which produced it.

More important, perhaps, a critical attitude is justified because the trends hypothesized are very one-sided. For example, there is good evidence for a secular rationalization of utopian and ideological symbol systems (though, not necessarily behavior). But, and this is the one-sidedness, there is also good evidence for the persistence of non-rational and irrational symbol systems. There is good evidence: for the erosion of socialist and communist appeal in the West in recent decades; but also for its persistence; for a declining impact of older ideologies on power, but also for their persistent and even increased impact under certain conditions. In short, the theory is very selective in what it chooses to explain and to ignore. And it explains what it chooses to explain much less than perfectly.

What are the sorts of factors used by these writers to explain what they mean by the decline of ideology? Professor LaPalombara writes, "I come away from this literature with the impression that moral imperatives must necessarily give way before the growing avalanche of washing machines, refrigerators and television sets." [26] But I think this must have been written in a moment of exasperation, for it is neither accurate nor fair. Certainly, economic factors like growth in real income, stage of industrialization and weakening of class lines, differences and identities are used. (If that is Marxian, so much the worse for the non-Marxians.) But other factors include increasing formal education, decline of religious identities, reduction in isolation and alienation of rural, ethnic and migrant groups from dominant economic and political elites, increasing acceptance and use of social science and, finally the growth of bureaucratic organizations and a new technical-professional-managerial middle class. In general, I would characterize this laundry-list of factors as containing essentially technological, economic, social and administrative factors. What is left out? Politics and ideology on the one hand; culture, the family and national character on the other. Yet much recent work on the sociology of ideology shows you can't leave the latter of these out and have an adequate theoretical framework.[27] Without them you cannot expect to predict adequately.

[26] LaPalombara, *op. cit.*, p. 4.

[27] I have in mind here the work mainly of anthropologists, psychologists, and linguists. For summary of the contribution of the "irrationalist stream of thought" to the recent study of ideologies see Birnbaum, *op. cit.*, pp. 95–96 and items in the bibliography under I.5–I.9 [pp. 133–138]. A book which more than any other sums up this aspect is Erik H. Erikson, *Childhood and Society* (New York, 1950).

Perhaps because of disciplinary identities or whatever, I perceive the papers presented to this panel as emphasizing the factors left out. For example, Professor Christoph emphasizes the differences in political ideology between Great Britain and the Continent. The differences between Britain, France and Germany can hardly be explained in terms of "modernization," that is, factors included in the end-of-ideology theory. Christoph explains them in terms of English history, political culture and national character. British political culture, the family and national character are also, he implies, at the heart of the immense persistence (even stagnation) of British political thought. Pierce makes several observations of the same sort from his French vantage. Secker's analysis of trends in German political ideology breathes with a sense of German history, and its political-cultural themes of authoritarianism, militarism and oligarchy.

Professors LaPalombara and Pierce discuss more the consequences of changes in political leadership and ideology—and understandably enough, since within the period covered these are the two countries having the most significant (though hardly revolutionary) regimes and ideological shifts. However, during the period studied these countries are not designed to show what a powerful independent factor a change in political leadership and ideology can be in a society. They are too stable for that. Both history and comparative studies accord much better case materials for showing the impact of ideology.[28]

Of course, one can turn this around and criticize the end-of-ideology theory for an absence of correlation between the explanatory factors which are in the theory and ideology. For example, Germany, Italy and France have all had their "eco-

[28] Recent comparative studies of economic and political modernization have shown the impact of political and ideological leadership in a way that is most impressive to me. For example, see Clark Kerr, John T. Dunlop, Frederick Harbison and Charles A. Myers, *Industrialism and Industrial Man*, (Cambridge, Mass., 1960); and, S. N. Eisenstadt, *The Political Systems of Empires* (Glencoe, Illinois, 1963).

nomic miracle." But, according to Pierce, absolute utopianism persists strongly in the French socialist party but not in Italy and Germany.

What has been the impact upon political ideology of the slow *detente* between Washington and Moscow and the declining influence of the U.S. in Europe? None of the authors tries to draw this link. Yet I am curious and, after all, it is a political factor.

V

The End of Ideology Theory as Ideology

The end-of-ideology writers write not just as sociologists or social scientists but as journalists and an international anti-totalitarian ideological cabal.[29] Their work is ideology but, like almost all Western ideologies since the 18th century, with a heavy "scientific" component to give respectability and a sense of truth. Several questions arise. What is the nature of their ideology? Who are the ideologists and who is their reference group? How does one explain it? What consequences might it have? I cannot really answer these questions. However, several panelists have advanced hypotheses on one or the other question. I would like to comment and add a few ideas of my own.

First, as regards the nature of the ideology, Professor Pierce's discussion of the ideas of Camus, Weil and Aron makes clear certain ideological differences from Bell, Lipset, and Shils. He suggests to me the idea of distinguishing between American and French schools of thought. The differences lie in the French writers' basic value commitments to individual liberty and the right to criticize society, their anticlericalism, and, more important, their creation of new values

[29] The ideology is most clearly visible in Daniel Bell, *The End of Ideology* (Glencoe, Illinois, 1960). For some facts on the cabal see p. 18.

and principles of moral conduct more concerned with the problems of individual identity in modern society than with the problems of society as such. The American writers have not criticized American society or its Catholic Church and have attacked sociologists concerned with individual liberty and problems of identity like David Riesman and William H. Whyte. Although very productive, the end-of-ideology writers certainly have not been ethically creative. Assuming Professor Pierce is right in saying a hostility to ideological politics would have conservative consequences unless it is ethically creative and liberates people, the work of the American school definitely would be conservative. (Since I know only bits and pieces of the work of these French writers, my remaining remarks apply only to the Americans.)

Professor LaPalombara, referring to the American School, calls them intellectual Marxists and ideological anti-Marxists. Although this apparent paradox is interesting, I think the former point is simply wrong, the latter a half-truth and an inadequate characterization of this ideology. I would characterize the ideology as a synthesis of Marxian and liberal styles of belief and value around a central core of managerialism.[30]

Basically, the American version of the ideology is a defense of contemporary organizational society against both socialist

[30] From *Marxism* these writers draw the ideas of ideology as strictly a dependent variable, stages of economic development as a major independent variable, laws of history leading to some inevitable future state and an eschatology concerning this future state. They also draw from Marxism a major commitment to social and economic equality. However, their eschatology is not socialist but vaguely equalitarian, democratic and managerial. From *liberalism* they draw the ideal of rational conduct and a distrust of feelings and large-scale government organization and planning in the present to change society's future. Other liberal themes are hostility to totalitarianism, a preference for political democracy and for a non-ideological, electoral politics in contrast to a politics of broad political movements, political ideologies or ideological party systems. From *managerialism* they draw a preference for administrative over political means, for gradual, manipulated social change over rapid change based upon political movements, a horror of conflict and disorder, scientism, a group emphasis on individual conformity and societal integration, and, finally, a great respect for technical-professional expertise.

and liberal intellectual critics. Lipset, Bell and Shils have actively counterattacked both C. Wright Mills' basically socialist attack upon the American managerial elites and the liberal attacks of Whyte and Riesman. Unlike Gaullist France, however, these writers do not seem to have any association with a particular regime or managerial group, but only a self-nominated reference group relationship to the "amanagerial evolution" now occurring in all Western societies.

The essential nature of the ideology may be most easily understood by contrasting these writers' analyses of utopias with that of a German democratic socialist of an earlier era, Karl Mannheim.

Mannheim believed the socialist-communist utopia a utopia but, because it was based on a dynamic theory of Western capitalist societies and an associated vision of planned, controlled economic and social change, more rational in the current situation than liberalism or any other utopia available. The end-of-ideology writers, at least the American school, see 19th century liberalism and socialism as equally emotional, irrational and irrelevant, reject planning in favor of decentralized pluralism and argue against rocking the boat in democratic-welfare states of the West. Structural-functionalism replaces a dynamic theory of current Western societies. What Mannheim called utopias, these writers call ideologies and label extremist. What Mannheim called ideologies, for example Catholicism, Protestantism or the organization-man myth, these writers either ignore or defend.

Mannheim felt that widespread insight into the truth about a society came dialectically from an active clash and then synthesis of conflicting ideological and utopian movements. He believed that political movements and some degree of ideological conflict between groups and classes were necessary, inevitable and, if held within rules of the democratic political game, desirable in order to enlighten the individual and to maintain adaptive modern societies. There was no end of either ideology or utopia. However, a sociology of knowledge would aid to expose the biases and other shortcomings of all the political opponents; and social science would assist the victorious political party in the selection of relevant national policy goals and effective ways and means. But social science was a supplement, *not* a substitute for more natural, human, political and social processes of change and adaptation. On the other hand, the end-of-ideology writers see truth about society originating with "objective" social science. The ordinary man doesn't want to be enlightened. Radical political clashes and criticism of conservative myths, illusions and idols cannot be held within democratic rules as shown in Weimar, and only expose us all to totalitarianism. Happily the age of utopias is ended anyway; only a few sick intellectuals need be sat upon. And, as for the sociology of knowledge, shelve it before it gives the profession a bad name.

Certainly the real issues here are profound and difficult ones. Without commenting on them further, I wish to end by questioning whether the biographical fact that two of these writers are disillusioned socialists (Shils was never one to my knowledge) helps us very much in explaining their ideology.[31] Certainly, the facts of biography shape an intellectual's product. However, whether the crucial biographical fact is these writers' socialism or whether, as I would guess, it is more that they are sociologists, Jews and ambitious, successful Americans which is crucial cannot be answered just out of the blue. Until more intensive and reliable biographical analysis is available, it may be well to try to explain the "end-of-ideology" ideology in a more impersonal way.

[31] For a most sensitive and scholarly analysis of how the facts of an intellectual's biography are blended with his view of the ideological, political, economic and social climate of his times in shaping his ideological product see Erik H. Erikson, *Young Man Luther: A Study in Psychoanalysis and History* (New York, 1958).

JOSEPH LAPALOMBARA

*Decline of Ideology: A Dissent and an Interpretation**†*

Introduction

With increasing frequency and self-assurance, the scientific objectivity of American social science is proclaimed by some of its prominent practitioners. Various explanations are offered for the onset of social science's Golden Age, but central to most of them is the claim that modern social science has managed to resolve Mannheim's Paradox,[1] namely, that in the

* From *The American Political Science Review*, Vol. LX, No. 1, 1966. Reprinted by permission of the author and The American Political Science Association.

† Research for this paper was made possible in part by assistance from the Office of International Programs of Michigan State University, and in part by support from the Stimson Fund of Yale University. In gathering information on the Italian situation, I had highly valuable assistance from Gloria Pirzio, Ammassari, of Rome.

[1] This term is used by Clifford Geertz in "Ideology as a Cultural System," in D. E. Apter (ed.), *Ideology and Discontent* (London, 1964), pp. 48 ff. Although the present paper was prepared in draft before that volume appeared, I have benefited immensely in its re-

pursuit of the truth the social scientist himself is handicapped by the narrow focus and distortions implicit in ideological thought. Presumably, the social scientist can now probe as dispassionately as physical scientists observe the structure of the atom or chemical reactions. For this reason, it is claimed by some that the ideologically liberated social scientists—at least in the United States—can expect to be coopted into the Scientific Culture, or that segment of society that is presumably aloof from and disdainful toward the moralistic speculations and the tender-heartedness of the literary intellectuals.

The behavioral "revolution" in political science may have run its course, but it has left in its wake both obscurantist criticisms of empiricism, on the one hand, and, on the other hand, an unquestioning belief in "science." Quite often the latter belief is not merely anti-historical and anti-philosophical but also uncritical about the extent to which empirical observations can be colored by the very orientation to values that one seeks to control in rigorous empirical research.

The claims of modern social scientists are greatly buttressed by the views of Talcott Parsons.[2] In response to criticisms of

---

vision from Geertz's perceptive essay. I have also profited from suggestions offered by my colleagues, Wendell Bell, James Mau and Sidney Tarrow; and particularly from William Delany, whose analytical critique of papers on this subject delivered at the 1964 Annual Meeting of the American Political Science Association ("The Role of Ideology: A Summation" [reprinted in this volume]) is itself a most insightful view of the problem.

[2] I do not mean to suggest that American sociology speaks with one voice on this subject. There is, on the other hand, the claim of scientific objectivity and objection to the intrusion of values into research. But, on the other hand, there is also growing concern with the "global" questions, a retreat from the scientism implicit in some functionalist formulations, and increased demands for the need to engage in ethically relevant social research. See, for example, Peter Berger, *Invitation to Sociology* (Garden City, N. Y., 1963); Maurice Stein and Arthur Vidich (eds.), *Sociology on Trial* (Englewood Cliffs, N. J., 1963).

It is also worth recalling that Max Weber, himself, to whom many claimants of the "scientific objectivity" of social science often turn for support, would never, in my view, have gone as far as some of our contemporaries in his brief for empirical science. As I read him, he considers his work offered by a group of scholars at Cornell University, Parsons asserts that the "break-through" in the behavioral sciences occurred in the United States in part because of that country's intellectual openness and receptivity. A critical cause of this latter quality, according to Parsons, is the American intellectual's ". . . relative immunity to the pressure to put problems in an ideological context," and thus his refusal to worry too much about "global" problems.[3] For Parsons, science and ideology are simply incompatible concepts.

This is not the place to explore the ideological underpinnings of Parsons' formulations, particularly since the reader can turn for this to Andrew Hacker's somewhat polemical but nevertheless extremely cogent analysis (which Parsons chooses essentially to evade).[4] It is worthwhile noting, however, that Parsons' refusal to be concerned with the "global" questions, and his claims for the scientific objectivity of his emerging general theory, underpin the claims of other social scientists who extol the "scientific" qualities of their disciplines.

One interesting extrapolation from these assumptions about

a *science* of culture to be both "meaningless" and "senseless." See Max Weber, *On the Methodology of the Social Sciences,* translated and edited by H. A. Finch (Glencoe, Illinois, 1949), pp. 49–112, and especially Part III. It is also possible to read Weber on the use of values in teaching as simply a strategy to be followed by scholars on the left who, in an authoritarian Bismarckian society, would be permitted to voice in the classroom only the values of the "Establishment." See, *ibid.,* pp. 1–47.

[3] Talcott Parsons, "The Point of View of the Author," in Max Black, (ed.), *The Social Theories of Talcott Parsons* (Englewood Cliffs, N. J., 1962), pp. 313–315, 360–362.

[4] Andrew Hacker, "Sociology and Ideology," in *ibid.,* pp. 289–310. In my view, Hacker raises most of the relevant questions about Parsons' seeming political "conservatism," and he underscores as well the essentially ideological reactions of Parsons to the work of someone like C. Wright Mills. Parsons' response to Hacker is to acknowledge that he (Parsons) is an "egghead," and a "liberal" whose views of American society and the functioning of the American political system are normatively unacceptable to Hacker and to ". . . a good many other American intellectuals, especially those who think more or less in Marxist terms. . . ." *Ibid.,* p. 350.

social science objectivity, and of the essential incompatibility of social science and normative orientations, is found in the so-called "decline of ideology" literature. Presumably, social-scientific generalizations have been made about the waning of ideology. The irony attaching to arguments in and against these "findings" is that they have themselves taken on many of the undeniable earmarks of *ideological* conflict. Thus, I wish to acknowledge that my own effort in this paper may be in part —and quite properly—identified as ideological. Indeed, the underlying theme of my argument here is that we have not, in fact, resolved the Mannheim Paradox and that perhaps the future of social science will be better served if we acknowledge this fact and face up to its intellectual and theoretical implications.

More particularly, however, I wish to deal in this paper with these topics: 1) what is it that is meant when social scientists write about the "decline of ideology"; 2) an examination of some empirical evidence from the West that strongly challenges some of the "findings" of these writers; and 3) a somewhat tentative ideological-social scientific interpretation of what these writings may represent in contemporary American society.

The Meaning of Ideology

It is abundantly clear that those who write about ideology's decline, with few exceptions,[5] intend a pejorative denotation

---

[5] One exception would be Otto Kirchheimer, who was greatly concerned about the possible consequence of, say, the emergence of the "catch-all" political party in a country like the West German Republic. See his "The Transformation of the European Party System," in Joseph LaPalombara and Myron Weiner (eds.), *Political Parties and Political Development* (Princeton, 1966). Cf. his "The Waning of Opposition in Parliamentary Regimes," *Social Research* 24 (1957), pp. 127–156. I am uncertain as to whether what Kirchheimer describes is a decline of ideol-

and connotation of the term. Taking their lead from Mannheim, these writers contend that ideological thought means at least that such ideas are "distorted," in the sense that they lack "congruence" with reality. Beyond this, however, they seem to support the Mannheim view that the lack of congruence may be either emotionally determined, and therefore the result of subconscious forces, or "conscious deception, where ideology is to be interpreted as a purposeful lie." [6]

It can be argued, of course, that one is free to define ideology as it happens to suit one's mood or purpose, and we have a vast literature demonstrating the considerable range of meaning that can be assigned to the concept.[7] But if one elects a definition that is based too heavily on the notion of willful or unintended deception or distortion, much of what social scientists generally identify as ideological would simply have to be ignored, or called something else. Moreover, if the central purpose of the analysis is to demonstrate something as significant as ideology's decline, it seems to me to be the essence of intellectual legerdemain, or downright slovenliness, to leave the definition of ideology vague, or to confuse the demonstrable decline of something one finds objectionable with presumably empirical generalizations about the gradual disappearance of something which is much broader in meaning.

ogy, but it is noteworthy that he was one of those who didn't think that what he saw was "good" for Western societies.

[6] Karl Mannheim, *Ideology and Utopia* (London, 1936), pp. 175–176. Mannheim's second chapter in this volume, pp. 49–96, from which the volume's title is derived, is of course the classic statement of the origins of the term "ideology," its particular and general formulations, its relationship to Marxism and its catalytic impact on the sociology of knowledge.

[7] The best recent short review of the literature that I have seen is Joseph J. Spengler, "Theory, Ideology, Non-Economic Values, and Politico-Economic Development," in Ralph Braibanti and J. J. Spengler (eds.), *Tradition, Values and Socio-Economic Development* (Durham, 1961), pp. 3–56, and especially Part V. Spengler himself opts for a somewhat pejorative definition which hinges on values that directly or indirectly impede a "rational" approach to the ends-means problem in economic development: see pp. 31–32.

JOSEPH LAPALOMBARA

My usage of ideology is quite close to the definition suggested by L. H. Garstin, in that it involves a philosophy of history, a view of man's present place in it, some estimate of probable lines of future development, and a set of prescriptions regarding how to hasten, retard, and/or modify that developmental direction.[8] While the concept, ideology, is certainly one of the most elusive in our vocabulary, we can say about it that, beyond the above, it tends to specify a set of values that are more or less coherent and that it seeks to link given patterns of action to the achievement or maintenance of a future, or existing, state of affairs. What make such formulations of particular interest to political scientists is that ideologies frequently insist that in order to achieve or maintain desired ends, deemed to be morally superior and therefore desirable for the entire collectivity, public authority is expected to intervene.

It is in this broad sense, then, that I am using the concept in this paper. This being the case, several caveats are in order. For example, an ideology may or may not be dogmatic; a relative lack of dogmatism does not necessarily make a given set of cognitions, preferences, expectations and prescriptions any the less ideological. An ideology may or may not be utopian. I assume that conservative movements of the last century or two, as well as the so-called Radical Right in the United States at present have strong ideological dimensions, notwithstanding their vociferous denials of utopias. Similarly, Catholicism is no less ideological in many of its political dimensions by reason of its rejection of the Enlightenment's assumptions concerning man's perfectibility. An ideology may or may not be attuned to

[8] L. H. Garstin, *Each Age Is a Dream: A Study in Ideologies* (New York, 1954), p. 3. I recognize that my usage here is quite broad and that it may be typical of what my friend, Giovanni Sartori, scores as the American tendency to assign to the concept, ideology, a very wide meaning, "without limits." Sartori argues that such definitions are "heuristically sterile and operationally fruitless" (personal communication to the author, November 16, 1965). Sartori may or may not be right; my point here is simply to break away from the extremely narrow definition implied in the "decline of ideology" literature.

the claimed rationality of modern science; the place of scientific thought in ideological formulations is an empirical question that should not be begged by the assumption that science and ideology are incompatible. Technocrats and others who enshrine the Managerial Society certainly engage in the most fundamental kind of ideological reasoning. Ideology may or may not emphasize rhetoric or flamboyant verbal formulations. The language of ideology is also an empirical question; it will surely be strongly influenced by the socio-historical context in which it evolves, and a decline or, better, change in rhetoric should not be confused with a decline in ideology itself.[9] Finally, an ideology may or may not be believed by those who articulate it. Whether an ideology is cynically used as a weapon or instrument of control; whether it emanates from subconscious needs or drives or is rationally formulated and incorporated into one's belief system; indeed, whether it is narrowly or widely, publicly or privately shared with third persons are also legitimate and fascinating questions that require careful investigation rather than *a priori* answers.

It seems to me that the "decline of ideology" writers[10] commit one or more of all of the errors implied above. For example, ideology is said to apply to passionately articulated prescriptions, evidently not to those which manifest calm ration-

[9] Much of the burden of Geertz's essay, *op. cit.,* is to alert the social scientist to the great need for viewing ideology within a framework of "symbolic action." See pp. 57 ff.

[10] I refer here primarily to the following: Raymond Aron, "Fin de l'age idéologique?" in T. W. Adorno and W. Dirks (eds.), *Sociologica* (Frankfurt, 1955), pp. 219–233; R. Aron, *The Opium of the Intellectuals* (New York, 1962 [reprinted in this volume]); Talcott Parsons, "An Approach to the Sociology of Knowledge," *Transactions of the Fourth World Congress of Sociology* (Milan and Stresa, 1959), pp. 25–49; Edward Shils, "The End of Ideology?" *Encounter 5* (November, 1955), 52–58 [reprinted in this volume]; S. M. Lipset, *Political Man* (Garden City, 1960), pp. 403–417 [Reprinted in this volume]; Daniel Bell; *The End of Ideology* (Glencoe, Ill., 1960), especially pp. 369–375 [Revised Edition, pp. 393–407, reprinted in this volume]; and S. M. Lipset, "The Changing Class Structure and Contemporary European Politics," *Daedalus* 93 (Winter, 1964), 271–303.

ality. As Daniel Bell puts it, "ideology is the conversion of ideas into social levers. . . . What gives ideology its force is its passion." [11] Lipset, in his personal postcript on ideology's passing, tells us that "Democracy in the Western world has been undergoing some important changes as serious intellectual conflicts among groups representing different values have declined sharply." [12] In the case of Aron, his passionate and intemperate attacks on the ideas of certain French intellectuals are so extreme as to represent not so much social science analysis as they do a fascinating example of the rhetorical aspect of ideological exchange.[13]

It seems equally apparent that what these writers mean by ideology is not any given set of values, beliefs, preferences, expectations and prescriptions regarding society but that *particular* set that we may variously associate with Orthodox Marxism, "Scientific Socialism," Bolshevism, Maoism, or in any case with strongly held and dogmatically articulated ideas regarding class conflict and revolution. Thus, "the exhaustion of political ideas in the West" refers to that particular case involving the disillusionment experienced by Marxist intellectuals when it became apparent that many of Marx's predictions were simply not borne out, and when the outrages of the Stalinist regime were publicly revealed. We need not document the evidence for the widespread disillusionment, or for the agonizing ideological reappraisals to which it has led. But, as I shall briefly document below, to limit the meaning of ideology to absolute utopias, to concentrate one's analytical attention upon what some Marxian socialists may be up to, and to equate certain changes in rhetoric with ideological decline is to narrow the meaning of the central concept to the point where it has very limited utility for the social scientist.

The writers I have in mind also seem to see ideology as a dependent phenomenon, whose rise and fall is conditioned by

[11] Bell, *op. cit.*, pp. 370, 371 [p. 96 in this volume].
[12] Lipset, *Political Man, op. cit.*, p. 403 [p. 70 in this volume].
[13] Aron, *The Opium of the Intellectuals, op. cit.*

a number of ecological factors, most of them economic. This curious determinism suggests that if there are marked differences in poverty and wealth—or in life styles—ideology emerges; if these differences are reduced, ideology (i.e., class-conflict ideology) declines. Thus, Lipset tells us that "Ideology and passion may no longer be necessary to sustain the class struggle within stable and affluent democracies." [14] At another place he says, "As differences in style of life are reduced, so are the tensions of stratification. And increased education enhances the propensity of different groups to 'tolerate' each other, to accept the complex idea that truth and error are not necessarily on one side." [15]

These writers are far too sophisticated to suggest that there is a simple correlation between increases in economic productivity or distribution and decline of ideology. They recognize, for example, that religious and other cleavages may cut against tendencies toward ideological quiescence. Nevertheless, I came away from this literature with the uncomfortable impression that these writers claim that moral imperatives, differences of opinion regarding the "good life," and opposing formulations regarding public policy must necessarily give way before the avalanche of popular education, the mass media and greater and greater numbers of washing machines, automobiles and television sets. How else judge the assertion—as clearly debatable as it is subjective and ideological—that ideology is in decline because "the fundamental problems of the Industrial Revolution have been solved." [16]

There are certainly thousands of European intellectuals, as well as tens of millions of other Europeans, who would react to the last quoted statement sardonically, or in sheer disbelief.

Since the generalizations about ideology's alleged decline apply to the West, and therefore to Europe as well as the North American continent, it may be instructive to look at one

[14] Lipset, *Political Man, op. cit.,* p. 417 [p. 86 in this volume].
[15] Lipset, "The Changing Class Structure . . ." *op. cit.,* p. 272.
[16] Lipset, *Political Man, op. cit.,* p. 406 [p. 73 in this volume].

of these countries, Italy, to see exactly how accurate these generalizations are. It should be noted that the time span I will consider are the years since World War II; my point will be that since generalizations for such a short period are so manifestly inaccurate, it is useless to lend any kind of serious attention to prognostications about where we will be a century or two from now. Keynes, I believe, authored the most appropriate aphorism about the "long run."

Ideology in Italy

The points I wish to stress about Italy can be briefly stated, although their detailed documentation would require more space than is available here. First, notwithstanding the existence within the Italian Communist party of both a "crisis of intellectuals" and a "crisis of ideology," there has recently occurred within that party a new ferment of ideas which in a certain sense has actually enriched rather than diminished attention to ideology. Second, if one bothers to look away from the Communist party (P.C.I.) and toward Christian Democracy (D.C.), it is possible to conclude that ideology in the latter is actually on the upswing. Third, and following from these two observations, the so-called decline-of-ideology theory is simply not valid for the Italian case.[17]

[17] A number of colleagues who were good enough to read this manuscript urge that the empirical evidence challenging the "decline" thesis should not be limited to Italy. Roger Masters and Giovanni Sartori point out, for example, that the U. S. would provide additional supportive evidence. Nils Elvander notes that Tingsten himself, in his analyses of the Swedish Social Democratic Party, became "caught up in the party, and when the battle was over he went on declaring ideology dead, not being able to see that it was revitalized again and again" (personal communication to the author, December 19, 1964). I am aware of this additional evidence and simply note that the Italian case is used here as an illustrative rather than exhaustive example.

Decline of Ideology: A Dissent and an Interpretation

The Italian Communist Party. The most frequent—and most wishful—interpretation of P.C.I. is that it is moving in a reformist direction that will eventuate in its accepting the existing system and limiting its demands to social, political and economic manipulations designed to effect needed, but not revolutionary, reforms from time to time. This view of the party is superficial in the sense that "reformism" dates back to 1944 when Palmiro Togliatti returned from Moscow articulating a moderate line which was as unnerving as it was unexpected. This line was carefully followed in the Constituent Assembly, which drafted the Italian Constitution, and in this broad sense the party has been "reformist" throughout the postwar years.

What has changed in recent years is neither the party's will to power nor its commitment to a basically socialist ideology. Rather, I would say that the changes include: 1) the party's use of extreme rhetoric; 2) its now openly expressed polycentrist view regarding the nature of the international socialist or communist movement; and 3) the party's notions regarding how the class struggle should be conducted in contemporary Italy. The debates and agonizing reappraisals that the party has experienced in recent years must be construed not as a sign of ideological decay but, rather, as a sign of ideological vigor which is largely responsible for the party's steady and increasing attraction at the polls.

The list of P.C.I. errors in prognosticating about Italian society is long and impressive; it led observers at Bologna not long ago to comment on what a "grotesque assumption" was the party's belief that only it possessed a scientifically infallible method for analyzing reality.[18] The errors included such things as predictions about the comparative rate of economic growth in Communist and free countries, expectations regarding the European Common Market, impending economic crises in cap-

---

[18] Paolo Covilla, Giorgio Galli, Luigi Pedrazzi, Alfonso Prandi and Franco Serra, "I Partiti Italiani tra il 1958 e il 1963." *Il Mulino,* 12 (April, 1963), p. 323.

italistic countries, etc. One observer of this pattern of inaccurate prognosticating notes that it was not until the middle of 1961 that the "Communists awoke from their dogmatic dream and almost in a flash learned that their judgments did not correspond to reality." [19]

The truth is that the alarm had sounded for P.C.I. several years before, and precisely at the VII Party Congress of 1956. It was here that the party's activities in the underdeveloped South first received a public airing. The critics of the party's *"Movimento di Rinascita"* in Southern Italy openly noted that the movement was in crisis and that the crisis grew out of the party's failure to adapt ideology and consequently policy to the concrete conditions of Southern Italy. Members of the Party itself scored it for its "sterile and negative" approach to national problems, for its rigid and doctrinaire adherence to fixed schemes, for its permitting the movement to lose whatever dynamism it may have had in earlier years.[20]

Both Togliatti and Giorgio Amendola (the latter considered the leader of the P.C.I.'s "reformist" wing) urged that the party must be flexible and overcome the inertia of pat formulations. They admitted that both the party and its trade-union wing seemed to be unprepared to confront the great changes in local conditions that had occurred in the years since 1945.[21] It is possible that, within the party's secret confines, this kind of self-appraisal had begun before 1956, but in those earlier days one would not have expected Togliatti to say publicly that the

[19] G. Tamburrano, "Lo Sviluppo del capitalismo e la crisi teorica dei comunisti italiani," *Tempi Moderni,* 5 (July-September, 1962), p. 22.

[20] See the editorial, "I Problemi del Mezzogiorno nei Congressi del PCI e del PSI," *Cronache Meridionali,* 4 (January-February, 1957), pp. 57–58. The struggle of the P. C. I. to make the necessary ideological, strategic and tactical changes in its approach to the Italian South is perceptively and exhaustively analyzed by Sidney Tarrow, *Peasant Communism in Southern Italy.* Ph.D. dissertation manuscript, Berkeley, University of California, 1965.

[21] "I Problemi del Mezzogiorno . . . ," *op. cit.,* p. 59. Cf. Giorgio Amendola, "I Comunisti per la rinascita del Mezzogiorno," *Cronache Meridionali* 4, (May, 1957), p. 279. See, also, P.C.I., *Tesi e documenti del Congresso del PCI,* (Rome, 1963), p. 138.

Decline of Ideology: A Dissent and an Interpretation

party was not keeping up with basic social and economic transformations in Italy or that it was necessary for that organization to engage in the kind of total reexamination that will finally sweep away "ancient and recent moldiness that impede the action of P.C.I." [22]

To be sure, removing, ideological mold is not easy for Communists, who tend to be ultraintellectual in a society where intellectual elegance is highly prized. One can therefore note in the party's literature the care—and the web-like logic—with which recent changes are reconciled with Marx and Lenin, and particularly with the writings of Antonio Gramsci, the intellectual fountainhead of Italian Communism, and a formidable dialectician whose work is too little known in the English-speaking world.[23] Nevertheless, the party's public posture has changed radically. The most recent and important indication of this change is the party's decision to seek alliances with elements of the middle class—peasants, small landowners, artisans, small and medium industrialists and even with entrepreneurs who are not involved with industrial monopolies.[24] The importance of this change should be strongly emphasized; the P.C.I. has managed in one stroke to shift largely to monopoly capitalism all of the attacks that had previously been leveled against an allegedly retrograde, decadent bourgeoisie. The party's open strategy is to attract to its ranks the mushrooming members of the middle and tertiary strata that large-scale industrial development tends to proliferate. The fire of opposition is no longer directed against proprietors in general but against the monopolists who allegedly exploit all others in society, who are oppressive, and who increase the degree of imbalance or disequilibrium in the social system.

This, then, is not the party of the Stalin Era. Not many who

[22] Abdon Alinovi, "Problemi della politica comunista nel Mezzogiorno," *Critica Marxista,* 1 (July-August, 1963), 4–8.

[23] Palmiro Togliatti, *Il Partito Communista Italiano* (Rome, 1961), p. 55; Antonio Gramsci, "Alcuni temi della questione meridionale," in *Antologia degli scrutti* (Rome, 1963), pp. 51, 69.

[24] Tamburrano, *op. cit.,* p. 23.

followed the antics of P.C.I. up to the Hungarian Rebellion would have predicted changes in orientation such as the ones so briefly summarized. The fascinating question to pose here, however, is whether what has happened represents a *decline* in P.C.I. ideology, or something else. If by decline is meant the abandonment of some of the rhetoric, the verbal symbols, the predictions and expectations voiced until the late fifties, there seems little doubt about the validity of such a judgment, although the more appropriate word would be *change*. However, if by decline is meant that P.C.I. is becoming bourgeois or "social-democratized," or that it is abandoning any commitment to ideological formulations, I believe one should hesitate before leaping to such a conclusion. As Palmiro Togliatti significantly put it, "There is no experience regarding the way in which the battle for socialism can or must be waged in a regime of advanced monopolistic state capitalism. . . . There do not even exist explicit prescriptions in the classics of our doctrine." [25]

Communist leaders who spearhead this reappraisal are not calling for ideological retreat but, rather, for a concerted search for new ideological underpinnings for party policies and actions. In noting that Marxism offers, at best, vague guides to party behavior in modern Italian society, these leaders seem to me to be a long way from abandoning such key concepts as class, dialectical conflict, the exploitative nature of monopoly capitalism, and the fundamental need for effecting structural—not mild, reformist—changes in the social system. They, are the millions of Italians who support them at the polls, are far from concluding, if this is the acid test for the inclination toward ideological decline, that the problems created by the Industrial Revolution have been largely solved.

The effort to attune the party's ideology to present Italian

[25] *Ibid.*, p. 69. See the important statement by Bruno Tentin, one of the most important of the party's young leaders, intellectuals and ideological architects, "Tendenze attuali del capitalismo italiano," in *Tendenze del capitalismo italiano: Atti del convegno economico dell'Instituto Gramsci* (Rome, 1962) p. 43 ff.

realities is a complementary side of the vigorous campaign for polycentrism which the party has been conducting within the international communist movement. Beginning in 1956, P.C.I. frankly asserted that the Soviet model could no longer be a specific guide to Communist parties in every country and that it would be necessary to find a "national path to socialism." Togliatti made this point forcefully in the last book he published before his death.[26] In November, 1961, the P.C.I. Secretariat formulated a resolution which said in part that "There do not exist and there cannot exist either a guiding party or state or one or more instances of centralized direction of the international Communist movement. Under existing conditions there must be and there must increasingly be a great articulation of the movement in a context of full independence of individual parties." [27]

These are brave words, and it is still much too early to conclude with any confidence what the result of the P.C.I.'s campaign will be.[28] What is important is the apparent P.C.I. conviction that it can come up with a new strategy—a new formula for achieving power—for Communist parties operating in Western European and other countries of advanced capitalism. It is important to bear in mind that, in doing this, the party purports to be able to provide an up-dated ideological rationale for action. Some of the "moldiness" of "Scientific Socialism" has certainly been scraped away. What remains, coupled with some of the newer ideas currently in ferment, amounts to much more ideology than one might detect from the simple notation that the language of the late forties and early fifties is no longer in vogue.

[26] Togliatti, *op. cit.,* p. 131.
[27] See "Problemi del dibattito tra partiti comunisti," *ibid.,* p. 16.
[28] The Italian Communists have pushed polycentrism very hard indeed, and do not react well to Soviet attempts to water it down. See, *L'Unita,* November 22, 1961, p. 11. On this general topic see the excellent analysis by Donald L. M. Blackmer, "The P.C.I. and the International Communist Movement," Massachusetts Institute of Technology, mimeographed.

Italian Christian Democracy. The genius of Alcide DeGasperi is that for a decade following the birth of the Italian Republic he was able to hold together within the Christian Democratic party (D.C.) strongly opposed ideological factions that managed to play down ideology in the interest of holding on to power. This was no mean achievement. Although the popular image of the D.C. is that of an opportunistic, anti-ideological "brokerage" party, the truth is that, from the outset, strong factions that would have emphasized ideology, even at the risk of splitting the party, had to be suppressed or defeated. DeGasperi's hegemonic control of the organization was secured only after he had managed to beat down early competition for leadership emanating from such ideologues as Giuseppe Dossetti, Amintore Fanfani and Giovanni Gronchi. One might well conclude that, in an age of alleged ideological decline and after a decade of enjoying the many fruits of political power, ideology would have become a much less salient issue within the D.C.

Exactly the opposite tendency is apparent, however. Since the death of DeGasperi, and the advent of Fanfani as a major party leader in 1954, the ideological debate has not only intensified but has also broken into public view, revealing a party organization under deep internal stress. I believe that the facts will clearly demonstrate that since that date the role of ideology within the D.C. has actually increased rather than diminished, and a few central occurrences will serve to bear out this conclusion.

In September, 1961, the D.C. held at San Pellegrino the first of three annual "ideological" conventions. They represented a long and successful effort on the part of those in the party who had fought for making the party ideologically coherent, something more than the "brokerage" party the D.C. had been under DeGasperi's leadership. Looming over these proceedings were two of the party's perennial dilemmas: First, to what extent should the D.C., a party drawing much of its strength from the political right, articulate a left-wing ideol-

ogy as a guide to policy? Second, how much ideological freedom could the party express *vis-à-vis* a Catholic Church to
which it must necessarily remain fairly closely tied? Those
who favored stronger articulation of a coherent left-wing ideology were strongly spurred by an undeniable gradual movement to the left by the Italian electorate, by the increasing
willingness of the Italian Socialist party to consider active coalition with the D.C., and certainly not least by the kinds of
ideological changes in the Vatican triggered by the innovating
papacy of John XXIII.

Speakers at the conferences reviewed the party's ideological
history, noting that at war's end it appeared that the party
would lead the country left and that, in those years, DeGasperi
himself stated that the old order based on the domination of
rural landowners and urban industrialists would not remain intact. But it was lamented that whenever the D.C. confronted
issues concerning which the party's ideology seemingly required socialist solutions, ideology was arrested in favor of not
pushing to the breaking point the ideological centrifugal tendencies within the organization. As Franco Malfatti, one of the
followers of Giuseppe Dossett and Amintore Fanfani, points
out, the revolutionary tone of early D.C. pronouncements was
gradually transformed into the muted notes of a purely formal-
istic democracy and of a great concentration of governmental
power at Rome.[29]

[29] Franco M. Malfatti, "La Democrazia Cristiana nelle sue affermazioni
programmatiche dalla suia ricostruxione ad oggi," in *Il Convegno di San
Pellegrino: Atti del I Convegno di Studi della D.C.* (Rome, 1962), pp.
325–341. For examples of the early, postwar ideological statements of the
party, see, for example, Alcide DeGasperi, "Le Lineo programmatiche
della D. C.," in I Congressi Nazionali della Democrazia Cristiana (Rome,
1959) p. 23; Gianni Baget Bozzo, "Il Dilemma della D.C. e del suo
prossimo Congresso," *Cronache Sociali* Vol. 3 (April 30, 1949), p. 17;
Achille Ardigo, "Classi sociali e sintesi politics," in *Il Convegno di San
Pellegrino . . . ," op. cit.,* pp. 135 ff. It should be noted that the periodi-
cal *Cronache Sociali,* cited above, was the most important publication for
those in the D.C. who, in the early postwar years, attempted to give the
party a clear-cut left-wing ideological cast. Until recently, full collections
of the magazine were extremely rare. The major articles from it, how-

As the D.C. moved self-consciously toward the "Opening to the Left" which would bring the Socialists into the government, the party's ideologues would no longer accept the De-Gasperi formula whereby all concern about or dedication to ideology was to be obscured in favor of the overriding value of party unity. At San Pellegrino, Malfatti put the new posture of the ideologues pointedly. "The problem of [party] unity," he said, "is a great one of fundamental importance but it is also a problem that runs the risk of losing all its value if used as a sedative, or as the Hymn of Garibaldi, every time there is conflict between clerical and anti-clerical elements." [30] If the party wished to be free of all internal ideological conflict, nothing would remain of it except an agreement "to hold power for power's sake." [31]

According to Achille Ardigo, a sociologist and longtime member of the party's national executive committee, the major milestones in the D.C.'s ideological evolution are the following: First, the development of the concept of the political autonomy of Catholics, unconstrained by specific direction by clerical forces. Second, the growth of the idea of the autonomous function of intermediate groups (such as family, community and social class) against the excesses of the centralizing, modern liberal state. Third, the defense and consolidation of liberty, in a government of laws, through an alliance of the democratic forces of the nation against political and ideological extremes. Fourth, the materialization of the ideology of the "new party" led by Amintore Fanfani. Finally, the emergence of a new concept of the state as an artifice of harmonious and planned development—the idea of the state as an instrument of dynamic intervention in the economic sphere and of the modification of the rights of property in favor of the well-

---

ever, are now available in a two-volume work, *Cronache Sociali* (Rome, 1961).

[30] Franco M. Malfatti, "L'Unita della D.C. e il problema delle tendenze," *Cronache Sociali*, 3 (February 15, 1949), p. 15.

[31] Ardigo, *op. cit.*, p. 145.

being of the collectivity. It is the evolution of this last, self-consciously ideological stage that permitted the party's recent shift to the left and the acceptance of coalition with the Socialists.[32]

One can identify many reasons for this shift to the left, including Italian voting patterns that have clearly led the D.C. in this direction. To the many social and economic pressures leading to the emergence of a Catholic Socialism, one would have to add the liberating impact of John XXIII's revolutionary encyclical, *Mater et Magistra*. In the light of this radical departure from the conservative, often reactionary, political utterances of Pius XII, it is easy to understand why the D.C. left should be spurred to a more purposeful and ideologically rationalized attack on Italian society's ills.

It is important to recognize that the San Pellegrino meetings mean not that the D.C. has moved left on a purely opportunistic basis, but, rather, on the basis of a "rediscovery" of the ideological formulations laid down by Dossetti and others in the late forties. To be sure the current ideology is not socialism and, indeed, leaders like Aldo Moro have been careful to distinguish D.C. ideology from socialism and communism. Nevertheless, the D.C. is today a dramatically less catch-all party than it was under DeGasperi. It now has a somewhat official and publicly articulated ideology. If ideology is in fact in significant decline elsewhere in Europe,[33] Italy will certainly have

[32] *Ibid.,* pp. 155–165.

[33] Exactly how much of the West is to be included in the generalization about ideology's decline is never made too clear. Lipset, for example, is careful to hedge his European generalizations by frequently excepting Italy and France. My point would be that if these two countries are excepted, as they should be, one can scarcely pretend to speak with justification about *European* trends. See Lipset, "The Changing Class Structure . . . ," *op. cit., passim.* Moreover, there is also rather persuasive evidence that Lipset's generalizations are not currently valid, if they ever were, for a country like West Germany. See H. P. Secher, "Current Ideological Emphasis in the Federal Republic of Germany," a paper delivered at the 1964 Annual Meeting of the American Political Science Association, Chicago, September 9–12, 1964. Note particularly the extensive, German-language bibliography on this subject contained in the

to be excepted from such easy generalizations. In the P.C.I., ideology has changed and appears to be vigorously reasserting itself; in the D.C. the era of suppressed ideology has passed, and ideological debate and commitment are clearly resurgent.

How, then, explain the imperfect, distorted and erroneous perceptions of the decline-of-ideology writers?

Interpretations of the Decline-of-Ideology Literatures

Several interpretations of the decline-of-ideology writings are possible, and I shall touch here on only two or three. First, one might simply dismiss this literature as reflecting a much too narrow focus on certain undeniable changes in the rhetoric, and even in the perceptions and prescriptions, of some contemporary Marxists. I say dismiss, rather than accord them serious intellectual attention, because: a) the narrow focus fails to include a broader conceptual framework that would permit comparative analytic attention to other aspects of Marxian and non-Marxian ideologies, and b) many of the observations limited to the crisis or travail experienced by Marxists since the Hungarian Rebellion and the XX Congress of the CPSU amount to nothing more than propaganda slogans.

Second, it is possible to sidestep the fascinating subject of broader comparative ideological analysis and concentrate instead on the central proposition that runs through much of this writing, namely, that ideology tends to wane as societies reach levels of social and economic modernization typified by several Western countries. It seems to me, however, that any attempt

---

footnotes of this paper. In any event, the burden of Secher's argument is that German ideology is on the upswing, both in the SPD and in the Catholic sectors of the CDU/CSU.

to assess these writings in such terms is fraught with a number of difficulties that can only be briefly mentioned here. For example, one will have to come to grips with Mannheim, who remains, after all, the first and most prominent scholar to touch on almost every aspect of the arguments mustered by contemporary writers, including the proposition that the birth and death of ideology depends on certain social, economic and "ecological" factors.

But, Mannheim, as I have noted, intends a pejorative definition of ideology, thus greatly narrowing its application. For systems of ideas that are *not* incongruent with empirical realities, he uses the term "utopia." However, if I read him correctly, Mannheim's final test for deciding whether a system of ideas is ideological or utopian is almost invariably *post facto* in the sense that what one identifies as yesterday's ideology becomes tomorrow's utopia when it can be shown that, somewhere in space and time, prescriptions or transcendent ideas turned out not to be incongruent with potential "social realities." [34] The pragmatic test is deceptively simple: If it works, it's utopian; if it doesn't, it's ideological. Outside of ascribing super-rational powers to the "omniscient observer," there is no readily apparent way of identifying the very thing one wishes to measure, except after the fact.

Beyond this conceptual problem, there are others implied by the "more modernization-less ideology" formulation. Such generalizations involve secular trends that span centuries.

[34] See Mannheim, *op. cit.*, Ch. 4, "The Utopian Mentality." Mannheim notes that, "Ideologies are the situationally transcedent ideas which never succeed *de facto* in the realization of their projected content. . . . Utopias too transcend the social situation. . . . But they are not ideologies, i.e., they are not ideologies in the measure and in so far as they succeed through counteractivity in transforming the existing historical reality into one more in accord with their own conceptions" (pp. 176, 177). Mannheim later refines the definition of utopia, trying to tie it to the issue of incongruence from "the point of view of a given social order which is already in existence." Needless to add, it is ideology's decline that Mannheim applauds, and the decline of utopia that he greatly fears because the latter, he says, would make man nothing more than a "thing" unable to shape or understand history: *ibid.*, p. 236 [p. 26 in this volume].

Thus, even if one can reach an acceptable working definition of ideology, the matter of measuring these trends—to say nothing of projecting them into the future—seems to me to involve a degree of precision in historical data gathering and measurement that is only a little better today (and in some ways much worse) than it was in Mannheim's time. My own impression about such long-range trends is that, despite some interesting changes in the symbology of ideology, we are far from seeing the end in Europe of ideology as I have defined it or, indeed, of ideology defined as dogmatic, inflexible, passionately articulated perceptions of reality and prescriptions for the future. Furthermore, since the long-term trend line is not unequivocally established, we cannot say whether short-term phenomena are part of a downward plunging graph line or merely a cyclical dip in a line which may be essentially flat or rising.

It also seems to me that the proposition we are discussing here suffers all of the limitations (which I have detailed elsewhere)[35] that one can identify with a good deal of the recent writing about political development. This formulation seems to rest on the assumption (or hope) that socio-economic-political development is moving in a deterministic, unilinear, culture-specific direction, whereby the future will consist of national histories that are monotonous repetitions of the "Anglo-American" story. In short, the decline-of-ideology writers seem to believe that "they" are becoming more and more like "us."

This leads to a possible third interpretation of the literature, namely, that most of this writing is not social science but, ironically, simply more ideology. The French scholar, Jean Meynaud, reacts in this summary way to the "decline" writers: "In reality, the deep intent of this theory is to establish that in wealthy societies socialism is definitely eclipsed. With many persons it [the theory of decline] is a rather banal aspect of

---

[35] See my (ed.), *Bureaucracy and Political Development* (Princeton, 1963), Ch. 2; and my "Public Administration and Political Change: A Theoretical Overview," in Charles Press and Alan Arian (eds.), *Empathy and Ideology: Knowledges of Administrative Innovation* (forthcoming).

anti-communism or, if one prefers, of a new version of conservative opportunism." [36] This view is strongly echoed by William Delany who says, "The end-of-ideology writers write not just as sociologists or social scientists but as journalists and an anti-totalitarian ideological cabal. Their work is ideology cabal. Their work is ideology but, like almost all Western ideologies since the 18th century, with a heavy 'scientific' component to give respectability and a sense of truth." [37]

These are admittedly harsh judgments. And yet, when one confronts the waning-ideology literature with actual developments in Western Europe, the gap between fact and "scientific" findings suggests exactly such evaluations. Indeed, it is entirely possible that, in the case of some of the decline writers, what they see may be little more than autobiographical projections, which may be fine for some novelists but is clearly quite sticky for social scientists. In any event, in so far as social science analysis of ideology is concerned, it is more than a little difficult to agree with an appraisal of the social sciences which begins by confiding that the American social scientist has been co-opted into something called the "establishment," and then goes on to say about "establishment" members:

Theirs is an alienation brought about by "superior wisdom," that is, by the ability to penetrate the ideologies of others and thereby to emancipate themselves. In this group is the social scientist, who is the objective observer. He penetrates all of the disguises created by the untrained mind or the ideological mind and attaches himself to the image of the wise. He represents the "establishment." [38]

I suppose that, if there is an American "establishment" and if the social scientist has come to play such a prominent role in it, one would expect that in the rationalization and defense of

[36] Jean Meynaud, "Apatia e responsibilita dei cittadini," *Tempi Moderni*, 5 (April-June, 1962), p. 33.

[37] William Delany, "The End of Ideology: A Summation," *op. cit.*, p. 11 [p. 311 in this volume].

[38] Apter, *op. cit.*, pp. 37–38.

his well-ordered world the social scientists's words are likely to take on typically ideological overtones. In any event, it is difficult to imagine how the social scientist in the United States would now go about rebutting the reiterated Russian claim that Western social science is not much more than thinly veiled bourgeois ideology.[39]

This leads to a few concluding remarks about the extent to which phenomena associated with the alleged decline of ideology reflect in great measure certain kinds of adaptations to the crisis confronting Western intellectuals. The Italian case will serve as one concrete illustration of this, although similar patterns can also be explicated for other Western countries.

At the end of World War II, Italian intellectuals—like their counterparts elsewhere in Western Europe—felt deeply involved in a concerted and apparently promising effort to transform Italian society. This was a period in which "The sacred texts were dusted off and the people were enlightened in order to create the maximum degree of consensus and to realize the maximum degree of support and conversions."[40] But romantic notions of socialist revolution—widely fostered by intellectuals—were of very short duration. Failure of Italian society to move directly toward socialism caught many intellectuals flat-footed. They remained tied to a permanent anti-Fascism which led them to ritualistic rhetorical statements about Italian society's ills and the paths to salvation.[41] For almost fifteen years, these intellectuals repeated with startling monotony themes and prescriptions which were simply out of joint as far as the changing conditions of Italian society were

[39] See A. A. Zvorykin, "The Social Sciences in the U.S.S.R.: Achievements and Trends," *International Social Science Journal*, 16 (No. 4, 1964), pp. 588–602. J. S. Roucek, "The Soviet Brand of Sociology," *International Journal of Comparative Sociology*, 1 (1961), pp. 211–219.

[40] Antonio Carbonaro and Luciano Gallino, "Sociologia e ideologie ufficiali," *Tempi Moderni*, 4 (January-March, 1961), p. 31.

[41] Nicola Matteucci, "Pensare in prospettiva," *Tempi Moderni*, 4 (April-June, 1961), p. 32. Cf. the important editorial, "Valori e miti della societa italiana dell'ultimo ventennio, 1940–1960," *ibid.* (October-December, 1961), p. 22.

concerned. In this sense, certainly, Aron and others are right in scoring the stultifying consequences of doctrinaire ideological formulations.

These were years of demoralization for intellectuals who expected revolutionary change and were treated instead to a great deal of temporizing under DeGasperi; but the intellectuals were also blinded to certain social and economic changes that made the traditional rhetoric of Marxism alien to growing numbers of Italians. The irony in all of this is that the intellectuals were the last to appreciate the need for new rhetoric and, indeed, for new ideological formulations. They had been preceded by political leaders not only in the Communist party, but in the ranks of Christian Democracy as well. The politicians evidently quickly understood that no large-scale intervention of the public sector in any kind of development was likely to proceed for long without some kind of *ideological* justification.

To some extent, the isolation of intellectuals from social realities was encouraged by the P.C.I. In keeping the party's intellectuals organizationally separated from mass members, the P.C.I. was able to capitalize on a tendency which is deeply rooted in Italian culture. As Guiducci points out, Italian intellectuals were strongly influenced by the Crocian idea that they were a caste apart, superior to and removed from the masses, and thus failed to maintain an open and realistic contact with the broader population. Even in a context of deep ideological commitment, they managed to adhere to "a position which is traditional with the Italian man of culture, estranged as he is from reality, tied as he is to a culture which is literary and humanistic in the narrowest sense of the words." [42]

The striking thing about Italy in recent years is that the country's intellectuals (largely of the left, but also of the right) seem to be emerging from the kind of isolation Gui-

---

[42] Roberto Guiducci, *Socialismo e verita* (Turin, 1956), pp. 23 ff. Cf. Gaetano Arfe, "La Responsibilita degli intellettuali," *Tempi Moderni,* 4 (January-March, 1961), pp. 31–32; Paolo Prandstraller, *Intellettuali e democrazia* (Rome, 1963).

ducci mentions. Their confrontation of the realities of Italian society has not led, however, to a decline of ideology. Rather, I would suggest that what has happened involves in part ideological clarification and in part the framing of new ideologies to which striking numbers of Italian and European intellectuals, are those of the welfare state and of economic planning. As volve substituting new myths for old. The new myths, which form the core of the ideological structure of many intellectuals, are those of the welfare state and of economic planning. As Henri Jarme rightly puts it. "The myth of planning is only the socialist variant of the myth of progress." [43] But such myths, if Italy is any test, attract more than segments of former orthodox Marxists; they are woven as well into the kind of new ideology that Christian Democrats create.

To be sure, the emergence of new myths creates new symbols and vocabulary. This sort of change should not be construed, however, as an end of ideology. As Giovanni Sartori notes, "Granted that in an affluent society the intensity of ideology will decrease, a lessening of its intensity should not be confused with a withering away of ideology itself. . . . The temperature of ideology may cool down but this fact does not imply that a society will lose the habit of perceiving political problems in an unrealistic or doctrinaire fashion; and it implies even less that a party system will turn to a pragmatic approach." [44]

Two points are relevant here. First, it is obvious that many Italian intellectuals seem to have rediscovered a valid—or at least personally satisfying—function in society, namely, providing an ideological rationale, as well as rational alternatives, for economic planning activity. Second, in achieving this redefinition of role, the intellectual seems to have reaffirmed his responsibility for creating the ideological system within which

---

[43] Henri Jarme, "Le mythe politique du socialisme democratique," *Cahiers Internationaux de Sociologie*, 33 (July-December, 1962), p. 29.

[44] Giovanni Sartori, "European Political Parties: The Case of Polarized Pluralism," in J. LaPalombara and M. Weiner, *op. cit.*

contemporary activity is justified. Needless to say, some of these intellectuals will phrase ideology in the language of science and rationality, whether they are in favor of radical change or of the preservation of the status quo. There is certainly little evidence in Italy, in any event, that, say, a commitment to social science miraculously resolves the nagging problem of Mannheim's Paradox, nor, indeed, that it should.

When we turn to the decline-of-ideology writers, it is possible to detect that they, too, are in search of a definable role in contemporary American society. Whether that role involves the use of social science to criticize America's failings or to extol its consensual or managerial character is a fascinating empirical question. But surely the exploration of this problem would require of a mature social science a certain amount of caution and humility regarding the danger of translating highly selective data gathering or personal predilections or ambitions into sweeping historical projections and "scientific" generalizations. Clifford Geertz, I believe, has put this most succinctly: "We may wait as long for the 'end of ideology' as the positivists have waited for the end of religion." [45]

[45] Geertz, *op. cit.*, p. 51.

MICHAEL HARRINGTON

❧

The Anti-Ideology Ideologues *

Speaking of the great upheavals between 1930 and 1950, Daniel Bell wrote, "For the radical intellectual who had articulated the revolutionary impulses of the past century and a half, all this has meant an end to chiliastic hopes, to millenarianism, to apocalyptic thinking—and to ideology."

The end of ideology is a shorthand way of saying the end of socialism, at least as that idea was conceived of by the nineteenth-century party of the poor. In one sense, Bell rends a straw man. He defines ideology as a passionate, oversimplified program for the immediate incarnation of an abstraction, and it is not surprising that he (or anyone else) would greet the passing of such an anachronism. But there is more than a tautology at stake. For Bell must include a very substantive argument in his analysis: "The old political economic radicalism (pre-occupied with such matters as the socialization of industry) has lost its meaning. Socialism arose as an irreverent movement for the de-mystification of the capitalist ideology. But then, it in turn did not notice its own irrelevance and itself became an ideology."

In short, Bell refashions Mannheim's theory of the transition from revolutionary utopia to self-satisfied ideology. The

* Reprinted with permission of The Macmillan Company and Weidenfeld & Nicolson Ltd. from *The Accidental Century* by Michael Harrington. Copyright © Michael Harrington 1965. Title supplied by the author.

The Anti-Ideology Ideologues

issue is no longer that of the very structure of power (that would be "the old political economic radicalism"). The poor, the once-poor, are now fairly contented. The real problems are those of the quality of life: leisure, mass communications, and the like.

Bell is not one of the cynical detractors of the party of the poor. A convinced reformer with a sympathy for the tradition which he criticizes, he is concerned for the emergence of a new utopia, purged of the old arrogances (he even calls his hope "socialism"). But then, one must confront the basic issues he raises. First of all, is it true that the "old" radicalism is now irrelevant? Has social development so far departed from the predicted patterns that the classic analyses simply no longer apply?

Secondly, and even more basically, if not only the old ideologies, but the conflict of classes that provoked them as well, are finished and done with, where is the political equivalent of poverty that will motivate the new utopia? Where, in a time of centralizing, concentrating power in every advanced nation, is there a substitute for the creativity of misery?

The Future of Socialism, by C.A.R. Crosland, was published in 1956. It is one of the most brilliant and thoughtful books of Social Democratic rethinking to have been published in the West. In his study, Crosland makes a point quite similar to Bell's: that the traditional socialist formulations have lost their meaning through the integration of the workers' movement into a reformed society. He took the countervailing power of the unions as one of his cases in point, and the American experience as a classic demonstration. Writing about the situation in coal, steel, and automobiles, Crosland said, "Even in those industries traditionally considered the citadels of capitalist power, the Trade Union strength is now overwhelming."

Even as Crosland was theorizing, approximately half of the jobs in the American coal industry were being canceled out and the union was powerless to do anything about it (in fact, the union aided the process). The automobile workers de-

343

clined in membership in the same period, and within three years of the publication of *The Future of Socialism,* the steelworkers were forced to wage a six-month strike to protect the very existence of a quarter of a million jobs. Indeed, far from being "overwhelming," labor strength in the United States consistently declined throughout the decade of the fifties and into the sixties. Organized union membership dropped, both in absolute numbers and as a percentage of the total working force.

The issue here is not a quarrel over a footnote but the underestimation of a revolution. It is in America that automation and cybernation first became a massive social force, a chaotic planner of unemployment, regional decay, and a new relation between labor and business. It proved that what technology can integrate, technology can dis-integrate. The immediate result was not a return to the generalized crisis of the 1930s and most of the nineteenth century, but a chronic, nagging, new pattern of wasted human and material resources.

One might even speculatively generalize this situation. If the first Industrial Revolution called into life that utopian movement that eventually ameliorated society sufficiently to make utopia unnecessary, what will the second industrial revolution do? An unprecedented, urbanized environment is emerging in the United States, and Europe is not far behind. Is it possible that this upheaval could once more goad people into action? Is it conceivable that the theories of the happy integration of Western society are themselves as transitory as the theories of its increasing proletarianization?

In any case, it would seem at least premature under such circumstances to declare the old radicalism utterly irrelevant. It is, as the last chapter noted, one of the most basic tendencies of the contemporary technological revolution to collectivize economic and social life. In the Megalopolis, the characteristic habitat of mid-twentieth-century man, one cannot take a drink of water or move a step without entering into a web of collective relationships. The advanced economies of Europe have recognized this interdependence by opting for one or another form of state planning.

This issue, once again, is not whether the West will be collectivized, but how and by whom. And this problem suspiciously resembles the old-fashioned questions that Friedrich Engels used to put in popular form for the socialist movement. How, he asked, can an essentially social system of production be directed by essentially private decision makers? A hundred years later, a technology not subject to conscious and democratic controls is making a minor shambles out of the integration of some of the workers.

Thus far, this second industrial revolution has mainly affected the semiskilled and the unskilled. In part, this has seemed to corroborate the various theories of the passing of the poor. More and more heavy industrial jobs have been mechanized, automated, or cybernated. There is a vast migration from secondary occupations (factory labor) to tertiary ones (the office and service trades) just as the nineteenth century saw a movement from primary occupations (agriculture, raw materials) to secondary ones. But the process will not stop at the factory. Menial office jobs are now being abolished; middle management's turn could come tomorrow.

It would be foolish to think that the mere existence of a crying need for the conscious socialization of the modern economy will create an effective movement with that end in view. In the United States, the first response of the labor movement has been more or less conservative. Some unions, classically the United Mine Workers, accepted the change as inevitable, bade farewell to a good part of the membership, and retrenched in those areas that the whim of technology and fuel consumption still allowed them. Others, like the United Automobile Workers, called for a much more effective counterattack, yet it did not materialize on a national, political scale.

There is much, then, that is indeterminate. Consider two contrasting possibilities: that this same technological revolution could produce the most decadent poor the world has known in modern times; or a new kind of internal opposition.

George Orwell's *1984* has been widely characterized as a repudiation of its author's socialist convictions. He denied the charge, but more significantly, such an interpretation cannot be demonstrated in his novel. His tyrants are not tortured Dostoevskians whose blind faith in absolute freedom led them to totalitarianism. On the contrary, they are determined, thoughtful antiutopians who detest freedom and solidarity. But Orwell was an extraordinarily candid man, and in his book he presents an image of the decadence of the poor.

The "proles" of *1984* are so impotent and helpless that they are not even subjected to totalitarian discipline. This is an important distinction between Orwell's version of the future and Huxley's. In the *Brave New World,* the mass has been reduced to a vegetable existence, but they are well fed. They are creatures of the future, a new kind of slave. In *1984,* the proletarians still exist, but more than that they have retrogressed to the brute levels of existnce of early capitalism.

"And even when they became discontented, as they sometimes did," Orwell's hero writes of the proles, "their discontent led nowhere, because, being without general ideas, they could only focus on their specific grievances." "Left to themselves, like cattle turned loose upon the plains of Argentina, they had reverted to a style of life that appeared to be natural to them, a sort of ancestral pattern. They were born, they grew up in the gutters, they went to work at twelve, they passed through a brief blossoming period of beauty and sexual desire, they married at twenty, they were middle-aged at thirty, they died, for the most part at sixty."

Orwell pictured this retrogression as the outcome of totalitarianism and permanent war. But something like it could be a consequence of technology of abundance.

Already in the American mid-sixties, nearly a third of the young people were without the high-school education that the skill level of the society required as a minimum. There was widespread youth unemployment and underemployment, most

particularly among Negroes who were the double victims of
poverty and racism. There were those who talked of a new
"underclass," of a "non-revolutionary proletariat" (both
phrases are Gunnar Myrdal's). This mode of existence was not
based on the solidarity of vast numbers in a single plant, but
upon the disintegration of life in the streets. Its protests were
not organized movements, but the urban *jacquerie,* mob violence like the Harlem riots of 1964.

If this tendency continued, it could produce a tragic, rather
than contented, definition of the decadence of the poor. At the
top of the society, there would be a bureaucratic elite; beneath
them, technicians and skilled, organized workers; and, at the
very bottom, the class of janitors and the jobless, those who
perform those functions too menial even to bother mechaniz-
ing or automating. And such a group would indeed have an
Orwellian hopelessness. They would suffer a poverty that had
been purged of poverty's one virtue, that of forcing men to
fight against their misery.

Or, perhaps there would be another consequence of the
technological revolution: the emergence of an educated opposition.

In the fifties, as noted before, blue-collar work bore the
brunt of automation and cybernation. But in the sixties, the
distinct possibility appeared that the machines would more and
more replace clerks and even middle-level executives. If this
trend were to persist, if a working-class insecurity were to in-
trude upon middle-class life (and, in the past, one of the most
essential differences between the two existences was that the
one was cyclic and unstable, the other much less so), a new
stratum of society might be energized to seek basic and structural reforms. There would be an obvious danger that such a
development would be technocratic and authoritarian, carried
on, as in *1984,* at the expense of the "proles." But, as the
teachers' union in France, and more recently in the United
States, and the engineers' union in Britain demonstrate, this
need not be the case.

347

It is, of course, impossible even to hazard a serious prediction with so many variables, technical and human, involved. Yet, just as some of the unemployed leagues of the American thirties sold "life memberships," perhaps some of the proclaimers of the finished and unideological society will have mistaken a passing historical moment for an entire future. The thesis of the integration of the party of the poor into the life of affluence and bureaucracy waits for confirmation upon the disintegration of the rest of the century.

But, assuming for a moment that the internal opposition of misery has ceased to matter in the West, a huge question remains: Where will society find the political equivalent for poverty?

The echo of William James's quest for a moral equivalent of war is, of course, intentional. James was not in favor of organized slaughter. Yet he understood that war touched something profound in men. It was an outlet for deep frustrations, an occasion of almost utopian fraternity behind the lines. Similarly with poverty. It would be insane to wish to maintain human misery in order to preserve the creativity born of despair. But, if there is no longer a militant poor to teach the rich, where then will the West discover its practical idealism?

Long ago, William Morris anticipated this problem, though certainly not in its contemporary form. He asked, "Whether the Society of Inequality might not accept the quasi-socialist machinery . . . and work for the purposes of upholding society in a somewhat shorn condition, maybe, but a safe one . . ." That, after all, is one description of an integrated society as is Huxley's *Brave New World*. In it, who has any motive for freedom?

The answer to this question given by Bell and many other end-of-ideology-ists is essentially that the advanced Western societies have reached (or are reaching) such a consensus that passionate political conflict is no longer a necessity. The big issues of freedom have been resolved, and if society settles down to a "stolid acceptance of things as they are" (Barrington Moore's phrase), that reality is good enough for all but incurable romantics. As Seymour Martin Lipset puts this mood, "the workers have achieved industrial and political citizenship; the conservatives have accepted the welfare state; and the democratic left has recognized that an increase in over-all state power carries with it more dangers to freedom than solutions for economic problems."

Or, as Bell said, "the old politico-economic radicalism (preoccupied with such matters as the socialization of industry) has lost its meaning . . ."

Within these assumptions, the poor (or, more precisely, the ex-poor, since "the workers have achieved industrial and political citizenship") surrendered their *élan* out of good common sense. Why sacrifice to create a new world when the present one is more or less satisfying? The basic material and social questions have been settled to the satisfaction, if not according to the ideal, of all major groups. After the wars, revolutions, fascisms, and depressions of the century, history has turned out to be sportsmanlike after all. All retire for the celebration, for everyone has won.

But this static assumption may be untrue. Indeed, I assert that it *is* untrue. And if this is the case, the end of ideology, if it is in fact taking place, is a catastrophe.

Some of the evidence for the accidental, and continuing revolution of these times has already been stated. In the cold decadence of capitalism, one can see that the Western economic structures are now, and have been for some time, in process of basic modification. The fragility of the "industrial citizenship" of hundreds of thousands of American coal miners, automobile workers, and steelworkers has been remarked. The present effect and enormous future potential of automation and cybernation will be described later.

But here there is no point rehearsing, or anticipating, statistics and data. It seems clear enough that the technological revolution of this century is far from over—and therefore the social and economic revolution remains on the agenda.

Indeed, one might even suspect that the idea of the end of ideology is a product of the Indian summer of the old-fashioned Industrial Revolution, the first one. During the fifties, it was possible to look back on the accomplishments—and relative political consensus—of the last stages of the factory age without looking forward to the radical dislocations of the automating and cybernating age. From such a point of contemplation, basic change and its corresponding social conflict were the fate of the developing, but not the advanced, societies, and the West could busy itself with exporting its wisdom to those historical unfortunates.

But if the accidental revolution is a present fact, then the end of ideology would mean the beginning of decadence.

Under such conditions, there would be the most basic options to make, and no humanely oriented class or group to make them. Who will direct the concentrated economic power and with what priorities? Will planning be totalitarian, technocratic, or democratic? Will cities simply sprawl and sprawl and sprawl, abolishing the landscape? Will the new leisure take the form of the old unemployment; will it be manipulated by advertising or will it be creative? The list of momentous, fundamental, and unavoidable questions could be prolonged almost indefinitely.

Businessmen and bureaucrats are notoriously unprepared for the creation of a new, and anticapitalist, social order. Should they continue to back into one, it would almost undoubtedly combine the worst of the past and future. The expoor, the end-of-ideology-ists say, are so content that they have abandoned all but an occasional rhetorical reference to the Good Society. And the new poor are more like Orwell's proles than Marx's proletarians.

Who, then, will decide the shape of the new civilization? By far and large, the proclaimers of the end of ideology are men of the moderate, democratic Left. They happily assume that the passing of the simplifications of the once-oppressed will open up the way for a tolerant consideration of the unfinished business of the West, the questions of the quality of life. Even granting their complacency about the way in which the advanced nations have permanently adjusted their economies, these theorists have no group, outside of a few intellectuals, that is impelled to make their cautious utopia a cause in the way that poverty provoked the old utopia.

But then, history has not granted the complacent premises. Technology bids to transform the second half of the century as vigorously as it did the first. And correcting these theories for their omission of an upheaval, a grim possibility emerges: an insistent, revolutionary situation without any revolutionists, a society urgently requiring movement but without an Archimedian point of leverage in the lives of men.

STEVEN KELMAN

The Feud Among the Radicals*

When Yale assistant professor of history Staughton Lynd last year branded fellow civil-rights activist Bayard Rustin a "labor lieutenant of capitalism," and a liberal professor at an Eastern college countered that Lynd is "on the very margin of sanity," some observers of the factional struggles of the American Left were tempted to yawn and wonder why radicals always seem to fight each other more than their common foes. But the exchange was really the opening dialogue in the final act of a drama.

The action is taking place, not in a void—the locale of so many American radical debates since the 'thirties—but in an atmosphere made congenial by a revived campus "New Left," by the burgeoning attack on American involvement in Vietnam, and above all by the determination of the black one-tenth of the nation to join the Great Society. The predicament of today's small band of American radicals concerns the tactics they are going to use in promoting their programs. Should they work for a coalition of the largely powerless Negro masses and poor people, with groups already sharing power—the labor unions, liberal organizations like the Americans for Democratic Action, and progressive religious movements? Or should they reject alliances with such forces and attempt instead to organize those "unspoiled" by power as a potential revolutionary force independent of "The Establishment"?

To the public, such debates on the radical fringe seem no more than ludicrous. Will any appreciable number of people follow either path? Are today's radical disputes any different from the obscure infighting of the 'thirties between Socialists, Trotskyites, Communists, Lovestonites, and other shades of left-wing opinion?

The answer is yes. We should not be misled by the experiences of the 'thirties into ignoring the present-day radicals. The radicals of the late 'thirties remained more or less in the wilderness of theory because their potential constituency, the workers, already belonged to F.D.R. They could do unionizing work, but the workers invariably resisted attempts to make such unions tools of one or another radical faction.

On the other hand, today's potential radical following—the urban poor and the Southern Negro—is as yet unclaimed (or, as John Lindsay's election in New York shows, old claims are in flux). Furthermore, today's poor are still largely invisible amidst American affluence, while during the Depression everybody was working to end distress because everybody was involved. The isolation of today's poor, underlined by the outbreaks of destructiveness in Harlem and Watts, makes radical solutions to their problems seem necessary.

The Left of the 'thirties was mesmerized by words. While serious economic problems beset the country, many remained caught in the irrelevancies of such questions as whether the Soviet Union was a "degenerate workers' state" or a "managerialist bureaucracy." In contrast, the Left of the 'sixties prides itself on its belief in action first. The coalition vs. independent-action debate of the 'sixties, in fact, got started only after a few years of radical action. The Left built itself up testing its relevancy in the field.

The Immorality of Alliance

Radicals have always divided up on the basis of their answer to one important question: is it possible to achieve "meaningful" (i.e., radical) change within the existing political structure? American radicalism today might roughly be divided into three parts according to the answer to this question. There are the *Can'ts,* the *Cans,* and (of considerably less importance than the others) the *Communists.*

Can'ts believe that the existing society is so corrupt that alliance with any established group is dangerous, useless, and immoral. Existing groups, in the words of the Can't publication *Freedom North,* are "so integrated into the existing structure that they function as enemies of social change." Can'ts specialize in making comparisons between America today and Nazi Germany. Many agree with Staughton Lynd that "socialism . . . is likely to come by way of resistance to fascism." With Armageddon approaching, Can'ts feel it is frivolous to try to do anything basic about our problems now.

Cans, on the other hand, are radicalism's matchmakers. As radicals, they are maximalists in their demands, but they are willing to accept less than total victory in every confrontation. Cans do not shrink from basic and caustic criticism of current institutions, but they maintain that the tool for change is available in the form of political democracy. Bayard Rustin, for example, prefaces his Can program with the remark, "Needless to say, I am assuming that the forms of political democracy exist in America, however imperfectly. . . ." Cans base their radical plans on the swing to the Left which they forecast, once groups now excluded from political power—the Negroes and the poor—get their "one man, one vote."

The Communists (or, to be more precise, the Moscow Communists) fall outside either group because theirs is essentially

an opportunistic policy. Ideologically, they are Can'ts. But politically, they are often Cans. Recently, for example, American
Communist party leader Gus Hall warned against the classic
Can't pitfall of "being tied down by abstractions or slogans
that sound radical but do not correspond to . . . what is possible," and Henry Winston, another ranking Communist
official, took the coalitionist line that "equal rights can be attained only by enlisting the support of the peace organizations,
the trade-union movement, and other democratic forces." This
"realistic" position is of course designed to serve the purposes
of the Communist party, which can then claim credit for
everything that happens of which they approve.

As the battle positions form, the troops line up more and
more behind two men, Bayard Rustin and Staughton Lynd—
each of whom, curiously enough, often seems like a general
leading a brigade which rightfully should belong to the other
side.

The followers of Bayard Rustin have been caricatured as the
radicals in gray-flannel suits, and denounced as academic types
who have either never seen a picket line or have forgotten
what it used to be like. But Rustin does not fit these stereotypes. He is rather a tall, graying Negro revolutionary, a non-
racialist and a pacifist, who boasts twenty-four civil rights and
"political" arrests (including a long stretch during World
War II as a conscientious objector). When I succeeded in getting to speak with him—an appointment squeezed into
Rustin's perpetual round of meetings, conferences, speaking
engagements—I was astonished to find that he is so active that
he has had little time or inclination to follow the voluminous
literature radicals pour out and the debates swirling around his
name.

Rustin is not an intellectual. Unlike many other radicals, he
does little writing. When he speaks he prefers to talk to local
audiences rather than at $100-a-plate fund-raising affairs. A
friendly observer on the liberal Left has commented that
Rustin's main virtue is his ability to put reasonable proposals

into revolutionary rhetoric. When he does write, his purpose is to set out a course of action. Rustin's long article in a 1965 issue of *Commentary,* "From Protest to Politics," set out the new Can course of political action, articulating positions he had begun to develop tactically at the 1963 civil-rights March on Washington and the 1964 Democratic Convention. These positions represented a departure from Rustin's earlier advocacy of direct action ("placing down our black bodies and stopping traffic") as the primary civil-rights technique.

He was born in 1910 in West Chester, Pennsylvania (ironically, this is near the place where today's radical Students for a Democratic Society—SDS—set up one of their first projects aimed at "organizing the poor"). After graduating from high school, he worked at odd jobs to earn money for college. At City College, he earned money singing folk songs with Leadbelly and Josh White. His radical and civil-rights activity has taken him around the world. As early as 1941 he became the first field secretary of the then just-formed Congress of Racial Equality. In 1947 he participated in the first freedom ride ever held. In North Carolina, the destination of the ride, he was arrested and sentenced to thirty days on a chain gang. Rustin's story of his experiences in the New York *Post* led North Carolina to abolish chain gangs.

Organization is Rustin's forte. He was Martin Luther King's strategist and ghost writer when King was first gaining fame. He planned the Montgomery bus boycott and drew up the design for King's Southern Christian Leadership Conference. More recently, he organized both the 1963 March on Washington and the 1964 New York City school boycott. Like President Johnson, he is a man proud above all of results. He flashes results—jobs created for the poor, laws passed, discriminatory practices ended—with a sense of satisfaction.

Because of his long and distinguished career in the radical movement, it is difficult for Rustin's opponents on the Left to attack him head-on. Instead they use guerrilla tactics. The most unkind cuts of all are almost always preceded by references to the old comrade Bayard they all knew and loved, mixed with shock that he has abandoned the people for the guiles of the power structure.

From Method to Mesmerism

And who is leading the pack of holier-than-the-Master disciples? Can'ts have been portrayed as the beatniks of the 'sixties, oversexed bearded slobs whose main concern is to *épater le bourgeois*. But Staughton Lynd, the general of the Can't forces, is nothing like that. Professor at Yale, Lynd seems an unlikely candidate for the role of assailant of the established order. When I spoke to him, the thirty-six-year-old Quaker—feet lazily propped on the wooden desk in his newly installed cubbyhole office in Yale's Trumbull College—answered in slow, deliberated phrases in which each word seemed carefully weighed to make sure that it would offend nobody. He almost appeared to be thinking for the first time about some of the problems on which I was questioning him. He spices his speech with such quaint Americanisms as "okey-dokey," and the Quaker expression "folk" for "people." In his published historical writings as well, Lynd is methodical and contemplative. His background in the solid professional gentry extends from New York City's Ethical Culture and Fieldston schools to Harvard.

"As long as I've known him, Staughton's been some form of Marxist," an old classmate says. In 1948 Lynd, still too young to vote, supported Norman Thomas rather than Henry Wallace for President because the latter was a "bourgeois party" candidate. In 1954 Lynd and his wife joined a Georgia cooperative community run by ex-conscientious objectors. He left the community in 1957 to do graduate work at Columbia, where he got a doctorate in American history for the thesis,

"The Revolution and the Common Man: Farm Tenants in New York During the American Revolution." He got his first teaching assignment at Spelman College, a Negro women's school in Georgia. In 1964 he came to Yale.

Lynd's self-proclaimed intellectual role is that of New Left philosophical synthesizer. "I've tried to teach pacifism to Marxists, Marxism to the pacifists, and Christianity to both," he told me. Defying all the best rules of radical obscurantism, he once defined his political credo as simply as this: "The time we live in . . . is the Period of Transition from Capitalism to Socialism. . . . I consider myself a radical in that I applaud the coming of socialism, and seek to assist rather than resist it."

Up until 1964 Lynd's life seemed much like a rerun out of 1840-vintage Transcendentalism, but in the summer of 1964 he got his first activist experience as director of the Mississippi Freedom Schools. It wasn't until a year later that he was arrested for the first time. Although on this occasion Lynd was literally on the receiving end of a can of red paint, he is still for the most part sheltered from the day-to-day tribulations of the radical activists.

But his spiritual home is in the fray. His skills as an organizer are recognized by all. As a Chicago SDS leader observed, "Nothing much happens without Staughton." And a crowd does something strange to Lynd—the easygoing academic is transformed into the kind of bogeyman good at scaring big businessmen and little children. Many people who knew Lynd when he was younger, and who have described him as "shy," "a poor speaker," and even "a bit pedantic" are surprised at his talents with crowds. But it is not so much Lynd's delivery that is extraordinary (a Yale student who has debated with him commented, "Even the shocking statements are made in a mild way") as what he says: in a crowd of militant revolutionaries, he can act as the conciliator; in a mixed group of militants and moderates such as are usually present at anti-War-in-Vietnam rallies, he can delight the extremists and try to move the moderates by a mixture of sweeping moralisms, bold-sounding attacks on targets as diverse as Yale and American Secretaries of State, and calls to action which, at the moment they are uttered sound like just the thing needed to stop the "shame."

In addition to the generals, each side has its folk heroes. A Can't demigod is Bob Moses of the Student Nonviolent Coordinating Committee (SNCC), who showed his militant opposition to the idea of "manipulative" leadership by changing his name to Bob Parris and leaving Mississippi when he felt he was becoming too idolized by local blacks. The Cans have Michael Harrington, a former member of the Catholic Worker movement and current Socialist party leader who wrote his angry book on the American poor, *The Other America,* only to have President Kennedy read it and dream up the War on Poverty.

The personalities are diverse, and the language is anything but sedate. The Can'ts have revolutionary-sounding journals like *Liberation* and *Free Student,* as well as the less strident *Studies on the Left* and the tabloid weekly *National Guardian.* (These publications, aided by a few newspapermen who lazily picked up their expression, have succeeded in having their position dubbed the New Left.) The Cans can answer back only in the Socialist party's *New America* and in the bimonthly *Dissent,* but they have the advantage of access to liberal publications like *Commentary, The New Leader,* and even that Establishment bastion, *The New York Times Magazine.*

Cans have labeled their opponents "kamikaze radicals," "messianists," and even "reactionaries." Can'ts have replied that Cans are "court socialists" in the palace of power, unwilling to offend "the good man in the White House." Cans have been attacked as "former radicals" and even "sell-outs." At times this is meant literally: a California SNCC journal suggested that Rustin agreed to sell out in exchange for a $50,000 grant from the AFL-CIO to his A. Philip Randolph Institute. The Can coalition has been described as a "coalition with the Marines." At an open-air rally, Harrington, who had recently written an article attacking Communists in the peace movement, was derisively called "Colonel Harrington of the War on Poverty."

Beyond C. Wright Mills

This tendency to be diverted by colorful language often obscures one basic difference in the views of the Cans and Can'ts: their different conceptions of the meaning and uses of power. The Cans have an unambiguous attitude toward power. They feel it is nothing to shirk, provided it is based on democratic consent. To them gaining political power is *the* aim of all political action.

The Can'ts are not at all sure. The dual origin of today's New Left in the anarchist and Marxist traditions leaves them unclear as to whether they want to *take* power or *annihilate* it. This double attitude becomes apparent in the actions which New Left thinkers have proposed as alternatives to Rustin's coalitionism. Sometimes their purpose seems to be to *escape* from power, sometimes to *grab* power by a minority putsch, sometimes merely to *test* the purity of their forces against temptations to "cop out" to the power structure.

These different attitudes toward power help explain the seeming contradiction in the fact that Negroes like Rustin, who have *experienced* the evils of the society which they are trying to change, seem to be less extreme in their position than middle-class whites like Lynd, who have grown up with the best America has to offer. The middle-class "community organizers" of SNCC and SDS don't mind romantically living "among the poor" on 50 cents a day. For them it is a "happening"; for the poor, it is something they've been doing all their lives, and who is to blame them if they don't like it. Lynd can afford to be extreme; he has no personal stake in the success of his programs. The poor, and people like Rustin who have known poverty, do.

So Rustin has carefully developed a scenario for bringing about the adoption of the clearly defined Can program. He takes as his point of departure the pluralistic model of American society developed by liberal sociologists in the 'fifties to answer C. Wright Mills' attempt to prove in *The Power Elite* that a group "few in number and weighty beyond comparison," outside public control, exerts all real power in the United States.

According to the pluralistic-society theorists, countless interest and voting groups—the unions, business, churches, farmers, etc.—compete for, share, and thus atomize power. This view, which nonchalantly ignored unorganized groups (such as Southern Negroes), has been updated by Rustin. According to him and to many Cans, the United States is a pluralistic society which must be made *more* "plural."

In other words, democracy in America is not yet perfected. Not only are some groups excluded from political participation, but also economic power is concentrated in too small a group. However, the basic instrument for change is there, and the powerless of today can become the powerful of tomorrow by using it. That instrument is politics. To a strategist like Rustin, the question is one of numbers:

A handful of Negroes, acting alone, could integrate a lunch counter by strategically locating their bodies so as *directly* to interrupt the operation of the proprietor's will; their numbers were relatively unimportant. In politics, however, such a confrontation is difficult because the interests involved are merely *represented.* . . . In arriving at a political decision, numbers and organizations are crucial, especially for the economically disenfranchised.

For Rustin, the turning point in the realization that it was time for the civil-rights movement to turn from "protest to politics" and from lunch counters to "numbers and organizations" was the mass demonstrations at Birmingham and the March on Washington in 1963. In Birmingham the entire Negro community, rather than a small educated elite, was in the streets. In Washington a coalition of Negro, church, liberal, and labor groups amassed 250,000 demonstrators. These were mass efforts with more than token goals.

The civil-rights movement, Rustin reasoned, could now use the strength it had acquired in ten years of localized pressure to turn to the more substantial problems which both Cans and Can'ts agree are at the heart of the "Negro question"—economic problems. And, in focusing on economics, the civil-rights movement could emerge from a self-restrictive racial ghetto. Automation, medical care, the quality of urban life, housing, and mass transit are not issues which face Negroes or even poor people alone: they face most Americans.

As Rustin turned his vision from small direct-action protest toward mass protest and the resulting political action to change society, he immediately was forced to realize the fact that

. . . The country's twenty million black people cannot win political power alone. We need allies. The future of the Negro struggle depends on whether the contradictions of this society can be resolved by a coalition of progressive forces which becomes the effective political majority in the United States.

And the proposed elements of the coalition are, like Barkis, willing. As early as December, 1963, in an article in the AFL-CIO's *American Federationist,* labor's leading political theorist, Gus Tyler, held before the rights movement the tantalizing possibility of a "simultaneous expansion of jobs and freedom" arising from a Negro-labor alliance. Cans have been heartened by the agreement of civil-rights and labor leaders on a three-point program of Congressional priorities: a $2 minimum wage (what one Can has called "the single most potent *civil-rights* proposal ever to come before Congress), repeal of 14 (b) of the Taft-Hartley Act, and expanded unemployment insurance. Cans are counting on their voter drives and the unions' organizing drives to provide the power base for a swing to the left. Meanwhile they have rejoiced at the presence of Catholic nuns at Selma and the important support of the California clergy for a strike of AFL-CIO organized grape pickers in that state.

Redemption Through Success

The goal of Can action is to *shift the center of power* by placing the votes and influence of Negroes and the poor behind a new progressive majority force, eventually realigning the two parties so that the "alliance of New Dealers and Slave Dealers" within the Democratic party is broken, and making it the instrument of the Negro-labor-liberal coalition. Rustin argues that the Negroes will of necessity be a radical influence in the coalition, because even if most Negroes—in their hearts— "seek only to enjoy the fruits of American society as it now exists," they will find this goal impossible. Rustin says: "The young Negro who would demonstrate his way into the labor market may be motivated by a thoroughly bourgeois ambition and thoroughly 'capitalist' considerations, but he will end up having to favor a great expansion of the public sector of the economy."

The Cans are counting on redeeming their radicalism, not by verbal militance, but by success. Rustin can boast of his work in opening up the building trades unions to Negroes. "How many jobs have these fellows produced?" he asks of the Can'ts. Radicals of the Can persuasion will continue to press for massive government programs of slum clearance, urban development, public housing, hospital and park construction, and the creation of new towns. Though such a program is still "this side of radicalism" (to use Michael Harrington's phrase), it would be an important radical breakthrough in that it would necessitate national planning. It is at this point, says Harrington, that the radical forces in the coalition could press for the "basic transformations" which the poor need today, but which the "entire society will require tomorrow if it is to make its revolutionary technology humane."

So the Cans are busy trying to build.

But not without sniping. Hal Draper, a leftover from the 'thirties and a Berkeley perennial, has quipped that the Can theory of coalition leading to realignment "has an excellent chance of coming true if Mary Poppins joins the LID" (the League for Industrial Democracy, a leading Can "educational organization"). But the more fundamental criticism of the coalition concept by the Can'ts is not its impracticability but its political immorality.

Staughton Lynd has summed up this objection in the epigram "Coalitionism is Elitism": "its assumption is that major political decisions are made by deals between the representatives of the interests included in the coalition. . . . Men like Rustin will become the national spokesmen who sell the line agreed on behind doors to the faithful followers in the streets."

This conclusion about the alleged antidemocratic nature of coalitionism was reached at the 1964 Democratic National Convention at Atlantic City. To the Can'ts, the turning point was when the credentials of the all-white official Mississippi Delegation were challenged by the Mississippi Freedom Democratic Party (MFDP), an independent political grouping organized by SNCC. The Democratic hierarchy came up with a compromise: the MFDP would get two at-large seats, and a resolution requiring abolition of racial discrimination in delegate selection would be adopted.

SNC leaders opposed the compromise, carrying the majority of MFDP delegates with them and out of the convention. Rustin, along with Martin Luther King, Roy Wilkins, James Farmer, and others, fought for its acceptance, arguing that it was the best solution obtainable and that allies in the liberal would begin to govern. The transfer of allegiance would apply, to begin with, only to specific acts. Those refusing to pay taxes might pay them to the continental congress.

This would go on until Johnson and "the Tuesday lunch club that runs this country" resign!

This comic opera version of a *coup d'état,* carried on by a handful of Can'ts presumably in the name of the "objective interests" of mankind, shows at its purest how the Can'ts turn the corner toward totalitarianism. Imagine the twenty-seven millions who voted for Goldwater setting up their own government, occupying SAC, and dropping The Bomb on Peking. Lynd's "parallel structure" ideas could lead to a potential putsch by any kind of disgruntled political faction.

But there is also Lynd-the-Anarchist, sounding like a modern Pied Piper of Hamlin, leading the discontented from current corruption to parallelistic purity. He idyllically exhorts the alienated: "Let the teacher leave the university and teach in Freedom Schools; let the reporter quit his job on a metropolitan daily and start a community newspaper."

When used in this manner, the parallel structure is not really a political device at all. It is rather a "counter-community," an oasis of fraternity in a land of materialism. People elected by Negroes as representatives to state or national legislatures, suggests Lynd, should "decline" to take their seats, and serve as a "symbol" of rejection of existing government, presumably staying home to create some local "parallel structure."

It Boils Down to Style

If the creation of such havens of happiness is the goal of SDS and SNCC in their organization of the poet, the poor people

wing of the Democrats would be necessary in the future. Lynd objected to Rustin's contention that "national considerations" —the need of the Negro for allies—must play a role in the decision; by that, Lynd felt, Rustin meant that the "plain people in Mississippi" were not "competent to decide" on the matter.

The Democractic "power structure" was thus thrown in the same lot as the Mississippi racists. Both, said SNCC, wanted to keep the Negro "at the back of the bus." The lesson, SNCC leader Bob Moses said later, was that "responsible" groups in society were not responsible, that the destiny of America was not in the people's hands. And the villain of the Can't morality play was Rustin.

The Can'ts thus came to contest Rustin's view of American society as an incomplete democracy. To them this is a country ruled by an all-embracing "power structure" where even the "first-class citizens" (middle-class, white-collar, and industrial-working-class whites) do not have "any meaningful degree of control over the basic direction of American society or the values which now dominate it," in the words of one editor of *Studies on the Left.*

This Can't model of what they call, with obvious awe mixed with scorn, "The System," is essentially, if not always overtly, Marxist. Indeed, the ideological Marxists have indignantly asked why today's Can't New Left uses pussyfooting terms like "Establishment" and "power structure" when it means—or at least *should* mean—capitalism.

The answer is that the Can'ts don't quite *mean* capitalism. Capitalism is part of what they mean, but the whole is more accurately described as "power." They have updated C. Wright Mills to make the "power elite" a fiendish, but demoniacally brilliant, octopus which is frantically trying to devour any radical movement emerging to the surface.

Playing Checkers the Can't Way

So a fundamental reason that Can'ts refuse to enter into coalitions with liberals or unions is that these have *power*. They are part of the same Establishment that General Motors and Governor Wallace are part of. In fact, the New Left's most significant contribution to modern political paranoia is their increasingly prominent belief (strangely parallel to that of the John Birch Society) that The System against which they are railing is none other than American liberalism.

But, lest they be accused of reverting to the old leftism of the Communists in the early 'thirties, who used such terms as "Social Fascist" in describing Social Democrats, the Can'ts shrink from such terminology, preferring instead a new term of their invention, "corporate liberalism." It is the "corporate liberals," said SDS President Carl Oglesby at an antiwar rally last November, who rule America.

This all is pretty cagey. The corporations rule the country; the assignment of the liberal and labor unions is to stop ("co-opt" in the current parlance) radicalism by producing watered-down reform. Thus the cabal keeps all power in its hands and prevents The People from making any decisions affecting their lives.

But, in their attempted synthesis of Marxism, pacifism, and anarchism, the Can'ts end up unsure as to what they want to do about society. Meanwhile, they cover up lack of decision with slogans like "Let the People Decide"—it is they, not us, say the Can'ts, who should come up with programs and conclude what to do.

The heart of the ambiguity in this attitude lies in Lynd's concept of The Unrepresented. Behind this idea is the old anarcho-Rousseauian belief that majority-rule democracy is insufficient because it does not include the whole community in

sharing power. A minority is defeated, period. It can try to become a majority, but as long as it isn't, it doesn't make policy.

For someone who cannot stand such a situation, there are two possible courses of action. One is to *renounce* the idea of power and to withdraw into a new community created by people who share your beliefs and style of life. The other is to *grab* power—to become the government—through a minority putsch supported by a small number of self-chosen saviors. Lynd has toyed with both anarchistic and authoritarian courses of action in his chief contribution to Can't political thought, the "parallel structure."

Parallel structures are institutions set up outside the existing community ("community" in the broad sense of "social unit"). They are the refuge of The Unrepresented. The Southern Negro cannot participate in either major party, so he creates a "parallel party" (after the Atlantic City Convention in 1964, the Mississippi Freedom Democratic Party started describing itself in such terms). This is one thing in Mississippi or Alabama, where the Negroes are literally disenfranchised. But what if the majority of the people are in favor of, say, the war in Vietnam? This still leaves the minority unrepresented (because "the majority rules"). So, according to Lynd, The Unrepresented should form a parallel *government* to end the war. If you don't follow this logic, you've never played checkers with someone who knocks over the board when he starts losing.

Lynd offers the Continental Congress of 1774 as an excellent example of a parallel government growing into the real government. According to Lynd-the-Authoritarian, those opposed to the Vietnam war should unite with those involved with SNCC and SDS community work to convene a new Continental Congress.

Resolutions would be adopted and the form of treaties ratified; emissaries of the congress could seek to make direct contact with the people of other countries. In effect the continental congress involved are likely to view the whole thing as a cruel hoax perpetrated on them by middle-class rebels. What can the counter-community *do,* for example, about poverty? The government has the money; The Establishment has the jobs. But the Can'ts refuse to deal with The Other Government or The Establishment. It is, if nothing else, unfair to the poor to use them as the vehicle for the Can'ts in his search for an elusive counter-community. Notes Marxist professor of history William A. Williams:

A community is a community is a community. It is not a sect. It is not Plato's in-group of philosopher kings. It is not a secular congregation carefully selected according to a priori standards. And least of all is it a marching and chowder society organized by incipient nihilists to give themselves comfort and company.

When Can'ts try to apply their mélange of anarchism and authoritarianism in practical action, the results are, not unpredictably, strange. For example, they had an opportunity at their August 1964 Assembly of Unrepresented People to show the world the new higher form of democracy, baptized by SDS "participatory democracy." Witness this hair-raising (but friendly) description which appeared in *Liberation:*

Decision is neither voting nor consensus. In fact, decisions in the usual sense don't occur. Policies are set and action determined by those who, in the maelstrom of discussion and debate, exert the most influence through courage, articulateness, reasonableness, and sensitivity to the feelings of the group. Influence is enhanced by image characteristics such as reputation, looks and style of living that appeal to young people. . . . Thus, the Assembly's activities were not leaderless, formless, and decisionless. The leaders were the most influential; they set the dominant modes and forms, which were the policies; their actions were the decisions.

This seems like "choosing" (if the process could be called that) a virtual dictator on the basis of political sex appeal. Could it conceivably be the basis for anything but an ingroup of initiates?

As can be seen, the dominant mode of these Can't attempts at political action is *style*. Decisions are made by those who have the best image, and protest is generally along such lines too. This can have tragic results, as has become apparent in the, if nothing else, heroic "strike" of Mississippi Delta plantation workers organized by the SNCC-controlled Mississippi Freedom Labor Union (MFLU). MFLU has remained true to the Can't tradition by refusing affiliation or alliance with the AFL-CIO while still asking for no-strings contributions from AFL-CIO unions. The MFLU workers have been persuaded to stop work until their demands for $1.25-an-hour wages and union recognition are met. The trouble is that this valiant protest involves at most five of more than one hundred plantations on the Delta. With so few workers out, it is child's play for the planters to bring in labor from other plantations. Under such conditions, the strike can theoretically go on forever without any results. Meanwhile, the striking workers have been reduced to a diet of food from the North and freedom songs from SNCC.

Pop-Art Guerrilla Warriors

There is something in the Can't psyche which is unable to accept the objective existence of success. For three years, SNCC devoted virtually all its energy to desegregating public accommodations. After a lot of fighting, they achieved a little desegregating. Then came the Civil Rights Act of 1964, which legislated access to *all* such accommodations. Suddenly all they had worked for became a hoax: public accommodations did not really matter if you did not have the money to use them. So next SNCC turned its attention to voter registration. The workers risked their lives working on it and got a pitifully few Negroes registered. Then came the Voting Rights Act of 1965.

Suddenly voting lost its importance; it was described as "a delusion and a snare" as long as The System remained.

This is why Cans often call Can'ts reactionaries. Their attitudes, say the Cans, lead to giving up the struggle, often giving up politics, and resigning themselves to no change at all. Their conservative view of society (everyone is The Establishment; nobody is ready to move except us) leads to quietism.

Disillusioned that the workers or the poor have "let them down" by not making a revolution, some Can'ts give up trying to change the society and make their rebellion totally personal. They try to dissociate themselves from what they had previously tried to change by personal "affirmations" such as unconventional dress or speech. For example, at a Vietnam rally last year at Berkeley, one self-proclaimed "novelist" came on stage, dressed in an army uniform and helmet, to give his solution for Vietnam. The solution consisted of gleeful repetition of a four-letter word interspersed with harmonica music. The apolitical Can'ts prophesy with glee world-wide race war and the destruction of Western civilization, thus assuming the role of "pop-art guerrilla warriors," in Irving Howe's words. But their incantations often turn into a catharsis for a segment of the middle class which, in the end, enjoys the activities of the apolitical Can'ts as entertainment.

Meanwhile, among those still engaged in politics, the struggle goes on. The Can'ts continue with their invective and their organizing. As the war in Vietnam has escalated, the Can'ts have accused the Cans of agreeing to be quiet on "U.S. imperialism" in Vietnam and elsewhere as the price for their coalition—a coalition which thus becomes, by extension, a "coalition with the Marines."

This accusation has occasioned some of Lynd's most hysterical attacks on Rustin, since Lynd considers attack on American foreign policy as one—if not *the*—foremost goal of any radical movement.

While the Can'ts shout, the Cans are able to keep relatively restrained. For they know that even independent radical organizing efforts will help them and increase their strength in any coalition. This is why Rustin can say that he is grateful for SDS community organizing and local third parties, but still add that on a national level coalitionism is the only answer.

One wonders what ever became of the End of Ideology. In 1960 Professor Daniel Bell, the Columbia sociologist, wrote a book documenting "the exhaustion of political ideas in the 'fifties." Bell spoke of a world where old ideological battles were over, where men debated, not about doctrines, but about allocation of resources.

That was the 'fifties. The 'sixties have now passed their halfway mark and it seems that perhaps Bell's death sentence was a bit premature. Clark Kissinger of the SDS disputes Bell in the direct New Left manner: "When they proclaim the end of ideology, it's like an old man proclaiming the end of sex. Because he doesn't feel it anymore, he thinks it's disappeared."

Whatever else can be said about the radicals, one thing stands out. *They* feel it.

DONALD CLARK HODGES

The End of
"The End of Ideology" *

What is the evidence for the increasingly fashionable thesis of
the gradual extinction in the West? Is the evidence actually as
strong as it appears? Intellectual spokesmen for the thesis of
an end of ideology in this country point to the convergence of
a regenerate capitalism and a liberalized, affluent socialism
leading to a new social order that will take us one step beyond
the Welfare State. A rosier picture was never painted. And,
perhaps, neither a more misleading one. That ideological controversy is in the process of disappearing is one thing; that this
statement entails a decline of ideology is something quite
different.

How does this post-bourgeois panacea compare with evidence for the counterthesis that ideology is now waxing
stronger than ever? In answer to this question let us examine
the arguments for an end of ideology from Mannheim and
Aron through Feuer, Molnar, Kerr, Bell, and Lipset. Let us,
then, assess the evidence in the light of data which their arguments either neglect altogether or otherwise fail to analyze.
Although ideology has been defined differently by these vari-

* Reprinted by permission of the author and publisher from *The
American Journal of Economics and Sociology,* Vol. 26, No. 2, 1967.

ous thinkers, there is more than a family resemblance between its several uses. One may isolate its common denominator which can be identified with the more or less conscious deceptions and disguises of human interest groups. The question is the extent to which increasing enlightenment and affluence have created a new society in which efforts to disguise partisan interests and to manipulate and outwit rival groups now take the form of cooperation toward a common goal, and whether this consensus signifies the decline of ideology or rather the triumph of one ideology over all its rivals.

I

We may begin by taking a fresh look at the arguments for a secular decline in ideology. First there is the argument for the emergence of the intelligentsia as a politically independent stratum committed to the ideal of objective or disinterested knowledge. This thesis was originally developed by Mannheim, *Ideology and Utopia* (1936). In the course of affiliating themselves with the classes in power, intellectuals have become the ideological spokesmen for vested interests, whereas those intellectuals who have chosen to make common cause with oppressed and disaffected classes have championed utopias of one kind or another. Under ideologies Mannheim includes all those misrepresentations concerning the status quo that make it appear more favorable to our interests than it actually is; under utopias, those statements about a future condition that make the present appear less favorable to our interests than is warranted, though a prospect that is destined to become actual. However, there is still another course open to intellectuals, short of vacillating from one side to another, or taking a middle-of-the-road position, namely, a consciousness

374

of their own independent role as a social stratum. No other group in society is better situated, for example, to develop a total orientation, an objective knowledge of man's social condition that rises above the distorted and partial perspective of the social classes. Indeed, the historic mission of the intellectuals includes not only the development of ideological and utopian modes of thought, but also the fullest possible synthesis of the tendencies of an epoch. And this latter mode of thought, which can be accurately termed scientific, is to that extent beyond both ideology and utopia.

The tendency of our age, according to Mannheim, is toward the complete destruction of all spiritual vistas and their replacement by a prosaic or matter-of-fact attitude corresponding to the increasing absorption of intellectuals by private and public bureaucracies. This theme is further developed in his subsequent volume, *Essays on the Sociology of Culture* (1956). Concerning the contemporary situation of the intelligentsia and its foreseeable role in our society, he predicts the decline of a relatively free or liberal intelligentsia along with the comparative and critical outlook which a condition of polycentric viewpoint imposes. Free thought and inquiry have had, after all, a very short and turbulent history and have been but passing interludes between periods of centralized and uniform culture. Increasing specialization in our times calls for a growing army of intellectual functionaries, while the retailing of knowledge in standard packages inhibits the questioning spirit. One may anticipate, therefore, a shrinking in the range and depth of free inquiry, which is also losing its social basis through the decline of the old independent middle class. As the condition of the uncommitted and independent critic becomes much more precarious, one may expect the corresponding rise of a new type of thought control. Yet this trend is not only inevitable, according to Mannheim, but even hopeful. Far from involving a renascence of ideology and utopian thought, it signifies their suppression. Although a new scholasticism

375

may be the outcome, it will be a closed system based on technical and scientific knowledge rather than upon the fanciful flights of speculation.

Second, we must consider the increasing number, prosperity and influence of intellectually trained and enlightened persons under conditions of affluence. The intelligentsia, consisting of salaried white-collar workers, men of letters, and members of the liberal professions, has never before been more numerous, emancipated, influential, and nearer to the centers of power than it has become in our own day. Intellectuals in the older and honorary sense—men of letters and members of the liberal professions—are more apt to be influential in the economically underdeveloped countries than in more affluent societies. On the one hand, their comparative influence in society decreases vis-à-vis the technical and bureaucratic sections of the intelligentsia. In backward countries anyone is an intellectual who has a university degree; there is no distinction between the intellectuals and the intelligentsia as a whole. There, men of letters and members of the liberal professions are frequently more influential than their more practical-minded colleagues. However, the destiny of intellectuals is for them to become transformed into administrators and subordinated to the enterprise which employs them. Since the State ranks knowledge of a useful kind above the pursuit of culture and intellectual accomplishments for their own sakes, the administrators tend to become the favored sons. As in the past, the most frustrated segments of the intelligentsia continue to show sympathy for the myths of the radical, socialist, and communist Left. And it is precisely these political myths that constitute the opium of the intellectuals, according to Raymon Aron's book of that title (1955).

Although the revolutions of the twentieth century have been conceived and carried out by intellectuals, the bureaucratic and technical intelligentsia has everywhere taken over power from them. Yet the affluent society increasingly offers employment to its displaced members. Consequently, from finding themselves alienated from the larger society, they are now in the process of becoming reintegrated into it. Ideology and especially the political myths of the Left increasingly lose their appeal. The ideological captivity of intellectuals to the interests of other classes interferes with their increasing stake in society and tends to give way before it. Thus the two great societies of our time, the U.S. and the U.S.S.R., have witnessed not only an artificial suppression of ideological differences through the imposition of unanimous adherence to the principles of their regimes, but also the natural or spontaneous withering away of ideology owing to the fact that the intellectuals have come into their own and that dissident ideologies no longer "pay." As the economic sources of frustration for intellectuals are gradually overcome, the intellectuals have less and less need for ideological opiates. Political issues as voiced by intellectuals are becoming less and less controversial.

Marxism, according to Aron, is the last great ideology prior to the end of the ideological age. What people increasingly agree upon is the need for a system that increases the volume of collective resources, the GNP, and reduces the disparity of status between groups with a minimum of delay and friction. Consensus instead of conflict is the goal of modern advanced societies. By comparison with the bitter ideological struggles of the 20s and 30s, the disputes of the 50s are more like fencing matches.

Third, there is the life-affirming, socially liberating, pleasure-loving, and anti-ideological bias of scientific intellectuals. In *Psychoanalysis and Ethics* (1955), Lewis Feuer gives supporting psychological evidence for Mannheim's thesis that ideological modes of thought are self-alienating forms of ideation rooted in repression. No man is free to think or to act who allows himself to become captive to ideas instead of to the irreplaceable and unconditioned drives of the human organism. Anxiety-induced or ideological behavior is psychologically unauthentic. Unlike Mannheim, who distinguishes between ideologies and utopias, Feuer lumps them together as projected

377

wish-fulfillments where knowledge is unavailable. More specifically, an ideology is any world view or overview based on one's social and political feelings, the result of a conscious or unconscious effort to impose our will upon the universe or upon human history. The upshot of Feuer's psychoanalysis of ethical statements is that a man without an ideology is almost as rare today as a man without any political allegiance. At the same time, men are becoming ever more aware of ideational tyranny and the sanctification of words and formulas which inhibit the satisfaction of basic human needs. Just as the age of religious wars was succeeded by a period of skepticism, so one may reasonably expect the present ideological age to issue in a countermovement beyond ideology.

Feuer also advances historical evidence for the thesis that the scientific-oriented intellectual since the Renaissance illustrates an anti-ideological instead of an ideologically based ethic. The general conclusion emerging from his historical investigations, *The Scientific Intellectual* (1963), is that scientific movements in the West have been predicated upon a socially liberating and pleasure-loving ethos. Contrary to the expectations of Freud and Max Weber, biographical studies fail to substantiate the now over-worked thesis that scientific intellectuals were largely Protestant ascetics who had successfully sublimated their lust for life. Feuer's own research into the lives of members of the Royal Society suggests a quite different interpretation, that they were less dominated by repressive modes of thought than by the urge to rise above religious and political hatreds and the oppressive sway of ideologies. His studies of scientific intellectuals among the medieval nominalists, the Copernican revolutionists, eighteenth-century Scots, nineteenth-century Jews, and the scientists of Napoleonic France provide further evidence for the thesis that science was far less of an opiate for them than an indispensable technique for controlling, reshaping, and enjoying the world. In this light, the current death wish and finimundialist orientation of the new scientific and civilian militarists in the service of the Cold War may be only a passing phase, a momentary setback in the long-run ascendancy of scientific intellectuals over the forces of darkness and superstition.

Fourth, we must consider the fact that ideologues have been eclipsed by the professionals of intellect or social engineers. Modern conditions of affluence demand the smooth running of the industrial machine, which is the job of social engineers rather than of intellectuals in the old sense. The task of these new experts is definitely not that of exerting ideological influence in the interests of a particular class, but rather of moderating conflicting interests and ambitions. The engineers of consensus serve the needs of all the people by preserving social equilibrium and further developing the mechanism of adjustment. In effect, the affluent society is classless and has no need for either conflict, ideologies, or intellectuals. At least that is the thesis defended by Thomas Molnar.[1] The intellectual is a passing phenomenon in modern history, according to Molnar, appearing as a social type not before the sixteenth century (subsequently pushed back to the thirteenth century) and disappearing into oblivion after the twentieth. In the past the man of education accepted the status quo imposed from above. In the future he may be expected to accept it as imposed by his social peers.

A causal connection has been suggested between the declining vehemence of ideological commitments and increasing prosperity. The rising expectations of transitional societies give rise to a host of grievances, resentments, and conflicts, and in response to the controversies bred by poverty in the midst of plenty the contenders for power tend to elaborate ideologies in self-justification. An intellectual leadership possessing the weapons required for ideological conflict crystallizes within each class; economics of scarcity are witness to the continuing struggles between classes and the corresponding ideologies of revolutionary, liberal, and conservative intellectuals. However,

[1] "Intellectuals, Experts, and the Classless Society," *Modern Age*, Winter, 1957–58.

just as economics of scarcity made possible the rise of the intellectuals, so the affluent society brings about their decline. Even in class societies intellectuals become increasingly dispensable with the conquest of political power by a dominant class, since then the second-zone intelligentsia of experts, bureaucrats, and social engineers are required to consolidate the victory. The role of intellectuals has been essentially critical and destructive both of the new and the old. In contrast, the contemporary social engineers endeavor to smooth the way for social and economic change. Planning and manipulation are less essential to their task, and they have little need to invent justifications and rationalizations in their own defense. The new elite of experts corresponds to Mannheim's self-aware, independent, and scientific-oriented intelligentsia that is no longer the tool of classes or the servant of class conflicts. The disappearance of the intellectual is a social blessing not a curse.

In *The Decline of the Intellectual* (1961), Molnar is still more explicit in identifying the intellectuals with a distinct and separate class in society whose fate is to be socially influential as long as freedom of expression exists and society is divided into hostile and competing classes. Since the overrriding tendency of our times is toward homogeneity and the regimentation of leisure, the intellectual has succumbed to the social engineers. Unlike Mannheim, however, Molnar does not anticipate a decline of ideology predicated upon the decline of the intellectual. On the contrary, he regards a future state beyond ideology as both impossible of realization and monstrous in conception. In fact, the depoliticization of the intellectuals is precisely a condition of universal indoctrination and intensified manipulation by a new breed of ideologically sophisticated but cynical professional persuaders.

Furthermore, the social engineer is himself an intellectual whose goal is ideological consensus rather than the end of ideology. His efforts, according to Molnar, are in effect ideological in fulfilling the task left undone by his predecessors. Like Julien Benda in *The Treason of the Intellectuals* (1928),

380

Molnar calls for a return to philosophy which would preserve the free, critical, and inquiring spirit that the intellectuals mis-used and the social engineers abused to establish their controls.

Fifth, the rule of administrator-intellectuals becomes in-creasingly benevolent as well as skilled. With the achievement of industrialization the intellectuals acquire a greater stake in society. They not only find employment but become more se-cure, more professional, more bureaucratic-minded, and corre-spondingly less ideologically motivated. The affluent intellec-tuals displace the struggling and resentful ones. At the same time these new-style or nonrevolutionary intellectuals become more sensitive to the wishes of the people. Unlike the old, transitional and revolutionary intellectuals, they hesitate to push the population to the limits of human endurance. The negotiator takes the place of the demagogue, while a benefi-cent political bureaucracy and economic oligarchy are sup-ported by the appreciative masses. Although the new realism is conservative, it is also popular.

This is also the theme of Kerr *et al, Industrialism and In-dustrial Man* (1960). In the natural history of elites it is the destiny of the revolutionary intellectuals to give way to the nonrevolutionary ones. The influence of a radical intelligentsia is limited to transitional periods on the road to industrializa-tion and the affluent society. Consequently it is political radi-calism, the ideology of the Left, that withers away. The sense of protest subsides as the cultural patterns of the world inter-mingle and ideological controversies give way to affluence. Education reduces the scarcity of skilled persons, which in turn reduces the differential between wages and salaries. Middle incomes make for a middle-class society in which riches and poverty are the exception. A leveling equality is the outcome both economically and culturally. Higher education and re-search are transformed into a major industry, and more and more other industries take on the characteristics of the university and its faculty. The model for the enterprise be-comes the university, a symptom of the increasing role of academicians in public life. Along with the rise of experts and academics, the middle bureaucracy of clerks and officials increases in number and influence. Intra-bureaucratic rivalries take the place of class warfare as battles tend to be fought in committees instead of on the streets. The typical avenue of individual expression becomes the new Bohemianism, itself intensely personal instead of social, and to that extent, non-ideological.

Finally, the consensus of bureaucratic society has effectively stifled ideologies of the Right as well as of the Left. Bell's *The End of Ideology* (1960) and Lipset's *Political Man* (1960) point to the characteristic movement of stable democracies in the West toward a post-politics phase of general consensus in which there ceases to be any fundamental difference in principle between the democratic left- and right-wing parties. Where the socialists are the moderates and the conservatives accept the Welfare State, there is no longer a role for ideological thinking. The triumph of the radical intelligentsia through the democratic social revolution in the West has meant an end to domestic politics for the intellectuals. In the future political controversies will tend to take a peaceful course and to be waged without ideologies. If anything, the increasing conformity and political apathy of American voters suggests a strengthening of consensus. The exhaustion and obsolescence of ideologies is not limited to the radical intelligentsia alone, but applies generally to all intellectuals in the affluent society, including the bulk of the workers who have won their fight for citizenship. Actually, ideologies still have a major appeal only in the newly emergent nations suffering from economic backwardness, population explosion, and extreme poverty.

II

Is the foregoing evidence as strong as it appears? More specifically, what criticism, if any, can be advanced against the foregoing arguments for a decline of ideology?

To begin, Mannheim illogically concludes from the increasing self-awareness, positivism, and sociological realism of intellectuals that ideologies, no less than utopias, are in process of disappearing. He fails to consider that intellectuals have an increasing stake in modern societies and a corresponding incentive to develop ideologies through advertising, industrial psychology, and social engineering techniques. Although the intellectuals may be themselves undeceived, they are well paid for misleading others. Moreover, it is in their own collective interest to do so. The rise of an enlightened intelligentsia does not logically imply an end to intellectually supported or induced superstition. Whatever may be said for an end of utopian thinking and for the corresponding disappearance of political radicalism, arguments for an end to ideology have to be predicated upon a different set of facts. In brief, my criticism of Mannheim is two fold: he confuses the emancipation and independence of intellectuals from self-alienating modes of ideation with the emancipation of the masses from utopias and ideologies; and he fails to consider that the newly organized power of the intelligentsia is largely limited to the professionals who exploit ideological thinking in their own self-interest.

Aron also makes an unwarranted leap from the new position of prominence of the intelligentsia to the self-emancipation of the human mind from ideological bondage. However, the end of ideological self-alienation for the intelligentsia does not imply an end to ideology for society as a whole. Nor does the end of politics and the emergence of a broad consensus

383

among the population imply a decline of ideology. On the contrary, the evidence indicates that political conflicts are becoming less ideological precisely because of the all-pervasive self-emancipation of the intelligentsia without also considering the evidence for the increasing exploitation by intellectuals of ideologies and self-alienating modes of thought. The rise of the intellectuals is positively correlated in our time with a tendency beyond utopia, it is true, but toward ideology. Feuer mistakenly concludes from the anti-ideological tendencies within the scientific intelligentsia that a scientific education is a liberating force in general. Actually there seems to be a positive correlation in this country and the U.S.S.R. between increasing scientific education for the intellectuals and the increasing propagation by intellectuals of ideologies for mass consumption. Feuer's category, the scientific intellectual, is misleading because of its ambiguity. Thus it ranges all the way from intellectuals who are scientists in the narrow sense of the mathematical and physical sciences, through so-called social scientists who are to a considerable extent still ideological in their thinking, to professional intellectuals of every hue and color who have received a scientific education. Those in this last sub-category, whose professional job it is to defend and propagate ideologies in our day, are not without considerable influence upon scientific intellectuals in the strict sense. Not only does Feuer confuse evidence with illustration in his thesis, but also the different meanings of the basic categories he uses.

Molnar is flatly mistaken about a classless society in the West. The tendencies toward social leveling have not gone hand in hand with any economic leveling of the kind he imagines to exist in the United States. On the contrary, social leveling appears to function as a compensatory mechanism, as a new-style opiate of the masses designed to improve human relations and to bring about consensus. Thus we may agree with Molnar that not only poverty, conflict, and rising expectations generate ideologies. The ideal of a smoothly running industrial machine also masks and serves special group interests and, to that extent, is likewise ideological. There are ideologies of affluence as well as scarcity, of consensus as well as conflict, of moderation as well as extremism. Granted that engineers and experts tend to displace the radical, liberal, and old-style conservative intellectuals, they are hardly less politicized than Benda's treasonable clerks. Their post-party and post-parliamentary politics are political in a new sense. Precisely because they are less and less economically dependent upon the old social classes, they have ushered in a new age of ideology even more self-alienating than the old—at least for the bulk of the citizens. Their ideology of consensus is self-justifying, unlike the old ideologies that supported the interests of classes other than the new class of intellectuals.

The word intellectual in Molnar's privileged use of it is evidently too narrow to cover both its current meanings and the related term intelligentsia. There is little doubt that intellectuals in pre-industrial and rapidly developing countries tend to function primarily as men of letters, liberal professors and ideologues generally, and that in economically developed countries they tend to function rather as technical engineers and bureaucratic administrators. This is the basis of Harry J. Benda's distinction between the old and new intellectuals in his essay on "Non-Western Intelligentsias as Political Elites," reprinted in John H. Kautsky's *Political Change in Underdeveloped Countries* (1962). Edward Shils' essay in the same volume, "The Intellectuals in the Political Development of the New States," is even more specific in distinguishing between the mandarins or traditional intellectuals, the politicized or oppositional intellectuals, whether conservative or revolutionary, and the intellectual bureaucrats or functionaries enjoying actual power. The term intellectual may be used in a preferred sense for the ideological or politicized intellectuals, but the word intelligentsia is broad enough to include these other species as well. What is misleading about Molnar's thesis is not so much his use of the term intellectual for the politicized variety from the thirteenth to the twentieth century, but rather his failure to stress the common bonds uniting different types of intellectuals within the intelligentsia. Actually the intelligentsia is at the peak of power and influence when its members share in political power, and this influence is greatest in the case of social engineers. Since the decline of the intelligentsia is decidedly not a phenomenon of our time, the alleged decline of the intellectual is misleading even as a formulation of Molnar's own thesis.

Kerr *et al* are unduly optimistic about the income-leveling and job-upgrading tendencies of industrialization and automation in particular. Contrary to the evidence concerning the impact of automation upon the labor force, they assume both that new, more, and increasingly technical jobs can be provided and that the bulk of the labor force possesses the native ability and intelligence to be upgraded. The new masters may be more skilled and beneficent then the old, but they are still limited by the increasing superfluousness of the permanent industrial reserve army of the unemployed and its psychological incapacities for adaptation to the new technology. It is one thing to argue that the conditions of the masses tend to improve under the welfare legislation sponsored by the intelligentsia. It is something else to conclude from this that a general leveling of incomes is taking place. Despite the decreasing scarcity of educated and skilled labor, the price for its services is unlikely to be governed by the market when all other prices tend to be administered. With the undisputed rule of the intelligentsia not far away, there are strong reasons for believing that the price system it administers will be increasingly favorable rather than unfavorable to the incomes of the salariat. Absolute poverty may become a thing of the past, but increasing relative poverty is still a more than likely possibility for the future. Since the rise of the intellectuals will not be altogether undisputed, ideologies will be necessary to consolidate their power. An increasing amount of consensus and teamwork is required for the efficient operation of automated industries, so that ideologies will be increasingly in demand within industry.

A planned economy precludes industrial strikes, lockouts, slowdowns, and labor unrest. Consequently the labor force must be increasingly persuaded that the new social order represents the optimum of social justice. It is simply false that the Welfare State of the emergent intelligentsia has no need of ideology or even a decreasing need. Although there is some evidence that personal radicalism in the form of a new Bohemianism may serve as a counterargument to the increasing conservatism of economic planning in a bureaucratically administered society, as more and more individuals seek this outlet, it, too, tends to become ideological.

It is an unwarranted leap from the thesis of a decline in ideological obfuscation on the part of intellectuals to the thesis that the age of ideology fades. Actually the new science of society and corresponding sociology of knowledge emancipates primarily the intelligentsia who are now more than ever *called* upon to make use of this knowledge in manipulating the masses. Civil religions and secular political myths and formulas have actually increased in influence with the decline of the older theologies. The tendencies toward realism of the new power elite are confined principally to the intellectuals and holders of college degrees. A new age of faith replaces the old. Ideology and consensus are not invariably at loggerheads, especially when consensus itself is symptomatic of a total victory of ideology.

Bell and Lipset confuse the case for increasing conformity and general consensus with the evidence for the end of ideology. Actually this growing consensus is symptomatic of the increasing power of ideology over the lives of citizens. Secondly, they confuse the exhaustion of ideologies for the radical intelligentsia and intellectuals generally with the obsolescence and disutility of ideologies as instruments of social coherence. On the contrary, ideologies have never been more useful or influential than they have now become with the help of mass media. That Bell and Lipset underestimate the role of ideology in the mass society is evident from their failure to discuss the

387

role of the bulk of the intelligentsia in disseminating the myths of modern democracies. Here we may agree with Harold Rosenberg's concluding comments in *The Tradition of the New* (1959) concerning the emergence in America of a self-conscious intellectual caste of post-radical critics who have solved their economic problem by volunteering as organization men and ideologists of the white-collar world. Although for themselves the only vital issues remaining for society are "self" and "alienation," they do not hesitate daily to manipulate people as though they were objects, to organize them as if they were chattel, and to reshape their ideas in the mold of newfangled ideologies. Contrary to Bell and Lipset, the end of ideology occurs only within two comparatively narrow circles: the new intelligentsia of bureaucrats, technocrats, and ideocrats; and the disillusioned and exhausted ex-militants of the Left.

MICHAEL NOVAK

❧

An End of Ideology *

One would have thought, a few years ago, that the age of ideology was at an end. But now young people have discovered that pragmatism, too, has the characteristics and effects of an ideology. They have observed, in particular, its low resistance to a new, toughened strain of tyranny. Technological progress, they recognize, demands stability and unity over periods of time long enough to bring plans and projections to fulfillment; it thus depends upon control over natural resources, industrial facilities, future human desires, and world conditions. Any government dedicated to the uses of advanced technology finds it in the national interest to produce and to enforce stability ("controlled dynamic growth") on a worldwide scale.

Thus university students have been among the first to discern and to condemn the dangers of the philosophy heretofore dominant in the intellectual life of this country. Many among the brightest and most emotionally mature students, as studies like that of Joseph B. Katz have shown, are won over by the experiences, emotions and arguments that have given birth to "the New Left." These are the students who rebel most strongly against liberal professors, liberal journals, and the general civility and temperateness of liberalism. Moreover, so sharp is this rebellion that communication between "Old Left"

* Reprinted with permission from *Commonweal*, March 8, 1968. Copyright © 1968 Commonweal Publishing Company, Inc.

and "New Left" is scarcely possible. Fundamental presuppositions have been changed. Basic value judgments are made differently. If we had an accurate map of what is at stake, perhaps it would become possible to disagree with clarity and precision, instead of with rudeness, contempt, and theological odium.

The argument of the students, naturally enough, is grounded in what they see and hear daily at the universities. The war in Vietnam has taught them that their professors share the basic values and interests of the American government and of the leaders of the new technological industries, whatever the highly publicized public differences between academy and town on questions of procedure. Thus the recent statement by fourteen "moderates"—some of them giants in academic life—justifying present United States policy in Asia reaches the students as no surprise. They have long known what William Pfaff recently wrote in *Commonweal:* that the war in Vietnam is essentially a pragmatist's war, essentially a liberal war. Protest against the war was slow in coming, precisely because it fitted the American intellectual temper so well. Richard Rovere's recent account of his own dilemma in *The New Yorker* illustrates the point.

What, then, is the American intellectual temper as students perceive it? First, let us be clear that we are talking about a minority of students, although probably the most significant minority in terms of perception and talent; and a growing minority. Secondly, we need a context in which the argument is not unduly loaded against either the older intellectual community or the radical students.

Historically, "the movement" is at best five or six years old. The young do not have a full-blown theory by which to situate their own position over against alternatives. They arrive upon the scene when there seems to be a vast consensus, a tradition that has been appropriated with growing extension and solidity since at least the first days of the New Deal. That tradition is anti-metaphysical; it values compromise and adjustment; it prides itself upon its diagnosis of "real" interests and its estimate of immediate "realizable" possibilities; it thinks itself, in a word, unusually "realistic." As the young see it, however, this tradition has been operative with a social and political vision that has been reduced to automatic and trivial sequence. It is tired, repetitive in tactics and strategy, and increasingly out of contact with the dynamic energies of our time. The pragmatic tradition misread the conditions that resulted in the war in Vietnam and the conditions of despair and pride in the black community. Moreover, pragmatists seem blind to the fact that they, too, are ideologues. They neither defend nor criticize their own presuppositions, value judgments, predilected standards (like quantification), and political biases. They have tried so hard to be "objective" that they have failed to examine their own subjectivity—including economic status and professional commitments—for sources of distortion. Because mathematics is "objective," they think they are.

The students spot plenty of distortion. An occasional paper of the Center for the Study of Democratic Institutions, *Students and Society,* for example, offers unusually clear student testimony on this point. The word for professors is "technocrat." The American intellectual community seems to prefer "how to" questions, questions of prediction and control. Such questions demand as much quantification as the material will bear ("and then some"). Effectively, this preference removes the intellectual community from facing value questions and questions of ends—these are "soft" questions and those who deal with them are considered unprofessional. Rewards go to hard-nosed analysts who provide the power of prediction and control.

Many professors do not seem sensitive to what their students are thinking or feeling; many would be surprised to think that, precisely as professors, they ought to be. Concentration is upon "objective" materials. Much worse, the limits of reality, for academic purposes, are established by professional circles in

391

each discipline; what is important to such a circle is important, what is irrelevant to it does not, professionally, exist. The gap between the professional disciplines and the real world—where "real" means of concern to living human beings—could grow to great lengths before professionals would notice. But students have noticed. And to them specialization seems to be an escape from responsibilities as a human being. Professors perform their professional tasks, and then retreat to their comfortable upper middle class homes and private lives, like kept women of the American way of life. Their dignified phrases about truth and academic freedom could be claimed just as well by auto repairmen.

The close ties between major universities and the new technological industries, moreover, and the new dependence of state and national governments upon academic research and advice, have changed the role and character of the universities in society. In a rough way, the university is to our society what the church used to be: its spiritual center, its source of guidance and legitimation. Its duly ordained experts are the clergymen of the new era: Walter Rostow as *eminence grise*. We have not yet devised ways of guaranteeing the separation of university and state.

Radical students turn upon their professors as protestant reformers upon complacent and powerful medieval churchmen. The note of disappointed innocence is poignant: how *could* you, *you* above all? The one hope of cutting through the American myths of cherry pie, freedom, and hard work lies in the university. Yet university professors appear to prefer the comfort of their sinecures to preaching the original revolutionary message of our land, the message transmitted through our bill of rights, our constitution, the Statue of Liberty's call to the oppressed and poor of the world.

It is important to make clear that the protest of the reformers is not merely a protest of activists against theoreticians. The student protestants are saying that the old *doctrines* are wrong, the theories are inadequate, the professors are blind to too many realities of life. The reformation is theoretical as well as practical. We have to revise our *conception* of knowledge and of the role of science, our *view* of ourselves and of our world. The issues involved, in fact, sound like metaphysical or theological issues.

Gut Reactions

The students, however, have been well taught by pragmatic teachers; they do not know how to raise metaphysical questions; they retreat, instead, to gut reactions. They look at the war, the ghettos, the increasing reaction of right-wing and liberal forces of "law and order," and they *feel* indignation. The corruption riven through American life by the interests of the comfortable is so palpable they can taste it and smell it. "All you have to do is open your eyes, man. If it don't make you feel sick, ain't nothin' no one can do for you." When one young man I know loses his bitterness—the center upon which he now pivots his personality—he pulls out a wrinkled photograph of babies disfigured by napalm: his Spanish Jesus mutilated on the cross. Among the students there is an unmentioned litmus test: they study you to see if you feel what they feel. Liberals who talk "realistically" and "pragmatically," radicals believe, cannot possibly feel what their words imply; they know not what they do.

Yet the young are trapped. They reject the technocrats but have pitifully few intellectual alternatives. When John Dewey and other great architects of the current pragmatic realism were teaching, they at least carried with them, implicitly but powerfully, the humanistic tradition of their own earlier schooling; they advised their students, however, not to bother with the old masters of the prescientific era. Some among the second generation of behavioral scientists, political scientists,

393

social scientists, and analytical humanists, consequently, speak only one intellectual language. In rejecting that language, the present generation of students finds itself mute about its most urgent feelings. They do not wish to be anti-intellectual, but the one available intellectual language is abhorrent to them. Moreover, it is impossible for them to return to the classics, the great books, or the humanists—the recovery of a tradition that has now lapsed would turn them into historians, whereas it is the present and the future they most want to absorb and to comprehend. Had they the language, one feels, many of them would like to articulate clearly what is happening now, and thus produce new classics expressing our own new cultural era. Mute instead, they can only say that those over thirty don't understand.

And surely they are right in feeling in their bones a new culture coming to birth. They need a vision of man adequate to the new time, and a political and social theory adequate to that vision. It ill becomes the older generation, which (over-burdened by vast wars) has since 1932 provided so little by way of long-range vision or creative political and social theory, to demand that the students produce the longed-for vision and program in one stroke: instant ideology. The radical students need help. Specifically, they need fresh theories, new intellectual tools, openness to breakthroughs and readiness for originality. In many cases, all they need is someone to help them to articulate what they have already experienced and cannot quite say.

Thus, for example, the radicals speak in indignant tones of corruption, sickness, and selling out; but they do not really mean to say that they think of themselves as pure, or that total purity of motive and conscience is possible for a human being. The vision of man which they seek must be utopian in the sense that it is an alternative to the present series of pragmatic adjustments and gives promise of a new cultural epoch. It need not be utopian in the sense that it represents a naïve innocence about man. Reflecting on the first five or six years of the movement, the radicals have learned that you can't trust anyone *under* 30, either; not even yourself.

The radicals recognize that the rugged individualism of Ayn Rand, the inner-directed personality by David Riesman, and the natural, atomic individual imagined by John Stuart Mill and the English empirical tradition are not now (if they ever were) viable models of human behavior. The social sciences—and political events—have taught them too well that the supposedly private, autonomous world of the self is in fact conditioned and shaped by the institutions in which human beings live, move, and have their being. The sense of reality is, itself, a social product. Consequently, the radicals aspire to political consciousness in the proper sense: to become conscious of one's own identity is to become aware of institutional power already at work in oneself. The road to personal liberation is not private or through meditation, but political. Awareness grows through conscious, reflective, accurate action. The separation between thought and action, which present university life enforces, seems to the students illegitimate; and they argue the case on theoretical grounds.

The students seek fresh theories at many crucial places in the analysis of social reality. For example, when older liberals speak of "academic freedom and academic decorum" in connection with recent demonstrations on campuses, they are thinking of McCarthyism, loyalty oaths, and the disruptive techniques of the Nazis in the 1920s. But the students are thinking of the enormous power of television and newspapers to establish the mainstream of public discourse. They see clearly how the honeyed discourse of public officials—which is ordinarily reported straight—instantly smothers the imaginations and emotions of all within their reach, and how a sweet coating is put upon all intentions and actions of the United States. The inherent respectability of official sources gains a multiplied, overwhelming power, and the entire burden of counter-argument, unmasking, and reporting of contradictory interpretations passes over onto the few who are equipped for it. Commonly, the mass media cannot follow the subtleties of the argument; moreover, officials merely announce; dissenters must document. Thus, a time-lag of days, weeks, or months may be required before a rebuttal can be published. Worse, the very structure of the mass media makes dissenters seem querulous, nitpicking, obsessed; officials are encouraged to pose as noble and long-suffering.

The balance of power in the formation of public opinion has been altered by the advent of television. The society of independent, rational individuals envisaged by John Stuart Mill does not exist. The fate of all is bound up with the interpretation of events given by the mass media, by the image projected, and by the political power which results. The few with access to further information cannot compete with the many. Moreover, it is not so much "further information" that is at stake; it is the "image," the symbolic presentation of values, presuppositions, angle of vision, frame of reference, that is established by the media. In a society with respect for its political institutions, officials have only to act with decorum and energy in order to benefit by such respect and to have their views established as true until proven false.

Thus people are at the mercy of their government in a new and frightening way. The forces of "law and order"—army and police—are so powerful in the United States that no conceivable challenge could be raised against them. The technological society demands unity and thus the whole apparatus is concentrated in an awesome way in the hands of the federal government. "Freedom of speech," therefore, can no longer be governed merely by standards of decorum. The assumption that officials are speaking the truth can no longer be safely entertained by those who value their liberty. The credibility gap is not due to the personality of President Johnson; it now inheres in the office and in all public offices.

What, then, does freedom of speech mean in a technological society? How can one defend oneself against McCarthyism on the one hand, and official newspeak on the other? The solution of the students has been to violate the taboos of decorum and thus embrace Vice President Humphrey, the CIA, Dow Chemical and other enemies in an ugly scene, hoping that the unpopularity of the radicals will rub off on those embraced. They want to make the heretofore bland and respectable wear that tag which most alarms American sensibilities: "controversial."

This tactic suggests that it would be an advance in academic freedom never to allow a public official to share the privileges of academic discourse, unless followed immediately by a devil's advocate in open debate. We desperately need protection against our government, its agencies, and its industrial allies. We desperately need a theory of free speech and tolerance which takes account of advances in technology, in expanded population, and in industrial wealth and power. We need defense against the owners, advertisers, and official users of the mass media, and against those who rely upon traditional decorum and the need for law and order to make effective public challenge impossible. Given television and affluence, a government no longer needs a brazen Gestapo; it can win acquiescence by granting bread and circuses and announcing noble sentiments.

Thus many seeds of immense theoretical importance are germinating in the consciousness of the young. Never was it so clear that the role of the teacher—and today of the publicist—is as Plato described it: that of a midwife. Professors are not the fathers of the new consciousness, they are only the midwives, looking on with alert and critical wonder at what the young, seeded who knows how or where, bring forth.

Praise for *Return to the Secret Garden*

"This is an atmospheric, beautiful read I thoroughly enjoyed."

—*South Wales Evening Post*

"Wonderfully satisfying."

—*Carousel*

"It takes some of the best features of the original and puts them into a familiar yet strikingly altered setting."

—*This Fleeting Dream*

"Holly Webb succeeds beautifully with her sequel."

—*Angels & Urchins*

"It is a great read, compelling and engaging."

—*Powered by Reading*

RETURN TO

THE

SECRET

GARDEN

RETURN TO

THE SECRET GARDEN

HOLLY WEBB

sourcebooks
jabberwocky

Published by Sourcebooks Jabberwocky, an imprint of Sourcebooks, Inc.
P.O. Box 4410, Naperville, Illinois 60567-4410
(630) 961-3900
Fax: (630) 961-2168
www.sourcebooks.com

Originally published as Return to the Secret Garden in 2015 in the United Kingdom by Scholastic Children's Books, an imprint of Scholastic Ltd.

Library of Congress Cataloging-in-Publication Data

Names: Webb, Holly, author.
Title: Return to the secret garden / Holly Webb.
Description: Naperville, Illinois : Sourcebooks Jabberwocky, [2016] | "Originally published...in 2015 in the United Kingdom by Scholastic Children's Books, an imprint of Scholastic Ltd."--Copyright page. | Summary: As World War II begins, London orphan Emmie is unhappy to be evacuated to an old mansion in the Yorkshire countryside until she starts discovering the secrets of the house--a boy crying at night, a diary written by a girl named Mary, and a very secret garden.
Identifiers: LCCN 2015044674 | (13 : alk. paper)
Subjects: | CYAC: Orphans--Fiction. | Gardens--Fiction. | World War, 1939-1945--Evacuation of civilians--Great Britain--Fiction. | Yorkshire (England)--History--20th century--Fiction. | Great Britain--History--George VI, 1936-1952--Fiction.
Classification: LCC PZ7.W3687 Re 2016 | DDC [Fic]--dc23 LC record available at https://lccn.loc.gov/2015044674

Source of Production: Worzalla, Stevens Point, Wisconsin, USA
Date of Production: September 2016
Run Number: 5007515

Printed and bound in the United States of America.
WOZ 10 9 8 7 6 5 4 3 2 1

For my mother.

It's 1939, and a group of children have been evacuated to Misselthwaite Manor. Emmie is far from happy to have been separated from her cat and sent to a huge, old mansion. But soon, she starts discovering the secrets of the house—a boy crying at night, a diary written by a girl named Mary, and a garden.

A very secret garden…

CHAPTER

One

THE CHILDREN MARCHED DOWN THE street in a long line of twos, and only one of them looked back. The others didn't turn because they didn't need to. There was nothing to look back for. Everything they owned was with them—a few clothes, a battered, shapeless stuffed toy here and there. Each of them carried a paper bag and a gas mask, and that was all they had.

Emmie trailed, peering over her shoulder, so that Arthur, behind her, gave her a shove to tell her to keep up. She kicked him swiftly and walked backward instead, still trying to see.

But Lucy wasn't there. *It was stupid to expect that she would be anyway,* Emmie thought. Lucy hardly ever came out onto the street. She was shy, and she hated loud noises. Emmie still stared though, hoping to see the small, black cat peering after her around the corner of the tall house. Lucy had probably fled out into the backyard, Emmie decided miserably. She kicked Arthur again because he was smirking at her—and because she felt like it.

"Emmeline Hatton!"

Emmie whipped around with a sigh. Of course Miss Dearlove hadn't seen Arthur giving her a push. She never did see. "Me, miss?" she asked innocently, trying to look as though she didn't know what was the matter.

The matron glared at her. "No, the other Emmeline Hatton. Of course you! You bad-tempered little girl, how dare you kick Arthur like that?"

"He pushed me…" Emmie started to say, but Miss Dearlove didn't bother to listen. She grabbed Emmie by the arm and hauled her up to the front of the line. She was a tiny lady, not actually much bigger than Emmie, but Emmie didn't dare pull away. She had known Miss Dearlove forever. The matron was like a busy little clockwork train, wound up into a clicking fuss of pure crossness. It was best not to get in her way—but somehow Emmie always did.

"You can walk here with Miss Rose and the babies since you can't be trusted to behave like a ten-year-old. Why is it always you? And after your ridiculous behavior this morning as well. As if we haven't got enough to worry about." She glanced down at her watch. "Miss Rose, we need to hurry. The station's bound to be busy, and there isn't that much time to spare." She scuttled down to the end of the line again with one last growled "Behave!" to Emmie.

Miss Rose was usually less bad-tempered than the matron, but even she eyed Emmie and sighed. "Today of all days, Emmie? I would have thought you'd have more sense."

"He shoved me," Emmie muttered. She knew that wasn't quite true, but she wasn't letting them have the last word. "It isn't fair. Why do I always get into trouble?" She walked down the street next to Miss Rose, seething and muttering to herself. If she huffed and growled, she wouldn't cry, and she wasn't going to give Arthur Banks the satisfaction of that, however much Miss Rose frowned.

They had been told the day before that they were leaving. Miss Dearlove had stood up at the end of breakfast and explained that since war was expected to be declared within a few days, the Craven Home for Orphaned Children would be evacuated "somewhere safe."

No one knew what evacuation meant, except that it was vaguely connected with the rows of brown boxes on the shelves in the schoolroom, which contained the gas masks. Once a week for the last few months, they had pulled the masks on and sat staring at each other, snout-nosed and goggle-eyed. After the first few tries, Arthur had figured out how to make a rude noise, a sort of farting snort around the rubber facepiece. He did it every time now, and they all laughed. Even Miss Dearlove didn't sound that cross when she told him off.

But Emmie had dreamed of those huge, round eyes almost every night since. The glass lenses of the masks leaned over her, stooping down close and staring. The gas masks were supposed to help them breathe, Miss Dearlove said, but when Emmie thought of her mask, sealed away in its flimsy cardboard box, she found her breath catching in her throat. Where was this gas going to come from anyway? No one had said. Arthur and his friend Joey said it would be dropped by planes, but all the gas that Emmie knew about came in pipes to the kitchen for the stoves. She didn't see how it could be carried in a plane. *If only someone would explain*, she thought bitterly, kicking at a crack in the pavement as they marched on. Where were they going—and why? What was happening? No one told them anything. They didn't need to know. They just got packed up like their clothes and sent away...

"Look." The little girl Emmie had been shoved next to tugged at her sleeve.

"What?" Emmie muttered, not looking.

"Over there." Ruby pointed across the road. "See, Emmie, there! Do you think they're being evacuated too?"

Emmie turned and saw that they were passing a school, where a long column of children was lining up on the playground. They were carrying an assortment of battered cases and brown paper bags, and there were labels tied onto their coats.

"I suppose so."

"Just like us..." Ruby said thoughtfully. "I didn't know everybody was."

"We have to get out of the cities—in case of planes flying over," Emmie said vaguely. "All the children do." That was what the boys had thought anyway. They had been lurking around the matron's sitting room, listening to the news broadcasts, so Emmie supposed it was possible they were right. The children on the playground did look a lot like them, except that there were mothers huddling around them and even a few fathers. They were pushing packets of sandwiches into children's pockets, hugging them, and running along beside them as the line of children started to snake out onto the street. The children marched away, following two older boys who had a banner with the school's name stitched onto it. *Almost like a procession*, Emmie thought.

Some of the schoolchildren were crying, Emmie noticed. A lot of the smaller ones were clinging to their mothers, pale faced and bewildered. They didn't seem to know what was happening either. But some of the others looked happy, swinging their cases as if they were off on holiday. Perhaps they were—they might end up at the seaside.

Emmie blinked thoughtfully. She was almost sure she'd never

been out of London. Until now, she hadn't really thought about where they were going. She'd been too worried about what they were leaving behind. Maybe those two boys in the line with grins all over their faces were right. It was an adventure...

But almost all the mothers were brushing tears away quickly with the sides of their hands so as not to be seen. Emmie shivered. She supposed the children from the Home were lucky—all the adults they knew were coming with them. It didn't make her feel lucky though. She tried to remember the softness of Lucy's head bumping against her fingers, the warmth of her breath as the little cat nuzzled against her. But all she could hear was Ruby, grumbling because she was tired and her shoes were too tight.

They hadn't gone all that far, but the streets were so much busier than the quiet area around the Craven Home. Even Emmie felt tired, with so many people pressing around her and the constant roar of cars and carts and buses along the bustling street. On any other day, it would have been fun to stand on one of those islands in the road and watch and wonder where all these people were streaming off to. Today, Emmie wished she was back sitting in the window of her dormitory, peering out at the street to see the grocer's van and a car every so often. She'd wished for something to happen, something exciting, and now it had.

"We're almost there, Ruby," Miss Rose said soothingly. "The

station's just along the road there. Do you see? The clock tower and the name underneath: King's Cross."

The station was huge, with two great, curving arched windows across the front, like tunnel mouths.

"London and North Eastern Railway? Are we going northeast then, miss?" Emmie demanded sharply, looking at the rest of the white letters along the roof. But Miss Rose ignored her, starting to hurry the line of children across the road. A policeman waved them over, holding up a line of buses and smiling down at little Ruby clutching her faded bear.

There were other lines of children converging on the station now. Hundreds of them, marching along like little ants. More and more poured out of buses, labeled, carrying parcels and bags and battered cases. Emmie had never seen so many people her own age before. How many were going out of London?

Miss Rose slowed as she walked them past the scattering of shops around the front of the great building and glanced around anxiously for Miss Dearlove.

"What is it?" Emmie asked. Miss Rose looked so suddenly uncertain. All the staff at the Home had been brisk and decided about the move, brushing away questions and urging the children to complete their meager packing. Now for the first time, Emmie wondered if they were as confused and worried as the children.

Mrs. Evans, the cook, was clutching her big, black handbag against her front like a shield.

"Nothing, Emmie!" Miss Rose replied sharply. She was glancing back and forth between the sandbags built up around the doorway and a flight of steps down—still with a sign to the Underground but blocked off with a great pile of bits of broken stone. She glanced down at Emmie with a bright smile that showed her teeth. "I just wasn't quite sure which door we were to take, that's all. We must expect everything to look a little different in wartime, mustn't we?" she added in a comforting, singsong voice as though Emmie had been the scared one.

Miss Rose didn't allow herself to be daunted by the huge space inside the station or the milling crowd of children. She straightened her shoulders and hurried them in, then started counting everybody again in case one of the twenty orphans had disappeared on the way. Emmie didn't think any of them would have dared. Not with those planes coming—and the gas. She had thought about running away before—on days when nothing happened and no one spoke to her. But that had been before she found Lucy.

Miss Dearlove marched over to a man in a station uniform. He frowned down at his list and eventually pointed across to one of the farthest platforms. Then he checked his watch and pointed again, flapping his hands.

The matron came trotting back to them and caught Emmie's hand, pulling at her sharply. "We haven't much time. Come along, all of you. No dawdling. There are only so many extra trains for the evacuated schools," she added to Miss Rose. "The timetable is all upset. If we miss this one, we'll have to wait hours." She glanced irritably down at Emmie as she spoke, as if it were her fault that they were late.

The train was already steaming as the children hurtled onto the platform and a porter flung the doors open for them, bundling them in as Miss Rose and Miss Dearlove and Mrs. Evans wrestled with bags and food baskets.

Emmie collapsed onto a padded seat, clutching her brown paper bag of clothes and staring out the window. She could see another train at the next platform with a girl gazing back at her. She smiled faintly, recognizing the strange girl's expression of fear and excitement. There was even something of her own sickening loneliness. Perhaps that girl had never been out of London either. Perhaps she'd never been on a train. But maybe, just perhaps, the train was taking her toward something new and different. Things might be better—even though she'd had to leave so much behind.

The girl waved at her, and Emmie lifted her hand slowly as their train shuddered and creaked and began to pull out of the station, out of London, heading for somewhere else.

Emmie leaned back against the scratchy velour of the seat. She was facing the window, but she was hardly looking at the green banks next to the tracks that the train was racing through. She wondered where that other girl's train had been going. She had looked nice—no, not nice. *Nice* was what Miss Dearlove and Miss Rose were always encouraging them to be. *Play nicely. Now, that isn't nice. Is it, Emmie? Nice little girls don't behave like that.*

The only other girl Emmie's age at the Craven Home had left when they were both about five. Louisa had been very nice indeed, and that was why she had been adopted. It had been made quite clear to Emmie that if only she had been more like Louisa, she might have been adopted too. But she was much too old for that now. And she didn't care anyway.

Emmie ran her hand over the arm of the seat, and tears stung the corners of her eyes. The dark, dusty stuff reminded her of Lucy's fur.

Whenever one of the younger, sweeter, *nicer* children was taken away to have a proper home, or when Miss Dearlove snapped at her for being ungrateful, or the boys teased her for being skinny and pale and ugly, Emmie would simply shrug and stare. Miss Dearlove called her insolent, and Arthur had smacked her ears for *giving him that look.*

She'd stare until Miss Dearlove flounced away or the boys grew bored. And then she'd sneak upstairs to the little window on the landing outside the girls' dormitory. There was a large cupboard half in front of it, full of musty blankets and spare clothes, and a skinny, ugly, little person could squeeze behind the cupboard and open the window—and climb out onto the rusted iron fire escape without anyone knowing where she had gone.

The first few times Emmie had been out there in the days just after she'd found the window, she sat there alone, gazing out across the roofs below. She loved the view—watching the clouds streaked with red as the sun went down. Even on the days when London was choked in fog, she had imagined the sky and the rooftops beneath the layers of gray. If she leaned against the railings, she could just see a slice of the road and watch for passersby and wonder where they were going—and where she would go one day. She'd even taken a few steps down the fragile, old metal staircase. But then common sense had sent her slinking back again. She had nowhere to go. She couldn't leave.

Emmie had been out on the fire escape on a February afternoon when she first saw her. It had been almost dark and icy cold, especially because Emmie wasn't wearing a coat. She couldn't sneak her coat upstairs, not without someone stopping to ask her why. But being cold was worth it—for time alone to think and watch the sky.

She had felt as though she were all alone in the city. A purplish light had soaked through the sky, and wisps of cloud floated by, looking almost close enough to touch. Emmie leaned against the metal railings, feeling the hard cold of the iron bite into her cheek and knowing she should go in before they missed her.

Something had made her stay. Afterward, she thought she'd known something was going to happen. There was the faintest creaking on the metal steps, and a darker patch of shadow slunk onto the tiny landing where Emmie was curled.

"A cat!" she whispered. The cat was tiny—hardly more than a kitten—and shy. It hesitated at the edge of the landing, watching her suspiciously. She caught a gleam of light reflected in its eyes. Why had it come all the way up here?

Emmie moved her hand cautiously toward her pocket, trying not to move suddenly and scare the cat away. She had hidden a sandwich in her handkerchief—fish paste. She hated it, but they were supposed to finish everything that was on their plates. Usually she dropped the scraps off the fire escape, but she'd forgotten. She held back a laugh. Perhaps this cat had eaten her leftovers before. Perhaps that was why it had come.

She opened her handkerchief and wrinkled her nose at the smell. But there was a scuffling in the darkness—the cat had moved. It could smell the fish paste too. Someone turned on the light inside, and both Emmie and the cat froze. But no one saw the open window. There was a quick patter of footsteps up the stairs, and one of the little girls disappeared into the dormitory.

With the light on, Emmie could see the cat—tiny and skinny, like her. It was hunched at the corner of the metal floor, eyes fixed on the wrapped sandwich, but too scared to come closer.

Slowly, Emmie put the handkerchief down between them and unfolded it properly to let the little thing have a glimpse of the food. Then she wriggled farther back against the wall of the house.

"You may as well eat it," she whispered. "I won't. You can have it." She watched the cat curiously. It was nothing like the cats she had seen in the schoolroom books. They were plump and cushiony, with long, white whiskers. This creature looked half-starved, and it couldn't resist the sandwich for long. It darted forward and began to tear at the bread, glancing over at Emmie every so often to check that she wasn't moving.

When the sandwich was gone, the cat sniffed at the handkerchief and even licked it, as if the flavor of the fish paste had soaked into the cotton.

Then it turned and whisked away, skinny tail held low, and Emmie leaned over to watch it scurry down the steps.

The next night, she had only bread and butter, but the cat

didn't seem to mind. It ate the whole slice, and then when Emmie held out her fingers, it sniffed them curiously before it darted away.

Emmie kept taking her scraps out to the fire escape, and the cat kept turning up. As soon as she climbed out of the window, a small, dark shape would appear, faster and faster each time. There were days she couldn't get out, of course—days when Miss Dearlove decided on a "brisk walk" or the inspectors came. But it only took seconds for Emmie to slip behind the cupboard and open the window a crack and drop her scraps out onto the fire escape.

It was an odd feeling, waiting and hoping for a glimpse of black fur. It wasn't even as if the cat stayed for long, not for those first few days anyway. She—Emmie was only guessing it was a she, but "it" all the time sounded mean—would eat whatever Emmie had brought, and then when she was sure all the food was gone, she would hurry back to whatever she had been doing. *Sniffing around the trash bins, probably,* Emmie thought.

It seemed strange to mind so much, to sit in lessons and hope the cat would turn up, but Emmie found that she thought about the cat more than she thought of anything else. She had never had a pet or known any sort of animal. The Craven Home only had the occasional mouse, and then only in the kitchens, where the children weren't really supposed to go. There wasn't any chance of taming a mouse with crumbs, even if Emmie had wanted to. Knowing that the cat came to see her, or her sandwiches, tugged at something inside Emmie. The cat wanted her, even if it was only for food. It needed her—and she needed it too.

In the third week, the cat climbed into Emmie's lap when she wasn't fast enough unwrapping another fish-paste sandwich, and Emmie named her Lucy.

"Emmie! Emmie!" Someone pulled at her hand, and Emmie realized Ruby was talking to her.

"Don't you want a sandwich?" Ruby pushed one into her hand, and Emmie stared down at it, trying not to gag. It was fish paste.

"No!" she said sharply, and shoved it back at Ruby. Then she caught Miss Rose's eye and added, "No, thank you. I'm not hungry."

"There's plain bread and butter, Emmie." Miss Rose passed her another paper packet. She went on gently. "You need to eat something. It'll be hours more yet. It's a long way."

Emmie nodded. She was too miserable even to ask again where they were going, in case she started to cry.

"Missing that scrawny cat?" Joey leaned over, speaking through a mouthful of sandwich, and Emmie pressed herself back against the seat disgustedly. If only they hadn't all seen. She had kept Lucy a secret for weeks, but the little cat grew tamer and a tiny bit plumper, and she was clever enough to figure out that Emmie— and more food—were inside the house.

Miss Dearlove shooed her out, but Miss Rose seemed to like cats. When she saw Lucy sitting on a windowsill or sneaking along the passage by the schoolroom, she smiled faintly and looked the other way instead of chasing the little cat outside again. And the cook liked her—Lucy had the sense to catch a mouse and drop it in front of Mrs. Evans's feet. After that, Emmie would occasionally see a saucer of milk in the yard at the bottom of the fire escape—a saucer where there had once been milk anyway.

How could they have made her leave Lucy behind if what everyone said was true and London was going to be flattened by bombs? And the gas. Emmie had heard Miss Rose and the cook saying that all the mailboxes were being painted with special gas-detecting paint, so they'd glow yellow instead of red if there was gas floating in the streets. It sounded as though it was going to happen any day now. What would happen to Lucy if that was real?

Emmie shivered and closed her eyes for a second. She could see Lucy lying on the little iron landing of the fire escape, basking in the sun. The little cat liked to stretch out on her side, showing off her rusty reddish black underneath. Sometimes she even lay on her back with her paws in the air. She'd wave them, as if she was inviting Emmie to rub the fluff of her belly. And then if Emmie dared, half the time Lucy would pounce on her and bat at her wrist. But Emmie didn't mind the scratches.

The other children had petted Lucy and even fed her scraps, but she seemed to remember that Emmie had been her first protector, and she always came back to the fire escape.

Emmie had found a basket the night before while they were packing. It was in that same cupboard of odds and ends that stood in front of their window. There must have been a cat once before—or perhaps it was meant for picnics in the park, although Emmie wasn't sure anyone at the Home had ever done something so lovely. She hadn't asked Miss Dearlove or Miss Rose if they could take the cat. She hadn't even thought about it. It had been so clear to her that Lucy could not be left behind. She'd simply been grateful that she wouldn't have to carry Lucy in her arms or tie a string around her neck. She didn't think the cat would like being on a train.

But before breakfast wasn't Lucy's time to appear slinking through the kitchen or creeping up to the top of the iron staircase. Emmie had hurried through the press of twenty excited, bewildered children, dropping paper bags and gas masks and winter coats that smelled of mothballs—because even though it was a sweltering September day, who knew how long they'd be away for? Miss Dearlove raced around, spooning porridge into the little ones, sewing buttons back on, and in between, dashing back into the kitchen to screech at Mrs. Evans about twenty sandwiches.

In the passage outside the kitchen, she came on Emmie

with a fingerful of beef dripping, trying to persuade Lucy into the lidded basket. The little cat had her front paws in, and Emmie was wondering if she should just take a chance and shove the rest of her in too.

"Emmie! For pity's sake, why haven't you got your coat on? We're about to leave! What's in that basket? You've not put your clothes in there, have you? You should have them in a parcel, like the others."

Emmie glanced around at her, and Miss Dearlove sucked in her cheeks.

Lucy saw that Emmie was distracted and took her chance to launch out of the basket.

"No!" Emmie squeaked. "Oh, miss, catch her!" And she flung herself full length, grabbing the thin, black cat, who to Miss Dearlove looked just as scruffy and ugly as the little girl. Emmie was sallow skinned and thinner than ever, since she'd been hiding away half her food to feed the cat. Emmie's hair had wisped its way out of her thin braids already, and her arms were all scratched.

"That disgusting stray! I might have known…" Then the matron stopped and stared at the basket. "Emmie Hatton, did you think you were taking that creature with you?"

Emmie crawled clumsily onto her knees and stood up slowly, gripping the squirming cat in her arms. She stood there, wincing as Lucy flailed her claws and pulled several more threads out of her cardigan. The cat didn't care that she was being saved. She was hungry, and she had not liked the basket at all.

"We have to," Emmie whispered, her greenish eyes widening as she stared back at Miss Dearlove. It wasn't one of her purposeful stares—she wasn't trying to make Miss Dearlove angry. This was a round-eyed look of panic and disbelief. They couldn't leave the cat behind. It would be too cruel. "The bombs…" she faltered.

"We are not taking a cat, certainly not a dirty stray like that. Why, even proper pets are…" Miss Dearlove trailed off, shaking her head. "Get going, Emmie. We've a train to catch that's taking us halfway across the country! You're making us late. Now come along." Miss Dearlove went to seize Lucy from Emmie's arms, but Emmie screamed and darted back, and Lucy hissed, not even sure who to be angry with. She fought and bit and scratched, and at last Emmie let go of her with a despairing cry as the cat streaked away through the kitchen and the scullery and out.

"At last! Now get out to the hallway and find your coat. We should have left by now. Mrs. Evans, are you ready? The children are lining up," Miss Dearlove added to the cook, who was standing in the kitchen doorway watching.

But Emmie crouched to pick up the basket, gazing into it as if she almost couldn't believe it was empty.

"Put that down!" snapped Miss Dearlove, taking the handle.

Emmie jerked away, snatching it back. "No! I have to go and get her. We have to bring her with us!"

The matron grabbed the basket, and with her other hand, she slapped Emmie across the cheek. Emmie dropped the cat basket and leaned against the wall, tears seeping from the corners of her eyes. She wasn't crying because Miss Dearlove had hit her, even though it hurt, but because she'd realized that it was true. They meant it. They really were leaving Lucy behind.

"I couldn't help it," she heard Miss Dearlove murmur to the cook. "Dratted child, she does it on purpose. Bring her, will you, Mrs. Evans? I need to go and lock up."

Emmie felt Mrs. Evans's arm slide around her shoulders, and the cook's dry fingers stroked her scarlet cheek. She could hear the old woman tutting gently, but her voice seemed to come from a long way away.

"Come along, sweetheart. You come on now. Don't you worry about that little cat. She'll be next door, stealing a kipper for her breakfast, I expect. Time we were on our way."

CHAPTER
Two

E MMIE CLIMBED WEARILY OUT OF the train, her gas mask bumping against her hip and the tiresome brown paper bag clutched in her arms. They had been shut away in the stuffy compartments for hours, and even though they had changed trains at York, they hadn't had time for anything except a rush to the coatrooms. Her legs felt stiff, almost like pins and needles, and her dress was clammy, sticking across her back.

The children and the three women stood rather helplessly, gazing around the platform, until Miss Dearlove shook herself and straightened her shoulders. "There'll be someone to meet us. Into line, come along." She crouched down and picked up Ruby, who was worn out and swaying on her feet, the bear dangling perilously from her hand.

The train suddenly sputtered and creaked away with a great

heave, leaving them alone at the tiny station. It was unbelievably quiet as the noise of the train faded, even quieter than the back-street they were used to, where there was always a faint rumble of traffic. Here there was silence—except for a soft jingling of harness from beyond the tiny station building. The late-afternoon sun hung low, and there were bees murmuring over the grassy bank on the other side of the tracks.

A porter came hurrying up the platform with a luggage cart from where he'd been unloading some wooden crates from the baggage car at the head of the train.

"Miss Dearlove? Th' car's outside for thee."

The children gaped at him, confused by his broad Yorkshire accent. Miss Dearlove smiled gratefully and followed him through the little ticket office and out to the yard beyond, where a strange mixture of vehicles stood waiting.

A man in a smart, dark uniform with a peaked cap nodded to Miss Dearlove and then gently wrestled Ruby from her arms, propping her against his shoulder. Ruby was so exhausted that she simply eyed him for a moment and then thumped her head onto his jacket. The man eyed the children thoughtfully. "I reckon we can fit them all in th' cars, miss. We brought the cart for th' baggage." He eyed the children's bags, then glanced back at the horse-drawn wagon, shook his head, and smiled. "Bags won't fill, will they?"

Miss Dearlove looked around at the weary line of children behind her and sighed. "We couldn't bring very much with us. Miss Sowerby said in the telegram that bedding and such would be provided."

"Reckon there'll be enough." He snorted, and the man standing by the next car laughed.

"I dunno. Sleeping nose to tail, tha'll be." The children stared at him, not understanding. Did he mean they'd have to share beds? The man beckoned to Emmie and pointed into the second car, an enormous cream-and-black Austin. "Squash up in there, lass. Reckon there's room for seven or eight of you small ones in th' back."

Emmie clambered into the car, and the men pushed the others in after her, piling the little ones on the older children's laps. Emmie cringed as Tommy, one of the smallest boys, was pushed onto her lap. He was damp, and he smelled. She wasn't surprised—they'd been on the train all day, after all. She just tugged his coat farther around his bottom and wrinkled her nose.

She peered out the window around Tommy's knitted hood as they rolled away, the motion of the car smooth and quick, nothing like the jolting train. The station—Thwaite, it had said on the sign—seemed to be part of a tiny village. The car sped through what seemed hardly more than a church and a few white-painted cottages. But every little house had a garden bursting out over the fences. It was like nothing Emmie had ever seen before, and for a moment—a tiny, surprising, treacherous moment—she liked it.

The car wound along a narrow, tree-lined road, gradually climbing until the tall hedges opened out into a vast field of brownish green. Emmie stared, and Tommy let out a squeak of surprise. It was like the park near the Home, but a thousand times more—a great, endless space of low bushes, gray and brown and faintly purple. "What is it?" Tommy whispered.

"I don't know," Emmie admitted. "A field? There's sheep over there."

Tommy pressed his nose and his plump little hands against the window. "They're not fluffy..."

Emmie nodded. She'd never seen a real sheep, but there was a painting on the wall in the sitting room at the Home, and the sheep in it were whiter and softer looking. "Perhaps they're goats then. I don't know, do I?"

The colors deepened as the sun went down, and Emmie shivered. There was so much space. Sky everywhere. No streets. Even when they went to the park—which was only once a week or so—there were still buildings all around. This openness was frightening. It felt wrong, and it went on and on, without an end that she could see. Where were they going? What sort of place would be in the middle of the emptiness? Emmie gulped as they passed over a tiny stream rushing over rocks. Tommy laughed excitedly, pointing at the water, but Emmie flinched as the car bumped over the little humped bridge.

"Not far now," the man called back through the glass panel that divided the front and the back seats. "We're passing over the moor, and there's the drive up to the house. See the trees?"

The dim golden light flickered and turned greenish as they rushed into a tunnel of great trees looming over the road. Emmie leaned forward to see out the front.

"Here, look. This is where you're staying." The car broke out of the shady tunnel and pulled up in a stone courtyard at the front of a great, gray house, shadowy and dim in the evening light.

The children bundled out and stood huddled by the cars, even the smallest ones gazing silently at the house.

"It's a palace," muttered Arthur, and for once, Emmie didn't sneer at him. She thought maybe he was right. The gray stone walls surrounded the courtyard on three sides. The house wasn't very tall, and there were no turrets or towers, but it looked *old*. The great blocks of dark stone were softened at the edges, and the windows were small and patched into tiny squares. The low evening sun glittered in the little panes, shining out under spidery trails of creeper.

The cars drew away, moving slowly off around one side and leaving the children and the three women watching as a huge wooden door opened in front of them. The light was bright, and for a moment, the figure in the doorway showed only black, and Tommy stepped back into Emmie, clutching at her coat. But then the woman hurried down the steps, smiling and holding out her hands.

"You're here at last! Oh, you poor things, you must be exhausted. Welcome to Misselthwaite Manor."

Emmie lay in the high, carved wooden bed, watching the nightlight burning in its saucer of water and peering at the room. The night-light hardly gave enough light to see by, so it was half looking, half remembering in a strange jumble of the day.

She was tired, but she'd slept on the train, and now she felt oddly restless. Ruby was fast asleep across the room, snuffling into her bear—and that was odd, for a start. Emmie was used to one huge room with eight girls in it, although this room would have been about the size of the dormitory, if they took all the furniture out.

The candle flame jumped a little, and a creature glimmered in the light for a second—a horse with a thin, arched neck and a jeweled bridle. The walls were covered in them, pictures made out of fabric, all castles and horses and dogs. Emmie had never seen anything like them before. She had never seen anything like this house.

They had been hurried inside, the woman who had welcomed them explaining worriedly that they'd been told they mustn't show lights because of the new blackout regulations, but she'd thought they might trip over the furniture if she didn't turn the light on. A maid in uniform shut the door behind them with a slam, and the friendly woman shook Miss Dearlove's hand and beamed at Miss Rose and Mrs. Evans and the children.

"Mrs. Craven?" Miss Dearlove asked rather uncertainly.

"Oh! Yes, I'm so sorry. I'm Mrs. Craven. I wish my husband could be here to welcome you too, but he went to London this morning. You probably passed his train going the other way." She gave a little laugh, but it sounded odd, as though she didn't think her joke was that funny. "He retired from the navy when his father died, you see, but now that war is about to be declared, he's reenlisting."

"Craven," Emmie whispered to Joey, who happened to be standing next to her. He was staring openmouthed at a suit of armor that was standing up against the stone wall. If the hall hadn't been full of armor and weapons, it would have looked like a church. It was big enough. "The same name as the Home? Is that why we're here, you reckon?"

Joey dragged himself away from the armor and the spears crossed over each other on the wall and looked down at her in disgust. He was only a year older than she was, but he was a lot taller. "'Course it is, stupid. This is the place, isn't it? Didn't you ever read that sign on the front of the Home? *Founded by Mr. Archibald Craven of Misselthwaite Manor, in gratitude for the recovery of his son, Colin?* Misselthwaite, that's what she just said. Besides, I've seen her before."

He nodded at the smiling woman, who was now talking to Miss Dearlove and Miss Rose and pointing at the stairs. *They were working out where to put all the children,* Emmie thought. The man driving the car must have been teasing them, saying they'd have to sleep nose to tail. Surely a house like this would have enough beds.

"And you would have too if you weren't so dim." Joey poked her in the ribs. "She comes to visit. She's one of the Board." The Board came twice a year, which meant the children polishing their shoes and even more frantic hair-brushing than usual, and Miss Rose panicking in case someone had made a mistake in their workbooks.

"You might have said," Emmie muttered, but Joey only rolled his eyes. She hadn't recognized Mrs. Craven, but now she decided it might be because she had only seen her in a tailored suit and a smart hat, not an old tweed skirt and a cardigan. Miss Dearlove obviously hadn't known her straight off either.

It was very strange, Emmie thought sleepily, to have no idea what would happen tomorrow. She was used to things being always the same. She lay staring toward the wall and hoping to see the horse leap again.

All they had been told was that they were to stay mostly in this part of the house—not that Emmie thought she would ever be able to find her way out of it anyway. After they'd had supper, they had been led back through the huge hall, up a polished wooden staircase, in and out of corridors, down a few steps here, and around a corner. The house was like a rabbit warren, all passages. Emmie had wondered wearily if they might lose Ruby or one of the other little ones tagging along at the end of the line.

The red-cheeked woman who had shown them to their rooms had smiled at Emmie and told her that the country air would be good for her because she was far too thin.

"All bones," she added, patting Emmie's cheek. Emmie had scowled. She knew she was too thin. Everyone always said so. She was even thinner because she'd been saving her food for Lucy. Thinking of the little cat waiting for her on the fire escape only made Emmie scowl harder.

"Take that look off your face, Emmeline," Miss Dearlove snapped. "Say you're sorry to Miss Sowerby."

"Emmeline, there's a pretty name." Miss Sowerby seemed to be one of those people it was hard to offend. She just went on smiling, even when Emmie growled her apology. "You'll have this room, dear." She looked around it thoughtfully as she drew the curtains closed. "These curtains are good an' thick. We should be safe for this dratted blackout. Mr. Craven went marching around the house last night, trying to see if there was a chink of light showing anywhere, but how do we keep a hundred rooms all covered up? Not that we use all the rooms, o' course. Most of the second floor is under dust sheets. Now, we've put another bed over here for one of th' smaller ones." She glanced down at Emmie again, still beaming. "We've had no little girls at Misselthwaite for many a year. Mr. and Mrs. Craven have two boys. I expect you'll meet Jack tomorrow. He must be about the same age as you."

Emmie nodded and didn't say that she thought she had met him already. She wasn't sure, of course. But there had been a face peering down at them from a little flight of stairs as they followed Miss Sowerby through yet another passage. A thin, angry face, with a scowl that Emmie didn't realize looked a great deal like her own.

The boy had seen Emmie watching and stuck out his tongue. Everyone else had been so friendly, so sweetly concerned, that his furious face almost made Emmie feel better. She didn't care if the boy was rude. She could be just as rude back. She'd glanced around to check for Miss Dearlove and stuck out her own tongue, waggling it at him gleefully.

Emmie smiled in the darkness, thinking of the surprise on the boy's face. Obviously, he hated them being here. Well, she hated being here too, and she didn't care who knew it.

CHAPTER

Three

EMMIE HAD HOPED THAT WITH the upheaval of the move, lessons might be forgotten for a while. Especially as not all the staff had come with them to Misselthwaite. Miss Rose and Miss Dearlove were managing on their own without the two younger nursery nurses, who had gone together to train in one of the great London hospitals. But Miss Rose had enterprisingly sent a trunk full of books ahead of them, and a room farther along the passage had been set out as a schoolroom, with a strange assortment of heavy wooden tables and unmatched chairs.

Emmie stared grimly down at her historical reader. Couldn't they have forgotten this one? She didn't mind the stories so much, but she knew them practically by heart, along with all the doodles and scratches and bent corners. She had personally drawn a mustache and a silly hat on Queen Elizabeth I, and now every time she turned that page, it made her feel guilty.

She wasn't even sure that Miss Rose would notice if she slipped out. The teacher was too busy trying to cheer up Tommy, who'd wet his bed because he was too scared to get up in the dark and was sure he was going to be sent back. He was too small to understand that there was no one to be sent back to.

Emmie propped her chin on her hand and stared vaguely down at the page, letting the words sway between the lines and float into each other. The sun streamed through the deep-set windows and made bars of light on the wooden table. She could see tiny specks of dust floating in the air. There were birds outside; she could hear them—different ones. Back in London they were mostly pigeons, and she had no idea what these were. Perhaps they could persuade Miss Rose to go on a nature walk? Emmie wondered sleepily. She had taken them to count the wildflowers in the park once.

Or they could explore the house—wouldn't looking at all the paintings and the suits of armor tell them about history anyway? It would be better than reading about King Alfred and the cakes all over again. Emmie wasn't sure when Misselthwaite had been built, but it must have been hundreds of years old. Miss Sowerby might tell them. Or even Mrs. Craven. She'd asked Miss Dearlove to tell her anything she could do to help. Emmie had heard her.

"Have you finished, Emmie?"

Emmie's elbow slipped as she jumped, and she banged her wrist against the edge of the table. She didn't look up at Arthur and Joey on the other side of the table because she knew they'd be smirking. Being eleven instead of ten made them think they were so clever. "No, miss," she muttered, cupping her hand over the bruise and sucking her lips over her teeth. She'd hit her wrist right on the bone.

"Stop dreaming and get on then, please."

Emmie turned away from the sun patches on the wood and gazed at the pages again, her eyes blurred and stinging.

"We can go out?" Emmie repeated, eyeing Miss Sowerby suspiciously. She was sure that this couldn't be right. "On our own? Anywhere in the gardens?"

"Anywhere." Miss Sowerby nodded and then laughed at Arthur and Joey, who were suddenly gobbling down the last of their soup. "Use th' stairs at th' end of this passage, and they'll take you down to th' side door. These are your rooms on this passage, you see. You're not to go running all over the house. But the gardens, you can explore. Mind you listen to th' gardeners. If they tell thee to keep off, you keep off."

"And be back by two," Miss Dearlove added. "For afternoon lessons." She sounded suddenly anxious, as though she thought she might lose them. "We're trusting you three older ones. The littler children will stay closer to the house with Miss Rose and me."

"How are we to know when it's two o'clock?" Joey asked suddenly, and Arthur elbowed him in the side. Emmie scowled. None of them had wristwatches, of course. She looked crossly at Miss Rose and Miss Dearlove. Now they wouldn't be allowed to go.

"There's a clock in the little tower over the courtyard," Miss Sowerby told them calmly. "Go by that. You'll hear it chime the hours and the quarters." She gave Arthur a sharp glance. "Don't you ask me where th' courtyard be, boy. Use some gumption. Go an' find it!"

Arthur and Joey raced away. Emmie could hear them clattering down the wooden staircase. She wanted to bolt the rest of her food and run after them, but she held herself back, spooning up the last of the soup. She was almost sure that she would be stopped somehow. If she rushed and looked excited, someone was sure to call her and make her stay in after all. Even as she walked down the stairs and heaved at the heavy door, she was still waiting for Miss Dearlove to yank her back.

But no one did. Emmie stood hesitating in the doorway, staring out at the garden. It seemed strange for the sun to be so bright.

With war being declared and all the whispers about London being bombed, everything had felt gray—even the view from the train windows. Even the moor had been tinted gray and violet in the evening sun, faded with shadows and her misery over leaving Lucy.

Now she stood blinking at the whiteness of the gravel walk that led between the clipped yew trees. The yews were almost black in the sunlight, and the creeper growing up the stone wall of the old house blazed a wild green. Emmie put out her hand and rubbed one of the leaves, running it through her shaking fingers. She'd thought it would be rough, but instead it felt soft, almost soapy.

This was like another world, fresh and brilliantly alive, and then she remembered that it was hers only for an hour.

Emmie pulled the door shut behind her with a bang. She could hear the boys shouting and whooping somewhere in the distance, and she deliberately turned away from the noise. She wanted to explore by herself. The path seemed made to run down, leading to a thick, dark hedge trimmed into an archway. Beyond, Emmie could see more of the tempting green. She slipped through, catching her breath as the closed walk opened up into a stretch of perfect lawn. The grass looked like a carpet, clipped short, and she crouched down, running her hands over it and smiling to herself.

Then she turned, glancing back at the house. Could anyone see her? She could just imagine Miss Dearlove rolling her eyes at

Emmie stroking the grass… But the small diamond-paned windows glittered in the sun, and she couldn't see anyone looking out. Wasn't she away from their part of the house now anyway? She frowned. The place was so big that it was hard to tell. But the gardens were huge too—she could see that now. Walls and hedges and terraces divided up the great space, almost like rooms in a house. But on this higher bit of ground, she could see how far the gardens spread out—for miles, it looked like. Even if someone did glance out of a window, Emmie was almost sure they wouldn't see her. She felt deliciously small and secret. There was no one in sight, no one at all.

She stood up and stretched out her arms, feeling the sun on her hands and wrists—her cardigan was on the small side, and the sleeves rode up. She went a few steps farther, enough to look down the slope at the end of the lawn. Set into the side of the bank were steps of a crumbly, gray stone that was golden in the sun. They led down to a pool, darkly gleaming and scattered with white, waxen-looking flowers.

Emmie hurried down the steps to crouch at the edge of the water. Little golden fish hovered below the surface, and as her shadow fell across the pond, they swam lazily toward her. Perhaps they hoped she'd come to feed them, Emmie thought, and she sat down heavily on the stone paving, suddenly reminded of Lucy and how angry she was and how she hated it here. She hated it, but she'd forgotten. How long had Lucy waited on the fire escape the day before? Had she found enough to eat, scavenging from someone else?

Emmie stared into the water, wishing that there were a little black cat sitting here too, watching those fish. Or stretched out basking on the sun-warmed stone. Her fingers twitched, wanting dark fur to stroke.

She sprang up angrily, scattering the golden fish, and stalked away, past the pool and the glittering fountain. The sun and the scents of the flowers and the spicy smell of the yew hedges had made her forget how lost she felt. But she didn't belong here. She didn't belong *anywhere*. Emmie sped up, running along the edge of the pool. She swiped blindly at the flowers in the long bed down the side of the water garden, raising a gust of sharp lemon scent and a hum of bees. The garden was bordered by another dark hedge, and she darted through an archway at the corner, fists clenched, furious with the perfection, the trimmed prettiness of it all. She would rather be hiding away from everyone else on a broken, old iron fire escape. She didn't care how beautiful the place was.

Someone laughed, and Emmie heard running footsteps close by. She turned away sharply, not wanting the boys to find her. She was on a brick path now, less grand than the stone terraces around the fountain. One side was bordered by the hedge, and the other by a long brick wall trailing gleaming curtains of ivy. The ivy was flowering in clouds of tufted yellow balls, and bees droned in and out of it. Emmie had no idea what the dark leaves were, but she liked the gleam of them, and she slowed a little to watch the bees, sharply buzzing little ones and great, fat, sleepy, furry things that lurched from flower to flower.

She was about to hurry on, realizing that the boys must have been heading back to the house, when a sharp trilling song sounded above her head, and she stepped back, staring up in surprise. At first, Emmie thought Arthur or Joey had somehow climbed on top of the wall, but there was no one there—only a tiny, red-breasted bird, peering curiously at her out of the ivy.

"A robin!" Emmie stared at him. She didn't think she'd ever seen one for real before. She had seen Christmas cards, and Miss Rose had shown them how to draw a Christmas robin, but for some reason, Emmie had assumed that robins were part of the same storybook Christmas as parties and toys and stockings and camels.

The little bird leaned farther out to look at her, with his head to one side. He was grayish and soft looking, and the breeze ruffled the red fluff of his breast feathers. He trilled again, staring at her with bright, black-bead eyes.

"You know I'm new," Emmie whispered. "New and different. There hasn't been a little girl here for years and years, Miss Sowerby said." She took a step closer and watched as the robin's beak shimmered and trembled with the bright notes. It was magical. Then he stopped and looked at her sideways, proud and shy at the same time, and Emmie screwed up her face and whistled back to him.

"I have to go," she murmured. "They said we had to be on time for lessons, and I might be late already. It isn't that I want to go," she assured him and then stopped herself. Why was she talking to a bird? But his eyes were so bright and knowing. She was almost sure he understood. He fluttered up a few branches, perched on top of the wall, and then darted away with a flick of his tail.

Emmie turned and ran back along the path, through the hedge, and along the terrace past the fountain, racing back up the stairs to fling herself pink cheeked and breathless into the schoolroom.

"Goodness!" Miss Rose stared at her, and Arthur and Joey smirked angelically.

"I got lost," Emmie said quickly. "I couldn't find the right door."

A boy standing next to Miss Rose gave a tiny snort, and Miss Rose seemed to remember that he was there. "Yes. Jack, this is Emmie—she's ten, like you."

Emmie suppressed a sigh. She had always hated that there was no one her own age at the Craven Home, but she wasn't going to be friendly with this boy—the boy who'd been making faces around the banisters—just because he was ten. Especially not if everybody wanted her to...

"Emmie, this is Jack, Mrs. Craven's son. He was at boarding school, but he's had the measles, so he's staying home for now."

"I'm going back," the boy snapped. "Any day."

"Of course." Miss Rose smiled. "But for the moment, Jack will be doing some lessons with us."

The boy rolled his eyes, and Joey, Arthur, and Emmie watched him suspiciously—united for once in their dislike of this stranger. A stranger who actually belonged in this house.

"Boarding school?" Arthur muttered to Joey, as Jack slid into a seat across the table. "Those people are weird."

Jack glared at Arthur, but he didn't say anything. He was silent for the whole morning, working swiftly through the math questions that Miss Rose assigned them and shoving them in front of her when she came back from the table where the smaller ones were copying their letters. Miss Rose looked taken aback, as if she hadn't expected him to polish the work off so quickly. Emmie and the other boys stared at him in disgust. Posh *and* clever, then.

Jack looked down his nose, and as soon as Miss Rose announced in a relieved voice that it was half past three, he slipped out of his seat and disappeared.

"Stuck-up little so-and-so," Joey growled under his breath, and Emmie nodded, which surprised them both.

CHAPTER

Four

THERE HAD BEEN NO CHURCH that morning—only hymns and Miss Dearlove reading from the book of Bible stories and looking twitchily at the little clock on the mantelpiece and falling over her words. Then at eleven, they had trooped downstairs to the servants' hall, squeezing in among the maids and gardeners. The cook and Mrs. Evans had made tea, but hardly anyone was drinking it. Instead, they perched uncomfortably on the chairs gathered around the polished wooden radio. *The whole house must be there,* Emmie thought, trying to count the servants without letting anyone see that she was staring. Miss Dearlove had explained to them at breakfast that the prime minister was going to speak and that it was very important. The matron hadn't said quite how, but she was jumpy and nervous, and even friendly Miss Sowerby looked anxious.

As the words, "This is London..." echoed through the sunny room, Emmie saw that Mrs. Craven and Jack had slipped in too, and one of the gardeners had swiftly given up his chair for her. Mrs. Craven smiled at Jack and patted his arm. He leaned against her shoulder, darting cold glances at the other children. Arthur and Joey were rolling a marble along the crack between the flagstones, and Tommy was whining to Miss Rose that he was hungry.

But as the broadcast went on, even the smallest ones grew silent, frozen by the dreadful sense of sadness and frustration in the voice coming from the radio cabinet. Miss Dearlove was clutching Ruby on her lap, and Emmie saw her rest her face in Ruby's hair for a moment. Emmie was so shocked that it took her several seconds to understand what Mr. Chamberlain had said.

And that consequently this country is at war with Germany.

It was almost an anticlimax—Emmie already *knew* that. That was why they had been dragged out of London, wasn't it? Had they all been hoping that it wouldn't happen after all? Emmie glanced around under her eyelashes at the men and women in the room. Their fear felt so real that she was almost sure she could touch it. She jumped a little as the miserable voice died away and a great pealing of bells rang out—and all the frozen statues in the room shifted and gasped, and the maids turned to hug each other. Several of them were crying.

"Shhh, listen." Miss Sowerby nodded toward the radio again,

where a man was now solemnly repeating instructions about air-raid sirens and shelters. "The cellar. We'll have to use the cellar. It's the safest place." She looked over at Mrs. Craven, who nodded and gave a little cough.

"We'll start this afternoon. I shouldn't think they'd come here, but in case…"

"We could build some bunks, ma'am," one of the gardeners suggested. "Better get some hurricane lanterns down there."

And then everyone stumbled to their feet, hauling up the confused children to stand for "God Save the King." No one sang, only listened, heads bowed. Emmie wondered if the king was still in London, and the young princesses, or had they been evacuated too?

Emmie was probably supposed to be in the cellars now, but she'd slipped out to the gardens again instead. Miss Dearlove had said that after lunch they could all help to clean and dust. But even with lanterns, Emmie couldn't bear to be down there in the dark and shadows. They'd slept two nights at Misselthwaite Manor now, and she'd seen how strange and dark it was, even aboveground. The little night-light on her bedside table had seemed nothing against the weight of the darkness outside the windows.

The Yorkshire nights were black in a way that Emmie was sure London never could be, and the stars looked cold. But London's streetlights had been turned out now. Miss Dearlove had explained that to them when Ruby complained she hated the dark. This was war. All the country was pitch-black to give the bombers nothing to see. The thought made Emmie shiver and run to the light and the warmth of the gardens.

She ran her fingers along the brick wall that edged the path and then rubbed them together, brushing away the powdery redness. This path ran all along the side of the kitchen gardens and the orchard, Emmie knew now. She still hadn't explored all of the gardens, not even half of them, probably. But the kitchen gardens were interesting. There were plants under strange glass bells and tall wooden towers with what looked like beans hanging off them. The gardens seemed like good places to hide and spy and investigate, and Emmie had been down this path a few times now.

The wall was soft and worn, with fat cushions of faded velvet moss between the bricks. The door to the kitchen garden was open, and she peered around it curiously. She didn't think anyone would be here, so she wouldn't have to skirt around the edges of the garden, trying not to be seen.

All the gardeners had been in the servants' hall. Even those who were married and spent Sundays at their own cottages had come to listen to the prime minister's message. The cellars would be for them and their families too, if there should be an air raid. Everyone was down there now, planning how to furnish the rooms and strengthen the ceiling beams, considering whether the coal chute could be turned into an emergency door in case the house collapsed on top of them. When the butler said that, everyone else had turned to stare at him in horror, and he'd reddened and looked apologetically at Emmie and the other children.

But then he shrugged. It happened. He had fought on the Somme in the Great War, and he had seen the craters. The bombs they were talking of these days... Of course, there was no airfield nearby—yet—and they were a long way from York or any other town, but they were not far from the coast. Everyone had nodded and swallowed and tried not to think about the weight of stone above their heads.

No one had told the children they were not to explore these working gardens, but Emmie had only peered around the doors until now because gardeners had always been in there working. They were not unfriendly. One of them had smiled at her and asked her how she was settling in. She'd just given him her stare. Emmie had been avoiding company, unlike Arthur and Joey, who'd taken less than a day to discover there were apples and plums in the orchard, and gardeners who might look the other way while the boys climbed the trees, particularly if they'd help with the weeding or pick up stones in return.

Now the gardens were deserted, sun warmed, and silent. She could wander along the little paths and peer at the vegetables—most of which she didn't recognize since she'd only seen them boiled to within an inch of their lives. Perhaps she would see the robin again, she thought, glancing around hopefully. Birds ate vegetables, didn't they? He had been on the ivy-covered part of the wall when she saw him before, very close to here.

Padding quietly along, Emmie walked around a thicket of beans, the last few pods still dangling from their frame, and nearly tripped over a man tying up the stems. She skipped back, gasping, and then took another hurried step back when he looked up at her.

"Who are you?"

Emmie was silent for a moment. It wasn't the Yorkshire accent that made him hard to understand. The tight skin of the scars that covered one side of his face had pulled his mouth sideways and slurred his voice. She swallowed. "I'm allowed to be here."

"Never said tha' weren't."

"Why aren't you with the others? Building bunks and...and things." Emmie shrugged vaguely.

"Bunks?" He frowned at her.

"They're making the cellars into an air-raid shelter. Because now we're at war." It was the first time she had said it. Somehow, she felt it ought to have been more dramatic.

"Are we?" he muttered. "That why th'art here then? One of those evacuee children Mrs. Craven mentioned?"

"Yes. Didn't you go and listen to the radio this morning? I thought everybody did."

"Happen everybody doesn't want t'know."

Cautiously, Emmie moved a step closer to him. She wanted to ask what had happened to his face, but she couldn't think of a way to say it politely. She suspected he'd been injured in the Great War—like the lame man who came to the Home every few weeks to sharpen knives. She was just trying to frame the words when a little streak of red and gray fluttered past and landed between her and the man, glancing back and forth between them curiously.

"Oh, the robin!" Emmie crouched down to look at him closer.

"Tha' knows him then?" The man looked at her thoughtfully.

"I saw him yesterday. He was sitting in all those green leaves on the wall."

"Ivy, that is."

Emmie ignored him. She was trying to chirrup at the robin, who was looking at her with his head on one side, quite confused.

"I don't think I'm making the right noises..."

"Nor do I."

"Well, there's no need to be rude." Emmie glared at him, and then the robin shot up into the air and landed on the man's shoulder, its little scaly claws digging into his velveteen waistcoat.

"Tha'll fright him wi' that sharp voice," the man said, his own voice very gentle and soft under the strange slurring.

"Sorry…" Emmie dropped her voice to a whisper. "Why does he sit on you? Does he like you?"

"Known him from the egg, I suppose. He hatched out here in this garden—or one close by, at any rate. And I move slow." His face twisted a little, and the scars crinkled. Emmie tried not to grimace, but her eyes flickered and her mouth twisted in a moment of disgust.

"Even slower now," he added in a growl under his breath. And suddenly he heaved himself up so that the robin sprang away from his shoulder, spreading out his wings like little gray fans to catch the air. The man grabbed at a wooden crutch that had been laid down beside him. Emmie had thought the crutch was some sort of garden tool, but now as he stomped down the path leaning on it, she saw that part of his leg was made of metal. The robin swooped around his head, chittering fiercely as the gardener headed for the door at the other end of the garden, and then it fluttered away over the wall.

Emmie stared after them, wishing she hadn't made a face. She hadn't meant to. She'd liked the man, even if he had been as grumpy as she was. She could see that she'd made him angry—or sad. And she longed for the robin to land on her shoulder too.

She trailed around the vegetable beds for a little longer, hoping at least to see the robin again, but he had disappeared. There were only a couple of blackbirds, pecking hopefully at a fruit net, and they swooped away almost as soon as she saw them.

"I suppose I ought to go back," Emmie murmured, trying to speak softly like the gardener had said. If she stayed out long enough to make them worry, Miss Dearlove might keep her indoors the next day. If she was lucky, everyone had been too busy and anxious to notice she wasn't there. She ran along the path to the shrubbery, laughing a little as she felt the wind blowing her hair back.

Then she stopped, pressing herself back against the scratchy yew hedge and straightening her face to proper wartime seriousness. Mrs. Craven was walking toward her.

Emmie ducked her head politely, hoping that the lady would just walk past, but she didn't. She stopped and leaned down to talk.

"Are you having fun running about?"

"I didn't mean to," Emmie said hurriedly.

"Oh, I wasn't saying you shouldn't. It's lovely to see you running about." She swallowed. "I hope all that doesn't change."

Emmie looked up cautiously, not sure if this was meant for her to hear. Mrs. Craven sounded more as if she were talking to herself.

"Were you exploring the gardens?"

"Yes. I was looking at the vegetables. I met a gardener," Emmie added. "He made a robin sit on his shoulder."

"Oh! That would be Mr. Sowerby. He can charm the birds out of the trees—when he tries." She looked down at Emmie in surprise. "Did he speak to you?"

"He told me my voice was too sharp," Emmie said, frowning. "And that he knew the robin when he was an egg. Mr. Sowerby... like Miss Sowerby in the house?"

"Yes, her brother." Mrs. Craven put her hand on Emmie's shoulder. "He doesn't talk to people much these days. Don't be upset if he barks at you."

"Did he hurt his leg in the war?"

"At the very end of the war." Mrs. Craven sighed. "It's never healed properly. It hurts him. And he remembers things." She tried to smile at Emmie. "I know it was a long time ago. Long before you were born, or my Jack, or even David. But it doesn't feel all that long sometimes."

Emmie nodded. Miss Dearlove probably wouldn't want her talking to Mrs. Craven at all, but she wanted to know. Now was her chance to know more than Joey and Arthur. "David?" she asked politely. "Is that another of your children? I only knew there was Jack."

Mrs. Craven glanced down again, blinking, almost as if she'd forgotten that Emmie was there. "Yes. Of course, you've not met him. My older son, he's gone to join the Royal Air Force." She pressed her hand against her mouth for a moment and murmured something to Emmie about enjoying the day. Then she hurried away down the path and whisked around the hedge, but Emmie could see that she was still standing there. She was hiding—like Emmie did when she was trying not to cry.

Shaken, Emmie crept away, trying not to let the gravel scrunch under her shoes, and slipped in through the side door to find the others. Perhaps there were worse things than being afraid of the dark.

Emmie kicked at Ruby's bear, which was lying on the floor by her little cot bed. She could hear Ruby and the others laughing and squealing as they chased each other across the lawn below the window.

Of course Miss Dearlove *had* noticed that Emmie wasn't helping in the cellars the day before. Miss Rose had even gone to look for her, so they said, when she turned up *looking like butter wouldn't melt after we'd been worrying ourselves sick over you all after-noon.* Emmie thought that they looked downright cross rather than worried, but for once she'd had the sense not to say so.

After breakfast this morning, Miss Dearlove had confined her to her room, given her dust cloths and some wax polish, and told her to tidy up. Emmie had rubbed a little of the polish into the dark wooden table by her bed, so that the room smelled pleasantly of lavender and they couldn't say she hadn't tried—and then she'd gone back to looking out the window.

Even the misty, purplish slopes of the moor looked welcoming, now that she was shut up. But listening to the others playing only made her feel grumpier when she had to stay indoors for a whole day. Miss Dearlove had said she would let Emmie out for lessons, but that wasn't much better than being stuck in her bedroom, although it gave her a chance to scowl at Jack across the table. His smug, despising face meant she couldn't even look at him without scowling.

Emmie sighed and plopped down on Ruby's bed, which creaked painfully and sagged a bit. Then she picked up the bear, stroked him a little to say sorry, and sat him up against the pillow.

What was she going to *do*? Even though Miss Rose's boring lessons seemed to go on for hours, they actually didn't take up much of the day. Since the two nurses who'd cared for the younger children back at the Home hadn't come with them, Miss Rose was too busy looking after the little ones to teach anyone very much. So Emmie would be stuck in this room for hours. She couldn't even read, because the books were all in the schoolroom. There had to be something in here to do!

Emmie got up and stood in the middle of the room, watching the tiny specks of dust falling in the sunlight from the window. She supposed she could actually dust and polish the furniture, like she'd been told… It would pass the time anyway. Sighing, she went to fetch the jar of polish from the little bedside table and leaned over to pick up the rags, which had slipped down underneath it. Crouched down like that, she noticed for the first time that the table had a drawer. She wasn't really expecting to find anything interesting in it, but there might be an old pack of cards so she could play solitaire.

She tugged at the drawer. It stuck, as though no one had tried to open it for years, and then flew open sharply so that the faded notebooks inside slid around.

Emmie sighed. The books didn't look very exciting. There were three of them, all with faded cloth covers. They looked like the book Miss Dearlove made the laundry lists in.

She pulled one out and flicked through it. The notebook was full of tiny, closely written notes, but not a laundry list. It was more like a story. And even though the writing was old-fashioned and scratchy, the spelling was quite bad. Bad enough to make Emmie snicker. She realized then that the books were diaries—a child's diaries, she was almost sure. She had never heard of a child writing in a diary, but there were dates written here and there. It was the story of someone's life. Suddenly interested, she dug around in the drawer and got out all three books, searching through them to find the earliest dates.

The most faded book of the three was red, its cloth faded to pink in patches and the spine a little split. Emmie smiled to herself when she saw the date written on the opening page—January 1910. This was the first.

Something was written in faint brown ink on the inside of the cover. She picked the notebook up and took it over to the light of the window to read.

Mary Lennox
Misselthwaite Manor

This is not my book, but no one wants it, so I am making it my diary. No one will care.

Mary Lennox... Emmie rolled the name around on her tongue. She liked it. So this was a girl's diary. Someone around her own age? That angry, scrawled writing made her think so.

Emmie forgot entirely about polishing and put the later diaries back into the drawer. Then she lay down on top of her bed with the limp notebook propped against the pillow. One of the pages was coming loose from the stitching, and as she slid it back in, a few words seemed to leap at her.

> *Soft, scarlet feathers and thin, spindly little legs... I wish he would make friends with me... I haven't a friend of my own...*

Emmie stared at the page, swallowing hard. She felt as though something hard were lodged in her throat. This Mary had felt the same way she did—and she had seen a robin in the garden too. Perhaps her robin was the great-great-great-grandfather of Emmie's.

But if she had lived here, and this great, huge house was really her home, why *didn't* Miss Mary have any friends? *She must have been so rich*, Emmie thought. She must have had everything she ever wanted. Emmie turned back through the pages to the beginning of the diary, frowning to herself.

> *I do not like this place, and I do not want to stay here. But I have nowhere else to go.*

Even in the faded ink, the words seemed to shimmer on the page, and Emmie stroked her fingers across them. Someone else had felt so much like she did.

She could hear feet walking quickly in the passageway outside, so Emmie slapped the book shut and stuffed it back in the drawer. Then she snatched up the cloth and began to rub it over the carved post at the corner of her bed, with a cross, pinched expression on her face—just as they expected.

Miss Rose opened the door and sighed very faintly. "Come on, Emmie. Lessons."

Emmie stalked after her to the schoolroom, but her scowl was only to keep up appearances. If those notebooks were in her room, then they were hers, weren't they? No one could mind her reading them. Not that she was going to ask anyway. She was almost sure that Miss Mary, whoever she was, wouldn't mind.

"Stop daydreaming, Emmie!" Miss Rose tapped her nails on the table in front of Emmie's book, and Emmie blinked at her. She had been thinking about the robin, the rich orange-red of his feathers, and the way he'd looked at her with his head sideways, as though he thought she was interesting. Hardly anybody ever thought she was interesting. She was just a nuisance, except to Lucy. It was stupid for a bird to make her remember a cat, but he did. He'd looked at her the same way Lucy had—curious and a little bit suspicious. Emmie had tamed Lucy. Perhaps she could tame the robin too?

"Dolly Daydream!" Joey whispered, smirking. "What were you thinking about, then?"

Emmie rolled her eyes at him. As if she'd tell.

"She's dreaming about that stupid cat again." Arthur poked her arm with his pencil. "Weren't you? See, she was. She's gone red." He was bored and teasing Emmie was worth it, if he could make her lose her temper.

"Wasn't…" Emmie muttered, hating the way she blushed so easily. Why shouldn't she think about Lucy? "And what if I was anyway?"

"What cat?" Jack asked, and they all stared at him. He didn't speak during their lessons unless Miss Rose asked him a direct question. For the last two days, he had trudged into the school-room with a haughty look on his face and slid out again as soon as he could. He'd never spoken to any of them before.

"She had a cat back in London," Arthur said after a moment of silence. "Skinny black thing, a stray. Fed it half your food, didn't you, Emmie? That's why she's so skinny too."

"And then she made an almighty fuss when Miss Dearlove wouldn't let her bring it with us," Joey added. "She cried."

Arthur sniggered. "She's going to cry again. Look."

Emmie dug her fingers into her palms hard, so the nails left purple half-moons in the skin. "I'm not." She swallowed the tears back with a huge effort and glared, not at Joey and Arthur, but at Jack. This was his fault. He'd asked. They might have left her alone if he hadn't asked.

He gazed back at her, his gray eyes hard, like shining stones. "So you left your cat behind?"

Emmie didn't answer him. She didn't trust him.

"You know what's happening to cats and dogs in London, don't you?"

Arthur leaned farther over the table, glancing back toward Miss Rose, who was busy counting wooden bricks with the smaller ones. "What? There haven't been bombs yet. We'd have heard about it."

"Destroyed. All of them." Jack was still staring at Emmie. "*Killed.* Because there isn't going to be enough food to feed them. And because they'll be so scared of the bombs they'll go mad. There was a leaflet sent out about it back in the summer, telling people it was the best thing to do. A leaflet from the government, like all those leaflets about shelters and gas masks. Thousands of cats and dogs are getting put down. They take them to the vets, and the vets—"

"That isn't true," Emmie burst out. "You're just saying it because...because you hate us."

Jack shrugged. "I do hate you. But it's still true. It made my mother cry when she read about it in the newspaper. Some duchess was trying to get people to send them all to her country house, but it's too late now." He smiled triumphantly, and Emmie could only shake her head. It was horrible. It couldn't be true. But the duchess part made it all sound real. How could he make that up?

"Lucy wasn't a proper pet..." she whispered. "No one would take her to the vet."

He shrugged. "I bet they're catching strays too."

"Why would they?" Joey broke in suddenly. "Stop sniffing, Emmie. He's just saying it because he wants to see you cry."

Emmie looked around at Joey, her eyes hot and blurred with tears. Was he actually sticking up for her?

"No one could catch that skinny thing except for you anyway. She'll be all right. Bet she can run faster than a bomb."

Arthur nodded and then snickered. "And she'll be all right in the blackout, won't she? She'll fit right in."

Emmie snorted tearily. It was an odd feeling, having them on her side for once.

"Think what you like. No skin off my nose." Jack glanced up at them, and his eyes glittered. He dropped his voice. "Anyway, she knows I'm right."

Mary Lennox
Misselthwaite Manor
14th January 1910

I have been out into the gardens because there is nothing else for me to do. It is much colder here, and everything is gray, even the sky. There is a fountain, but it hasn't any water in it, just a lot of dead leaves.

There was a bird sitting in one of the trees. I asked an old man who is one of the gardeners, and he told me that the bird is a robin. The bird chirped at me, and it almost felt like he was talking to me. He had a gray body, a front covered in soft, scarlet feathers, and thin, spindly little legs. He isn't like any bird I saw in India. When I first saw him, he was sitting on the very highest branch of a tree over a wall. I think he was in the garden that has been locked up for years and years.

Martha, the maid, told me about this locked garden, and one of the gardeners did too. I tried to ask him where the door was, but he was cross and said I was meddlesome.

I want to see the garden, but it doesn't have a door, or not that I can find, and I walked all the way around. There are two kitchen gardens and then the orchard, but there is another garden beyond that with no way to get inside at all.

I'm almost sure the robin was in the locked garden. I am going to find the door, or perhaps I shall climb over the wall. Then I could see the robin again. He sang so loudly, and he liked me, I think. I wish he would make friends with me.

I don't think I have ever had a friend, and I should like one.

CHAPTER

Five

EMMIE WRIGGLED FARTHER UNDER THE quilt, fighting to stay asleep. She was warm, and if she woke up, she would know how dark it was. The wind was screaming around the house, blowing down off the great, purple slope of the moor. It howled in the chimney like a wild beast, and Emmie didn't want to wake up and have to think about it. She pulled the quilt right over her head, and that warm, breathless darkness felt safe. But it was too hot and stuffy to stay huddled underneath for long. She burrowed out like a mouse and lay twitching and listening to the wind and Ruby's thin, little snore. The diary slithered slowly down the heaped patchwork quilt and thumped onto the floor, but Emmie felt too edgy to reach down and pick it up.

The wild beast noises were dying down now, but they were still eerie. Just strange little hiccupping cries. What made the wind do that? Perhaps it was an owl sitting on the windowsill and wailing. Arthur had seen one, swooping down low over the courtyard—or he said he had.

Emmie shivered, even though the room was so warm, and waited to hear the *tap-tap-tap* of a beak. She was awake now; it was no good pretending she wasn't. She sat up, wrapping her arms around her knees and listening. No matter how many times she told herself the noise was only the wind, it still sounded as though something was trying to force its way in. She jumped and gasped for breath as the windows rattled again.

Then the wind dropped to a still calm that was just as frightening. The empty space where the sound had been echoed around her. Emmie buried her face in the quilt over her knees and waited for the wind to roar and slam itself against the walls again.

But it didn't. Instead, a thin, sobbing wail echoed down the passageway, so quiet and sad that it made Emmie gasp and whimper herself.

That was not the wind. She'd heard it earlier too, she realized, but she had thought the stifled gasps were part of the storm battling down from the moor. Now she was almost sure the noise wasn't an owl either. It was somebody crying.

She peered over at Ruby. No, she was definitely fast asleep. Miss Rose and Miss Dearlove slept next door to the smaller children's rooms, so if one of the little ones was crying, surely they'd have got up to see what was the matter. But she couldn't hear footsteps or anyone talking. Just the sobs, worn-out and miserable. As though whoever was making them didn't expect anyone to come. They were only crying because they couldn't not.

Emmie shuddered. What if only she could hear the noise because it was a ghost crying in the dark? The house was old and full of enough history to be haunted. Then she wrinkled her nose thoughtfully. If there was even a rumor of a ghost at Misselthwaite, that stuck-up Jack would have told her and Arthur and Joey. He would have done his best to scare them silly. In fact, she was quite surprised that he hadn't invented a ghost and dressed up in a sheet to try to frighten them. But still—in the dark, it was hard not to believe in ghosts.

Another weary cry whispered into the room, and Emmie got out of bed. She wasn't sure if she was going to see what was the matter, or if she was going to tell whoever it was to shut up. She just couldn't listen to that sad noise any more.

The manor had electric lights in most of the rooms, but because there were so many windows and the staff hadn't been able to fit proper blackout curtains over all of them, the children had been given candlesticks to carry if they needed to visit the lavatory at the end of the hallway. Emmie lit her candle from the night-light flame and marched out into the hallway, clicking the door shut gently behind her. The hall looked even darker than her bedroom. The blackness seemed to rush in on the small flame of her candle, as if it would like to swallow it. Huge, gray shadow-monsters loomed up the walls as Emmie began to walk toward the noise. It didn't help to know that they were only her shadows, thrown by the leaping candle flame. What if the candle blew out? Then the shadows might leap on her.

Emmie knew that was stupid, but she couldn't help believing it anyway, just a little. Breathing fast, she cupped her hand painfully close around the flame and hurried down the hall, trying to figure out which door the crying was coming from.

She got all the way to the little staircase where Jack had hidden on the first night. Was that really only three nights ago? But then the noise seemed hard to pin down, as though it was echoing back from somewhere else. But perhaps that was only the wind… Emmie stood hesitating at the bottom of the steps, wondering whether to go up. But the wind had died down again, and the night was peaceful. Had she just imagined the crying?

The candle flame skittered sideways in a sudden draft, and Emmie gasped as the shadows flung themselves in great tearing leaps around the paneled staircase. Perhaps the crying had stopped because the ghost was right behind her now. It had tempted her in…

She shut her eyes tight, wishing for Lucy, Miss Rose, even Miss Dearlove—anyone. But there was only the faint creak of the floorboards as she shifted her weight. She was all alone, and the night was still. Perhaps no one had been crying after all.

26th January 1910

I am sure it was magic.

The robin showed me the key, buried in the hole, but something had made him look for worms just there, just then. I might not have picked it up, because it looked so worn and rusted and dirty. But I had to, because I knew it was the key to the garden that had been locked for ten years. I still couldn't find the door, but the key in my pocket made me think that one day I would.

It happened when I went out to skip with the rope that Martha's mother sent me. I had never seen a skipping rope, but Martha showed me. She can skip to a hundred. I can't skip to more than thirty before I get tired, but I will get better. I skipped almost all the way down the walk by the locked garden, and the robin came to watch me.

He sat on the top of the wall and sang to make me look at him, and it was magic, because that meant I was watching when the wind blew through the ivy. He made me look, and I saw the brown metal of the door handle, just for a second. The door was painted green like all the others, but so faded and worn and covered in ivy that I never knew it was there. The ivy hangs down like a thick curtain. I crept underneath it and opened the door with the key—the only key, and I have it!

It was so still. So quiet, but then no one has stepped inside it for ten years. Only the birds have been there. Everything was covered in great, gray trails of roses. They've climbed and clambered over the trees and the benches and the statues, and they've even gone snaking out over the grass in some places. They've grown everywhere, but I think they're dead. They look so dry and gray. I wish they weren't. I wish I'd seen the garden as it was ten years ago, with all the roses flowering. But then it wouldn't have been so covered up with roses, and it wouldn't be so quiet and secret and mine. I can act out my own stories there, and no one will watch me or laugh. I have been digging around the bulbs—and there are hundreds, maybe even thousands of them, all sending up little green points. I pulled the grass away to help them breathe. I don't know what to do to help the roses though. I don't know how to make them grow.

I asked the gardener about roses, but he snarled at me again. He is the most bad-tempered person I have ever met. He might even be sulkier than me. The housekeeper said I was nasty tempered. I heard her, and Martha is always saying how strange I am. But in my secret garden, I am only me, and no one minds.

And I have the key—the only key! I'm keeping it in the drawer where I hide this diary to make sure no one sees.

Emmie gripped the pages tighter, breathing fast, her heart jumping. Mary had a place all of her own—a secret, like Lucy had been Emmie's secret. And now the diaries were in Emmie's drawer. In *her* bedside table. So maybe the key…

She sat up in bed, the diary almost sliding off her knees, and then glanced quickly over at Ruby. Had she woken her? But Ruby was still a small hump under her bedclothes, which wasn't surprising. Emmie wasn't sure quite what time it was, but she knew it was very early. When she'd woken up, she'd almost been scared to open her eyes, in case she'd still see the same shadow-haunted darkness, but even through the heavy curtains, a faint light had turned the room an early-morning gray.

Now the light was growing brighter, quite bright enough to see that there was definitely no key hidden in the drawer under the diaries. But this must be the place Mary had meant. Still, it had been a long time ago, Emmie thought, pushing the drawer closed with a sigh. Almost thirty years. Who knew what had happened to the key—and to the door and the garden.

Emmie's heart jumped. Was it still a secret? She knew where it was. Mary had written that it was the garden beyond the orchard. She could go and see.

Perhaps Arthur and Joey had already found it, Emmie thought with a sharp jolt of disappointment. They had climbed the trees, after all. Perhaps they had looked over into the secret garden.

She tried to remember the ivy-covered wall along the path. Had she seen a door? She had been into the kitchen gardens where she'd seen Mr. Sowerby. She was almost sure that she had walked through all three, but she had kept away from the orchard because Arthur and Joey were there.

She would go and look today. Maybe even now, before breakfast. No one had said that they couldn't go out early, Emmie reasoned to herself, slipping out of bed again and dressing as quietly as she could.

She padded down the passageway barefooted, just as she had done the night before. No wind was howling at the windows now. The storm had blown itself out, and she could see the pearly sky deepening to blue.

Emmie glanced up at the little staircase again, frowning. Perhaps the wind made strange noises down the chimneys because of the way they were built. In the daylight, the whimpering sounds seemed unlikely. Emmie shook off the haunting little cries and stepped cautiously down the side stairs. The key was in the door, a heavy, black iron key that made her think of Mary and the door to the garden. Emmie's fingers slipped on it in her eagerness to turn it. She hauled the door open, dragged on her shoes, and dashed out down the gravel path, forgetting to be quiet. She shoved through the shrubbery gate and ran as fast as she could through the trees, the shortest way to the long path outside the walled gardens. Emmie was sure this was where Mary had described the door being. It was where she had been skipping when she saw the wind blow aside the ivy.

As she came onto the path alongside the great wall, Emmie stopped running. It seemed too important to run. She couldn't come at the secret garden in a rush. She almost felt as though she needed to creep up on it, in case it had disappeared like something in a fairy tale.

She came toward the end of the wall, where Mary had written that the ivy was thicker and more overgrown than anywhere else, and looked around furtively. But everywhere was deserted this early in the morning. Perhaps she was the only one awake. The ivy still hung over the wall in a great, heavy curtain, and there was more of it here. Emmie could feel her heart suddenly thumping all through her as she stepped onto the flower bed behind a gnarled lilac tree and felt under the ivy for the door handle. The ivy rustled against her fingers, and the flowers smelled odd, but she hardly cared—for there, under her fingers, was a smooth, brass doorknob, worn silken with use.

Emmie stopped, rubbing her fingers over the smooth metal. Would it open? Would she be able to get inside without the key? She stood hesitating, trails of ivy draped over and around her, not quite daring to turn the handle in case she was still shut out.

At last she let out a sharp, frightened gasp and wrenched the handle around. The door creaked a little and caught, and then opened inward. Emmie ducked right beneath the trails of ivy and stepped into the secret garden.

A rush of scent and twittering and early-morning wet grass wrapped around her.

Mary's description of the garden—wild and overgrown and winter gray—was still strong in Emmie's mind, so what struck her all at once were the brightness and the scent of roses. They were not dead after all. They still poured themselves from tree to tree in great trailing curtains, and there seemed to be flowers all around her.

Emmie closed the green door and leaned against it, staring around. The garden looked to be about the same size as the kitchen gardens. Perhaps it had been built as one originally, before it was made into a rose garden? But instead of neatly edged beds, full of late lettuce, there were trees all around the walls—apples and peaches and plums—with just enough of each fruit still on the branches for Emmie to see what they were. Between the trees there was a lawn, but this wasn't a smooth carpet of green like the terrace that ran down to the fishpond. Instead, the grass was broken up here and there with clusters of tall evergreen bushes and arched trellises for the roses, each one like a frame for a carved stone seat or a statue or a huge urn spilling over with flowers.

She wandered breathlessly under the arches, reaching up every so often to touch a rose and laughing as they shed their petals on her face and shoulders. The summer had been long and hot, and many of the roses had already bloomed, with just the odd late blossom left here and there, but Emmie would have found it hard to believe that there could be more flowers. She seemed to be wrapped in them—roses overhead, and spilling out of the flowerbeds was a great mass of lilies so strongly scented that she could almost see the perfume in the air.

The early-morning sun was brighter now, warming her through the skimpy sleeves of her cardigan. Emmie smiled to herself and began to whirl around, spinning like a top, lifting her chin and closing her eyes so she saw only a rich, orange glow from the sun under her eyelids. The scents of the garden swirled around her, and she spun on until she staggered, dizzy and giggling. Then she slowed down, stepping gently from foot to foot as she twirled and listened to the hum of bees and the tiny birds twittering in among the vines.

The garden couldn't be a secret now, Emmie realized, as she stopped to lean dizzily against a great tree, a tree that had no leaves of its own but was so wrapped in climbing roses that it seemed more alive than ever. Mary had described a garden that had been abandoned. Now the grass had been trimmed, and although the roses still scrambled wildly everywhere, they had been shaped around the trees and statues. Even though the door had been hidden, it was no longer locked.

"She let other people in," Emmie whispered to herself regretfully. She had so wanted it to be her secret too. She could have hidden herself away.

But she could still come here, she decided. Now, so early in the morning, the garden was hers. There would be other times too. And if someone came, it wasn't as if there was nowhere to hide. Emmie smiled to herself, touching the petals of a fat, crimson-purple rose. The petals were layered together so tightly that even her small fingers wouldn't slip between them.

It wasn't a secret garden anymore—but it could still be her garden full of secrets.

Over the next few days, Emmie went to the garden whenever she could, prowling around and looking at the statues and the flowers. Sometimes she pinched away the dying flowers on the roses—not because she knew it was the right thing to do, but because she didn't like the faded colors and the sickly sweet smell of the browned flowers. She piled the dead flowers in a corner behind one of the statues, so they didn't show.

The robin watched her, often perching in the trees above her head and twittering, she thought with approval. "You like me being here, don't you?" she asked him once, hurrying past with an old basket full of rose heads. She had found the basket behind one of the greenhouses, and she'd also brought a little pair of sewing scissors that she'd found abandoned in the schoolroom. They were good for snipping away the flowers, and no one missed them. The real garden tools were all locked away in the sheds.

The robin came closer to her every day. Once, he even sat on the basket. She was almost sure he made his home in an overgrown corner of the garden. There was a tiny statue of a boy playing a flute, almost hidden by vines, their leaves orange and golden now that autumn was coming. In the spring, it would be the perfect place for a nest.

On the days she'd been in the garden, Emmie came back to the house for breakfast in a hurry, forgetful of the time and with petals in her hair. Somehow, the garden made it easier to put up with Arthur's smirking face or Ruby whining for help with her buttons. Emmie went back to the garden in her head, wandering among the lilies and roses or stretching out on the sun-warmed stone of the seats. Then she would surprise Ruby by twirling her around and hugging her once the dress was all buttoned up.

Often Emmie just sat, curled up under the great dead tree. She leaned against the seamed bark, gazing around and imagining it all as Mary had seen it, dark and dead in winter. How long would she and the others be here? No one had said. Would she see the garden in winter too? Emmie was still reading the diary, but being out in the gardens made her tired, and she never managed to puzzle her way through much of the ornate handwriting before she fell asleep.

Walking around the garden and admiring the flowers made her wonder what all their names were, and if there was someone she could ask. Mary mentioned several different sorts of flowers and things she had planted with Dickon, the boy who lived on the moor. But Emmie wasn't sure of any of the names. She would have liked to talk to the gardener with the false leg, Mr. Sowerby, but even though she saw him again in the kitchen gardens, she didn't go up to him.

How could she explain what she wanted to know and why? What if he realized what she was doing and told her the garden was private and she mustn't go in there again? She still would, but it would take the shine off her secret. Besides, Emmie's stomach squirmed when she thought of the way she had looked at his face. She didn't know how to say she hadn't meant to grimace. Or that she'd only meant it for a fraction of a second. She wasn't sure there was a proper way to say that.

The garden felt more like it belonged to her every day, with every fallen leaf she gathered up. Emmie hated the thought that one morning she might walk in and find someone else already there. For the first few mornings, she peered fearfully around the door, trying to hear if there were voices or if one of the gardeners was whistling inside. But no one seemed to know about the garden, even though she occasionally saw that more deadheading had been done than she could have managed, that the heavy-headed lilies had been carefully tied up with twine, that the leaves falling from the apple trees had been raked away. The garden was loved, but no one ever seemed to go into it. No one except Emmie, sneaking in like a thief.

Until the golden, sunny afternoon when she sauntered out after they'd had lessons and saw Mrs. Craven walking down the long path by the brick wall with a letter in her hand.

Emmie knew where she was going. She knew, but she had to watch anyway, biting her lip and wishing and wishing it wasn't going to happen. But it did. Almost without looking, Mrs. Craven put out her hand to sweep the ivy away and then slipped in through the green door. She left it standing open, as if she didn't care whether the garden was secret or not. Emmie stood on the path by the lilac tree, watching and waiting, her fists clenched and her teeth bared like an angry little cat. She stood there for a half hour, hating. When she heard footsteps in the garden, she pressed herself back against the wall behind the lilac and tried not to snarl as Mrs. Craven sauntered by, leaving a trail of some sweet, flowery perfume. It made Emmie want to cough.

As soon as Mrs. Craven had disappeared around the corner of the path, Emmie sneaked back in. She expected that somehow the garden would look different—that she would be able to see the way it had been spoiled. But the roses were blooming just the same.

Emmie lay down on the grass behind a veil of small, pink roses. Mrs. Craven had been sitting on a bench in one of the alcoves, and most of the time she'd had her eyes closed—Emmie had looked. She hadn't picked any flowers or even walked around. But still the secret garden felt different, as though it had woken up from a dream—or Emmie had. Misselthwaite was Mrs. Craven's house, and her husband's and Jack's. Not one part of it was Emmie's. It never had been.

"I shouldn't ever have thought it was my garden," she whispered to herself, pressing her face into the crook of her elbow. She had pretended it was hers. In her head, she had moved one of the statues that she didn't like. She had planted a great drift of purple daisies in and out of the white lilies and built a little summerhouse with its walls all made of roses and the sweet honeysuckle she'd seen clambering up a sunny patch of wall by the green door.

She had imagined herself curled up in a chair, a wicker chair covered in cushions, like the ones that stood on the terrace in front of the grand rooms of the house. Golden honey-smelling flowers grew over their heads, thrumming with bees. Lucy had been stretched out asleep on her lap, a safe, contented Lucy who belonged, like she did. They had been happy.

And now it was all gone. Lucy had never even been in the garden. Lucy had probably been destroyed, like that boy had said. Emmie didn't even have a cat curled up with her on a rusty, old fire escape anymore, let alone in a house made of flowers. It was all a silly, empty daydream. Emmie wailed, forgetting to be quiet and secret. It didn't matter anyway. The garden was broken. The secret was gone.

She wept, tears streaming down her cheeks and trickling into the grass.

"Lass. Lass. Look at me."

Emmie rolled over, gasping, as someone caught her arm. She hadn't even heard him coming.

"Whatever's the matter?"

It was the gardener, Mr. Sowerby, looking down at her with the unscarred side of his face pink and worried.

Emmie wanted to howl again and run—but she couldn't. If she did that, he might think it was because she was frightened of him, and she wasn't. She just desperately wished that everyone would leave her alone. She pulled away from him, hunched up, and curled into a ball with her face hidden in her knees.

"Did someone hurt thee?"

Emmie managed to shake her head as much as she could curled up. "Go away," she sobbed. "Leave me alone."

He was silent for a while, so silent that she almost wondered if he'd gone. But when she looked up, he had settled himself uncomfortably on a little white bench under one of the rose arches. He was rubbing his leg as though it hurt.

"Isn't that a false leg?" Emmie asked shakily. "It can't be hurting. You can't even feel if you rub it."

"Tell that to th' leg," he muttered. "Now, what's making thee take on so?" Then his gaze sharpened, and he stopped massaging his leg and leaned forward to look at her properly. "Is it you? Been deadheading the roses?"

Emmie dropped her head again. "Wasn't it right? They were brown. I wanted to make room for the others, the little ones that were just opening out."

He chuckled, such a surprising noise that Emmie looked up and stared at him. He had bright-blue eyes, she noticed, now that she was looking past the scars. Sky-blue eyes and dark-red hair curling out from under his cap.

"Tha's been doing a grand job of it, lass. Don't tha' worry."

"I didn't know where to put the brown bits," Emmie admitted. "I hid them behind the statue over there. That one of the girl with the silly smile." Then she sighed, rubbing her hands across her sore eyes. Now even that secret was gone.

He nodded and then leaned back against the bench, drawing a piece of wood and a knife from his pocket. He opened the knife and began to shave tiny flecks of wood away, shaping something. He didn't talk to Emmie, but he must have sensed her edging closer to the bench.

"What is it?" she asked at last. She couldn't quite see—the carving was tiny.

He opened up his hand and showed her, and Emmie laughed. The robin was peeking out at her, head on one side, tail feathers practically twitching.

"It's the robin, the one who lives in this garden, isn't it?" She reached out one finger, wanting to stroke it, and then looked up at him pleadingly. "If I told you what she looked like, do you think you could make a cat? I'd do more helping in the garden, whatever you wanted. You'd just have to show me. I promise I'd do it."

"A cat, is it?"

"Maybe only a kitten. I don't think she ever had enough food to grow much."

"Like thee then."

Emmie sighed. "I'm fatter now. I used to give some of my food to Lucy. That's my cat's name. I didn't mind." Her voice shook. "She'd love it here. They keep giving us milk. I'd smuggle it out to her. And the porridge, it's nicer here."

"A real little cat, then?" He was frowning now, and Emmie nodded. She thought he was cross.

"I never wanted to leave her! I had her all ready to go in a basket. I wanted to bring her with us, away from the bombs, but Miss Dearlove said she was disgusting, and she wasn't. She was a love. She was all mine."

Suddenly she couldn't bear his eyes on her, and she stumbled up, grabbing at the bench and meaning to run away. But he caught at her hand. "Stay. Tell me about tha' little cat."

His voice was so gentle and coaxing that Emmie paused, half-ready to run like a little wild thing. His hand was rough from working in the garden, but he wasn't holding her tight. If she'd pulled hard, she could easily have got away. But she didn't. She stayed, like the robin, who'd perched on the gardener's shoulder.

"Tell us about her..." He patted the bench, and Emmie settled in the corner, drawing up her knees.

"She's black," Emmie began. Then she closed her eyes, trying to make a picture of Lucy in her head. It was getting harder and harder to see her. "Black all over and quite thin. Arthur and Joey said she was skinny," she added, and her scowl came back, just for a moment, drawing two deep lines above her nose. Then she sighed, and her face smoothed out again. "Even her whiskers are black. The only color's her eyes, and they're yellowy green. They shine. They even glow sometimes when it's dark on the fire escape."

"That's where thee found her, then?"

"It's my place," Emmie explained. "No one goes there except for me." She shivered and opened her eyes to look at him. "No one's in that house now at all. It's empty. I don't know when we'll go back."

"Does tha' miss it?"

Emmie shook her head. "No. I-I like it here…" She said it slowly, as if she were only just working it out for herself. "I love this garden especially," she added. "I thought it was a secret."

She was looking out across the garden, so she didn't see him glance up, his eyes widening.

"A secret?" His voice was wistful, and he glanced up at the covering of roses and then the neatly cut grass as if he was seeing something different.

"No one else came. Like the fire escape, only better. Much better." Emmie sighed. "Except that I didn't have Lucy. I don't even know where she is." She wriggled up and put her hand on his knee. "Do you know the boy who lives here? Jack?"

He nodded.

"He said cats in London are being destroyed. Because there won't be enough food." Her voice wobbled. "Lucy doesn't eat much. I gave her a bit, and I think Mrs. Evans in the kitchen did too. Mostly she took stuff out of trash bins." She hesitated, not wanting to ask, in case he told her the truth. But then she remembered how the robin had perched on his shoulder, and she trusted him. *This man understood about creatures*, she thought. "Do you think she's still there? What if someone…" She couldn't say it.

"Cats is clever," he murmured. "And they likes their own place. She knows where to hide herself away, doesn't she?"

Emmie nodded, remembering the way that Lucy had appeared on the fire escape, almost out of nowhere. "But there's no one to feed her."

"She'll get by. Is that why tha' were crying? Worrying about th' little cat?"

"I could remember her properly here. I wanted a house for her…" She looked around at him suspiciously, in case he was laughing. But he was watching her, his face grave, and remembering.

"Tha' reminds me of another little lass," he said, stretching out his leg as though it ached.

Emmie eyed him curiously, wanting to ask who he meant, but even though he was gazing out across the garden, she thought he was seeing something different. It was as though he had forgotten she was there. She watched him silently, seeing his mouth twist in a remembering smile.

Then at last, the gardener sighed and glanced down at her and slapped his knees. "I better get on. Only came in here after I heard thee wailing. Be of good faith, lass. Tha' cat will be waiting for thee when tha' goes back." He stood up, limping back to the wheelbarrow he'd left on the path, and Emmie watched him go. He didn't have his crutch today, so his leg must have been feeling better.

She turned back sharply as something rustled behind her. Was it the robin again? She peered at the bushes, hoping to see his black eyes glittering among the leaves. But instead, there was a boy, guiltily half stooping behind the great dead tree.

"You!" Emmie sprang up. "What are you doing? Were you listening? Were you spying on me?"

Jack had looked almost apologetic when she first saw him, but now he straightened up and marched out from behind the tree with a haughty expression. "I wasn't spying. This is my garden. This is my *house*. I can go anywhere I like."

"I hate you," Emmie snarled. She clenched her fists. If she scratched her nails down his face, as she longed to, she'd be in such trouble. "It isn't your garden."

"It's all mine." He waved a lordly hand around at the tree and the roses. "All of it. You're not to come in here again."

"It isn't yours," Emmie said again, trying to sound sure. "Mr. Sowerby said I could be here. You ask him!"

"He is a servant," Jack pronounced grandly. "It's not up to him to say."

"I don't believe you." Emmie shook her head. Jack's mother hadn't spoken about the sullen, lonely gardener in that way at all.

"What were you doing anyway?" Emmie demanded, feeling braver. "Why were you hiding?"

"I wasn't hiding. You just didn't see me." But Jack had gone red, and Emmie knew he was lying. She guessed he had been in the garden to try to avoid Joey and Arthur. They were bigger than he was, and he hadn't made himself very popular by snickering during lessons whenever they got the answers wrong.

Jack caught the little smirk on her face, and the red faded out of his cheeks, leaving them pale with fury. "Get out!" he spat. "Go away! All of you, leave me alone! This is my house!" Then he plunged past, shoving her sideways, and ran out through the green door and onto the path.

Emmie gazed after him, feeling oddly guilty. Jack had spied on her and tried to tell her she couldn't be in the garden. Then he'd shouted at her and knocked her into a rose arch. She had a great, long scratch down her leg to prove it. So why did she wish that she'd been nicer?

3rd February 1910

I have told my secret. I never thought I would, but Martha's brother, Dickon, is more like a wild moor animal than a boy. He promises he will never tell, and I believe him. He's used to keeping all the nests and burrows that he finds out on the moor secret from the other boys. He says they might steal the birds' eggs if he told. So I can trust him.

I went out through the gate from the laurel walk into the woods. I heard whistling, and I thought it might be another sort of bird, but it was Dickon playing on a wooden pipe. He made me remember the snake charmers in India, but instead he was playing to two rabbits, a bird that's called a pheasant, and a little red squirrel in the tree above his head. They came so close that the rabbits were sitting by his feet.

He had brought the seeds and the garden tools that Martha had asked him to buy with the money my uncle gave me. He was explaining how I should plant them, but then he said it would be better to show me, and where was my garden? I didn't know what to say. But I liked him, he smiled so. Perhaps he had charmed me with his pipe playing too.

I took him into the garden. I wanted someone to tell me if the roses were still alive, and they are! A few are brown and gray all through, but most of them are wick. This is the word that means they are green and alive inside. We are going to make the garden wake up properly. It needs the weeds dug up and all the dead wood cut away from the rose trees. Dickon says when they all flower in the summer, there will be fountains of roses. I cannot wait to see.

4th February 1910

Yesterday was the strangest day. I have spent so many weeks at Misselthwaite never seeing anyone but Martha and Mrs. Medlock, the housekeeper, and Ben Weatherstaff, the gardener. Then, in one day, I meet Dickon and am summoned to see my uncle, and in the night of the same day, I find out who has been crying.

There is a boy here named Colin, and no one ever told me. They have been keeping it a secret because Colin made them. He doesn't like anyone to see him or know about him. He has been very ill, and he says he is going to die before he grows up. He is certainly very pale and ill looking. Martha knew about him all the time and never told me! It's no wonder that she was so panicked when I said I had heard another child cry. She tried to tell me it was the scullery maid crying because her tooth hurt, but I knew that wasn't the truth. I am not angry with Martha though. All the servants thought they would be sent away if they ever spoke about him.

I went back to Colin's room this afternoon. He made Martha bring me. We talked and talked, and I told him about Dickon. In the middle of us talking and laughing together, Mrs. Medlock and the doctor came in. They were so surprised that I almost laughed out loud. The doctor stopped like a statue and nearly tripped Mrs. Medlock. I was worried Mrs. Medlock would be angry with me again, like she was when I came too close to Colin's rooms before. I understand now why she dragged me away. But Colin told them both that I was his cousin and that he liked me. He likes me! He is very bad-tempered and ill, but then I am bad-tempered too, I suppose.

Martha, Ben Weatherstaff, Dickon, Colin, and the robin. Five friends.

CHAPTER

Six

"EMMIE. EMMIE."

Emmie turned over, murmuring in her sleep, and then shivered. Months had passed since they'd arrived at Misselthwaite, and now it was winter. She had two sweaters on over her nightgown and a pair of huge, woolly socks, but she was still cold. It had been almost too cold to read Mary's diary the evening before. She had managed only a few pages before her fingers froze.

"What is it?" she asked Ruby, peering grumpily at the little girl from under her nest of blankets. For the last few days, Emmie had only felt warm when she was asleep.

"I'm cold," Ruby said pleadingly. "Can I get in with you?"

Emmie eyed her for a second. Ruby's face looked pinched with cold in the candlelight, and she was shivering. "Why don't you have your blankets around you? Don't stand there like that. The floor's freezing. Come on, fetch your blankets. And get in fast!"

Ruby scurried obediently to strip her bed and appeared back at Emmie's bedside looking wider than she was tall, wound in at least three blankets. She scrambled in next to the older girl, and Emmie stretched the extra covers over the two of them like a tent. She could hardly breathe, but it was better than being cold.

There was frost on the inside of the windows again, she expected. And the snow was piled up around the window frames so they could hardly see out. The garden had been smoothed into a strange landscape of lumps and hills, with paths cut through by the few gardeners who were left.

At first, Emmie had thought winters in Yorkshire must always be like this, but Miss Sowerby promised them it wasn't so. There were five-foot drifts out on the moor, and most of the estate workers had temporarily moved into the manor. It was easier to keep everyone warm in one place.

"Tell me again about the fish," Ruby whispered, snuggling up to Emmie.

Emmie shuddered as Ruby's icy nose pressed against her cheek. "Again?"

"Please, Emmie…"

Emmie gave a sleepy groan and wrapped her arm around Ruby. The littler girl was like a hot-water bottle.

Ruby was supposed to stay close to the house with Miss Rose and the other younger children when they went outside, but the five-year-old was good at slipping away. She loved the huge pond, and she spent hours watching the fish—even though she'd been told she mustn't play by the water. Miss Rose was terrified she'd fall in.

A few weeks after they'd arrived at Misselthwaite, Emmie had gone to admire the fish and found Ruby there too. She was crouched at the very edge of the pool, peering down into the water. Beside her on the stone slabs was a pile of bread crumbs.

Emmie was about to march over and tell the little girl to get back to her own place, but then she realized if she came up behind Ruby and surprised her, she'd probably fall into the pond and Emmie would be the one blamed for it.

So she sat down next to her instead and threw one of Ruby's crumbs into the water. A glowing orange fish surged up to snatch it, and Ruby looked around.

"You aren't supposed to be here," Emmie pointed out.

"I like feeding the fish. They're funny."

"Miss Rose is probably looking for you."

Ruby shrugged, and her mouth straightened into a sulky line. "Not a baby," she muttered. "Sam the gardener saw me feeding the fish, and he said it saved him a job. There's some special fish food. He said he'd show me where it is if I promised I'd be careful. He's really busy. I'm *helping*." Her bottom lip wobbled, and Emmie nodded quickly.

"All right, then! Don't start that." Ruby probably was helping. They all were now. Arthur and Joey had picked the fruit in the orchard. Emmie helped Mr. Sowerby in the secret garden—and in the kitchen gardens too. He'd asked her, and he'd even dug out an ancient pair of Wellington boots that almost fit so she could dig without caking her sandals in mud. Miss Rose and Miss Dearlove took turns helping with the cooking. Emmie expected that before long they'd all be eating in the servants' hall to save work. Four of the gardeners had already left to join the war effort—and several of the maids too. Even the smaller children helped with sweeping the floors, and Mrs. Craven was talking about shutting up some of the rooms, covering everything in dust sheets until… No one was really sure "until" what.

"Please, Emmie. Tell me what the fish are doing," Ruby whispered, breathing warm, damp breath into Emmie's ear.

Emmie started, blinking back from her vague half dream of that day by the water. She'd almost fallen back to sleep, and she gave a regretful little groan as she realized all over again how cold it was.

"All right." She yawned and tried to remember the story that had comforted Ruby the week before, when she'd run down to the pool and seen that the patchy covering of ice was solid—so thick that this time it didn't break when she tapped it. She had been distraught, certain that the fish would all freeze to death. The panicked look on her face had made Emmie think of Lucy, tearing open the old memories all over again.

"The fish are down at the bottom of the pool, sleeping," she murmured, and she felt Ruby snuggle up against her side. "It's cold and dark, but the fish don't mind. They're sleeping, dreaming of the sunshine. Every so often, they flick their fins, just a little, to keep themselves warm."

"Tell about the gold sparkling," Ruby whispered.

Emmie smiled to herself, proud that Ruby had remembered her story. "Even though it's so dark under the ice, the fish can see each other's golden scales glittering, and that reminds them that the sun will come back and melt the ice in the springtime."

She yawned and added, "And tomorrow we'll go and sweep the snow off the top of the pool and take that old football we put there out of the ice to let the air in. And deep down at the bottom of the pool, the fish will all sniff and say, *Smells like snow again.* And they'll just flip their tails once and go back to sleep."

Ruby chuckled, wriggling delightedly at the thought of the little squeaky, fishy voices.

"Now go to sleep," Emmie mumbled. "S'late."

CHAPTER

Seven

I FOUND THEM! I FOUND THEM!" Emmie raced through the kitchen garden, yelling with delight, skidding and sliding on the icy brick paths until she almost crashed into Mr. Sowerby raking a patch of earth.

He straightened up clumsily, staring down at her and grinning. "What did tha' find?"

Emmie panted. She could tell it was a good day. He was smiling, and he didn't have his crutch. She no longer paid attention to his scars. They were just as much a part of him as his heavy boots and velveteen waistcoat, but there were days when she could tell from the set of his shoulders that it was best to run on by.

Emmie put her hand on his arm and looked up at him pleadingly. "Come and see? Please? It's a good thing. You'll be happy."

He shook his head at her. "Another one as wants me to be

happy. Tha' and Mrs. Craven. Tha' would have me dancing." But he propped the rake against the wall and limped after her, while she skipped backward in front of him, beckoning and giggling to herself.

"I've been looking for so long," Emmie explained. "I almost didn't believe you." She ran ahead of him along the path to the secret garden, and then came back to grab his hand and hurry him after her. She hadn't listened to Jack telling her not to go back in. *The gardens belonged to the gardener more than to one spoiled boy,* Emmie thought.

Mr. Sowerby needed her to help anyway, now that it was only him and a couple of elderly men drafted from the village to look after the huge expanse of gardens around Misselthwaite Manor. There was a chance that the lawns might have to be dug up and planted with vegetables, but Emmie wasn't sure if the gardeners would be able to manage any more.

"Look!" She dragged Mr. Sowerby across the snowy grass to the white bench under the rose arbor and crouched down, pointing at a clump of white spears, edged in green and just nudging out of the snow. "Look at them! Are these snowdrops, like you said? They don't look like that drawing in the plant catalog, but they're new. I walked around looking yesterday, and they weren't here then."

"Ah... Th' first ones. It's sheltered here." Mr. Sowerby

reached down and cupped the flowers in one of his big hands. Emmie watched, holding her breath. "They won't be all th' way out for a couple more days. These are th' buds. They's late, this year. With the snow like it is." He straightened up and looked around the white garden, sighing with pleasure. The sigh eased out of him like a long-held breath. Then he shook his head and clapped the snow from his gloves. "Crocuses soon. Primroses out in th' lanes, and then daffodils. Ah, it'll be a sight, lass. Daffies as far as tha' can see, there'll be."

Emmie stared at the snowy hummocks where the roses had been and sighed. "I can't see it. I don't think the snow's ever going away. It's been weeks. And you said we'd have the snowdrops in January!"

The gardener snorted. "Can't always be right, lass. Worst winter for forty year, they do say. Them poor snowdrops is doing their best. They can't show through a foot of snow, can they?"

"S'pose not." Emmie sighed. The snow had been fun at first. Jack had a sled, and he had even made temporary peace with Joey and Arthur, because it was more fun with someone to push. Emmie had a few goes, but she and Jack were still pretending that the other one didn't exist, which made it hard to go shrieking down a snow slope with him. Emmie had slipped away after a while. She helped Ruby and the other little ones skid around on two old metal tea trays from the kitchen instead, squealing and tumbling and tipping each other over.

But now the snow just meant that every time they went outside, they came back wet. Everyone had chilblains, itching and burning on their fingers and toes. The whole house, huge as it was, seemed to smell of damp wool. Drying racks were spread in front of every fire, sucking up the warmth before it got into the rooms. There was a lot less snow than there had been—the road from Thwaite was clear again—but the gardens were still wrapped in white stillness. Even the robin seemed quieter than usual. Whenever Emmie saw him, he was fluffed out and grumpy looking, as though the cold was getting to him too.

"Emmie! Emmie! Where are you? You have to come! Emmie!"

"That's Arthur yelling." Emmie turned to look anxiously at the wall that bordered the path. The garden wasn't a complete secret, like it had been that spring and summer so many years before, but the door was still hidden. It was her refuge, and Mary's as well. Emmie didn't want to show Arthur the door under the ivy.

"Let him go by," Mr. Sowerby murmured. "He'll be in th' laurel walk in a moment. Then tha' can dart out and run after him."

Emmie nodded and crunched quietly over the snow to the green door, leaning against it and listening. Then she eased the door open and slipped out onto the path with a quick wave to the gardener. Mr. Sowerby stood there, tucking his hands under his arms for warmth and smiling after her. Then he began to limp slowly in her footsteps to the door.

"What is it?" Emmie called, running after Arthur and hissing as her rubber boots skidded on the ice.

Arthur was hanging over the gate to the woods, staring out as if he thought she might have gone that way.

"I'm not that stupid," Emmie said sharply. "There are still drifts out there that could half bury us."

"The road's clear!" Arthur seized her hand. "You've got to come back to the house. Mr. Craven's here on leave. Lieutenant Craven, he is now."

"So?" Emmie frowned and then looked hopeful. Now that butter and sugar had been rationed, even the plainest cake was a treat. She couldn't see any other reason she should be interested in Mr. Craven's movements. Except that she was a little curious to see Jack's father. "Does that mean there's cake?"

"No, stupid. He wants to see you. Come on. I said I'd fetch you. He's waiting."

He tugged at her hand and began to run back along the path through the shrubbery. Emmie followed, still protesting.

"But why? He doesn't even know who I am."

"He does," Arthur called back over his shoulder. "I saw him.

I saw the car, and I wanted to know who he was. I was in the hall, watching. He said, did I know where Emmie was, and could I fetch you. Right away. He knew your name all right."

They reached the side door, stopping to knock the snow off their boots, and then peeled off their layers of coats and scarves.

Emmie stared anxiously at her reddened finger, wondering if she had done something wrong. *I can't think what. Why else would he want to see me though?* She had Lieutenant Craven in her head as the tall hero that Jack obviously worshipped. She had seen that even from the few words the boy grudgingly spoke during lessons.

Miss Sowerby pounced on her at the top of the stairs and sighed about Emmie's hair, which was all sticking out of its braid, but she didn't make Emmie comb it out. She hurried her along the hallways as eagerly as Arthur had. These were the grander parts of the house, the corridors that the children had never been into. Thick curtains were drawn over most of the windows. Even before the war had started, it had been hard to keep enough servants to care for so large a house. Now, with so many of them gone off to enlist or to do war work, the endless task of opening the curtains and closing them before the blackout had been allowed to lapse. The passages were dim, even in the bright snow light, and faces glimmered out of dark portraits as Emmie was hurried by.

A fire had been lit in Lieutenant Craven's small study, which was full of rather dusty velvet-covered chairs.

The room had been shut up while he was away. It smelled musty, and there was a fine layer of dust on the huge wooden desk. Standing in front of the fire was a thin, tired-looking man in a dark uniform with glittering buttons.

Emmie was used to seeing Mrs. Craven worried about food, or there not being enough blankets, or the possibility that the second gardener's youngest boy had scarlet fever. She had never seen her smile like this before. The light from the window glowed behind her, but her thin, pale face was lit up from inside, so that she shone like the paintings in the passageway.

Emmie ducked her head, embarrassed. She felt as if she were intruding.

"Emmie?" Lieutenant Craven sounded as uncertain as she was.

"Yes," she whispered back, staring at her knitted socks.

"I've brought you something."

Emmie looked up, frowning. "Me? You don't even know who I am."

"Mr. Sowerby wrote to me about you. He wrote to me that he'd found you crying in the garden, and you told him about your cat."

Emmie scowled, ashamed for a moment that someone else

knew. She had spent so long trying to hide herself away so no one saw her. Jack had crowed over her tears, and now Mr. Sowerby had written it in a letter to this stranger in uniform. She looked up, about to say something angry, but then she caught his eyes. The same dark-gray eyes as Jack's, fringed with black lashes.

She clenched her fists, her nails digging into her palms. "I miss her," she muttered, trying to be polite and only managing fierce instead of angry.

"Emmie, look." Mrs. Craven stood up and put an arm around her shoulders, pushing Emmie gently over to the armchair by the fire. On the chair was a basket—a wicker picnic basket, much like the one she had tried to bring Lucy in months before.

"Is it a cake?" Emmie asked, bewildered.

Lieutenant Craven laughed. "Look and see."

Emmie shook her head stubbornly. He was laughing at her.

He stopped smiling and came closer, squatting down next to the basket. "Mr. Sowerby wrote to me. He told me how you'd fought to bring your little cat. He said the first time he saw you, you looked completely lost, wandering around the gardens as though you'd never seen flowers before." He looked down at the basket, his dark brows drawing together. "You don't understand what it's like to be away from here, Emmie. This is my home. I've lived here always. Everything in me is tied up with Misselthwaite, even when I go away.

"Letters are like a glimpse of home for me. I read them over and over. I could see this lost little girl in my gardens. Even though I'd never met you, I'd read about you so often. I knew you, and I liked you because Mr. Sowerby likes you." He smiled to himself. "He knew what he was doing, telling me about you in the garden and the cat left behind." Lieutenant Craven glanced at the basket and reached out one hand as if he was going to pat it. Then he drew his fingers back cautiously.

"I've got a week's leave, that's all, but I had to spend last night in London because I couldn't get a train until this morning. So I went to the Home. Your Miss Dearlove had written to me as well. She's been worried about leaving the building empty and wanted someone to check that all the windows were still secured. To make sure no one had broken in."

Emmie nodded, still unsure what this had to do with her.

"I walked all around the building, you see. Making sure everything was all right. Into the yard and up the fire escape."

Emmie gasped, suddenly breathless. She felt like she had that time she'd had a fight with Arthur. She'd raked her nails right down his face, and he punched her in the stomach.

"Did you see her?" she whispered, forcing the words out.

He nodded. "She must have heard me thumping about on the fire escape. Perhaps she thought I was you." He snorted. "*She* was so quiet that I didn't even notice her until she was on the step below me. I tried to grab her. Goodness knows what I'd have done if I'd caught her. Put her in my pocket?"

"She ran away?" Emmie came closer, putting her hand on his sleeve. "Was she all right? Was she thin?"

He nodded. "Very thin, I'm afraid. So I went back to the hotel and borrowed a flashlight, and they managed to find me some fish-paste sandwiches. I told them I'd missed lunch."

"Fish paste?" Emmie echoed, looking at the basket and wrapping her arms tightly around her middle. She felt as though she were holding herself together, holding everything in. Did he mean what she thought he meant, or was she making up a stupid story again—like the house she'd imagined for herself and Lucy in the garden, her pretty honeysuckle house?

Emmie wanted to run and tear at the fastenings of the basket. But what if there was only a cake in there after all—or fish-paste sandwiches?

"Mmm-hmm. I'm glad I thought of it. She was tricky to catch, though at least it wasn't too hard to see her against the snow."

"You...you mean it? You're not just teasing me?" Emmie asked, stepping closer.

He snorted and held out one hand so she could see the deep, red scratch across the back. "I'd be careful when you get her out.

She's cross about the basket." He nodded at Emmie. "I sat on that fire escape in the snow with a plate of fish-paste sandwiches, waving them about like a clown."

"And she came back?" Emmie took a step closer.

"It took her a while. She came out from behind the trash bins in the yard. She didn't want to come anywhere near me, but she couldn't resist the smell of the food. She's very thin. She might leap out when you open the basket, Emmie. She didn't want to go in there at all, and she's been shut up since yesterday afternoon. I didn't dare open it again. I just lifted the lid a fraction and stuck in more sandwiches. I know that sounds cruel," he added apologetically, "but I didn't want to lose her in the hotel or, even worse, in a train. I wouldn't have put it past her to escape at some station in the middle of nowhere."

"Lucy?" Emmie whispered, crouching down in front of the chair. What if it was the wrong cat? What if this was all some stupid joke? Jack would do that, and this was Jack's father. She scowled at the basket, trying not to be too hopeful.

There was no sound, except a faint creaking of the basket, as if something inside had moved just a little. The darkness behind the strands of wicker shifted slightly.

Emmie smiled faintly, almost believing that it was true. She could imagine Lucy glaring suspiciously through the wicker. She was surprised Lieutenant Craven only had one scratch. Carefully, she began to thread the wicker catches back through their loops, and then she lifted the lid just a little. A pair of green eyes shone out of the shadows of the basket, and Lucy hissed at her.

Emmie sat back on her heels. "It's open," she whispered. "You can come out now." She desperately wanted to throw the lid back and hug Lucy tight, but the little cat had been in the dark for so long.

Lucy had curled up at the back of the basket, full of distrust, but now she crept forward. A small, dark muzzle appeared out of the gap, fringed with black whiskers and with a faint smell of concentrated fish.

"Hello, puss," Emmie said, her voice very low and calm—like Mr. Sowerby talking to the robin.

Lucy edged out a little farther, so that all of her small black head was free. She darted a glance sideways at the Cravens, and Emmie was almost sure that Lucy recognized Lieutenant Craven as the person who had stuffed her into the basket. She practically spit.

"It was the only way he could bring you," Emmie explained gently. "I know you didn't like it. But if you come out, you could have some milk." She added out of the corner of her mouth, "I'll give her what would be my bread and milk at teatime. I don't like bread and milk anyway."

"She can have her own allowance of milk," Mrs. Craven murmured. "We'll stretch to it. It isn't rationed yet, and anyway, we get it from the farm. And she'll deserve it if she can catch mice."

"She did catch a couple of them at the Home," Emmie assured her. "But then she left a dead mouse in one of Mrs. Evans's slippers, so nobody was very grateful." She lifted the lid a little more, and the dark ears flickered. "Lucy…come out, sweetness… I never thought I'd see you again. I thought someone would take you away, and… and I don't know what." She did, but she wasn't going to say it.

The black cat suddenly erupted out of the basket, hissing, and Lieutenant Craven took several steps backward, making his wife laugh.

"She's already drawn blood once," he pointed out, shrugging.

Lucy scrabbled and clawed and landed in Emmie's lap, where she sat hunched up and rigid, with her ears laid back, glaring around the room.

"Shhh, shhh, puss…" Emmie muttered, spilling out a stream of soothing nonsense words to calm the furious cat down. "It's all right… Yes, horrible basket. Shall we put it in the fire, yes, shall we, mmm? I don't mean it," she went on, flicking her eyes sideways to Lieutenant Craven. "Probably you have to give it back. Yes, yes, he does…"

"Where did you find a cat basket?" Mrs. Craven asked him in a whisper.

"It's a very expensive hamper, *actually*. And I went and bought it at Fortnum's when I realized I'd need something to put her in. What was in it might have to be your Christmas present for the next several years."

Mrs. Craven pressed her hand over her mouth, laughing at him.

"And Mr. Sowerby can have the basket," Lieutenant Craven added. "If he can get the stink of fish out of it."

Lucy's ears were still flat, but now she was sniffing cautiously at Emmie's fingers. "It is me," Emmie promised, running one hand down Lucy's back. She could feel the cat's ribs under her dull fur. "You're starving," she whispered, her eyes stinging with tears. She looked around at Lieutenant Craven. "I don't think she'll ever be grateful, but I am. You don't know how much. I think you rescued her just in time. I don't suppose people are throwing away as much food as they did before. She's even skinnier than she used to be. Thank you." Emmie nodded her head to him, almost bowing. She didn't know how to say it better, but she wished she could.

Lieutenant Craven half bowed back to her very smartly. Emmie supposed he was used to doing that sort of thing on ships. "I only wish I could have brought her sooner," he said, smiling. "I worried about her too, when I was on the ship and thinking of you all. Would she go with you now, do you reckon? She doesn't want to be anywhere near me—or the basket."

Emmie ran her hand over Lucy's back again and then down from behind her ears, so that the thin cat shivered and stretched a little and nestled closer. Emmie nodded. "Could I take the basket though? I know she doesn't like it now, but she might want it to hide in. She does like little, dark places. I really don't think Mr. Sowerby would want it. The smell won't go away. Fish paste doesn't." Then she swallowed, pulling Lucy tight under her chin and feeling the soft warmth of her domed head. "I don't have any money."

Lieutenant Craven blinked at her as though he didn't understand.

"For the basket—or the expensive things you had to buy in it..."

"But you've been working in the gardens," Mrs. Craven broke in, and Emmie saw her kick her husband very gently, as if she was giving him a sign.

"Mr. Sowerby said so. And with so many of the gardeners away in the war effort, he said you children were a blessing," Lieutenant Craven agreed. "You've earned a basket. You can owe me the rest," he added, grinning at her, and Emmie nodded. She knew he was joking, but she didn't care. She did owe him. She knew that.

As she walked away from the study with Lucy still tense in her arms, Emmie thought about keeping a cat in a house with a hundred rooms. How would she ever know where Lucy was? Emmie waited for her to wriggle and fight and jump away, but Lucy sat still, as daunted by the huge house as Emmie had been.

Miss Sowerby was polishing a table at the end of the passage, even though, as the housekeeper, that was a job she wouldn't usually do. Emmie quickened her step, and Miss Sowerby dropped the cloth as soon as Emmie appeared and beamed at her. "He found th' little cat for you then?"

"You knew about Lucy too?" Emmie muttered. "Did Mr. Sowerby tell you?" He was her brother, Emmie supposed. They would talk.

Miss Sowerby peered down at Lucy, cringing in Emmie's arms, and made a soft, *prrrping* noise to her. "And desperate for someone to love. Go an' show her to Miss Dearlove. Tell her Master Craven brought her for thee. But nicely. Don't tha' smirk."

"I wouldn't," Emmie said quickly. "It's too important. I wouldn't. Miss Sowerby, can I really keep her in the house? She's never been a proper house cat. She doesn't know about…about being clean. What if she makes a mess?"

The housekeeper sighed and looked thoughtfully at the two skinny little creatures. "She'll learn, I expect. If she makes a mess, you come t' me, and I'll help thee clean up."

Emmie nodded. She could feel Lucy relaxing a little, the hammering of her heart slowing. She followed Miss Sowerby through the house to the servants' hall, gently murmuring to Lucy about how much she was loved and how many mice she could catch in the dusty old house.

They came upon Jack in the dim passageway that led to the servants' hall and the kitchen, clutching a thick piece of bread and butter. Miss Sowerby clicked her tongue at him.

"You'll spoil tha' dinner!"

But Jack didn't even look at her. He glared at Emmie. "My father came home. He's been away for months, and all he wanted was to talk to you."

Emmie glared back. "It was important."

Lucy's whiskers twitched, and she leaned a little out of Emmie's arms, catching the scent of the butter. Jack stepped back, staring at her wide-eyed.

"Your cat!"

"He found her. Your father did. He had to go to the Home, and he saw Lucy, so he brought her back." She swallowed, trying to think of something nice to say. Jack was horrible, but his father wasn't. "It was very kind of him," she managed primly.

"I don't know why he bothered," Jack muttered angrily, barging past. "That looks more like a rat to me."

"Jack Craven!" Miss Sowerby snapped. "Apologize."

But Jack was already gone, racing up the passageway and

slamming the door at the bottom of the stairs. Miss Sowerby sighed and ushered Emmie into the servants' hall.

"There she is!" Arthur swung around from the table as he saw them at the door. "What did he want? Emmie! Your cat!"

"Lieutenant Craven found her," Emmie said simply. She gave Miss Dearlove a pleading look. "He went and found her, miss. Mr. Sowerby, the gardener, wrote to him and said he knew I missed her. Lieutenant Craven brought her all the way here in a hamper." She bit her lip and forced herself to sound humble. "Please may I keep her?" Deep in Lucy's fur, her fingers were crossed. If Miss Dearlove said no, it didn't matter. Emmie was keeping her anyway. And Miss Dearlove could hardly send Lucy back. But it was the right thing to ask. For Lucy, she'd do it, however much she hated to speak sweetly and beg.

Emmie buried her face in Lucy's fur and looked sideways at the matron, trying to see what she would do. Miss Dearlove's fingers clenched on the soup spoon she was holding, and then she dropped it in her bowl with a clinking sound.

"He went to the Home?" she murmured. "I wrote to him…"

"He checked all around." Emmie nodded. "He said the windows weren't broken. And then he sat on the fire escape. He had sandwiches."

Miss Dearlove shook her head wearily. "You'll have to keep her then. He's the owner of the house, Emmie. If he fetched her, I can't tell you no."

Emmie swallowed and didn't look at her. She couldn't keep herself from looking happy, and she was sure Miss Dearlove would think she was being rude. "Thank you, Miss Dearlove." And then she added quickly, "I promise I'll keep her out of your way, miss."

"You'd better see if Mrs. Evans and Mrs. Martin have anything you can feed her."

Emmie nodded and hurried toward the kitchens.

"Miss Sowerby told us, Emmie." Mrs. Evans surged over to cluck at Lucy. "Isn't she thin, poor little dear…"

Mrs. Martin looked at Lucy doubtfully. "She's not much bigger than a mouse herself. Is tha' sure she can hunt?"

"That mouse was in my slippers, Betty. I'm telling you," Mrs. Evans assured her grimly. "Sit down here, Emmie. I'll find her a saucer for some milk, and you eat this soup." She rubbed one red finger under Lucy's chin. "Go on, girl. You'll have to let go of her some time."

"I still can't really believe I've got her," Emmie admitted in a halting whisper.

Mrs. Evans fetched a cracked saucer from the back of a shelf and went into the larder to pour in the milk. She put it down next to the table, and Emmie ran her hand down Lucy's fur again and loosened her fingers. She waited for Lucy to spring away, but the cat darted her head sideways and licked at the fur on her shoulder.

It was as if she was pretending not to notice the milk—or at any rate, not right away.

After a few seconds of washing, she peered down at the milk and jumped elegantly from Emmie's knee to sniff at it, and then she began to lap furiously, forgetting all her dignity and splashing her whiskers in the saucer.

At last she licked at the china, her little tongue rasping over the glaze, and then stood up, arching her back high. She licked the drops of milk off her whiskers and stalked across the kitchen. Emmie held her breath, but all Lucy did was jump onto the basket chair that Mrs. Martin kept for the moments she could sit down. It stood up against the wall next to a kitchen chair, with a cushion added, for Mrs. Evans. Lucy sat in the middle of the basket chair, staring around coolly.

"Look at her!" Mrs. Martin laughed "Cheeky little beggar! Rulin' the roost she'll be. Give her a day or so."

"You don't think she'll run away?" Emmie said hopefully.

Mrs. Evans gave a sniff. "Nonsense. She knows she's fallen on her feet. Look at her. Cat knows which side her bread's buttered on, Emmie."

Emmie giggled. "She does like bread and butter."

"She likes everything," Mrs. Evans muttered. "I remember. Mind, Emmie, she's not to get into the larder."

Lieutenant Craven had only a week before he had to go back to his ship, the destroyer HMS *Grafton*, which was moored in Harwich, farther down the north coast from Misselthwaite. From there, they sailed out to patrol the water between Germany and Holland, hunting for merchant ships carrying materials that Germany could use for the war effort.

Emmie met him several times, tramping around the gardens in his navy-issue raincoat and boots, almost always with Mrs. Craven's arm wrapped in his. Jack darted about beside them, dashing off and then back again, as if there were a string holding them all together, and he couldn't be pulled too far away from his father.

Lieutenant Craven smiled at her each time, and Emmie thought he would like to stroke Lucy, but the little cat laid her ears flat whenever she saw him. She felt like saying thank you again—or doing something to show how grateful she was—but it was hard with Jack scowling at her. She always just smiled and hurried past.

A couple of days after Lieutenant Craven had arrived, Emmie slipped into the secret garden to look at the snowdrops again, Lucy padding after her and shivering. She pulled up short, finding Lieutenant Craven sitting on the bench under the rose arch with Mr. Sowerby beside him.

"How is she?" he called, nodding at Lucy.

"She doesn't like the snow much. She keeps shaking it off her paws." Emmie looked around the garden rather sadly. "Don't you wish you could see it better? It's mostly still under snow."

Lieutenant Craven snorted a little. "If I can see it in my tiny quarters on the ship, how much easier do you think it is when I'm actually here?" He closed his eyes and pulled his hands out of the deep pockets of his coat to point. "Yellow climbing rose up that wall. Blue and white columbines in the bed underneath, and the pink oriental poppies around the statue of Atalanta. Pink roses around the sundial, white roses up the wall behind, and those little pink things I can't remember the name of across the front." He opened his eyes again and looked at her. He was smiling, but he still looked sad. "I could go all around the garden. I see it all the time."

Emmie nodded and reached down to pick up Lucy, who was prowling miserably around her feet. The cat followed her whenever she went outside, but the melting snow left her wet and skinnier than ever. Emmie had even asked Miss Sowerby if she could clean something, so as to have a job indoors.

"Poor little creature." Lieutenant Craven leaned over to look at her. "She looks fatter though."

"Little minx," Mr. Sowerby said coaxingly, holding the back of his hand so Lucy could sniff at it.

Lucy wriggled and sprang out of Emmie's arms to walk along the arm of the bench and rub her face against Mr. Sowerby's damp sleeve.

Emmie watched, trying not to feel jealous. Mrs. Craven had told her that Mr. Sowerby was an animal charmer, but until now she had only seen him with the robin. Her face set, and she took a step back, not even realizing that she was doing it.

Lucy whisked back along the arm and padded quickly after Emmie, laying her ears back as the cold of the snow hit her paws. She rubbed the edge of her chin along the top of Emmie's Wellington boot and purred, a deep, thrumming sound that was almost too loud for such a thin body. It was the first time Emmie had heard her purr. Not even back in London had she done it. Emmie stared at her and then at Mr. Sowerby, her mouth open in surprise. Then she crouched down in the snow and ran her mittens over Lucy's back again and again, while the little cat went on purring.

Mr. Sowerby chuckled. "Don't tha' fear, little lass. She belongs to thee."

"It's doing it again." Emmie sat up cautiously. Lucy was curled behind her knees, and she didn't want to push her off the bed by accident. "That noise."

Lucy stood up and stretched and marched up Emmie's legs to nuzzle her face.

"You're so heavy. Greedy puss," Emmie murmured lovingly. Lucy probably wouldn't ever be a big cat, but after a month of proper meals, there was a covering over her bones and her fur was almost glossy. She looked loved.

A thin, sobbing cry made Lucy lay back her ears, and Emmie gasped. "You heard that too! It is real, then… I haven't heard it for weeks, and the last time I almost decided I'd just made it up or it was half a dream." She glanced over at Ruby, but the littler girl was fast asleep. Emmie picked Lucy up, snuggling the cat against her shoulder, and wrapped a blanket around them both like a shawl. "I can't manage you and a blanket and a candle," she muttered, looking at the night-light doubtfully. "But I think it's starting to get light. A little bit."

The passageway was almost entirely dark, and Emmie shuffled along with one hand on the wooden paneling, feeling for doors and the gap where the stairs were. "It is real," she muttered every so often when she heard another stifled whimper and Lucy twitched. "It's real. It's not a ghost, and I'm not making it up. This isn't a dream." She turned slowly as the crying came again. She had thought it was coming from the passage that led off sideways from theirs, but now she was almost sure the noise was above them, although she didn't quite see how. For one horrible moment, she looked up to the white ceiling, expecting to see a hunched, dark shape crouched above her and howling. But there wasn't, and Emmie shook her head crossly. That was a stupid idea out of a nightmare or a ghost story, like the ones Arthur and Joey tried to scare the little ones with.

"The stairs…" Emmie looked around, confused. She was sure this was the passage where Jack had pulled faces at her, so where was the staircase?

"Oh!" Emmie jumped as another gasping cry came almost next to her. Lucy sprang out of her arms and padded away, nosing at a door up ahead, one that was drawn nearly shut. The noise was so sad. Emmie guessed that the child was trying hard not to make a noise, but every so often, they couldn't help having to gasp for breath.

Behind the door were the stairs she had noticed before. She climbed them and found herself in a child's bedroom lit by a night-light just like her own.

Emmie blinked as she came up into the soft light of the candle. She saw Lucy spring onto the bed and nose forward curiously. And then the crying child sat up and stared.

"What are you doing here?" Jack said, but his voice was shaky and full of tears, and he didn't sound angry—only desperately sad.

"I heard you."

He slumped back onto his pillow. "Go away then. Go and tell everyone you heard me crying, so you can all laugh."

Emmie stood hesitating at the foot of his bed. She had solved the mystery, but she didn't feel proud of herself. It wasn't enough. She sighed. "Can I sit down? Please? This floor's cold."

"S'pose." He glanced at her over his shoulder, but he didn't sit up. Lucy sat down on his feet and started to wash her ears. Jack looked at them both uncertainly, as if he thought maybe he should kick them off his bed. "You should go back to your own room if you're cold," he growled.

"What's the matter?"

"Nothing."

"I heard you before, you know. I thought you were a ghost."

He snorted. "There isn't any such thing." Thinking that she was wrong seemed to cheer him up a bit, and he sat up again, moving his feet very carefully so as not to disturb the cat.

"If there were, it would be here." Emmie shrugged. "This place is so old that it ought to be full of ghosts."

"There is sort of a ghost in the garden."

Emmie's eyes widened. "Which garden?"

"The one where you were... Well, you know." He looked at her shiftily and gave a damp sniff.

"Where I was crying like you were just now, you mean?"

He nodded and looked away.

"What sort of ghost?"

"My grandmother." He sounded rather proud of it.

"Have you seen your grandmother's ghost?" Emmie squeaked.

"Not really seen… It's more of a feeling." He reached out cautiously to pat Lucy and then looked up at Emmie. "Do you think I'm making it up?"

"I don't know. What do you mean, a feeling?"

"She died in that garden. A branch broke off the tree while she was sitting on it."

Emmie nodded slowly. She had known some of that from the diary. It was why the garden had been locked up. But Mary had never written it out so clearly. Emmie supposed she should have realized that Jack was related to the people in the diary. This had always been the Cravens' house, after all.

"She came back to the garden."

Emmie watched his face—the clear, gray eyes shining in the candlelight. He didn't look as though he was trying to make fun of her.

"Is she still there?" she asked, whispering.

"My father thinks so. He took my brother and me there when we were only just born, to show us to her." His voice was shaking again, and Emmie saw him rub his eyes. They were shining with tears. She chewed her bottom lip for a moment and then edged a little closer, putting her hand close to his on Lucy's back. "When will your brother come home on leave?"

"No one knows," Jack said, his voice choked. "He doesn't know either. He sends letters, but they never say very much. He's almost finished his training now. He'll start flying sorties soon—that means attacks against the enemy."

"You must be proud of him then," Emmie suggested cautiously.

Jack only sniffed again. "I have to be, don't I? Everyone says that." He glared at her. "I'd rather he were here. I don't care. Right now in the middle of the night, I don't want to have a brother who's a hero. I just want him to be here. It's easier to be proud of him in the daytime. Now I just keep thinking of his plane getting shot down."

"That won't happen!" Emmie assured him, putting her hand on top of his, but he snatched it away furiously.

"How do you know? You don't know anything about it! Thousands and thousands of things could go wrong. What if he has to bail out?"

Emmie shrugged. She didn't know what that meant either.

He shook his head in frustration. "Uuurrgh! Jump! With his parachute. Do you know what that is?"

"Yes!" Thanks to Arthur and Joey going on and on about flying, she did. "I'm not stupid." She looked at him thoughtfully.

"You know, if you told the boys your brother was a pilot, they'd like you more."

He stared at her contemptuously. "Think I care?"

She shrugged again. "It was just a thought. Anyway, I suppose it doesn't matter. Aren't you going back to your posh school soon anyway?"

"Not allowed," he growled. "Doctor said I still have to get better. More."

"You look well enough." Emmie smiled to herself. "Maybe you should spend more time in the garden."

He frowned at her. "What's that supposed to mean?"

Emmie had forgotten for a moment that she wasn't supposed to have read the diaries. She leaned forward to stroke Lucy again while she thought what to say, but Jack flung himself back against the pillows. Lucy glared at him and dug her claws into the quilt.

"Did my mother tell you all those stupid stories?" Jack growled. "About the magic? It's all nonsense. Magic is just silly. How could a garden make someone better? It's just a bedtime story she used to tell me, that's all."

"I only meant that fresh air's meant to be good for you. Miss Dearlove always says so. But actually, I don't think it is nonsense." Emmie looked up at him and folded her arms stubbornly. "I believe in the magic. The garden brought Lucy back to me."

He laughed scornfully. "No, that was my father."

"I wished for her. Over and over. I dreamed of her in the garden with me, and now it's real. I imagined her sleeping there in the sun, and she does. She did today, while I was weeding around the bulbs coming up. She sat on the ledge at the bottom of the statue, and she had her eyes closed, and the sun shone on her whiskers. It came true."

"David used to play hide-and-seek with me in that garden," Jack muttered reluctantly. Emmie could see he didn't really want to tell her, but he had to say it to somebody. She just happened to be there. He'd turned his face away from her, so he was hard to hear.

"It would be so good for hide-and-seek," Emmie said, pretending not to notice there were tears on his face again. "There are so many places to hide. The birds are all in there in the bushes, and that's even though there are hardly any leaves yet. When it's summer, it'll be the safest place in England. Mr. Sowerby said that." She eyed Jack sideways and saw that he was still struggling not to cry. She kept on talking.

"The robin's looking for a place to build a nest already, did you know? I saw him darting in and out of the ivy, and another robin was with him. I'm sure they were looking for a place for her to lay her eggs. But I'm worried about Lucy. I don't think she really knows how to hunt birds yet—there weren't that many

around our street—but she'll learn. She's watching them already."
Emmie looked down at Lucy, stretched smugly on Jack's patch-
work quilt. "She loves it here. I don't think she'll ever want to be a
London cat again."

Then she stared very hard at Lucy's flicking tail.

It wasn't only Lucy. The newspapers in the servants' hall were
already full of stories about evacuees being collected by their parents and taken home because no bombs were falling on London
after all. What if Miss Dearlove and Miss Rose decided that they
should go back too? After five months away, Emmie found it hard
to imagine being shut up in city streets again.

She bit her lips together, her face twisting as she struggled to
hold in her own tears.

"What are you crying for?"

"Because I like it here too!" Emmie wailed. "I never meant to."
Lucy sat up and nudged against her arm, nibbling at Emmie's wrist
with her teeth. She hated it when anyone cried. It made her jumpy
and vicious.

"What a stupid thing to cry about." Jack sneered at her, his
mouth curling. "Even the cat thinks you should shut up. How can
you cry because you're happy?"

"You don't know anything. You don't know how lucky you
are," Emmie snapped. "You've got a family, even if you are worried

about them. I don't have anyone but Lucy, and I don't belong. You've got everything!"

He looked so surprised that it was almost funny. Emmie eyed him with her head tilted to one side. "Didn't you know we were all orphans? Or just not wanted anyway. We don't know. None of us know where we came from."

"That doesn't mean no one wanted you. Maybe there was an accident or something," he said uncomfortably.

Emmie shrugged. "Maybe. But to be honest, it's more likely my mother got in the family way when she shouldn't have."

He went red slowly, all the way to the tips of his ears, and Emmie giggled. She couldn't help it. He was so funny and horrified, and his pale skin went red in waves, like sloshing paint about. "I suppose I shouldn't have said that. It's true though."

"Aren't you embarrassed about it?" he whispered.

Emmie shrugged. "No. I'm cross with her. Or them—whatever happened. They shouldn't have given me up, even if I wasn't a pretty baby. I wish I had a place that was mine. That's why..." She trailed off and then sighed. "I pretended the garden was mine. No one ever seemed to go in it. It was a place just for me."

Jack looked sideways at her. "I could help you with that weeding," he muttered wearily. "You could show me where the robin's nest is."

"I think it's in the roses, in that dark, tangled bit in the corner just along from the bench."

He nodded. "That's a white rose. It's half-wild, but Mother loves it. David showed me a secret tunnel underneath it once, but I got stuck in the thorns. He had to pull me out." Jack yawned, wriggling down a little more on his pillows. "Did you see the robin fly in there?"

"Again and again," Emmie whispered, watching him struggle to keep his eyes open. His eyelids fluttered, thin and fragile looking and blue. She could tell he had been ill. "He must have a mate. Perhaps she's sitting in the nest already. Perhaps she'll lay eggs any day now, deep in the roses…"

Chapter

Eight

"I CAN'T SEE ANYTHING," JACK COMPLAINED, shifting grumpily on the painted metal bench. "And I'm cold. Can't we go in?"

"No. Shhhh. Any minute now, I bet." Emmie sat up higher, peering around them at the tangle of rose stems and ivy in the corner of the garden. That patch was wilder than the rest. Emmie thought that perhaps when Mary and Dickon and Colin rediscovered the garden, they had left that corner wild for the sake of the birds, and it had stayed that way. "It isn't that cold anyway. All the snow's gone." To Emmie, the spring sunshine felt delicious, even if it wasn't really warm. It made her cheerful. She kept finding unexpected things—first the snowdrops, and now primroses everywhere in little creamy clusters.

"So? I know it's gone. That doesn't make it summer, you know. The wind's still cold."

Emmie turned back to look at him, suddenly worried. Perhaps it was because he'd been so ill with measles. Maybe it really was too cold for him? She was used to sitting for hours on a freezing fire escape, after all. Even Lucy had preferred to stay inside today. She was curled up by the huge stove, charming Mrs. Evans into feeding her scraps.

"Don't look at me like that," Jack muttered, turning away from her. "I'm not sick. I'd have gone back to school ages ago, if they hadn't been evacuated so far away. And I'm stronger than you. I could beat you in a race."

A flutter of gray feathers caught Emmie's eye, and she reached behind her, grabbing at Jack's arm. "Look!" she whispered, leaning her head fiercely toward the gray rose stems. "Look! I told you."

The robin was perched among the faded stems, his fragile claws planted between the thorns and some little insect caught in his beak. He eyed the children suspiciously, and Emmie caught her breath. What if they were too close? What if he decided that he and his mate should not make their nest here after all? But he gave them one last stare and darted farther in, so that all they could see of him was a faint, dark movement in the coiling branches.

"He's feeding her," Jack said. "They've built the nest, and now he's bringing her food to build up her strength. Or maybe she's even laid the eggs already. I don't know… It might be too early."

Emmie turned around to look at him, wide-eyed. "You know all about nests?"

Jack shrugged. "Only what everybody knows. There are birds' nests all over the gardens."

Emmie sighed. "I didn't know. I thought it was special."

Jack looked uncomfortable. "I still wanted to see. I like him." Then he laughed. "He looked a bit like you just then. Sort of grumpy and suspicious."

"He isn't like that at all!" Emmie cried and then clapped her hand over her mouth, worrying that she'd frightened the robins. But there was no movement inside the clustered stems. "I know he's shy and strange now, but before he was so friendly. He used to come and watch me when I was exploring. It's just like…" She stopped short. She had been going to say that he was like the robin who'd shown Mary the way into the secret garden.

She was still sure that he was one of that long-ago robin's descendants. She had even imagined that the story was passed down among the robins, the same way that Mary had passed the story down to her through the diary. Perhaps they whispered it to their babies in the egg. This robin and his mate would tell their eggs. They could be telling it to them now, this very minute.

Emmie looked around to find Jack rolling his eyes at her. "Joey and Arthur are right, calling you Little Dolly Daydream. What were you going to say? About the robin?"

"Only that I wondered if there have always been robins nesting here," Emmie said quickly.

Jack looked as though he wasn't sure he believed her, but he didn't say so. "Come on. I have to move, or I'm going to freeze onto this bench."

Emmie got up, gasping as her stiffened knees gave. "Ow. Oh, ow…" She balanced on one leg, shaking her foot.

"You look like a stork." Jack snorted. "A stork that's going to fall over. Come on. Is there anything else new since yesterday?"

They had gotten into the habit of walking around the garden every day to point out the things that had changed and grown. Emmie strolled along the line of trees, peering for leaf buds. Perhaps they were a little larger than they had been the day before? Jack dashed ahead, sniffing like a spaniel, as though he could catch the scent of spring.

"Oh!" Emmie crouched down, and Jack came racing back to her. "These weren't here yesterday! But they must have been…" She frowned at the mound of heart-shaped emerald leaves clustered around the trunk of the bare apple tree. They seemed too bright for her to have missed them. She leaned closer, intrigued, and caught a wisp of sweetness that wasn't only the fresh scent of growing things. There were flowers buried among the leaves, she saw now—tiny, dark-purple flowers that seemed too small to send out so strong a perfume. Emmie sat back, frowning. They smelled oddly familiar.

"Violets." Jack squatted down next to her. "Mmm. Now I'm hungry."

"What?"

"Well, the sweets." He sighed at her, exasperated again. "You must have had them sometime. Or seen them in a sweet shop? Mother likes them. She has them in a little tin. Violet pastilles, I think they're called. They taste funny—sort of flowery."

Emmie shrugged. "Never heard of them." Sometimes Jack made her feel as if she didn't know anything. She didn't want to say that she had never been to a sweet shop. "Are they made of these?"

"Yes. And they make perfume too. Your Miss Dearlove wears it. It's horrible."

Emmie nodded, a smile lifting one corner of her mouth. That was what the smell was. "It's nicer on the flowers. On Miss Dearlove, it smells a bit musty."

Two days later, Emmie found a little tin sitting on her bed, white with a pattern of purple flowers painted on, flowers like the ones she had found in the garden. She could see that the tin said *Violet* on it, but she didn't understand most of the other words. She suspected they might be French. Emmie levered it open with her nails, sniffing as a wave of sugar and flowers poured out. Inside were tiny sweets, richly purple and pressed into the shape of flowers. She slipped one into her mouth, smiling in surprise at the intense sweetness. The sweet stayed in the side of her cheek all through afternoon lessons, until she crunched it as she chased Jack out into the garden. Emmie suspected that the tin might last her forever.

Emmie followed Jack anxiously along the passage. She could see his white shirt in the dim light; she had her eyes fixed on it. The house was so large, and although she had been all around the gardens, she had never explored much inside. "We aren't allowed," she'd told Jack when he first suggested it.

"I am. It's my house," Jack pointed out with his lordly air.

"Miss Sowerby said we weren't to."

"You can come if you're with me. And besides, what else are you going to do?" Jack waved at the window. The rain was so heavy that it seemed to be running down the glass in sheets. Lucy was sitting on the windowsill, staring out at it disapprovingly. As Jack marched to the door of the schoolroom, she sprang down and set off after him, waving her tail like a flag.

Emmie looked hesitantly around the room. It *was* Jack's house. She gave up worrying and chased after them down the passage, and then another passage and another, past suits of armor and strange, dark paintings, and hundreds and hundreds of doors.

"I'm lost," Emmie called anxiously, and Jack turned back to grin at her. "Where are we going anyway? I don't have any idea how to get back." Then she bit her lip worriedly, hoping she wasn't giving him ideas of running off and leaving her behind. Nobody would find her for years. She'd *die*, and by the time anyone thought to look for her, she'd just be a pile of bones. Emmie shuddered. Was that what was in all those old wooden chests they kept walking past?

"I don't either," Jack admitted cheerfully. "But I always get back in the end. No one really uses this part of the house. They haven't for years and years. Even before Mother had to shut parts up because of the war. It's like being explorers."

"You don't know where you're going?" Emmie gasped.

"No. I was going to show you the elephants, but I thought we'd get to them about three corners ago, and we haven't."

"Elephants?" Emmie was momentarily distracted from being furious with him.

"Carved ivory ones—there are ninety-six of them. I counted. Some of them are only as big as my thumbnail. They live in a cabinet in a room at this end of the house *somewhere*."

"Don't you mind being lost?" Emmie asked him. He didn't seem to be worried at all.

Jack shrugged. "I'll work out where we are eventually. And if I don't, someone will always come and find me."

Emmie supposed that actually someone would come and find her too. She just wasn't quite as sure of it as he was.

Jack looked around at the heavy wooden doors and then marched over to open one. Emmie had thought they might all be locked, but the door opened easily with only a faint wheezing creak.

"I wonder when anyone last came in here," Jack murmured, looking around the door. "It smells of dust." He put his hands in his pockets and strolled in, but Emmie thought perhaps he was only pretending not to care. The empty stillness of the room was daunting.

The rain made the room dimly gray, so that the furniture seemed to loom at them out of the shadows. There was a huge bed up against the wall, carved from black wood and draped with heavy, red-velvet curtains. Emmie couldn't imagine sleeping in it, swathed in the dark, dusty stuff. It would be impossible to breathe.

Lucy jumped up onto the gilt-embroidered coverlet and sneezed as a little cloud of dust puffed up under her paws.

Emmie followed her in cautiously, looking around. She almost expected the room's owner to appear and tell them to get out. It did seem like a room that had belonged to someone once. There were ornaments on the mantelpiece and, over by the window, a dressing table with more red velvet for a skirt. The mirror was dark with greenish spots. Emmie turned away from it suddenly, afraid that she might see another face behind her own.

The walls were covered in tapestries like the ones in Emmie's own room, but these hangings made a garden. Stiff, formal flowers twined all over them, and birds perched here and there. Emmie walked around the room examining the wall hangings and trying to see what the flowers were.

"There's a rabbit!" The little creature was hunched nervously in one corner under a tree covered with fruit. She turned to Jack, shaking her head. "Are all the rooms like this?" she murmured.

Jack nodded. "Mostly. I haven't explored all of them though. It's not as much fun on your own. David used to make trails," he added, his eyes widening as though he'd forgotten. "He had a ball of string, so we could follow it back."

Emmie rolled her eyes. "And you didn't think to bring one? I must say, your brother sounds a lot cleverer than you."

"He's better at everything than me." Jack's voice was small, and he didn't look at her. He just kept leaning on the windowsill and gazing down at the gardens in the rain. "We're not as far around as I thought we were. I can see the kitchen gardens. Look."

"I didn't mean it," Emmie said guiltily. "I mean, of course he's better at things than you. He's years older, isn't he?"

"Eight," Jack agreed. "But he used to let me follow him around when he was home for the holidays. He liked it. Dad used to say it was as if David had a puppy." He frowned suddenly and pulled away from the window. "I *have* been in this room before. I'd forgotten. It was years and years ago." He plunged across the room to a huge wardrobe standing in the corner farthest from the window and flung the doors open. "I thought so." Emmie peered over his shoulder. The bottom of the wardrobe was piled with round boxes, patterned and striped in faded colors, and fastened with ribbon. Jack fought with a bow and then lifted off the lid from the topmost box, grinning. "Can you imagine wearing this?"

He pulled out a hat that was so huge it looked more like a cake. Mrs. Evans and Mrs. Martin had been trying to find ideas to get around rationing by looking at old recipe books, but mostly it had just made them feel worse. Emmie had seen a whole page with drawings of elaborate desserts that looked like this hat. It was swathed in puffs of net and dotted with little silk flowers and ribbon rosettes. Jack reached out and perched it on Emmie's head, yanking it down around her ears and making her squeak. It was surprisingly heavy.

Jack pushed her over toward the spotted mirror on the dressing table, and Emmie let him. The hat might have belonged to Mary or to Colin's beautiful, tragic mother. Emmie wanted to see it. There were no such things as ghosts, she told herself.

There was so much hat that she could hardly see anything of herself underneath it. She was no more than a small, freckled nose and a pointed chin, sticking out under a pile of flowered net. Lucy sprang onto the dressing table and peered up at her worriedly.

"It's all right," Emmie murmured. "I know it looks like it's eating me, but it isn't. This hat is the silliest thing I've ever seen… Actually, no." She had turned around and caught Jack in an absurdly tall, gray top hat that was falling down around his ears. "That is. What else is in those boxes?"

Emmie was hidden, stretched out flat in the damp grass under one of the lilac bushes. It had dark pinkish-purple flowers, great fat clusters of them, and the scent was so sweet that Emmie wanted to drink it.

She could hear Jack tiptoeing around, looking for her. He thought he was being so clever, but she knew exactly where he was. The only thing that might give her away would be if Lucy decided to come and join in. The cat didn't understand hide-and-seek. If she decided to curl up under the lilac with Emmie, she'd purr and purr, and march around finding the best place to sit. But Lucy was sleeping in the sun on the edge of the statue. At least, Emmie thought she was. She rolled over a little, peering out past the fringe of long grass. There was still a puddle of black fur slopped languorously over the edge of the stone plinth. Lucy looked like she was melting.

The garden was so still in the early summer heat, with only Jack's footsteps breaking the silence. It was as if the weather was making up for the harsh winter and trying to fill everyone with sunlight. Making up for the bad news too. The newspapers seemed to get worse every day. The Germans had invaded Holland and Belgium, and now they had poured into France.

There was a British army in France too, the British Expeditionary Force, but it was a lot smaller than the wave of German soldiers and not properly prepared to fight. It was more of a gesture to show good faith to the French, Jack said. His mother had left a letter from Lieutenant Craven lying around, and Jack had read it. Emmie could tell when he was quoting his father. His voice went slower and deeper, and there were worried lines above his nose.

Jack lurched between crazy games—where he wanted to chase Emmie all over the house, or he planned to walk along the top of the kitchen garden wall without falling off, or launch Lucy in his toy sailboat across the pond—and moments of utter misery. He was anxious about his father, whose ship was guarding convoys on their way to Norway, and even more worried about his brother, David, who had been based in France flying a Hurricane to support the British Expeditionary Force.

Now all the planes had been pulled out of France to air bases on the coast, where they had to fly over the English Channel to give cover to the army instead. It made the war seem so much closer—that there were only twenty-one miles of sea to keep the Germans away.

The staff in the servants' hall had taken to sitting over the newspapers in the evenings and shaking their heads. The British Expeditionary Force didn't have enough tanks or heavy guns to stand up to the German army. Charlie Barker, one of the under-gardeners, had gone off to enlist back in September and had been sent to France with the Green Howards, one of the Yorkshire regiments. He'd written to Mr. Sowerby that hardly any of his battalion had pistols.

"Not even compasses," Mr. Sowerby had snarled, folding the letter with sharp, jerky movements of his hands and crumpling it as he stuffed it into his pocket. "How're the poor sods meant t' find their way back home? Runnin' like rabbits."

Emmie had never seen him so angry. For a few minutes, he was the same distant, growling figure she had first met so many months before.

Remembering, she edged back farther under the lilac bush and shivered a little in the chill of the shadow.

The green door in the wall banged open, and Emmie flinched, scraping her knees on the dry twigs. The quiet, bee-humming afternoon was broken as a figure blundered into the garden.

"Jack! Are you there? Jack! Oh please…"

Emmie heard him turn, his sandals hissing on the dry grass. He was still playing hide-and-seek. He waited for a moment, caught in the game. Then something made him run. He hurled himself at his mother.

It was the color of the paper. Emmie saw it a few seconds after Jack did. Even from the shadows under the lilac bush, she knew what it was. A telegram. Everyone knew what that color of paper meant. Mrs. Martin, the cook, had received a telegram to tell her that her son had been injured while he was fighting in the army in Norway, and she had refused to open the yellow envelope. She was quite certain that the message was to tell her that Will was dead.

She had sat holding it and staring at it and turning it over in her hands. Eventually, Mrs. Evans had sent Joey, telling him to fetch Mrs. Craven so she could open the envelope for the cook. Mrs. Evans had been so relieved that Will was only wounded that she had hugged everyone in the kitchen and used all the sugar ration to make cocoa.

"Is it David?" Jack was clinging to his mother's arm. Emmie wriggled farther back under the lilac bush. She shouldn't be here. This was secret, too much of a secret even to fit into the garden. She tried to stuff her fingers into her ears, but she couldn't make herself not hear.

"No." Mrs. Craven sat down suddenly on the grass, pulling Jack with her, half onto her lap. "No, darling. It's Dad."

Miss Sowerby told them the news properly at suppertime. She slipped into the servants' hall looking thinner and round shouldered, as though suddenly she wasn't young anymore. There were tears seeping through the smiling creases around her eyes.

She had known Lieutenant Craven since they were both children, since she was a clumsy little servant girl, too countrified really to work in such a smart house. She had watched over him when he was a bad-tempered, sickly child who wore out his nurse. He had screamed and shouted at her in the middle of the night. And then he had grown up when everyone had been so sure he never would.

"I never thought," she murmured, dropping into a chair next to Mrs. Martin. "After everythin' that happened… There was always a spark of something in him. They called it magic, the children, when they were small. Even with the war like it is, I never thought…"

"What happened?" Arthur whispered, his eyes round. They had known the Lieutenant was dead, but not from Emmie. They had seen Mrs. Craven's face as she ran calling through the gardens. She and Jack had stumbled together back into the house and shut themselves away in Lieutenant Craven's study.

"Is it certain?" Emmie asked at the same time. "It couldn't be a mistake?"

Miss Sowerby reached out to stroke her cheek. "I can't see it bein' wrong, Emmie. The telegram had his name, his number, an' all. It happened a week ago. There's a letter to follow, they said. It was th' Admiralty sent the telegram, they must know."

"A week? He was at Dunkirk then?" Joey leaned forward eagerly. "We thought that! When it came on the radio, we wondered if Lieutenant Craven might be there." He was smiling excitedly—it *had* been exciting, hearing it. Emmie and Ruby had hugged each other, and Ruby had done a little dance around the kitchen.

All those little ships, sailing off to France to rescue the brave soldiers and bring them home. Some of them had been fishing boats, the man on the radio had said. Some of them were the sort of boats that took people on outings at the seaside. Britain had called, and the men in those boats had answered, everyone said. The story had been so dramatic that the rescue felt almost like a victory, not the crushing defeat it really was.

Arthur ducked his head, his cheeks pink, suddenly remembering. "Sorry," he whispered.

Miss Sowerby only smiled at him, the tears slowly spreading down her cheeks.

"He was good at rescuing things," Emmie whispered. "If he'd go to all that trouble for Lucy, he'd make them pick up those poor soldiers from the water. That will be what happened. They were rescuing the soldiers."

Joey nodded. "Maybe a U-boat…" But then he snapped his mouth shut again, as Emmie and Miss Dearlove and Miss Rose all turned on him with a fierce glare. Miss Sowerby leaned forward, pressing her hands over her face, and Joey hunched down, trying to make himself look small.

"It's not a *story*," Emmie hissed, and Joey nodded, just a little apologetic twitch of his head. It was hard not to talk about it. He wanted to know. The news had caught everyone's imagination.

So many of the rooms were closed up and covered in dust sheets now that Mrs. Craven had taken to sitting downstairs in the kitchen or the servants' hall sometimes, especially to listen to the evening news. She said it was too lonely, hearing it upstairs on her own. But she didn't come down that evening, and neither did Jack.

Jack didn't appear at lessons the next day either. Emmie watched the door, hoping for him to slip in. She didn't know what she could say to him, but she hated the thought that he was hidden away again, desperate. Even more desperate now than he had been the night she went to find him in the dark.

"I expect Jack needs to be with his mother now," Miss Rose murmured. "We must leave them alone." She was looking at Emmie as she said it, and Emmie nodded, though inside she wanted to argue. What if Jack wanted someone else to talk to? Or needed someone, even if he didn't want them very much.

She wouldn't mind if he yelled at her again... Emmie leaned on her hand and stabbed her pencil at the page. Well, she would mind. But she wouldn't yell back, she promised herself.

He still has a mother, something whispered inside her. *You don't have anyone.*

"But I never did," she murmured to herself. "It isn't the same." Then she looked across at Arthur, expecting him to be smirking at her for talking to herself. But he was drawing tiny ships in the margins of his sums, and Joey was gazing into the distance across the room. For once, it could have been Emmie that teased them for daydreaming, but all she did was kick Joey gently under the table and nod sideways. Miss Dearlove was watching.

Emmie bolted her lunch down, eager to get out into the gardens, away from the brooding sadness of the house. The roses were coming out. She hadn't believed that there could be more flowers in the secret garden than when she had first seen it in September, but the buds were unfurling everywhere, lines of pink and white and blazing red bursting through the green. There were more every day.

She sped up as she ran down the paved walk by the gardens. There was a rose that climbed around the statue where Lucy liked to sleep, an early flowering one that Emmie had never seen open. Jack had told her that it was striped, dark red with white, and Emmie could see it in her head, like the stiff silk dress of the little girl in the painting that hung in their schoolroom.

Even Jack didn't know who the girl in the painting was, but she made Emmie laugh. She looked so cross. Her parents couldn't have been pleased with the portrait, Emmie thought. The poor painter must have tried to make her smile, or at least look grand and proud. But the girl's mouth was dragged into a determined line, and her eyes were snapping. She had wanted to be outside, Emmie was sure. Perhaps she had wanted to run around in the garden and stroke the petals of the striped roses, instead of being laced into that tight dress and made to stand still. Even the little dog in her arms was gazing wistfully out of the side of the frame. It wanted to dash around over the grass too.

Emmie twisted the brass handle under the ivy and eased the door open, slipping through and looking eagerly over at the statue. She darted across the lawn to see if the striped flowers had opened yet, but then a fluttering of pink caught her eye, and she spun around.

Mrs. Craven was lying on the grass under the great tree, her pink cotton dress the same color as the rose petals scattered around her. Fistfuls of them. Emmie stared at them, not understanding.

Mr. Sowerby always made sure that the bush just next to the tree was watered and carefully trimmed. The flowers had hardly opened, and now the bush was almost bare, a few buds limply trailing from the branches.

Mrs. Craven put one hand up to shield her eyes from the sun and squinted at Emmie as if she wasn't sure who this was in her garden. Her hand was scratched—there was a thin trickle of dark blood running down onto her wrist.

"You tore all the flowers off," Emmie whispered, shocked. "What did you do that for?"

Mrs. Craven didn't say anything. She just went on staring at Emmie as though she were a stranger.

Emmie stepped back, suddenly frightened. Mrs. Craven's face was so pale, and her eyes looked almost black.

"Come away, lass." Mr. Sowerby caught her arm, and Emmie gasped. She hadn't even heard him limping up behind her. "She needs us gone."

"But the roses—" Emmie whispered.

"Do as tha'rt told!" He pulled at her arm sharply, and Emmie cried out. He'd hurt her, even though she could see that he hadn't meant to. He hustled her back out the green door and onto the path. "I'm sorry, Emmie. Mrs. Craven needs th' garden now, doesn't tha' see it? Tha' just let her be. Did I hurt thee?"

"Yes." Emmie sniffed, rubbing her wrist. "A lot. When can I go and look at the roses?"

He shook his head and then rubbed a hand wearily across his reddened eyes. His scars looked darker. "No. Tha' can't. Didn't tha' listen? It's her place, hers and his, their secret. Leave her alone. Stay out."

Emmie gazed at him, dumbfounded, and then shook her head. "No! I can't... You don't mean it."

But he hardly seemed to hear her. He turned away and began to hobble up the path, back to the kitchen gardens.

"But who's going to look after the garden?" Emmie wailed. She ran after him, pulling at his jacket. "I help, don't I? Please? You can't make me stay away."

"I'll do it," he growled. "Get away with thee, child. Buzzing about like a wasp, th'art."

Emmie dropped back, staring after him with her eyes stinging. Even when she'd first arrived, he'd never spoken to her like that. It almost sounded as if he hated her. Emmie watched him until he limped into one of the kitchen gardens, and then she walked back to the door under the ivy. She wanted to sneak back in, and she didn't think Mrs. Craven was in a state to notice. But then the brass doorknob under her hand was cold. It seemed to have lost some of its worn, silken feel, that inviting golden softness that always tempted her in. Even in the hot June sunshine, the cold metal bit into her fingers, and Emmie stepped back.

She wasn't wanted.

Emmie lay on the warm stone slabs around the pool, with Lucy sitting next to her. Both of them were staring at the fish, and occasionally Lucy would put out a hopeful paw, then draw it back again. She wanted the little golden things so much, and she spent hours watching them, but she was afraid of the water.

"What if I can never go back?" Emmie whispered to her. "What if he meant for always?" She sat up, drawing her knees up under her chin, and closed her eyes, trying to see the garden in her head. But there was too much of it, too much to see and smell and touch. Even when she told it to herself as a story, only a hint of the magic came through. She needed to step through the door.

"I should have taken you with me," she muttered, running her hand over Lucy's sun-warmed fur. "No one ever tells you where to go." She looked over her shoulder at the long flower bed, blazing with pink lilies, and hissed through her teeth. The heat was bringing them all on. They were opening out like great cups— but it wasn't the same. "I *know* that rose would be out. I could go back. Mrs. Craven must have gone by now. And I don't think she'd mind if I was there anyway. She knows I love the garden. She told Lieutenant Craven how helpful I was." She rocked back and forth gently, hugging her knees. "I could go back," she whispered again. But she didn't get up. She could have—but she wouldn't.

2nd June 1910

Even the walls are covered now. Tiny creeping plants have seeded themselves in the cracks between the bricks and smothered them in flowers. White daisies, with each petal dipped in pink, and tiny yellow flowers that look like specks of gold. One of the statues has a great clump of violet-blue campanula trailing out of the wall behind her. It's grown all down over her shoulders like a cape of little bells.

There are so many columbines that I could gather armfuls and fill a vase in each room of the house if it wasn't such a pity to pick them. They must be named after the dancing girl in the stories, I'm sure. They dance and shake their frilly petals as the wind blows through them. Today I lay down next to the tallest purple delphiniums, the ones that are almost as tall as me, and stared up at the sky. I made patterns out of the clouds. Colin said I looked quite mad, and even Dickon was trying not to smile, but I don't care.

Emmie padded silently up the steps to Jack's room. She had been dreaming about the garden, Mary's garden. She had found the pages in the diary for the summer, all those years ago. She could see the garden as she read, and the words made it even harder not to be there. But she couldn't stop.

Then in her dream, she finally got in there again, but the garden kept changing, stretching out into tunnels of dark shadow. Emmie ran and ran to reach the bright sunlight and the roses, but could never escape the clinging grayness of the tunnel. She had woken up gasping, choking, to find Lucy stretched across her chest weighing her down—and grumpy when Emmie tried to move.

Too scared to go back to sleep, in case she slipped back into the shadows again, Emmie got out of bed. She would go and find

Jack, she decided. Maybe he wouldn't want to talk to her, but at least she could try. Lucy stood up and stared at her, and then clambered quickly into the warm spot that Emmie had left in the bed and curled up again.

The house was silent, and when she peered through the heavy curtains in the passageway outside Jack's room, the night was black. It must have been late, the middle of the night. Emmie paused at the top of the steps, chewing her lip and peering into the darkness of the room. Probably he was fast asleep. It was stupid to have come.

"What are you doing?"

Emmie nearly shrieked. Jack wasn't in bed. He was curled up on the wide stone windowsill, glaring at her. The moonlight glimmered on the side of his face. He looked cold and miserable.

"Why aren't you in bed?" she snapped, surprised into sharpness. She'd forgotten that his father had died and that she'd come all prepared to be nice to Jack.

"Why aren't you?"

Emmie shrugged. "I dreamed…something bad. I thought I'd come and see you. To see if you were all right…" She ducked her head, embarrassed. It sounded so stupid. How could he be?

"I am. Now go away."

Emmie swallowed down another sharp answer. "Do I have

to?" she asked, her voice almost pleading. "I don't want to dream it again. Can't I stay here for a little bit?"

"No."

"You don't have to be so mean."

"Yes, I do." Jack spat out each word, and Emmie suddenly recognized the way he was talking. He was all buttoned up. Even his mouth was tidy, the lips pressed together. His hands were folded in his lap, the knuckles white. If he let himself go, he was going to scream.

"It might be better if…"

"What?"

Emmie shook her head. "Nothing. I'll go then. Shall I?"

"Yes. Go away."

Emmie began to shuffle toward the steps, still looking at him, hoping that he'd change his mind. He watched her go. She could see the sharp glitter of his eyes in the light from the window. As she came to the top of the steps, Emmie was almost sure she saw him lean forward. Did he reach out one hand to snatch her back? But he said nothing. What would he do if she ran back and hugged him and curled up next to him on the windowsill? Probably push her off. Or cry. She wasn't sure which would be worse.

"Night," she murmured.

"Go away."

17th June 1910

Colin is doing a scientific experiment. He says there must be magic in the garden. I am sure he is right. I felt it, even from the first time that I opened the door. Perhaps it was because Colin's mother loved the garden so much, or because it was left on its own for so long. But the magic of growing things is in the garden, our secret garden. It does make something out of nothing, as Colin says. The garden is full of great, silken poppies that Dickon and I planted, but they were the tiniest black grains before. I remember tipping them out of the paper packet into my hand and thinking I would lose them all.

If the magic can do that, then it must be able to help Colin grow strong. Already he can stand up. He was sure he would never be able to walk, but he can manage a few steps now. If we believe, then perhaps the magic will make it come true. He will live to grow up.

I felt the magic; I know I did. It was in the green light shimmering through the leaves and the humming sound of the bees. Already the garden has made me stronger and happier. It must heal Colin too.

CHAPTER

Nine

WORKING IN THE KITCHEN GARDEN, Emmie could smell the roses. The scent wafted over the high wall, sweet and tempting. She sighed. She could go in—the door wasn't locked, and she was almost sure that Mrs. Craven was in the house. After the first few days of quiet strangeness, Jack's mother had gone back to being her old self, or seemed to have. She smiled at the children when she passed them. She went back to her volunteer work at the convalescent home in Thwaite, and she talked to everyone the way she always had.

But she didn't open up the garden. Emmie saw her going in there almost every afternoon. She had gloves on and tools with her. Sometimes she was even wheeling a barrow. Mr. Sowerby worked there too, but in the afternoons, he left her to be in the garden alone. Emmie wondered why Mrs. Craven never cried. Emmie didn't listen exactly, but it was like the roses. She was just across the wall, so she couldn't help hearing. Mrs. Craven didn't cry. Occasionally she sang very quietly, and Emmie wasn't quite sure of the song. *A nursery rhyme*, she thought.

Now she put out a hand and stroked the crumbling brick of the wall. It was comforting to be so close. She knew that the garden was still there, quiet and mysterious. But being this close made it so hard to stay away, knowing that she could just run along the path and sneak behind the ivy. She had the strangest feeling that the garden was lonely without her—that it needed her and Jack, playing hide-and-seek or tag, or stretched out in the grass watching the two robins fussing around their nest.

She had seen the male robin several times that afternoon, darting importantly over the wall, trailing worms almost as long as he was. The robins' first brood had hatched weeks before and flown the nest, but Jack had told her that there might be two lots of eggs, or even three. The robin was feeding his wife and his second clutch of children now. They had hatched just days before that afternoon of hide-and-seek. Now they must be fully feathered, almost as big as their parents. It was no wonder the robin looked harassed. Emmie watched him longingly, wishing she could swoop into the secret garden as easily as he could.

Jack still hadn't spoken to her since she'd gone to his room a week before. He hadn't come back to lessons, and Miss Rose hadn't said anything about it to his mother. Emmie didn't know what he was doing. She saw him in the distance occasionally, vanishing around the corner of a passageway or slipping behind a door. She'd tried running after him, but he always seemed to be just too far ahead. He knew the house well enough to disappear behind a tapestry or slide behind a suit of armor so that she'd never find him. He was determined to be left alone.

Emmie turned around and leaned against the wall, closing her eyes and feeling the sun-warmed brick against her back. She could see leaves dancing behind her eyelids, glowing in the sun and splashed with bright petals. She ached with longing deep inside. It hurt to be so close.

Her breath caught in a little surprised noise. She hadn't heard Lucy padding along the flagged path toward her. The cat wove lovingly around Emmie's boots, purring. Emmie picked her up, and she dug her claws in and out of the sleeve of Emmie's cardigan, her eyes closed to blissful slits. Then she abruptly wriggled onto Emmie's shoulder and sprang up to the top of the wall. She scrabbled a little as she reached the top and then glared triumphantly down at Emmie.

"Oh, Lucy…" Emmie sighed. "Not you too. It isn't fair."

The black cat padded smugly along the top of the wall for a

few steps and then stopped, her tail twitching slowly from side to side and her green gaze fixed.

Emmie watched her, suddenly anxious. What had she seen? It was probably just a butterfly. Lucy loved to chase them, sitting up on her haunches and batting at them with her long, black paws. "Don't eat it," Emmie whispered. She had eaten one yesterday, such a pretty one. The soft-blue wings had looked so strange sticking out of Lucy's furry mouth. And the cat hadn't even liked it much. She'd spat most of it back out.

"Oh no." Emmie stepped back and stretched up on tiptoe, trying to see over the wall, to see what Lucy was seeing. "No, you can't..."

Lucy wasn't listening to her. She was creeping along the top of the wall, her tail swishing.

The robin was perched in the tree on the other side of the wall. He was pecking at the bark. It looked like an insect was creeping around in the tiny cracks. He dragged it out triumphantly and fluttered away, and Lucy leaped down after him—on the other side of the wall.

"Lucy!" Emmie hissed. "Lucy, come back! You mustn't! You can't chase him. He's got babies..." Then she grimaced to herself. Lucy wasn't stupid. She would sneak across the grass, following the robin to the nest, and she would see that there were more of these soft, delicious, fluttery things. Jack and Emmie had shooed her away from the last clutch. Jack had even found several beetles one morning and put them down in a line in front of Lucy as a distraction. But there was no one to watch out for the robins now.

The little cat was all on her own in the garden, hunting.

"She'll eat them," Emmie moaned, scratching at the wall with her fingers, as if she could climb it too. "Lucy, come back…"

It was no good. She whirled around and raced through the rows of beans and tomatoes toward the path and the ivy and the door to the garden.

Even though she knew that it wasn't allowed, this time the brass handle didn't feel cold. The metal was warm and welcoming and buttery soft under her fingers. She twisted it eagerly, so eagerly she almost fell into the garden. As she dashed out onto the grass, searching anxiously for Lucy, she could feel something tight inside her easing away. The rustling, twittering quiet seemed to seep in under her skin.

Lucy was stalking across the grass toward the tangled corner where so many birds had nested. She seemed to consider each paw before she placed it down, and her shoulders were a little hunched, ready to spring.

Emmie ran after her, and Lucy glanced around, startled by the heavy footsteps.

"No! Shoo!" Emmie flapped her hands at the cat, and Lucy dodged her irritably, still intent on her hunting.

Then the robin fluttered out of the dense thicket with a sharp, stuttering trill, and Lucy turned away, sitting down in the grass as if she'd never meant anything. She even swiped one paw across her muzzle, licking at it and then looking at Emmie sideways, as if to say she'd only been washing. Nothing else.

Emmie smiled lovingly at her. She knew that Lucy would be straight back to the robin's nest as soon as she thought Emmie wasn't looking. Perhaps she should warn Mr. Sowerby? But he was still hardly talking. He didn't do much more than growl instructions when she asked him for garden jobs. Though he had patted her shoulder the day before when she'd shown him the basketful of peas that she had picked. He hadn't said anything, but she was almost sure that he was sorry—or *regretful*. He just couldn't bring himself to tell her so.

She crouched down, scooping Lucy into her arms. They would go and watch the fish in the lily pond. She knew Lucy couldn't catch those. She sighed and looked around at the roses. She couldn't stay. She knew it. The longer she stayed now, the harder it would be to tear herself away.

As she walked back across the lawn, she heard footsteps, quick and light—someone in the kitchen garden? Emmie whirled around, scanning the garden. She had played hide-and-seek in here so many times. Why couldn't she see anywhere to hide now? The handle was turning; she could hear that funny little squeak it made. Emmie stepped back, and another step, and another, and the door opened.

Mrs. Craven came in with a basket and pruning clippers in her hand. She had a straw hat on, shading her eyes, and Emmie was standing so frozen still that at first Mrs. Craven didn't notice the girl. She almost walked into Emmie and then stopped short, gasping and white-faced, as though she was truly frightened.

That was what Lieutenant Craven's death had done to her, Emmie realized, full of guilt. It was as if her skin had been stripped away. When that piece of yellow paper had dragged her life apart, she had lost all her protection, all her padding. Now everything hurt.

Mrs. Craven simply stared at her, and Emmie couldn't think what to say. She had missed the garden so much while she was exiled from it that she could understand how much Jack's mother needed to be there. She needed that calm sense of everything growing and flowering and just going on.

Looking at her now, Emmie almost agreed that the garden should be hers—though only almost.

"I'm sorry." Her voice was a squeak of nerves, and Lucy hissed crossly, suddenly clutched too tight.

Mrs. Craven shook her head. Either she simply couldn't bring herself to speak because she was too angry, or she was saying it didn't matter. Emmie couldn't tell.

"It was because of Lucy. I know I'm not supposed to be here. I stayed away even though I didn't want to. Really, I did! Please don't be upset..." Her voice trailed away. What a stupid thing to say.

The green door crashed open again, and Mr. Sowerby lurched through it, too fast and angry to balance himself properly. He almost fell, and Mrs. Craven grabbed his arm.

"What did I tell thee?" he roared at Emmie, and Lucy twisted and shot out of Emmie's arms, her ears flat against her narrow skull. She stalked away behind a stand of lilies and watched them all resentfully. "Stay away, I said!"

"I did!" Emmie yelled back, suddenly angry. "I did, for days and days! Even when I could have gone in without anyone seeing me, I stayed away."

"Don't shout at her," Mrs. Craven murmured, but the gardener was too angry to listen.

"So what are tha' doing here, then? Ungrateful, disobedient wench that th'art!"

"I'm not ungrateful!" Emmie screamed, clenching her fists. "I love it! How can you say I'm ungrateful? You don't know how I feel inside! You tore me out of my place!" She glared at him and then at Mrs. Craven, breathing fast and trying to think what she had meant. The words had come into her mouth without her thinking them first. "Yes, you did, twice. You dragged us all here, and I suppose that's fair because none of us liked the Home much and we had to be evacuated somewhere, so why not here? But it was different from everything, and I hated it, and I didn't have Lucy. It was only the garden that made it almost all right. Then I loved it, and I shouldn't have. And you tore me away again."

Mrs. Craven was staring at her still, but the white, set look had changed to a sort of puzzled fascination. As if she were trying to recognize something.

"She puts me in mind of thee," Mr. Sowerby muttered, rubbing one hand over the scarred side of his face. "A long time ago. Before all this." He passed his hand over his face again, as if he could rub the scars away. "Mean tempered."

"I'm not..." Emmie said, her voice quivering. It hurt more because it was almost true—she had been. She still was sometimes. But not like she had been before. Was she? Wasn't she better? The old Emmie would never have fussed over Ruby and her fish—or made such an effort to comfort Jack.

"I was mean tempered because I was lonely, even if I didn't know it," Mrs. Craven broke in quietly. "Emmie was lonely too. Colin—Lieutenant Craven, I mean... He did something special, bringing your little cat back to you."

Emmie eyed her worriedly, hoping that she wasn't about to cry. Her voice had shaken slightly as she spoke about him.

"And I've seen you with Jack. Considering how angry he was to have his home invaded by strangers, you must have put aside some of the meanness, at least. At any rate, there's been something—"

"It was the garden." Emmie twisted her hands over, feeling uncomfortable with this praise. "But I haven't seen Jack properly since...since his father... I did try. He didn't want to talk to me."

"He doesn't want to talk to anyone," his mother murmured. "I don't think he can yet."

Emmie nodded, and then her eyes widened. She turned and darted across the grass, grabbing at Lucy.

The black cat had slunk through the lilies while they were talking, making another stealthy attack on the robins' nest. She retreated behind the statue, sulking.

"I think I'll have to shut her indoors," Emmie said worriedly. "She'll hate it. She was never an indoor cat. She even went out in the snow. She didn't like it, but she just couldn't stay inside all the time. I don't know how to stop her. She never really noticed the first clutch hatching—she was too busy watching me and Jack—but now she knows they're there."

Mr. Sowerby frowned at her, drawing his one eyebrow down. "Was that why tha' came in here? To stop th' little cat?"

Emmie nodded. "She was in the kitchen garden with me, and she saw the robin go over the wall. She followed him, and I could see it in her eyes. She was so excited. All he could think about was worms and getting them to his babies. I don't think birds are clever enough to understand they're being hunted—or to do anything about it anyway. They haven't a hope."

"And that was the first time you've been in the garden since Mr. Sowerby told you to leave me in peace?" Mrs. Craven asked slowly, as if she was trying to understand.

"Yes." Emmie folded her arms and glared. "I did what he said. I thought about not doing it though. I almost went in a few times."

Mrs. Craven actually laughed. A short chuckle, nothing more, but Mr. Sowerby looked over at her in relieved surprise. "I stole this garden, Emmie, did you know? It was locked up. No one was supposed to go in it. I can't really complain if you do the same, can I?"

"You stole the garden?" Emmie stared at her and shook her head, not understanding. There was a hole in the story, and she couldn't quite draw it all back together. "You?" she murmured. "It was you? The girl who found the key? It was your secret garden?" *Before it was mine*, she wanted to say. "Then—you're Mary Lennox?"

Mrs. Craven—*Mary* Craven—smiled at her and nodded. "Did Miss Sowerby tell you the story?"

Now would be the time to confess about the diaries, but

Emmie wasn't sure what to say. She was still trying to piece every-thing together, to fill in the hole. The angry little girl from the diary—Emmie had never been able to think of her grown up, but of course she would be. She had stayed at Misselthwaite.

Emmie took in a sharp breath and caught Mrs. Craven's sleeve. "Colin! You said that it was Colin who brought Lucy back to me. You meant Lieutenant Craven. He was Colin…" Emmie's voice faltered, and she felt her eyes sting. It couldn't be right. Colin was the boy the garden had brought back to life. Surely the magic hadn't healed him for this?

Mary pressed one hand over her eyes for a moment and then nodded at Emmie. "He said he was going to live forever," she mur-mured. "We grew out of believing that the garden was full of magic, of course. But I think I still believed that he would…"

"It were a cruel waste," Mr. Sowerby muttered. "Sit down, Miss Mary." He took her arm and limped across to one of the stone benches, murmuring to her as if she were a wounded bird.

Emmie watched them, fascinated. Mary. And Dickon. The animal charmer. She felt as though she should have realized before. But how could she have seen the strong, cheerful boy that everyone on the moor had loved in this growling man?

"I shouldn't have shut you out of the garden," Mary said, beck-oning to her. "I'm sorry, Emmie. I didn't know." She took Emmie by the hand, pulling her gently to sit on the bench. Then she cupped her hand around Emmie's cheek and studied her face. "Look at you. The magic *was* still there. I should have seen that."

"So…I can come back?" Emmie whispered hopefully, looking up at her.

Dickon grunted. "If tha'rt here, tha' can work. There's weeds among th' lilies. And watch that little beggar of a cat." But he patted her shoulder and then gripped it, tight, and she knew that he meant it to be an apology.

"That robin Lucy was chasing must be the great-great-grandson of my robin," Mary said, looking dreamily around the garden. "He was so proud of himself and his beautiful red feathers. He was my first friend here. The first creature I actually *wanted* to like me."

Emmie glanced at her in surprise, recognizing the idea. "For me that was Lucy." Then she looked properly at Mary, seeing the soft, remembering look in her eyes, and murmured, "I'd better go. Miss Rose said I should keep an eye on Ruby." She got up and backed away slowly, chirruping to Lucy, who padded ungraciously from behind the statue of the foolish-looking girl.

At the door, Emmie turned to look back. Dickon was crouched close by the robins' nest, watching, and Mary was standing on the grass by the rose tree that she had destroyed. There were a few flowers on it, the buds that she had left behind now opened out. Emmie flinched for a second as Mary reached out to one of the pink-tinged flowers, thinking that she meant to tear it off. But all she did was run her fingers over the petals, and she was almost smiling.

Looking after Ruby had been made up as an excuse on the spot, but Emmie thought she might as well go and see if Ruby was by the lily pond. The fish would distract Lucy from robins. But as she hurried down the steps, she realized that the hunched-up figure by the water was Jack, not Ruby.

He sprang up at the sound of her footsteps, heavy in the still-too-big Wellingtons, and Emmie stood to the side of the steps to let him go. She had given up chasing him, but she wanted to sit by the water and think about what had just happened. Why should she be the one to run away?

Jack stopped at the bottom of the steps, looking up at her. He had the model Hurricane that David had sent him for Christmas in his hands—he almost always did. Emmie thought he carried it around with him like a talisman. She wondered if he pretended to himself that it was David's plane. Something deep inside Jack prayed that the fragile metal shell thousands of feet up would be protected if its tiny model was safe. The plane was wooden, made by one of the other pilots in the squadron. David had written that he'd asked the man to build the plane for Jack and paint it with the same camouflage pattern as David's own. The paint was rubbing away now from so much holding, the sharp lines of the brown and khaki paint smoothing into each other.

"They won't let him come home."

Emmie gaped at Jack. It had been days and days since he'd spoken to her. She had simply assumed that he would shove past her with a furious glare, as he had before. She was so surprised that for a moment she thought he was talking about his father, and she didn't know what to say. Then she saw the way he was cradling the plane.

"Your brother?"

"Mmm. He was hoping to get compassionate leave." His shoulders stiffened and hunched up. "Because of Dad."

"Oh..." She looked at him cautiously, wondering if he was still in that state where if someone was nice to him, he would cry and hate them for it. "I'm really sorry."

"Mmm. What was your nightmare about?"

Emmie blinked at him. She had almost forgotten. "Oh!" She chewed her bottom lip. "It's stupid. You'll laugh..."

"I won't. I promise."

"It was only that I couldn't get into the garden. I could see it, and it looked so sunny and beautiful, but I was stuck in all these shadows." She shivered, remembering.

"I had a dream like that about Dad," Jack said slowly. He sat down on the steps, and Emmie sat next to him. Lucy padded away to peer down into the water.

"You couldn't get to him?"

"Yes, and he needed me to pull him up out of the water, but I couldn't reach." He put his chin in his hands. "It wasn't like that, actually. Mum got the letter. It was a torpedo from a U-boat, but he didn't drown. The torpedo set off an explosion, and it killed Dad and the captain. They were on the bridge. Lots of sailors were killed too, but then everyone else was rescued by another destroyer. It's silly— Dad's ship had stopped to rescue survivors, and then they went and got hit themselves. If they hadn't stopped, he might still be all right."

He moved his hands up so they covered his face. His voice was muffled, and Emmie shifted closer to hear. "The destroyer that rescued the crew from Dad's ship had to sink her. They couldn't tow her back, not with everything that was going on, and she was too badly damaged anyway. So they used the guns on her. Dad loved that ship. He went down with her."

Emmie swallowed. "That's what they do in books, isn't it? It's like a hero thing to do."

"But this was real."

"I know. Sorry." Emmie leaned against him gently. It seemed easier for him to pull away if she did that. But he put his head down on her shoulder, and they sat, watching Lucy's tail beat on the stones as she imagined hunting fish.

Emmie stopped on the path outside the green-painted door. It was standing open behind the ivy. Jack's mother was in there. Emmie could hear her humming to herself.

"What's the matter?" Jack turned back to look at her. "She said you could go back in there. She doesn't mind, Emmie. She told me last night that she'd talked to you."

"It isn't that," Emmie muttered huskily. "I've got something… I need to go back and get something. I'll be back in a minute." She raced back through the shrubbery to the house, pounding up the stairs and into her room. Then she sat down on her bed, breathless and uncertain. She had to give the diaries back—they were Mary's. But Mary hadn't wanted them, had she? She'd probably forgotten all about them. She was busy with everything else. The faded little books had been in that drawer for nearly thirty years. If Emmie gave them back, she'd have to admit that she'd read them.

But most importantly, if she gave them back, she wouldn't be able to read them again. Emmie opened the drawer and ran her fingers over the worn covers regretfully. Mary from the diary was so like her. Emmie had imagined meeting her, talking with her—that grumpy, friendless girl torn away from everything she knew. Now she had met Mary, but she was no longer a girl. She couldn't talk to Mrs. Craven about how lonely she'd been, or the way the garden had come to feel like home.

Still, the diaries weren't hers. She stood up and began to walk slowly back along the passageway and down the stairs.

The sun was brighter than ever, and the heat hit her as soon as she stepped out of the heavy door onto the gravel path. Lucy came trotting toward her from among the yew trees, mewing loudly.

"Where have you been?" Emmie murmured, crouching down to stroke her. "I thought you were begging in the kitchens. Were you out mousing?" Lucy purred and rubbed against Emmie's ankles, her black fur shining in the sun. She was glossier every day, even if there weren't that many scraps for her to eat. She had adopted Mrs. Martin and kept bringing her small furry presents, usually in the middle of breakfast.

"Come with me," Emmie said coaxingly. She made chirruping noises as she crunched over the gravel, and Lucy bounded in front of her, darting off every so often to chase invisible bees.

"What were you doing?" Jack demanded, running over as he saw her duck under the ivy. "You were gone for ages."

"Like I said, I was getting something. For your mother." Emmie marched across the grass and thrust the little pile of notebooks at Mrs. Craven, who was deadheading roses. She blinked down at them in confusion.

"What are... Oh! Emmie, I'd forgotten these..." she murmured at last, turning the thin books over in her hands. "Of course, you're sleeping in my old room."

"I found them," Emmie admitted. "And I read them. I'm sorry. I didn't know... It seemed like such a long time ago. I never thought she was you."

Mary flicked through the pages, frowning at her own spiky writing. "So this is where you found the story about the garden and Colin and me? It wasn't that anyone told you?"

"I told her about Dad's mother haunting the garden," Jack put in, peering over his mother's arm at the diary. "Your writing's much worse than mine."

"Too many governesses gave up on me. I'm amazed you could read them, Emmie."

"You don't mind?" Emmie whispered worriedly.

Mary shook her head slowly. "No. No, I don't think I do. She seems a long way away, that girl. It's like Dickon said. I was a mean-tempered little thing. But I was so used to being on my own. All I had were servants who didn't like me because I had such spoiled ways. The garden changed everything. Well, you know that it did." She smiled at Emmie and sat down on the grass to look more carefully at the diaries. Jack crouched next to her, and Mary patted the grass, telling Emmie to sit too.

"Why did you stop writing a diary?" Emmie asked, curling up beside them cautiously, waiting for Mrs. Craven to change her mind and send her away.

"I didn't. But Colin's father—Uncle Archie, I called him— gave me a beautiful new diary as a present. Red leather, with a lock and a little golden key. I wore the key on a ribbon around my neck because it felt so special. Another secret. I wanted to write in that book instead, and I abandoned these. I wrote a diary all the way until the end of the war—the last war. And then I stopped." She sighed. "It was too hard to write about. Nothing like that had happened to us before. Misselthwaite was so quiet. We were protected from everything. The war broke into that— even into the garden."

"Dickon had to go and fight," Emmie whispered. "And Colin."

"Yes. Colin had been away before, to go to school, but Dickon had hardly been off the moor." Mary shuddered. "It was…unbe-lievable. But we thought at least it could never happen again." She began to turn over the pages, tracing a word with her finger here and there.

Jack huddled against her, and Emmie stared at the grass. They sat silently, listening to the birds, until at last Mary pointed to the page she was reading. "So much of the garden is the same. Look, that rose is still here. The dark-red one. I'm sure it still has the sweetest scent of them all." She smiled at Emmie. "Dickon cut some of those, you know. He gave them to your Miss Rose."

"Did he?" Emmie's eyes widened. "Yes! She had them in a vase in the schoolroom." She thought back, trying to remember if Miss Rose had said anything about the flowers. "Does that mean… If he's courting her, would she stay here when we go back?"

Jack sat up straight, staring at her. "You're going back? When?"

"I don't know… I mean, when the war ends. Lots of children went back already, didn't they?" Emmie tried to look as though she didn't care. "No one's said."

Mary folded the diary closed and slipped an arm around her shoulders. "I don't think the war is nearly over, and it isn't safe for you children to be in London. You won't be going back for a long while."

"You promise you'd tell us?" Emmie begged. She wasn't sure she could bear to be dragged back again, back to sitting on a fire escape and staring at the sky.

"I promise."

Chapter

Ten

"ARE THOSE GERMAN?" EMMIE ASKED anxiously, peering up at the sky.

"Yes!" Arthur said disgustedly. "Those are bombers. Junkers Ju 88, can't you tell?"

"No, I can't. You've got the binoculars. Can't I look?"

"You can see it without the binoculars," Jack pointed out. "Two massive engines—if they were Lancasters, you'd see four little ones. I suppose you could mix them up with Whitleys." His voice implied that maybe Emmie could, but he certainly couldn't. "But they don't have those little tail fins. And anyway, Emmie, these have black crosses painted on them. See? Under the wings and at the back of the fuselage."

"I think I can see." Emmie squinted up at the planes, black and menacing against the sunlight. The droning buzz of the engines sounded sinister, but perhaps that was only because she knew they were the enemy. "Do you reckon they're going to Linton, then?"

"Might be. Or Driffield. Here, give me a go with those." Joey grabbed the binoculars off Arthur, who made a face but didn't say anything. Joey had found the binoculars in the gun room, so he had first claim.

They'd heard the drone of the bombers overhead just as they were putting away their books, and they'd all hurtled out onto the terrace, where there was a good view.

"It looks like hundreds of them," Emmie murmured.

"Nope. Fifty or so." Arthur had his hands up, shielding his eyes from the sun. "I've never seen that many."

"God help the poor blighters wherever they are going..." Joey muttered. "Fifty? You're sure?"

Arthur shrugged. "Maybe more. Heavy bombers."

"I suppose they know at Driffield..." Jack murmured. "They'll have been spotted coming over, won't they?"

"Must have been." Joey lowered the binoculars. "Bet they've scrambled fighters from Leconfield already."

The drone was fading away now, the last of the heavy, dark planes disappearing across the moor.

"They're gone." Arthur sighed. "I wish we could have seen a dogfight."

Jack shuddered, but he didn't say anything, just slipped his hand into the pocket of his shorts. Emmie knew he had the wooden Hurricane in there, his talisman.

There were planes overhead almost every day now if it was good weather. Fighting weather. Since the beginning of July, the German Luftwaffe had been dropping bombs on the ships sailing in convoys in the English Channel. The Germans had attacked the merchant ships so fiercely that now they only sailed at night. They had bombed the naval bases and harbors heavily too, and the manufacturing towns where many of the weapons factories were. The first daylight raid of the war had come in early July, on the massive oil storage tanks at Hull, which even Emmie knew was in Yorkshire. The RAF couldn't fly their planes without fuel.

Jack's brother, David, was flying from an air base in Suffolk now. Jack kept scanning the newspapers, looking for anything about the air battles. There were so many accounts of planes shot down—from both the RAF and the Luftwaffe. The day before, Emmie had snatched the paper away from him because his hands were shaking.

"I wonder if they dropped any parachutists." Joey was still gazing out across the moor.

"We'd have seen." Jack turned back, looking up too.

"They found parachutes near Leeds," Joey reminded him stubbornly. "That was only yesterday."

"We know!" Emmie sighed. "You haven't stopped going on about it since."

"Well, there could be spies camping out on the moor for all we know." Joey adjusted the focus on the binoculars again.

"Why would they want to do that?" Jack frowned at him. "What could they report back—how the heather's flowering?"

"This is talking about the day before yesterday," Emmie murmured, clutching the newspaper that Jack had stuffed into her hands. "The day we saw all those German planes flying over the moor."

"It was a huge attack," Jack said huskily. He dropped down next to her under the tree. "There were hundreds of them. The ones we saw wiped out Great Driffield—all the hangars got flattened. They bombed the Whitleys standing on the airfield, blew them all up. There were a load more of them fighting over Sunderland, but there were attacks down south as well. There are more attacks every day now. Hitler's trying to wipe out our RAF so he can invade. That's what it says in here." He stabbed a finger at the newspaper. "David's squadron would have been fighting too. They'd have flown out from Martlesham. It's 11 Group that's really taking the pressure, this says. That's the squadrons in the southeast. That's him."

"He has to be safe," Emmie whispered. "It wouldn't be fair. Not both of them. Not him and your dad."

"I don't think anything's fair anymore." Jack swallowed.

Emmie smoothed the paper down over her skirt. "Does your mother know you're reading the newspapers?" she asked suddenly.

Jack shrugged and turned his head away, and Emmie knew that meant no. "This is Mrs. Martin's paper, isn't it? You swiped it from the kitchen."

"Mum won't let me see hers anymore," Jack said flatly. Then he looked back at Emmie and began to babble, as though the words were pouring out of him without permission. "They don't want me to know what it's like, her and Martha! They think I'm too young to understand. So all I get is Joey and Arthur taking turns being the Huns and racing around shooting each other down. Spouting about *kills* and *strafing* and *bailing out*..." He stopped, gasping for breath.

"David isn't telling me the truth either. He's stopped saying anything useful in his letters. I know they're not allowed to say much because of the censor reading their letters, but he used to write me proper letters, long ones, with funny stories about buzzing over sheep in fields or spilling soup all down his front when they had to scramble. Now all he says is he's all right and lots of love and look after Mum."

"Maybe he's just tired," Emmie suggested.

"I don't want him to be tired! He's got to fly! They've got seconds to spot the enemy aircraft, just seconds, Emmie! He can't even blink. He can't be tired." Jack dragged the wooden plane out of his pocket. "Lot of use this is going to be..." He laughed shakily, and Emmie looked at him sideways. His eyes had a strange, eerie glitter to them, and they looked huger than ever. *He didn't look like his brother at all,* Emmie thought vaguely. Jack was so like his father, with those great, black-lashed, gray eyes, and David was tall, with thick, brown hair like his mother's.

Emmie tried not to let herself shiver. Jack was sitting close enough to feel it if she did. But she could picture Jack's brother so clearly that it felt almost as if she knew him too. Jack had a photograph of David in his RAF uniform by his bed, and Emmie had looked at it often. It was strange how that one moment staring into the camera had caught so much about him. She knew how excited he was about becoming a pilot. How everything was a great joke, even being up in the air with nothing but a sheet of thin metal between him and the sky—and the guns. She knew how much Jack loved him.

It wasn't just the photograph, of course. Emmie had all the stories, everything Jack had told her. All those strange little moments that reminded him of his adored big brother. Even the garden made Jack think of hide-and-seek, or David laughing and swinging him around and around in the middle of the grass. It was like flying, David had said. That was what flying felt like... They'd gone so fast that Jack had gotten dizzy, and they fell over and lay on the grass together laughing.

Jack gripped the plane in his hands so tightly that Emmie heard it splinter.

"Be careful! You'll break it!"

But he jumped up, shoving it angrily back into his pocket. Then he grabbed her arm and pulled her after him out of the garden.

"Where are we going?"

"Down by the sheds. Dickon had a bonfire this morning, didn't he? He was burning leaves. I smelled them." He raced her through the kitchen gardens and out to the strip of ground between the gardens and the woods, where the gardeners' toolsheds were, along with the compost heaps and a patch of ashy ground for bonfires.

Jack crouched by the cindery mess and nodded. "Look, I thought so. There are still embers." He stirred them with a stick and blew, puffing out his cheeks so that a tiny flame licked up. "Emmie, help me get some of the dry stuff out of that wheelbarrow. Dickon didn't have time to burn it all."

He seized an armful of garden trimmings and cast them on the fire, still blowing. The green branches frazzled and sent off wisps of sharp-smelling smoke, but the dry grass and weeds crisped to gray at once, and the flames rose a little higher. Doubtfully, Emmie threw on another load. She loved watching the bonfires, but she wasn't sure this stuff was properly ready to burn. And the set look on Jack's face was frightening her.

"We're not supposed to..." she started to say. But then she gave up. Jack didn't care. And today, she wasn't sure anyone else would either.

"That's good enough," Jack muttered, looking at the flames. There was still a lot of sullen smoke, but the fire had a glowing orange heart, crisscrossed with burned twigs.

He pulled out the plane David had sent him and rubbed his fingers over the worn paint. He muttered something.

"What?" Emmie leaned closer, coughing a little as the smoke caught in her throat.

"I said, it isn't going to work." Jack looked around at her. "It was supposed to keep him safe. How can it? It's just a toy, Emmie! It can't do anything! He's going to die. Just like Dad..." He turned back to the fire, and before Emmie realized what he was doing, he crouched down and shoved the tiny plane into the crackling center. Then he stepped back, his eyes full of tears, cradling his burned hand.

"You can't do that!" Emmie screamed. "He gave it to you! Get it out!"

Jack shook his head. "It isn't going to work… I can't have it anymore. It makes me think about him. It hurts." He stared blindly at the fire and then stumbled away, leaving Emmie hovering at the edge of the fire.

"You mustn't do that." Emmie wept. The little airplane was charred already, its faded paint blackened. A few moments more and it would be gone. Emmie kicked at the fire with her boots, tearing apart the seething, spitting weeds. She grabbed a stick and pushed the burning toy out. It was half-gone already, one wing hardly there at all. Emmie ran to the rain barrel by the toolshed and seized a dipper of water. She flung it down on the plane, and it hissed, little cracks opening up along the wood. Sighing, she squatted down to look at it. The plane was ruined—hardly recognizable. But she picked it up anyway, folding her handkerchief carefully around it.

Even if Jack couldn't bear to look at it anymore, she would keep it. Someone had to remember and hope.

CHAPTER

Eleven

E MMIE. EMMIE. I DON'T LIKE it. It's shrieking at me. You've been so long washing." Ruby was curled in a ball in the corner of her bed, but as Emmie came into the bedroom, the little girl sprang up and ran at her. She clung tightly, with her arms around Emmie's middle.

"It's only the wind," Emmie said, half laughing. But she could feel Ruby shaking. She remembered being frightened by the crying of the wind in the chimney herself and realized with surprise that had only been a few months before. "I suppose you want to get in my bed then?"

Ruby nodded into Emmie's chest, but she didn't move, and she wouldn't let go. Emmie had to walk her over to the bed and sit down with her.

"I have to get my nightgown on, Ruby. Get in. Look, I won't

go anywhere. I promise. Hide under the covers. Lucy'll sit on you." She reached out around the littler girl to pull the blankets back, and Ruby hurled herself underneath them, burying her head under the pillow so that only the dark ends of her hair trailed out. Lucy pawed at it curiously and then tried clawing Ruby's arm. Ruby didn't come out from the pillow. She just scooped Lucy in and pulled the blankets up over both of them.

Emmie tried not to laugh. Ruby was big enough now to hate it when she thought people were laughing at her. She changed into her nightie and nudged Ruby over, wondering if once Ruby was asleep she could go and sleep in Ruby's bed. Two girls and a cat were going to be squashed in one bed.

"Is it really only the wind?" Ruby whispered into Emmie's neck.

"It's just the way the wind blows around the chimney, Ruby, honestly. I was scared of it too when we first came here. I've heard it before, and nothing ever happened to me, did it?"

"I suppose."

Emmie leaned back against the pillow, shifting a little to get herself comfortable next to Ruby and the cat. The rain lashed across the windows, rattling the glass. Emmie turned her head so she could see the tapestries, smiling at the white horse with the long, foolish nose, her favorite. The wind howled again, but Ruby only twitched a little. She was almost asleep. Emmie sighed. If they were still in London, the air-raid sirens would be wailing like that. Mrs. Evans had told them about the sirens when she came back from visiting her sister. The wind in the chimney sounded almost friendly tonight, especially since the room was warm. Lucy climbed out from under the blankets to purr by the pillow.

Emmie was almost asleep herself when she heard the door squeaking, a sharp, real noise, very different from the crying of the wind. Her heart thudded, even though she knew it couldn't be burglars or anything like that. But it was late, and deep down, she couldn't help but worry… She sat up on one elbow, gasping in a deep breath and hoping it wasn't Miss Rose or Miss Dearlove. They were sure to make Ruby move, and then she'd cry, and Emmie almost didn't mind her being there.

"Oh, it's you! Shhh, don't wake her."

Jack slid in around the door, his flashlight, his precious Christmas present, pointed down at the floor. "I couldn't sleep." He perched on the end of the bed and looked at Emmie sideways, a bit evasively. "It's really loud in my room. Much louder than here. The rain really smashes against the window. I couldn't sleep. And I thought maybe you'd be awake too."

"I almost was." Emmie yawned. "Ruby had a panic attack. I don't know what she thought the wind was—ghosts probably." She grinned at him. "For half a second, I thought you were one, or a murderer. It's that sort of night."

Jack nodded. "It is... Being up so late makes everything feel funny, doesn't it? Knowing everyone else is asleep—it changes things."

"What things?" Emmie blinked at him tiredly.

Jack shrugged and then turned to look at her. "Perhaps it makes it easier to talk. David used to let me talk to him if I woke up in the night. I think he was asleep a lot of the time though. All he did was grunt mostly."

Emmie giggled. "I could do that..."

"I really, really miss him. I burned his plane, Emmie. Why did I do something that stupid? He gave it to me."

Emmie sighed and wriggled farther away from Ruby so she could reach over to the bedside table. "You owe me a handkerchief," she murmured. "Miss Dearlove moaned at me for ages." She pulled the sad little parcel out and handed it to him. "It's not all there. A wing's gone. And the paint's sort of bubbled off."

Jack gaped at the plane, charred and broken in his hands, and then at Emmie. "You pulled it out? Why didn't you tell me?"

"Because you'd have put it straight back in, of course! I was waiting 'til I thought you'd want it. Sorry. Maybe I should have given it back to you before. But you still seemed...not ready for it."

Jack hunched up one shoulder at her, half shrug, half nod.

"Maybe you're right," he muttered. "Tonight's the first time I felt like Dad's death was real. Before, I kept screaming about it inside, trying to make it go away, but it isn't going to." He sighed, slow and shaky. "If she's in your bed, can I sleep in hers? No one'll mind."

Privately, Emmie thought Miss Dearlove would, but she didn't care. "Go on then. Don't blame me if Ruby jumps on you in the middle of the night and has a screaming fit though."

"It is the middle of the night."

"Shut up and go to sleep then." Emmie wriggled back down, curling herself around Ruby and smiling in the dark. The plane had been haunting her from inside that drawer. It still belonged to Jack, and she'd felt as if it wanted to go back to him. She peered across the room to the shadowy lump under the window. There was a hint of whiteness pressed against his face—her handkerchief, still wrapped around the plane.

Emmie surfaced slowly from the gray dream again. It came every so often, that terrible sense of longing and despair while she was shut away from the garden. She clenched her hands on the blankets, breathing fast. It wasn't real. Just a dream. "Only a dream," she muttered, repeating it to herself like a chant. "Only a dream."

Ruby huffed and wriggled and mewed like a kitten, and went back to sleep. Emmie sat up, rubbing at her arms.

"You're awake." Jack was kneeling on Ruby's bed, looking out of the window. "It's getting light."

"So it is." It must have been, since she could see him. She slid out of bed and went to stand next to him at the window. He'd opened it, she noticed. The smell of rain-wet garden eased around her, and she took in a deep breath, banishing the dream. "Shall we go out?" she asked suddenly.

Jack looked around at her. "Now?"

"Why not? You could put on Arthur's boots. They're by the side door." Emmie stood on tiptoe, resting her elbows on the windowsill. "I want to be out in it. I want to see the sun come up."

Jack scrambled off the bed, tucking the wrapped plane into the pocket of his too-small robe, and Emmie snatched the blanket off Ruby's bed. They crept out of the room and along the passage and down the stairs, pale and ghostly in the predawn light.

The bolts were stiff and shrieked. They stared at each other, round-eyed and frozen by the door, but no one came after them. Jack yanked the door open and grabbed her hand, and they went running out through the gardens. There was a faint pinkness at the lower edges of the sky, and the fishpond glimmered in the light of Jack's flashlight as they raced past.

The ivy rustled as Emmie reached for the handle, and the door swished over the grass. The garden was full of birds calling to each other as the children crept in. Emmie wanted to dance around on the wet grass, but she didn't. The garden wasn't theirs so early; they were visitors. They huddled next to each other on the bench, watching the trees and the statue and the sundial grow clearer and sharper as the darkness seeped out of the sky. Jack held the wooden plane in both hands, cradling it like a tiny bird.

A faint September mist swirled around their feet, and the birdsong faded to a chirrup here and there. Emmie thought she saw the robin perched in the rose arch overhead and peering down at them with curious beady eyes. But the light wasn't good enough to be sure.

"The sun's coming up," Jack whispered. "I've never seen it from outside before. It feels like magic. The sky's turned golden. I can feel everything in the garden. It's all reaching up for the light."

"Someone's coming," Emmie whispered, clutching his hand. "Jack, someone's coming. I can hear footsteps on the path. The door!"

It was probably only Dickon—or perhaps Jack's mother, come to look for him. But in the early-morning light, there was a breathless sense of something about to happen. Something strange or frightening or wonderful. Emmie couldn't tell which. Perhaps all of them at once.

The door shifted a little and then drew open, and a tall figure stepped through, coming out of the shadows.

"Who is it?" Emmie asked, her voice gone high and squeaky. But Jack was already gone. The little wooden plane and the handkerchief had slipped onto the bench. He was laughing and laughing, running across the grass toward his brother.

Emmie Hatton
Misselthwaite Manor
29th October 1940

Mrs. Craven gave me back the diaries. She said that she had loved reading them again, but now she thought I wanted them more than she did. She gave me a pencil too, a pretty one with a striped paper wrapper around it. She showed me the end of the diary and the empty pages, and even though she didn't say so, I know she meant for me to write in them myself. But I didn't know how to begin. I didn't have anything to write about, except that we have been here for a year. More than a year, now it's October. I wanted my diary to start with something special. I wanted something to happen, and now it has.

The Home has been bombed. Miss Dearlove told us this morning. It just isn't there anymore. Nothing is left at all. It wasn't just the Home; the bombs destroyed most of the street—but no one was killed. Everyone had gone to the shelters. She was shaking when she said it, and I suppose I ought to be shocked too. But London seems so far away. I almost can't remember the me that lived there.

We can never, ever go back. Mrs. Craven explained to all of us that the Home will be at Misselthwaite for always, not just while the war is on. She promised. That means that we belong here now.

About the Author

Holly Webb has written over one hundred books, including the critically acclaimed Rose series. She worked for five years as a children's fiction editor before deciding to become a writer. She lives in Reading with her husband and three small children.

Follow Holly on Twitter @HollyKateSkeet and visit her website at holly-webb.com.